Prosodic Weight

OXFORD STUDIES IN PHONOLOGY AND PHONETICS

GENERAL EDITORS:
Andrew Nevins, *University College London*; Keren Rice, *University of Toronto*

ADVISORY EDITORS: Stuart Davis, *Indiana University*, Heather Goad, *McGill University*, Carlos Gussenhoven, *Radboud University*, Haruo Kubozono, *National Institute for Japanese Language and Linguistics*, Sun-Ah Jun, *University of California, Los Angeles*, Maria-Rosa Lloret, *Universitat de Barcelona*, Douglas Pulleyblank, *University of British Columbia*, Rachid Ridouane, *Laboratoire de Phonétique et Phonologie, Paris*, Rachel Walker, *University of Southern California*

PUBLISHED

1
Morphological Length and Prosodically Defective Morphemes
Eva Zimmermann

2
The Phonetics and Phonology of Geminate Consonants
Edited by Haruo Kubozono

3
Prosodic Weight
Categories and Continua
Kevin M. Ryan

IN PREPARATION

Phonological Specification and Interface Interpretation
Edited by Bert Botma and Marc van Oostendorp

Doing Computational Phonology
Edited by Jeffrey Heinz

The Structure of Nasal-Stop Inventories
Eduardo Piñeros

Speech Timing
Implications for Theories of Phonology, Speech Production, and Speech Motor Control
Alice Turk and Stefanie Shattuck-Hufnagel

Phonological Templates in Development
Marilyn Vihman

Prosodic Weight

Categories and Continua

KEVIN M. RYAN

OXFORD
UNIVERSITY PRESS

OXFORD

UNIVERSITY PRESS

Great Clarendon Street, Oxford, OX2 6DP,
United Kingdom

Oxford University Press is a department of the University of Oxford.
It furthers the University's objective of excellence in research, scholarship,
and education by publishing worldwide. Oxford is a registered trade mark of
Oxford University Press in the UK and in certain other countries

First Edition published in 2019
Impression: 1

Published in the United States of America by Oxford University Press
198 Madison Avenue, New York, NY 10016, United States of America

British Library Cataloguing in Publication Data

Data available

Library of Congress Control Number: 2018953424

ISBN 978-0-19-881794-9

Printed and bound by
CPI Group (UK) Ltd, Croydon, CR0 4YY

Contents

Series preface   ix
Acknowledgments   xi
List of figures   xiii
Abbreviations and symbols   xv

1 Introduction   1
  1.1 Preamble   1
  1.2 Weight-sensitive systems in phonology   4
  1.3 Universals of weight   9
  1.4 Scope and aims of this book   13
  1.5 Overview of the constraint system for prominence mapping   17

2 Weight scales for stress   22
  2.1 Introduction   22
  2.2 Two theories of complex scales   27
  2.3 Core apparatus   29
      2.3.1 Moraic preliminaries   29
      2.3.2 Mapping between weight and stress   31
      2.3.3 Preliminary illustrations: Yana, Murik, Kelkar's Hindi   34
  2.4 MAIN→VV and similar constraints   36
  2.5 Coercion vs. Prominence: case studies   38
      2.5.1 V < VC < VV < VVC in Kashmiri: the Coercion analysis   38
      2.5.2 V < VC < VV < VVC in Pulaar: two problems for Coercion   42
      2.5.3 V < VC < VV < VVC in Pulaar: the Prominence analysis   47
      2.5.4 V < VC < VV in Chickasaw   49
      2.5.5 V < VC < VV in Klamath   52
      2.5.6 V < VC < VV in Maithili   55
      2.5.7 V < VC < VV in Yapese   57
      2.5.8 V < VC < VV in Finnish   57
      2.5.9 V < VC < VV < VVC in Nanti   58
      2.5.10 V < VC < VV in Tamil   60
      2.5.11 V < VC < VV (etc.) in Kara   62
      2.5.12 Coercion vs. Prominence beyond stress   63
  2.6 Geminates and stress   64
      2.6.1 Sixty-seven languages with VC < VV for stress: VG
            almost always aligns with VC   64
      2.6.2 VC < {VG, VV} in Cahuilla   66
      2.6.3 VC < {VG, VV} in Gupta's Hindi?   68
      2.6.4 VC < {VG, VV} in San'ani Arabic (and VC < VG in Amharic)   69

2.6.5 {VC, VG} < VV in Koasati and as the typological norm for VG in VC < VV systems 71

2.6.6 The weight of GV for stress 74

2.6.7 VG is arguably always heavy in V < VX systems (with special attention to Ngalakgan and Tashlhiyt Berber) 77

2.7 Alternative approaches to Skeletal Prominence 81

2.7.1 Vowel vs. Coda Prominence 81

2.7.2 The questionable existence of VV < VC for stress 83

2.7.3 Coda Prominence as an antidote to trimoraicity 86

2.8 Gradient weight for stress 88

2.8.1 VH ⪷ V ⪷ VC ⪷ VV in Hupa 88

2.8.2 V ⪷ VC ⪷ VV (etc.) in Yahi (Yana) 92

2.8.3 Skeletal structure in English 92

2.8.4 Other cases of gradient weight: Russian, Finnish, Italian, Spanish, and Portuguese 95

2.9 Conclusion 96

3 Prosodic minimality in isolation and in context 98

3.1 Introduction 98

3.2 Latin 102

3.2.1 Minimality as it applies to words in isolation 102

3.2.2 Minimality as it applies within cliticized structures 105

3.2.3 The interaction of minimality and resyllabification 108

3.2.4 Evidence for degenerate feet 111

3.2.5 Varying cliticizability 116

3.2.6 Latin minimality: conclusion 118

3.3 Māhārāṣṭrī Prakrit: gradient contextual prosodic minimality 120

3.4 Tamil 121

3.4.1 Overview of prosodic minimality in Tamil 122

3.4.2 Loanwords support the subminimality of VR 124

3.4.3 Rhotics are nongeminable in Tamil 124

3.4.4 VR is light in Tamil meter 126

3.4.5 The interaction of minimality and resyllabification 128

3.4.6 Analysis 130

3.4.7 The realization and sonority of Tamil coda rhotics 132

3.4.8 *μ/R: discussion 134

3.5 Conclusion 136

4 Quantitative meter: Categorical and gradient weight 137

4.1 Introduction 137

4.2 Variable weight due to optional processes 141

4.2.1 Optional resyllabification 141

4.2.2 Optional cluster or geminate compression 142

4.2.3 Optional correption in hiatus 143

4.2.4 Variable final vowel length 144

4.3   Superheavy avoidance   145
4.4   Gradient weight in meter I: positional discrepancies   147
    4.4.1   Kalevala Finnish   147
    4.4.2   Homeric Greek   149
    4.4.3   Tamil and other languages   150
4.5   Gradient weight in meter II: final indifference   151
    4.5.1   Homeric Greek   151
    4.5.2   Classical Latin   152
4.6   Interval Theory   153
4.7   Conclusion   158

5   Prosodic end-weight and the stress–weight interface   160
5.1   Introduction   160
5.2   Constructions exhibiting end-weight   161
5.3   Non-phonological factors in end-weight   165
5.4   Phonological factors not involving weight   167
5.5   Subsyllabic factors in end-weight   168
    5.5.1   Vowel length and quality   169
    5.5.2   Onset size and sonority   171
    5.5.3   Coda size and sonority   174
    5.5.4   Stress level   177
5.6   The syllable-count effect in end-weight   178
    5.6.1   The syllable-count effect in English   179
    5.6.2   The syllable-count effect in Latin   188
    5.6.3   The syllable-count effect in French   190
    5.6.4   The syllable-count effect: conclusion   192
5.7   Summary of prosodic factors in end-weight   193
5.8   Explanations for prosodic end-weight   194
    5.8.1   Final lengthening   194
    5.8.2   Rhythm   198
    5.8.3   Phonotactics   198
    5.8.4   Complexity   199
5.9   Phrasal stress as an explanation for end-weight   201
    5.9.1   Constraints   201
    5.9.2   Stress-modulated weight   210
    5.9.3   Multinomials   211
    5.9.4   Onset sonority   213
5.10 End-weight in compounds   217
5.11 The Rhythm Rule   220
5.12 Beginning-weight   222
    5.12.1 Overview of prosodic and syntactic beginning-weight 222
    5.12.2 A pilot study of prosodic beginning-weight in Turkish 226
5.13 Prosodic vs. syntactic end-weight   228
5.14 Prosodic end-weight beyond binomials   229
5.15 Conclusion   229

6 Conclusion and further issues   232
  6.1 The phonetics–phonology interface   233
  6.2 Opacity   237
  6.3 Onset effects and the domain of the weight percept   238
  6.4 Categorical vs. gradient weight   239

Appendix: Key constraints   247
References   249
Index   281

Series preface

The 'Oxford Studies in Phonology and Phonetics' series provides a platform for original research on sound structure in natural language within contemporary phonological theory and related areas of inquiry such as phonetic theory, morphological theory, the architecture of the grammar, and cognitive science. Contributors are encouraged to present their work in the context of contemporary theoretical issues in a manner accessible to a range of people, including phonologists, phoneticians, morphologists, psycholinguists, and cognitive scientists. Manuscripts should include a wealth of empirical examples, where relevant, and make full use of the possibilities for digital media that can be leveraged on a companion website with access to materials such as sound files, videos, extended databases, and software.

This is a companion series to 'Oxford Surveys in Phonology and Phonetics', which provides critical overviews of the major approaches to research topics of current interest, a discussion of their relative value, and an assessment of what degree of consensus exists about any one of them. The 'Studies' series will equally seek to combine empirical phenomena with theoretical frameworks, but its authors will propose an original line of argumentation, often as the inception or culmination of an ongoing original research program.

Weight has long been an important topic in the study of phonetics and phonology. In this book, Kevin M. Ryan provides a comprehensive analysis of prosodic weight: the categorization of syllables or larger prosodic constituents based on their patterning. Such categorization is often dichotomous (e.g. light vs. heavy) for certain phenomena, but can often be more complex, and Ryan demonstrates that factors such as length, complexity, and the onset contribute to scalar arrangements of weight, for constituents beyond the syllable such as the word and even the phrase. While most previous research on weight focuses on binary systems or the phonetic basis of categorization, this book places emphasis on the phonological analysis of complex and gradient scales for phenomena such as stress, prosodic minimality, quantitative meter, and prosodic end-weight. The book contributes thorough empirical and analytical depth, weaving together Optimality Theory analyses based on descriptive, typological data, as well as experimental and corpus-based statistics. The work stands for its fresh insights into traditionally studied languages, alongside the introduction of new sets of languages that have not figured into debates about the representation of weight.

Andrew Nevins
Keren Rice

Acknowledgments

Verse was first. I arrived at the topic of prosodic weight the same way that the field did historically, that is, from metrical verse. The codification of verse yielded the study of prosody, which in turn yielded the first formal theories of grammar. This happened first in India, but for me India happened first in Berkeley, where, as an undergraduate in 2002, I read Sanskrit with the Goldmans and Tamil with the Harts and decided to pursue phonology formally.

The present work has its origins in my 2011 UCLA dissertation 'Gradient weight in phonology', but only the sections on gradient weight in stress (§2.8), gradient weight in meter (§4.4), and Tamil minimality (§3.4)—less than a quarter of the present text— are direct descendants of that thesis, and they are reworked. Bruce Hayes and Kie Zuraw were my advisors at UCLA, and it is to them that I owe the greatest thanks for supporting and inspiring me during the early stages of this scholarship. Additionally, Matthew Gordon's and Donca Steriade's respective oeuvres on weight have been particularly influential, though it goes without saying that our views sometimes diverge. Gordon's work has in many ways served as my foundation, as evidenced by the 130 references to it below. The emphases of the present work have been shaped to some extent by a desire to complement rather than recapitulate this foundation, as described in §1.4.

I also wish to thank Adam Albright, Arto Anttila, Lev Blumenfeld, Megan Crowhurst, Robert Daland, Edward Flemming, Guilherme Garcia, Olav Hackstein, Jay Jasanoff, Paul Kiparsky, Paul de Lacy, Anya Lunden, Laura McPherson, Donka Minkova, Joe Pater, Russell Schuh, Stephanie Shih, Caley Smith, and Morgan Sonderegger, who contributed in various ways direct or indirect, as well as the 'Studies in Phonology and Phonetics' editors Andrew Nevins and Keren Rice. Additionally, Dieter Gunkel and Donca Steriade provided feedback on an earlier form of the manuscript. Needless to say, I bear full responsibility for any errors or omissions in the present version of the text. I gratefully acknowledge early support from a National Science Foundation graduate research fellowship and from a Humboldt Foundation fellowship for experienced researchers.

List of figures

1.1	Vowel duration as a function of onset complexity	7
1.2	Long vowels tend to cooccur with shorter onsets in English	7
1.3	Universals of weight	12
1.4	Euler diagram for the weights of selected rimes	19
2.1	The VC < VV ("Khalkha") criterion	24
2.2	The V < VX ("Latin") criterion	24
2.3	The energy of VV vs. VC	25
2.4	The V < VC < VV scale, as in Chickasaw	27
2.5	The V < {VC, VV} < VVC scale, as in Kelkar's Hindi	27
2.6	VC < VV stress systems and the categorization of VG	67
2.7	Hupa stress as a function of weight	89
2.8	Regression table for initial vs. peninitial weight effects in Hupa	90
2.9	Ratio scales for weight in σ_1 (top) and σ_2 (bottom) in Hupa	90
2.10	Real (left) and generated (right) rates of initial stress in Hupa	91
2.11	Weight coefficients of seven rime types in English simplex disyllables	94
2.12	Weight coefficients of four word-initial onset types in English	94
3.1	Prevocalic rates by part-of-speech for Latin C_0VC words	118
3.2	Weight in Kamban's epic (Tamil)	127
3.3	Regression table for rime placement in 908 lines of Kamban	128
3.4	Two tokens of Tamil /ɾ/ in the coda	132
3.5	Tamil /ɻ/ in the coda (372 ms window)	133
4.1	The typological range of quantity sensitivity in meter	138
4.2	Estimated compression rates for V__V(V) clusters in Latin	143
4.3	Intermediate weight with unimodal phonology	144
4.4	Superheavy incidence declines in Ṛg-Vedic cadences	146
4.5	Regression table for syllable weight in the *Kalevala*	148
4.6	Regression table for syllable weight in the *Iliad* and the *Odyssey*	150
4.7	Rime duration vs. strength propensity in Kamban's Tamil meter	150
4.8	Final indifference in Homer	152
4.9	Final indifference in Virgil	152
5.1	End-weight propensity vs. duration for five English front vowels	170
5.2	The sonority effect in end-weight	174

5.3   Vowel length before nasals vs. laterals in English   177

5.4 ΔAIC_c and random forests for syllable count in English binomials   182

5.5 ΔAIC_c and random forests for English personal name binomials   184

5.6   Syllable count in Latin binomials   190

5.7   Syllable count in French binomials   191

5.8   A stringent weight hierarchy   204

5.9 T_{ons} breaks the stringency hierarchy   215

5.10 A disjunctive solution to the onset sonority problem for stringency   216

5.11 End-weight among onset reduplicatives in English   218

5.12 The (reverse) syllable count effect in Turkish   227

6.1   Varying dichotomization of weight in Tamil vs. Finnish meters   241

6.2   Increasingly complex scales dissolving into gradience   242

6.3   A pathology of t-mapping   244

Abbreviations and symbols

Phonetic transcriptions and symbols generally follow the IPA (International Phonetic Alphabet). Classical languages such as Latin and Sanskrit are usually presented in standard romanization, which is close to the IPA, except most notably that vowel length is marked by macrons (e.g. ā = aː).

.	syllable boundary
#	word boundary
ˈ	primary stress (printed before syllable, e.g. baˈta = baTA)
ˌ	secondary stress (printed before syllable)
ˌˌ	tertiary stress (printed before syllable)
´	stress (with symbols, e.g. H́, ó, or orthographic forms), pitch accent, or lexical accent
ː	long vowel or consonant (same as macron)
ˑ	half-long vowel
|	boundary between feet or intervals
||	caesura
(...)	foot
[...]ω	prosodic word
<...>	extrametrical material
<	is lighter than
≤	is lighter than or equivalent to
≲	is lighter than, but not strictly
~	varies with
>	is heavier than, or yields via historical change
≫	strictly dominates (as of constraints)
≻	is more harmonic than (as of candidates)
◡	light syllable or position
—	heavy syllable or position
ə	schwa or reduced vowels in general
☞	winner (or, with 💣, should-be winner)
💣	erroneous winner
2sg.	second person singular
ā	same as [aː]
AIC$_c$	Akaike information criterion (corrected)
A(P)	adjective (phrase)

[± *approx*]	the feature approximant
β	coefficient in a regression
C	consonant
C_0	any number of consonants
C^1	at most one consonant
D(P)	determiner (phrase)
f	foot
f_0	fundamental frequency
G	geminate
gen.	genitive
GV	syllable with an onset geminate (e.g. [kːa])
H	heavy syllable
HG	Harmonic Grammar
$\mathcal{H}$	harmony
iff	if and only if
L	light syllable (or lateral)
μ	mora
maxent	maximum entropy
MCL	*muta cum liquida*
ms	milliseconds
N	sonorant
N(P)	noun (phrase)
OT	Optimality Theory
φ	node at the level of the prosodic word or higher
$φ_s$	strong φ
p	probability
PEH	phonetically effective heavy syllables
PFL	phrase-final lengthening
pl.	plural
P(P)	preposition (phrase)
PWd	prosodic word
R	rhotic
σ	syllable
$σ_{μμ}$	syllable with two or more moras
$σ_s$	strong or stressed syllable
σ́	stressed syllable
S	strong (position)
s	seconds

SE	standard error
sg.	singular
[± *son*]	the feature sonorant
SWP	stress-to-weight principle (penalize stressed lights)
T	obstruent
t	total perceptual energy of the weight domain
V (or V̆)	short vowel
V < VX	Latin criterion (light iff ends with V)
VC < VV	Khalkha criterion (heavy iff contains VV)
VG	rime closed by a geminate (e.g. [**ak**.ka])
V(P)	verb (phrase)
VV	long vowel or (heavy) diphthong
VX	rime comprising at least two timing slots
W	glide or weak (position)
WbyP	weight-by-position
WSP	weight-to-stress principle (penalize unstressed heavies)
$\chi^2(n)$	chi-square test with n degrees of freedom
X	segment of any type
×	position with any weight or grid mark
z	*z*-value in a logistic regression (β/SE)

1

Introduction

1.1 Preamble

The notion that syllables are divided into two categories, heavy and light, predates the introduction of writing in many traditions. This dichotomy was first evident from versification, but came also to be recognized in antiquity as critical for characterizing grammatical systems such as tone, stress, and morphology. In Sanskrit, for instance, heavy syllables are termed *guru* (cognate with *gravity*) and light syllables are termed *laghu* (cognate with *light*), and it is ultimately to Sanskrit rather than to Latin or Greek that anglophone phonologists owe the calques "heavy" and "light." Crucially, these terms are distinct from long (*dīrgha*) and short (*hrasva*), which refer to vowel or consonant length (e.g. short *i* vs. long *ī*, also notated [iː]). As Pāṇini specifies in his grammar, the Aṣṭādhyāyī (c. 500–300 BCE)—though the distinction is more ancient than that (Allen 1953)—a syllable is heavy if it contains a long vowel (which includes diphthongs) or a short vowel followed by a consonant cluster. The three relevant rules are given in (1) (Böhtlingk 1887, Vasu 1898).

(1) 1.4.10 hrasvaṃ laghu 'a short [vowel is] light [modulo 1.4.11]'
     1.4.11 saṃyoge guru 'before a consonant cluster, [a vowel is] heavy'
     1.4.12 dīrghaṃ ca 'and a long [vowel is also heavy]'

In modern terms, phonologists would usually say that a Sanskrit syllable is heavy if it contains a long vowel, diphthong, or CODA. For example, in *saṃyoga* 'cluster,' the first syllable is heavy. For Pāṇini, this is because the first vowel is followed by a cluster, namely, *my*. In modern terms, by contrast, one would say that the first syllable of *saṃyoga*, which is syllabified [səŋ.joː.gə], is heavy by virtue of ending with a consonant, that is, a coda. Pāṇini's characterization of weight is INTERVAL-based, where the interval is the span between the beginning of a vowel and the beginning of the following vowel (or, lacking a following vowel, the end of the constituent), while the alternative is SYLLABLE-based. The two systems are not always equivalent. For instance, the final syllable of *saṃyogam* 'cluster (accusative)' would be considered light as an interval but heavy as a syllable. This book assumes the syllable theory of weight, which is the standard approach in modern phonology (e.g. Jakobson 1971/1931, Trubetzkoy 1958, Allen 1973, Hyman 1977, 1985, McCarthy 1979b, Steriade 1982, Zec 1988, Hayes 1989, 1995, and numerous others; for recent article-length surveys, see Ryan 2016 and Gordon 2017). Nevertheless, Interval Theory is being revived in some quarters, as discussed in §4.6.

Prosodic Weight. First edition. Kevin M. Ryan.
© Kevin M. Ryan 2019. First published 2019 by Oxford University Press.

The Sanskrit grammarians distinguished between heavy and light syllables for both metrical and grammatical reasons. In verse, certain positions of the line are required to be filled by a syllable of a particular weight. For example, each line of the Sanskrit epic meter, the *śloka*, is sixteen syllables, of which the last four must be light-heavy-light-× (where × is a syllable of any weight). The first four lines (two verses) of the Bhagavad Gītā are given in (2). Note that *vacanam* in the fourth line ends with a light syllable. In this context, *m* is not a coda; rather, it RESYLLABIFIES with the following vowel, the usual treatment of C#V sequences in archaic Indo-European languages. Note also that *abra* in the fourth line—and in any instance in Sanskrit—is syllabified [ab.ra] (but cf. Kessler 1998). In this respect, Sanskrit differs from other languages, such as Latin and English, in which such a cluster is at least sometimes syllabified [a.bra].

(2) 1.1 dharmakṣetre kurukṣetre ‖ samavetā yuyutsavaḥ
      māmakāḥ pāṇḍavaś caiva ‖ kim akurvata sañjaya

    1.2 dṛṣṭvā tu pāṇḍavānīkam ‖ vyūḍham duryodhanas tadā
      ācāryam upasaṅgamya ‖ rājā vacanam abravīt

As one example of weight affecting morphology in Sanskrit, consider the reduplicated aorist, as in (3) (Whitney 1889:308–12). Each verb form comprises four morphemes, namely, the augment *a-*, the reduplicant, the root, and the suffix *-am*, which indicates the first person singular. The second column provides a syllabic parse with IPA transcription. The reduplicant copies a consonant and a vowel from the root, with some irrelevant adjustments to quality. The length of the copied vowel varies according to the distribution of weight in the product (surface form). If the root syllable is light (as syllabified with the suffix), the reduplicant is heavy. This is achieved by lengthening the copied vowel, as in (a–c). If the root begins with a cluster, as in (d–e), the vowel does not lengthen, as the cluster furnishes a coda for the reduplicant, rendering it heavy without lengthening. Finally, if the root syllable is heavy (in context), the reduplicant is light (f–h).[1] This trading off in syllable weight between the reduplicant and its base is a type of QUANTITATIVE COMPLEMENTARITY, as termed by McCarthy and Prince (1986); see also (11).

(3) a. a-rī-riṣ-am   [ə.ɻiː.ɻi.ṣəm]   'I have harmed'
     b. a-dū-duṣ-am   [ə.ɖuː.ɖu.ṣəm]   'I have spoiled'
     c. a-jī-jan-am   [ə.ɟiː.ɟə.nəm]   'I have begotten'

     d. a-ti-tras-am   [ə.t̪it̪.ɻə.səm]   'I have trembled'
     e. a-cu-krudh-am   [ə.cuk.ɻu.ɖʱəm]   'I have antagonized'

     f. a-bu-bhūṣ-am   [ə.bu.bʱuː.ṣəm]   'I have sought'
     g. a-ta-tams-am   [ə.t̪ə.t̪əŋ.səm]   'I have drawn'
     h. a-da-dakṣ-am   [ə.ɖə.ɖək.ṣəm]   'I have been skillful'

---

[1] If the root is both heavy-in-context and cluster-initial, as in *apapraccham* 'I have asked,' a heavy reduplicant is unavoidable. Lengthening would be doubly defeating in such cases.

Thus, both meter and morphology diagnose the same heavy vs. light distinction in Sanskrit, such that a syllable is heavy iff (if and only if) it contains a long vowel, diphthong, or coda. To generalize over these heavy types, it is commonly said that a heavy syllable comprises two MORAS, a mora being a unit of phonological length (the corresponding Sanskrit term being *mātrā* 'measure'). Canonically, a short vowel contributes one mora and a long vowel or diphthong contributes two (some analysts additionally recognize nonmoraic or trimoraic vowels; §2.3.1, §2.6.7). A coda canonically contributes one mora, though some systems treat (all or some) codas as nonmoraic (some analysts additionally recognize multimoraic codas; *ibid.*). Finally, onsets are irrelevant for weight in the foregoing examples. Nevertheless, I treat numerous cases below that support onsets as factors in weight elsewhere.

The same binary criterion for weight that is found in Sanskrit is also familiar from Latin. Once again, several systems converge on this classification, including the following. First, stress placement depends on weight. In words of three or more syllables, stress falls on the penult (second-to-last syllable) unless the penult is light, in which case it retreats to the antepenult (e.g. *praeféctīs*, *optā́tīs*, but *dígitīs*). Second, if a prosodic word is a monosyllable, it must be heavy (e.g. *dor*, *dā*, **da*; §3.1). Third, meters regulate the distribution of heavies and lights. For example, the penultimate syllable of a line of the epic meter, the hexameter, must be heavy.

Aside from this so-called LATIN CRITERION, which applies equally to Sanskrit and many other languages, another common binary criterion for weight treats a syllable as heavy iff it contains a long vowel or diphthong, ignoring the presence or absence of the coda. These are the two most frequent criteria, but numerous other schemes are attested, including sonority cutoffs, where only a subset of vowels or consonants induce heaviness. The specific criterion varies across languages and phenomena. Even within the same language, different processes often exhibit different criteria (Gordon 2006). But in every case, heavy syllables are aggregately longer or more sonorous than light syllables.

Beyond binary criteria, ternary and more complex scales for weight are also well attested. The most common ternary scale is $V < VC < VV$, as found in the stress systems of at least twenty languages (not counting extrametricality effects; Chapter 2) and additional cases from meter and end-weight (Chapters 4–5).[2] Quaternary $V < VC < VV < VVC$ is also encountered in several languages and systems. In Kashmiri (Morén 2000) and Pulaar (Niang 1997, Wiltshire 2006), for instance, stress falls on the leftmost instance of the heaviest grade from this scale that is available nonfinally in the word. Finally, some scales are highly complex and quantifiable, effectively dissolving, in the extreme case, into gradient continua of weight, as treated in §2.8 for stress, §4.4 for meter, and Chapter 5 for end-weight.

In summary, PROSODIC WEIGHT refers to the categorization or scalar arrangement of syllables or larger prosodic constituents based on their prosodic behavior. Such categorization is often dichotomous; for some processes, such as stress, it is usually so.

---

[2] V refers to a short vowel, VV a long vowel or (heavy) diphthong, and C a consonant. Onsets are omitted. Throughout, I arrange scales from lightest to heaviest.

But it is often more complex. While most previous research on weight focuses on binary systems or the phonetic basis of categorization, the present volume puts greater emphasis on the phonological analysis of complex and gradient scales. Complex scales are more widespread than previously appreciated and yield critical insights into otherwise thinly evidenced weight universals.

The remainder of the chapter comprises four sections, which respectively survey the range of weight-sensitive phenomena (§1.2), enumerate weight universals (§1.3), outline the book's scope and major findings (§1.4), and overview the weight-mapping apparatus (§1.5).

1.2 Weight-sensitive systems in phonology

Phonological weight plays a role in several grammatical systems, including stress, prosodic minimality, meter, end-weight, tone licensing, compensatory lengthening, syllable structure, reduplication, and (non-reduplicative) allomorphy. These areas are briefly surveyed in this section. More in-depth introductions to the first four areas are provided at the beginnings of the next four chapters, respectively.

First, as just mentioned for Latin, syllable weight can affect stress placement. Roughly 40 per cent of the world's stress systems are QUANTITY-SENSITIVE. Consider Khalkha Mongolian (Walker 1997). Khalkha has codas, but they do not count for weight. A syllable is heavy iff it contains a long vowel or diphthong, sometimes referred to as the KHALKHA CRITERION. Primary stress (notated by ' at the beginning of the syllable) is attracted to a heavy syllable anywhere in the word, as in (4). If multiple heavies cooccur, the rightmost nonfinal heavy receives primary stress. If no heavy is present, the initial syllable receives primary stress. Additionally, secondary stress (notated ˌ) occurs on any remaining heavies and optionally on the initial syllable if it lacks primary stress.

(4) a. ˈxada   'mountain'
     b. ˈunʃisan   'having read'
     c. ˌgaˈluː   'goose'
     d. ˌdoˈloːduˌgaːr   'seventh'
     e. ˌuˌlaːnˌbaːtˈriːnxan 'residents of Ulaanbaatar'
     f. ˈuitgarˌtae   'sad'
     g. ˈaːˌruːl   'dry cheese curds'

Second, prosodic minimality refers to the minimum legal size of a prosodic word. For example, in some languages, a prosodic word must be at least two syllables long. In others, prosodic words are permitted to be monosyllables, but only syllables of a certain size qualify. Consider Thurgovian Swiss German (Kraehenmann 2001, 2003, Muller 2001, Ringen and Vago 2011, Topintzi and Zimmermann 2014). A monosyllable in this dialect must contain a long vowel or complex coda, as in (5) (similarly in Icelandic; Kager 1999:268). The productivity of such a minimum is evident from repairs. In Thurgovian, a subminimal input is repaired by lengthening the vowel, as in (6). One can tell that the vowel is underlyingly short in such cases from suffixed forms such as the plural. Other evidence rules out an analysis in terms of shortening in suffixed forms.

(5) a. ʃilf   'reed'
     b. ʀuːʃ   'rouge'
     c. jakə   'to hunt'
     d. *ʃĩ, *ʃĩl, *ʀuʃ, *jak

(6) a. /has-e/   hase   'hares'
     b. /has/   haːs   'hare'
     c. /ttak-e/ ttake   'days'
     d. /ttak/   ttaːk   'day'

Prosodic minimality is sometimes also invoked for prosodic constituents above the prosodic word. For example, BinMin(φ, ω) requires a prosodic phrase to dominate at least two prosodic words (Selkirk 2011; see also Zec and Inkelas 1990, Inkelas and Zec 1995).

Third, weight is regulated in quantitative meter. For example, a verse of Vedic Sanskrit *gāyatrī* is given in (7). In this meter, which is related to the *śloka* meter in §1.1, a verse comprises three octosyllabic lines, and lines normally (with some exceptions) observe the weight template in (8), in which ᴗ notates a position that is typically light and _ one that is typically heavy (Oldenberg 1888, Arnold 1905). In fact, this schema is an oversimplification, as certain other tendencies apply, some of which are relational and therefore cannot be expressed by a unigram model. For example, the second and third positions are rarely both light (see also Kiparsky 2018).

(7) a. vá.ya.v ấ .yā.hi .dar.śa.ta   (Ṛg-Veda 1.2.1)
     b. i.mé .só.mā .á.raṃ.kr̥.tāḥ
     c. té.ṣām .pā.hi ś.ru.dhī́ .há.vam

(8) ×××ᴗ_ᴗ×

Other quantitative meters lack a fixed syllable count by virtue of allowing moraic substitutions. For example, the Sanskrit/Prakrit *āryā* meter contains lines of eight metra each, where most metra are required to be four moras (i.e. ᴗᴗᴗ, ᴗᴗ_, _ᴗᴗ, __, or ᴗ_ᴗ). Further restrictions apply; for example, odd-numbered metra cannot be ᴗ_ᴗ (§4.1).

Fourth, PROSODIC END-WEIGHT describes the tendency of prosodically heavier constituents to be localized domain-finally, all else being equal. This tendency is widespread cross-linguistically, but not universal. For example, in English and many other languages, coordinate phrases favor heavy-final orders, as in (9) (cf. e.g. Benor and Levy 2006, Mollin 2012, Morgan and Levy 2016). To a first approximation, this means that words with more syllables, longer vowels, and/or more complex margins are favored finally. This continues to hold when one controls for other factors influencing word order (including semantics, frequency, syntactic complexity, phonological complexity, etc.), through regression or experiments such as nonce-word ordering tasks. When constituents are monosyllables, as in (a–d), gradations of syllable weight are revealed. But end-weight also implicates the weight of larger prosodic constituents.

(9) a. pick and choose
     b. cap and gown
     c. tit for tat
     d. meet and greet
     e. dead or alive
     f. nook and cranny

Fifth, tone or pitch accent licensing is often treated as being weight-driven, usually in the sense that contour tones are confined to heavy syllables (e.g. Hyman 1985, Zec 1988, Zhang 2004, Gordon 2006). For example, in Thai, the full range of five tones (high, low, mid, rising, and falling) is available only on syllables with a long vowel or sonorant coda. The rimes V(ʔ) and VT (where T is an obstruent) support only two level tones, high and low (Gandour 1979). This Thai criterion, with its sensitivity to coda sonority, is perhaps the most widespread for tone licensing, unlike in stress and other systems, where it is also attested, but less commonly.

Sixth, compensatory alternations are usually taken to be weight-driven, in that they preserve mora count (e.g. Hayes 1989, Davis 2003, Beltzung 2008, Topintzi 2010, Kiparsky 2011). Perhaps the most common such pattern is the lengthening of a vowel to compensate for a lost coda, as in Ionic Greek *ēmi* 'am' (from earlier **esmi*; cf. Sanskrit *asmi*) or English *tooth* (Old English *tōþ*, from earlier Germanic **tanþ-*; cf. Sanskrit *dant-*). Consonant lengthening is another possible response, as in Aeolic *emmi* from **esmi*. Insofar as onsets do not bear weight, they are predicted not to participate in compensatory alternations, though several cases have been reported (e.g. Topintzi 2010 and references therein on Samothraki Greek, Pattani Malay, Trique, Trukese, Onondaga, etc.; cf. Loporcaro 1991:280, Kavitskaya 2002, Kiparsky 2011). Additionally, the duration or complexity of the onset trades gradiently with the duration of the vowel (Browman and Goldstein 1988, Katz 2010, 2012, Ryan 2014, Mai 2018). Figure 1.1 is based on the Buckeye corpus of conversational English (Pitt et al. 2007). It considers only primary stressed /ɪ/ in the initial syllables of disyllabic nouns. As onset size increases from zero to three consonants, /ɪ/ becomes shorter, the first two comparisons being significant (Mann-Whitney-Wilcoxon $p < .0001$). While this effect is phonetic, Ryan (2014), as here, maintains that onset complexity can affect weight in nearly every type of weight-sensitive phonological phenomenon. As an example of how onset-nucleus compensation plays out in the phonology of English, as onset complexity increases, the following vowel is increasingly less likely to be phonemically long (i.e. tense or diphthongal). Figure 1.2 is based on the initial syllables of all initially stressed, disyllabic nouns in CELEX (Baayen et al. 1993). The (near-)low vowels /æ, ɑ, ɔ/ are excluded, as their classification as long vs. short is less robust. The first two comparisons in Figure 1.2 are significant (Fisher's exact test $p < .0001$). Note the parallelism between phonetic trading off in Figure 1.1 and phonotactic trading off in Figure 1.2. The distinction between zero and one consonants is the most extreme, tapering off rapidly with greater onset complexity.

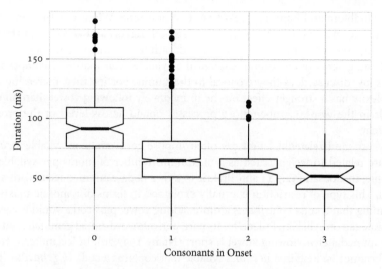

Figure 1.1 Primary stressed /ɪ/ in the initial syllable of a disyllabic noun is progressively shorter with progressively more complex onsets in the Buckeye corpus.

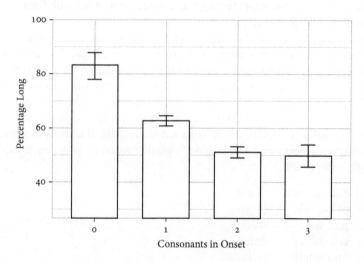

Figure 1.2 Long vowel incidence decreases as onset complexity increases. Based on the initial syllables of initially stressed, disyllabic nouns in English (CELEX).

Compensatory effects are documented also for prosodic constituents above the syllable. For example, even holding stress constant, the durations of two syllables composing a foot can trade off, as in Sami and Finnic languages (see Türk et al. 2018 for a survey) and in the Aŭciuki dialect of Belarusian and other Slavic languages (Borise 2017). Such effects can be phonologized in terms of moraic restrictions (Borise 2017, 2018). Moreover, as more material is added to the prosodic word, the constituents of that word are increasingly compressed, as with POLYSYLLABIC SHORTENING (Lehiste

1972, Lindblom and Rapp 1973, Port 1981, White 2002, White and Turk 2010). But this word-level DURATIONAL INVARIANCE ("smoothing" or "averaging" would be more apt)—regression towards the mean word duration by compressing long words or lengthening short ones—cannot explain the syllable- and foot-level compensatory effects just discussed, as they are local to their units. For instance, increasing onset complexity has a stronger effect on the immediately following vowel than on other vowels in the word. Compensatory processes obtain across levels of the prosodic hierarchy.

Seventh, and relatedly, languages often impose constraints on syllable structure that are related to weight, such as a maximum number of moras per syllable. For example, in Koasati (§2.7.1) and Prakrit (§3.3), a coda cannot cooccur with a long vowel. This type of restriction is usually explained in terms of a moraic maximum: Assuming that a coda contributes a mora, a long vowel plus coda would exceed the bimoraic cap on syllables. Pulaar, for its part, permits word-initial geminates, but only if the immediately following vowel is short (Niang 1997:70). In Icelandic, a stressed vowel cannot be long in a nonfinal syllable that contains a coda (e.g. *harður* 'hard'; **haːrður*), once again reflecting a bimoraic maximum for syllables (Kager 1999:268). In final position, a stressed vowel can be long before a simple coda, but not before a complex coda or geminate, reflecting the same constraint but with final consonant extrametricality (*ibid.*; §2.6.4).

Eighth, reduplication can be affected by weight. In Mokilese, for instance, the reduplicant must be a heavy syllable (McCarthy and Prince 1986, Blevins 1996). This heavy target is enforced on the surface by various strategies, as in (10). If the base is C-initial, copying the initial CVC is sufficient to ensure that the reduplicant is heavy (a–b). But if the base is C-initial and no following C is available to copy, the vowel must be lengthened, as in (c–d). If the base is V-initial, either a cluster must be copied (e) or, if no cluster is available, C must be lengthened (f). If a single C were copied but not lengthened before a V-initial base, it would resyllabify as an onset, yielding an illicit light reduplicant.

(10)   a. **pɔd**-.pɔ.dok   'planting'
      b. **pok**-.po.ki   'beating'
      c. **paː**-.pa   'weaving'
      d. **wiː**-.wi.a   'doing'
      e. **an.d**-an.dip   'spitting'
      f. **al.l**-a.lu   'walking'

Compare also quantitative complementarity in reduplication, as seen for Sanskrit in §1.1. Another case, from Ponapean, is exemplified in (11) (McCarthy and Prince 1986). If a monosyllabic base is heavy, the reduplicant is light (a–b). If the base is light, the reduplicant is heavy (c–d).

(11)   a. **du**-duːp   'dive'
      b. **ma**-mand   'tame'
      c. **paː**-pa   'weave'
      d. **lal**-lal   'make a sound'

Finally, (non-reduplicative) allomorphy is sometimes sensitive to the weight profile of the stem. Consider the Estonian genitive plural suffix of vowel-final stems in (12) (Mürk 1991, Kager 1996, Ryan 2016). In a word with no superheavy syllables, the suffix is -*te* when the base has an even number of syllables (a–b), and otherwise -*tte* (c). If the word contains a superheavy syllable, this parity is reversed (d–e). Kager (1996) analyzes this allomorphy as being foot-driven, as the parenthesized feet in (12) suggest. The suffix is geminated iff doing so would close a stressed syllable, making it heavy.

(12) a. (vísa)-**te**   'tough (gen. pl.)'
      b. (téle)(fòni)-**te**   'telephone (gen. pl.)'
      c. (pára)(jà-**tte**)   'suitable (gen. pl.)'
      d. (áas:)(tà-**tte**)   'year (gen. pl.)'
      e. (áat:)(riùmi)-**te**   'atrium (gen. pl.)'

While many cases of weight-sensitive allomorphy reduce to metrical structure, as in Estonian, it is not clear that this always holds. In Finnish, for instance, nominalizing -*ntV* has high and low allomorphs (-*nti* and -*nta* ~ -*ntä*, respectively; Anttila 2006). Anttila (2006) finds that the strongest predictor of the choice between these allomorphs is the weight of the ultima of the stem, not its stress or foot structure. Affix location may also be sensitive to weight. For example, in Amharic, a syllable is heavy iff it is closed by a geminate (Sande 2014, Sande and Hedding 2017). Adjective pluralization and verb iterativization is marked by an infixing CV reduplicant, but only if the base contains a geminate, in which case the reduplicant immediately precedes the geminate. If the base lacks a geminate, reduplication cannot be employed. As Sande (2014) argues, this attraction must be driven by weight, not stress: All bases have stress, but only those containing a heavy allow reduplication.

1.3 Universals of weight

This section reviews some properties of weight that hold across languages and processes. Some of these universals are non-controversial, though I adduce new evidence for nearly all of them in this book. Some, however, may not be widely acknowledged, such as the systematic reversal in the treatment of sonority between the onset and rime (see especially Gordon 2005 and Ryan 2014), or onset complexity effects, both of which receive further support from new studies here. I consider the nucleus, coda, and onset in turn. Each universal is labeled $x \leq y$, which indicates an implicational universal: If the weights of x and y are distinguished, x is lighter. Of course, x and y can also be conflated.

In the nucleus, greater length and sonority correlate with greater weight. Long vowels are if anything heavier than short vowels ($V \leq VV$), and full (or peripheral) vowels are if anything heavier than reduced (or central) vowels ($\partial \leq V$). Weight can be sensitive even to subphonemic duration, as with end-weight in Figure 5.2. In terms of sonority, lower is if anything heavier (notated "$I \leq A$"), with the exact cutoff(s) varying (e.g. de Lacy 2004:193). Note that duration and sonority are largely confounded in the nucleus, in that lower vowels are usually longer cross-linguistically

(Lehiste 1970, Westbury and Keating 1980), though height-conditioned length differences are not always significant (de Lacy 2007:294). When it comes to distinctive vowel length, however, there is perhaps no case in which a phonemically short vowel (e.g. [a]) outweighs a phonemically long vowel (e.g. [iː]) by virtue of the former's greater sonority.

The coda behaves like the nucleus, in that greater length/complexity and sonority correlate with greater weight. The presence vs. absence of a coda conditions heaviness in numerous cases ($\emptyset \leq C$), including several already discussed. Coda complexity can also affect weight ($C \leq CC$), though this is considerably less common. Most apparent cases of $C \leq CC$ can be attributed to final consonant extrametricality, such that the distinction is really $\emptyset \leq C$, ignoring the word-final consonant. Nevertheless, word-internal $C < CC$ is attested at least for stress (e.g. Hindi) and meter (e.g. Persian and Vedic Sanskrit) and is also characteristic of gradient systems (§2.8). Moreover, not all word-final complexity effects can be explained by extrametricality (e.g. English final $\emptyset < C < CC < CCC$ in §2.8.3). Additionally, coda sonority can condition weight, as found in stress, meter, end-weight, tone licensing, and syllable structure. I notate this generalization "$T \leq N$," though the cutoff need not coincide exactly with obstruents vs. sonorants.

While onsets are traditionally regarded as being inert with respect to weight, this book, like Topintzi's (2010) book on onset weight, supports a rather different outlook (see also Ryan 2014 and references therein). Onset weight is secure across the four metrical domains treated in detail in this book. In fact, weight effects based on sonority and complexity (as opposed to presence vs. absence) appear to be no less common for onsets than for codas. As in the coda, presence vs. absence can condition heaviness ($\emptyset \leq C$). Onset complexity effects ($C \leq CC$) are clear from gradient weight in stress, meter, and end-weight, as well as from categorical prosodic minimality and possibly categorical stress (Gordon 2005; cf. Topintzi 2010). Onset sonority can also affect weight in stress, meter, and end-weight, but in the opposite direction as in the coda: For the onset, less sonority correlates with greater weight ($N \leq T$). As with the coda, the sonority cutoff is not necessarily sonorants vs. obstruents, but can fall at other sonority divisions (e.g. voiced < voiceless). In short, universally across languages and systems, sonority contributes to weight in the rime, but detracts from it in the onset. On possible phonetic rationales for this reversal, see §5.9.4.

Related to the weight-augmenting effect of sonority in the rime, the whole rime VC is if anything lighter than the whole rime VV ($VC \leq VV$). The criterion $VC < VV$, that is, the Khalkha criterion, is common, but its reversal is arguably unattested for prominence mapping systems (see footnote d to Figure 1.3 and Chapter 2, especially §2.7.2, for further discussion). This (near-)universal continues to hold when further slots are appended to the rime, for example, $VCC \leq VVC$ and $VCCC \leq VVCC$. Thus, a V slot is universally heavier (if anything) than a C slot, owing to the former's greater sonority.

Next, consider geminates. Intervocalically, a geminate (e.g. [ap.pa]) is if anything heavier than a cluster (e.g. [ak.ta]). In fact, the two are almost always equivalent (cf. the Principle of Equal Weight for Codas; Tranel 1991), but some cases of C.C < G are attested for stress (e.g. Amharic, Cahuilla, San'ani Arabic). The reversal is arguably unattested (on two ostensible exceptions from Ngalakgan and Tashlhiyt Berber, see §2.6.7). CC ≤ G also appears to hold in margins (e.g. onset G vs. CC; Topintzi and Davis 2017).

Beyond geminates vs. clusters, one might ask more generally whether geminates are always moraic. In this book, I tentatively support the Moraic Theory of Geminates, though I do not wish to take a strong position on the question, since I do not address every potentially relevant case here (see the end of §2.6.4 for one type of case I do not address, as it concerns syllable structure). I do, however, reanalyze most of the claimed exceptions. First, in some stress systems, including Malayalam, Selkup, and at least a dozen other languages (§2.6.1), VG is light for stress (with VC), while VV is heavy. A traditional response to this situation has been to treat geminates as nonmoraic in such cases (cf. Selkirk 1990, Tranel 1991, Blevins 1995). However, as I analyze these cases in Chapter 2, they reflect attraction of stress to the long vowel, permitting geminates to remain moraic. Indeed, in some such cases, syllables closed by geminates attract secondary stress, corroborating their moraicity even when they yield stress to heavier VV. Cases of alleged nonmoraic geminates in margins are similarly reanalyzed here. In Leti, for instance, VV but not GV is said to condition stress (though the facts are not secure), as I analyze via long-vowel attraction (§2.6.6). Certain prosodic minima, including Leti and Thurgovian Swiss German, are said to treat geminates as nonmoraic, but the evidence is ambiguous in these cases, as addressed in §3.1. Thus, while it is not a specific aim of this book to defend the Moraic Theory of Geminates, because I adopt Vowel Prominence as a theory of VC < VV, most of the claimed exceptions to that theory are subject to reanalysis, potentially vindicating it.

The aforementioned universals are summarized in Figure 1.3. A checkmark indicates that the given polarity is attested at least once in the given phenomenon. The reversals of the universals (e.g. VV < V) are also shown in shaded rows. I include these to make explicit that the reversals are, for the most part, unattested, though some of the cells have footnotes. After all, a potential universal of the form $x \leq y$ is not undermined by its lack of attestation in a particular phenomenon; it is undermined only if its reversal is attested. Including both polarities of each pair makes explicit this distinction between "absence of evidence" and "evidence of absence." The "cat." and "grad." headers stand for categorical and gradient, respectively, and indicate whether the attested cases arise from categorical criteria/scales, gradient weight systems, both, or neither. This distinction is largely irrelevant for minimality and end-weight. Prosodic minimality is canonically categorical and prosodic end-weight is canonically gradient, though see §6.4 on exceptions to both.

An implied ceteris paribus clause accompanies all of these universals. They might be locally violated when another factor interferes. For example, in Huehuetla Tepehua, only a coda containing a sonorant is moraic, entailing that a simplex coda containing a sonorant (e.g. [an]) outweighs a complex coda containing only obstruents (e.g. [aɬtʃ]) (Kung 2007; §2.7.2). Certain VC therefore outweighs certain VCC_1, but this does not violate the C ≤ CC universal for codas, since the ostensible counterexamples are not in a containment relation. If sonority is held constant, C ≤ CC holds. As a second example, in Nanti, the rime [a] attracts primary stress away from the rime

[in], reflecting the precedence of nuclear sonority over coda presence for primary stress (Crowhurst and Michael 2005:78). While in this case a particular V outweighs a particular VC, Nanti exhibits V < VC when one controls for sonority.

Figure 1.3 is not exhaustive, especially as concerns near-universals. For instance, one might add that if a weight scale is ternary or greater, it almost always includes V < VC < VV, as in dozens of cases from stress and meter. V < VX < VXX (where X is C or V), for its part, is rare as a ternary weight scale, being attested, for instance, in

		Stress		Meter		Minimality	End-Weight
		cat.	grad.	cat.	grad.	cat.	grad.
Nucleus	V < VV	✓	✓	✓	✓	✓	✓
	VV < V						
	ə < V	✓					
	V < ə						
	I < A	✓	✓		✓		✓
	A < I						
Coda	Ø < C	✓	✓	✓	✓	✓	✓
	C < Ø						
	C < CC	✓	✓	✓	✓	✓	✓
	CC < C						
	T < N	✓	✓[a]		✓		✓
	N < T						
Onset	Ø < C	✓	✓		✓	✓	✓
	C < Ø						
	C < CC	[b]	✓		✓	✓	✓
	CC < C						
	N < T	✓	(✓)[c]		✓		✓
	T < N						
Other	VC < VV	✓	✓	✓	✓	✓	✓
	VV < VC	[d]					
	CC < G	✓				[e]	
	G < CC	[f]			(✓)[g]		

FIGURE 1.3 Universals of weight across metrical weight phenomena. A checkmark indicates that the given contrast is attested in the given phenomenon. Both orders of each contrast are presented to make explicit the universality of the polarities. The illicit polarity is shaded. Evidence from categorical ("cat.") vs. gradient ("grad.") systems is distinguished.

[a] Hinton and Luthin (2002) suggest this for Yahi (§2.8.2). Garcia (2017a) suggests it for English (§2.8.3).

[b] Gordon (2005) mentions Bislama and Nankina as potential cases, but they may not be secure (Topintzi 2010:223).

[c] Ryan (2014) suggests this for English.

[d] Potential counterexamples from Dutch, Tiberian Hebrew, and Huehuetla Tepehua are tempered in §2.7.2. A handful of cases from pitch accent systems have also been put forth (*ibid.*).

[e] Initial geminates count as heavy for prosodic minimality in some languages, though I am not aware of such a case in which initial clusters are also available, to compare CC (cf. Topintzi and Davis 2017).

[f] Geminates are claimed to be lighter than certain clusters in Ngalakgan, but see §2.6.7 for further considerations.

[g] Geminates, unlike clusters, optionally scan as light in Tashlhiyt Berber. On a possible vowel length confound, see §2.6.7.

Hindi stress per Kelkar (1968) and in various Indo-Iranian meters (including Hindi, Persian, and Vedic Sanskrit; Chapter 4).[3] As another near-universal, VG (i.e. a rime closed by a geminate) tends strongly to align with VC in weight, regardless of whether the Latin or Khalkha criterion is employed, though a few counterexamples are found (e.g. Amharic and San'ani Arabic; §2.6.4). In these counterexamples, geminates are heavier than clusters. As just discussed, geminates are arguably never lighter than clusters.

Furthermore, typological tendencies that are confined to specific phenomena are not addressed in this section, though they are treated in the relevant chapters below. For example, quantitative meters almost universally select the Latin criterion, though at least one case of the Khalkha criterion is established, in Nanti. A similarly strong skew between the two criteria is not found in the other phenomena. Finally, elements such as diphthongs and laryngeals are not addressed in this section, as they vary widely in their treatment. Diphthongs can be equivalent to V, VC, or VV in weight, though they usually align with VV. In Pulaar, for one, they align with VC as heavier than V but lighter than VV (as such, one might analyze them as vowel-glide sequences). Laryngeals also vary. In systems distinguishing V from VC, V? can join either category. Indeed, V? can even be lighter than V (as in Hupa) or heavier than VC (as in Cahuilla).

1.4 Scope and aims of this book

This book treats the phonology of weight in four grammatical systems, namely, stress, prosodic minimality, quantitative meter, and prosodic end-weight. All four are metrical systems in which mapping constraints relate weight to stress or phonological strength, either directly or via foot structure. In other words, all four exhibit a weight–strength interface. For stress, this is self-evident, as constraints regulate the coincidence of weight and stress. Quantitative meters are analyzed similarly, except that stress is replaced by metrical strength. Prosodic minimality, for its part, is usually taken to reflect the need for a prosodic word to be large enough to be footed, and hence bear stress. Finally, prosodic end-weight is argued here to be driven by the stress–weight interface on a phrasal scale, such that heavier constituents are drawn to loci of nuclear stress.

The chapters are ordered as such—stress, minimality, meter, end-weight—so that the exposition generally progresses from scales of lower to higher complexity. In particular, weight for stress is usually binary, though more complex and gradient scales are also well established. Prosodic minimality is typically binary. Quantitative meters too implicate binary criteria, but they often add to them gradient, intracategory weight effects. Finally, prosodic end-weight is thoroughly gradient. For these reasons, the first half of the book is dominated by Optimality Theory analyses based on descriptive, typological data, whereas the latter half is dominated by experimental and corpus-based statistics. In either case, however, the underlying constraint-based mechanics

---

[3] Eipomek stress is dubious as a case of this scale; see §2.1.

remain essentially the same, as explained presently. Within chapters, sections likewise tend to proceed in terms of increasing scalar complexity. For example, Chapter 2, on stress, treats binary and ternary systems before closing with gradient weight (§2.8). Prosodic end-weight, being the most complex, finds its proper place at the end.

As mentioned, the book focuses on metrical systems. Some other topics that are addressed under the rubric of weight in §1.2, such as tone licensing and syllable structure, are non-metrical, lacking a weight–strength interface. For example, recall Thai, in which a contour tone necessitates a long vowel or sonorant coda. The rationale for this restriction is that the rime must contain sufficient voiced material to realize the contour, tone (f_0) not being realized on voiceless material (Zhang 2004, Gordon 2006). But it does not reflect rhythm, as manifested in alternating strong and weak elements. I also do not pursue morphological topics here, such as allomorphy and reduplication.[4]

Similarly, this book treats only the phonology of weight, not its phonetic basis, except in passing, as relevant. This focus partly reflects a desire to avoid duplicating previous literature. In particular, Gordon's (2006) book *Syllable weight: phonetics, phonology, typology* extensively covers the phonetic interface of weight (see also dissertations such as Hubbard 1994, Ahn 2000, and Gordon 1999 and articles such as Broselow et al. 1997 and Gordon 2002b, among others). Gordon (2006, etc.) proposes that languages tend to select a binary criterion based on two desiderata, namely, PHONETIC EFFECTIVENESS (whereby the mean energy of heavies is rendered maximally distinct from that of lights) and PHONOLOGICAL SIMPLICITY (which favors criteria that do not involve disjunctions or multiple place predicates). The term "continua" in the present subtitle refers to gradient weight in phonology, which is not treated by the work just cited, and has been largely overlooked in research on syllable weight outside of my own work and some other recent articles (e.g. Garcia 2017b). On the one hand, research addressing the phonetic basis of weight seeks to determine how gradient phonetic measures such as duration or energy are mapped onto phonological categories such as heavy and light. On the other hand, gradient weight in phonology refers to phonologically diagnosed gradience, such as syllables varying along a continuum in their propensities to attract stress, to occupy strong positions in meter, to occur phrase-finally, and so forth. In some of these systems, such as prosodic end-weight in English, there is no heavy vs. light distinction of which to speak. The conclusion (Chapter 6) returns to the phonetics–phonology interface in the context of the constraint formalism developed in this book.

Though I define all constraints and introduce structural assumptions, including moraic theory, I do so fairly compactly, and generally assume familiarity with Optimality Theory (OT; Prince and Smolensky 1993/2004; for introductions, see Kager 1999, McCarthy 2002, 2011). To analyze gradient weight effects, I employ maximum entropy Harmonic Grammar (maxent HG; see Hayes and Wilson 2008 and references therein), which is closely related to OT, except that constraints are numerically

---

[4] End-weight can involve morphosyntax, but my discussion in Chapter 5 controls for morphosyntax, considering only the phonological aspect of end-weight.

weighted in maxent HG, yielding a probability distribution over candidates. To be sure, such probability distributions include those in which a single candidate wins (virtually) categorically, as in OT, but they cover variation as well. In either framework, however, the theory of weight-mapping, as outlined in §1.5, is the same. In particular, given the stringent formulation of predicates, markedness reversals such as VN < VT are no more possible in maxent HG than they are in OT. Maxent HG merely allows the modeling of both hard and soft contrasts. Moreover, it captures varying degrees of tendency, as when soft contrasts differ in their effect sizes.

Topics such as stress and prosodic minimality routinely come up in discussions of phonological weight, but about half of this book is dedicated to two topics that are often omitted from such discussions, namely, metrics and end-weight. Gordon (2006), for one, treats meter only briefly and does not address end-weight. Furthermore, my treatment of stress and prosodic minimality has different emphases from most previous work, in that the centerpiece of the stress chapter is the analysis of complex scales and the centerpiece of the prosodic minimality chapter is contextual minimality, that is, how minimality is implemented for constituents that are embedded in larger constituents.

This book is not conceived as a typological survey, though parts of it can serve that purpose. Rather, the focus here is on analytical issues. For survey purposes (e.g. for enumerating cases of a criterion), Gordon (2006) remains exemplary; one can also consult the growing online database StressTyp2 (Goedemans et al. 2017; cf. Kager 2012, Goedemans and van der Hulst 2013, and Heinz et al. 2016).

I now synopsize some of the key theoretical claims put forth in each chapter. I omit widely acknowledged generalizations here, which are treated at the beginning of each chapter.

Chapter 2: Weight scales for stress. The most common suprabinary skeletal scale is V < VC < VV, as found in at least twenty languages. I argue that a standard analysis of this scale, Coercion, is inadequate for most of these cases. Two alternative approaches are compared, namely, Vowel Prominence (e.g. STRESS→VV) and Coda Prominence (e.g. STRESS→CODA). The former is favored by several considerations, including its better coverage of secondary stress, its preclusion of the arguably pathological criterion VV < VC, its necessity for metrics and end-weight, and its compatibility with the Moraic Theory of Geminates. Concerning the last, geminate-closed VG almost always patterns like VC rather than VV in languages with VC < VV (in sixty-seven such languages surveyed, this holds about 90% of the time). Coercion and Coda Prominence require rejecting the moraicity of geminates in these languages, which include the likes of Finnish, Malayalam, and Pulaar, where independent evidence abounds for the moraicity of geminates, sometimes arising from the stress system itself. I take geminates always to be moraic for stress. Apparent counterexamples (beyond the Malayalam-type cases) such as Leti and Ngalakgan are reanalyzed. Finally, weight for stress can be gradient, as in English and several other languages. Gradient scales are both highly articulated and quantifiable, and often evince onset and sonority effects on weight. This chapter thus has three core theses: (1) Vowel Prominence is superior to both Coercion and Coda Prominence for capturing the stress typology; (2) Vowel Prominence usefully permits geminates to remain moraic in VG < VV systems, which abound; and (3) weight for stress is sometimes gradient, with various fine-grained aspects of syllable structure quantifiably affecting stress placement.

Chapter 3: Prosodic minimality in isolation and in context. To date, nearly all research on prosodic minimality considers the prosodic word in isolation. A contribution of this chapter is that it analyzes minima in the context of larger prosodic constituents, revealing new issues. In particular, resyllabification across words can threaten minima, to which languages can respond by (1) permitting degenerate prosodic words to stand on the surface, as in Classical Latin, (2) (largely) suppressing resyllabification iff it threatens minimality, as in Māhārāṣṭrī Prakrit, or (3) allowing resyllabification but repairing the resulting would-be degenerate prosodic word by lengthening or gemination, as in Tamil. A second contribution of this chapter is a detailed study of a VC minimum to which only certain coda consonants contribute, and not in a way that can be explained by sonority or phonotactics. To wit, in Tamil, coda rhotics are nonmoraic (for minimality and otherwise), despite being highly sonorous consonants.

Chapter 4: Quantitative meter: Categorical and gradient weight. Perhaps all quantitative meters involve a binary criterion (usually, but not always, the Latin criterion), but many (perhaps all) also treat weight as more complex in various ways. I distinguish between variable weight, which is caused by optional processes (e.g. variable cluster syllabification), and gradient weight, in which phonological structure is fixed but the meter evinces sensitivity to a continuum of weight. The latter is revealed in at least three ways. First, superheavies are sometimes avoided in cadences, as I demonstrate for Vedic Sanskrit. Second, different position types sometimes exhibit different tolerances for heavier or lighter heavies, permitting the diagnosis of an intra-heavy weight continuum, as I illustrate for Kalevala Finnish and Homeric Greek. Third, line-final position, traditionally regarded as indifferent to weight, in fact favors heavier heavies (or, in some meters, lighter lights), again revealing weight continua. Interval Theory (Steriade 2008, 2011, 2012) is examined at the end of this chapter.

Chapter 5: Prosodic end-weight and the stress–weight interface. Prosodic end-weight refers to the specifically phonological aspect of end-weight, as emerges when other factors influencing word order are controlled. I review eight principles of pros-odic end-weight, all of which align with the typology of weight more generally. I there-fore maintain that prosodic end-weight manifests bona fide phonological weight as opposed to, say, complexity or total duration. Several possible explanations for prosodic end-weight are considered, including final lengthening, complexity deferral, phonotactic or rhythmic optimization, and phrasal/nuclear stress. I argue that phrasal stress is the core motivation for prosodic end-weight, unifying its eight core pro-perties, while the other considerations are parochial at best. Thus, the weight–stress interface operates not only within words, but also in phrasal prosody. I extend the weight-mapping constraint apparatus to this phrasal context and discuss further iss-ues that it raises, including languages with beginning-weight rather than end-weight.

Chapter 6 concludes, summarizing key findings and raising issues for further research. This chapter elaborates on topics such as the phonetics–phonology interface, including the viability of a direct-interface approach to the weight predicate (*t*), the domain of the weight percept, the opacity of weight criteria, and explanations for the varying incidence of categoricity vs. gradience across weight-based phenomena.

1.5 Overview of the constraint system for prominence mapping

This book assumes the standard prosodic hierarchy that includes moras, syllables, feet, prosodic words, and so forth (e.g. Nespor and Vogel 1986, Hayes 1995, Selkirk 2011, and many others). The highest level of the prosodic hierarchy that I explicitly invoke is the recursive prosodic word (cf. the clitic group of Nespor and Vogel 1986). A simple example, *the cat*, is provided in (13). Chapters 2 and 3 offer more details on how moras and feet, respectively, are assigned. This section serves only to orient the book theoretically; it is not an introduction to these matters.

(13)

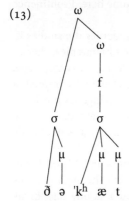

Chapter 5, on end-weight, treats still higher-level constituents, but generalizes over them via φ, which refers to any prosodic node at the level of the prosodic word or higher. When constituents such as feet are irrelevant, I omit them from tableaux, as in most of Chapter 2. Given this book's adoption of feet and its emphasis on scalar mapping as opposed to broader metrical theory, it makes little explicit use of the grid. One apparent exception is Chapter 5, which extensively invokes clash and lapse. However, the purpose there is to control for those factors, not to analyze them. Since lapse is sometimes cited as motivating end-weight, I control for any possible influence from it in order to distill effects that can only be attributed to weight, the object of that chapter.

Throughout the book, I invoke constraints that regulate the mapping between strong elements of different types. These constraints take the form of implications, $x \rightarrow y$, where x and y are (classes of) STRONG ELEMENTS, that is, constituents that can be prominent in metrical systems. They include stress, weight, and strength in poetic meter (also known as ICTUS), as in (14), to be refined presently (Ryan 2017b:606). Note that $x \rightarrow y$ is equivalent to $*x/\neg y$ "penalize any x that is not y." Both formulations are found in the literature. For example, STRESS-TO-WEIGHT (§2.3.2) is equivalent to $*P/\sigma_\mu$, where P is primary stress (Crowhurst and Michael 2005).

(14)

Type	Strong Element	Weak Element
Stress	Stressed	Unstressed
Meter	Strong	Weak
Weight	Heavy	Light

As stated, I assume that prominence mapping constraints invoke only strong elements. Thus, a constraint such as Stress→Light is precluded.[5] I do not restrict the type of element that can go in the protasis vs. apodosis of the conditional. Consider, for instance, a meter in which a weak position cannot contain a stressed syllable. Hanson and Kiparsky (1996) express this constraint as "W⇒¬P," meaning that a weak position cannot be prominent. This constraint invokes weak elements. But it could equivalently be formulated as Stress→Strong; as a rule, $x \rightarrow y \equiv \neg y \rightarrow \neg x$. These are notational variants, but Ryan (2017b) also presents an empirical argument for the no-weakness principle,[6] which I also tentatively assume here: Prominence mapping constraints refer only to strong elements.

I now elaborate on the taxonomy of strong elements that underlies the studies in this book. I assume throughout that they comprise stringency hierarchies, that is, they are expressed as subsets rather than as complements (Prince 1983:57f, 1999, de Lacy 2004). If strength is envisioned as a scale, strong elements comprise a contiguous subset of that scale that extends to its strong extreme. Stringency precludes the formulation of unattested grammars in which prominence is favored on weak elements over strong ones. For arguments for stringency over fixed ranking, see de Lacy (2004:148).

For stress (Chapter 2), I invoke two levels of strength, Stress and Main. Main refers to primary stress and is therefore a subset of Stress. On the apparent lack of necessity for the predicate Secondary *vel sim.*, which would, at any rate, break stringency (assuming that Main is also available), see §2.3.2.[7] No additional strength scale is needed for prosodic minimality (Chapter 3), which I analyze in terms of stress–weight mapping or foot form. For meter (Chapter 4), I adopt the most standard convention of generative metrics, which is to distinguish between strong and weak

---

[5] To be sure, there are languages in which stressed syllables are required to be light and even repaired to be such, but it is due to foot-form constraints, not prominence mapping (e.g. Zuraw 2018 on trochaic shortening). Similarly, de Lacy (2004) analyzes Kiriwina stress using a constraint that requires the weak syllable of a trochee to have a high vowel. As he makes clear, this constraint cannot be formulated more broadly as, say, Unstressed→High or NonHigh→Stress. In the present terminology, it is a foot-form rather than prominence mapping constraint, as discussed further in §2.3.2.

[6] It would not suffice to constrain mapped predicates to be of the same polarity. For example, among three-way mappings, constraints like Stress→(Strong→$\sigma_{\mu\mu}$) are attested, while those like Unstressed→(Weak→σ_μ) appear to be impossible (Ryan 2017b). No-weakness captures this asymmetry; polarity agreement does not.

[7] In principle, All, that is, any syllable, is also available as a predicate. This predicts the existence of languages in which all syllables are stressed. In practice, it is difficult to determine whether such languages exist: Given the relative nature of stress, a language in which all syllables bear some degree of stress would be unlikely to be described as such (though Macushi Carib is one example; Hawkins 1950). Moreover, even setting aside All, such a language is predicted by other standard metrical constraints. For example, combining moraic trochees with open-syllable lengthening can generate such a language.

positions (e.g. Halle and Keyser 1966, Prince 1989, Deo 2007, Deo and Kiparsky 2011, Hayes and Moore-Cantwell 2011, Hayes et al. 2012, Blumenfeld 2015, 2016b, Ryan 2017b, Kiparsky 2018; but for other approaches cf. Golston 1998, Golston and Riad 2000, 2005, Fabb and Halle 2008). In this book, I reserve the predicate Strong for strong positions in poetic meter. For prosodic end-weight (Chapter 5), I invoke φ_s, a strong node at the level of the prosodic word or higher. φ_s ultimately represents an extension of Stress, in the sense that Stress is the head of a foot, Main is the head of a prosodic word, and φ_s is any higher-level head.

Finally, weight itself is a dimension of strength, in that heavy elements can induce prominence in rhythmic systems. This book operationalizes weight classes as stringency hierarchies of syllables or segments. For example, $V_\mu[+son]_\mu \rightarrow$ Stress requires any syllable in which the second mora is a sonorant ([+son], which includes vowels) to bear stress. More or less inclusive feature matrices can be similarly specified (on features, see Chomsky and Halle 1968 and Hayes 2009), but given the no-weakness principle, they must, if referring to the rime, identify a section of the sonority scale that includes all more sonorous segments (on sonority, see Zec 1995, Parker 2002, 2012, de Lacy 2004). Figure 1.4 schematizes some legal weight predicates according to this system as an Euler diagram.

The notion of a universal sonority scale is not without controversy, in part because linguists invoke it for widely disparate phenomena (for discussion, see Parker 2002, 2012). In the present context, sonority is relevant only as it relates to the weight percept, which I take to be total perceptual energy (t), that is, "the integration of energy over time in the perceptual domain" (Gordon 2002b). I use the less precise term sonority in the context of segment classes because that is the convention in the field (e.g. Zec 1988, 1995, 2003, Kenstowicz 1994b, Anttila 1997a, 2010, Prince 1999, de Lacy 2004, Crowhurst and Michael 2005). Moreover, I employ only broad, generally accepted sonority contrasts, such as sonorant vs. obstruent and liquid vs. nasal. That said, it is total energy rather than sonority that ultimately grounds stringency scales for weight, a nuance that occasionally arises below. For example, in Tamil, /ɾ/ is more sonorous than /n/, but also lighter than it. In §3.4, I observe that

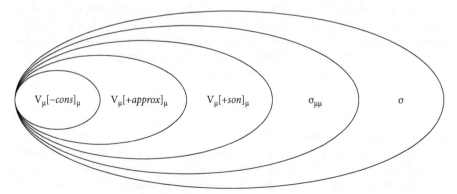

Figure 1.4 A partial stringent weight hierarchy for syllables, in which more embedded sets are heavier.

/ɾ/ is substantially shorter than /n/, meaning that its total energy is less even though its sonority is greater. In terms of the phonological analysis, I argue that rhotics do not project moras in Tamil. Similarly, /a/ does not outweigh /iː/ in any language, despite the former being more sonorous. Once again, moraicity—the discretization and phonologization of total energy (§6.1)—takes precedence over sonority.

As discussed in §1.3, sonority has the opposite effect in the onset: Lower sonority is heavier. For example, weight predicates might refer to [−*son*] or [−*voice*] in the onset. If predicates are expressed as syllable types, this raises the question of how onset and rime effects combine to form a unified stringency hierarchy. For example, in categorical weight systems sensitive to both onset and coda sonority, when the two are crossed (e.g. TVT vs. NVN), does the onset take priority (NVN < TVT) or does the coda (TVT < NVN)? Or do languages vary, say, as a function of language-specific phonetics? I am not aware of data speaking directly to this question. One might expect the coda to take precedence. After all, there are many cases in which coda presence vs. absence matters for weight while onset presence vs. absence is irrelevant. But for sonority, onset and coda effects are roughly equally frequent in the typology, and rarely both relevant for categorical weight. While some cases have been documented in which stress is sensitive to coda sonority, ignoring the onset (e.g. Kwak'wala, §2.1), others have been documented in which stress is sensitive to onset sonority, ignoring the coda (e.g. Tümpisa Shoshone, Dayley 1989; Karo, Gabas Jr. 1998, 1999, Topintzi 2010; cf. Blumenfeld 2006). Given this empirical unclarity, it would be premature to codify the coda as taking precedence over the onset in all respects. I therefore risk overgeneration rather than undergeneration, treating onset and rime effects as intersecting constraint families (Zuraw and Hayes 2017). I do so by leaving rime structure unspecified in weight-mapping constraints that invoke onsets (e.g. $T_{ons}{\rightarrow}$STRESS). Such constraints are still grounded by the sonority principle for onsets. See §5.9.4 for further discussion.

Finally, the present approach (with many others, e.g. de Lacy 2004, Crowhurst and Michael 2005) combines mora- and sonority-based weight. As such, it is more powerful than an approach in which sonority affects weight only via moraification. Consider, for instance, a language in which closed syllables are heavy only if closed by a sonorant, that is, VT < VN. One means of implementing this contrast is to confine coda moraicity to N, that is, $V_\mu T < V_\mu N_\mu$. In this book, feature-sensitive moraicity remains viable, but I also permit sonority to affect weight-sensitive phenomena even when moraicity is held constant, thanks to mapping constraints that relate sonority directly to other strength predicates such as stress. For example, even when $V_\mu T_\mu$ and $V_\mu N_\mu$ are both bimoraic, the latter might outweigh the former by virtue of $V_\mu[+son]_\mu{\rightarrow}$STRESS. At first blush, this extra power might seem redundant. Nevertheless, I motivate it at length in Chapter 2, adducing cases from stress and other systems in which sonority (including V vs. C) breaks ties between syllables that must otherwise be analyzed as bimoraic. To give a few examples, first, in Chickasaw, stress favors VV over VC, but VC remains heavy for secondary stress even when VC yields primary stress to VV. Therefore, one cannot analyze VC as monomoraic (§2.5.4). Second, in English prosodic end-weight, VV words outweigh VC words, even though both are bimoraic (e.g. *hem and haw, lock and key*; §5.5.3). Third, in

Homeric meter, the first position of a metron must be filled by a bimoraic syllable. But metron-initial heavies tend to be lighter heavies than heavies in other positions, revealing a rich weight scale (including VT < VN < VV) that cannot be analyzed via variable moraicity, lest VT and VN be parsable as light (§4.4.2). See also de Lacy (2004) and Crowhurst and Michael (2005) on weight contrasts between syllables that must be analyzed as monomoraic.

To conclude this overview of the weight-mapping apparatus, this book accomplishes prominence mapping by means of constraints relating metrical strength predicates to each other.[8] These constraints are stated as implications $x \rightarrow y$ "penalize each x that lacks the property y." By the no-weakness principle, x and y in such relations must be strong predicates. Moreover, a strong predicate is defined stringently, that is, as a set of elements such that for every element x_0 in the set, all elements heavier than x_0 are also in the set. Otherwise, I impose no restrictions on the protasis vs. apodosis of the conditional. For example, STRESS$\rightarrow \sigma_{\mu\mu}$ and $\sigma_{\mu\mu}\rightarrow$ STRESS are both viable. Strength scales include stress, weight, and ictus. Other possible strength predicates, such as tone (Zec 1999, de Lacy 2002b, Fabb and Halle 2008:254ff), are not explored in this book.

---

[8] As clarified above (footnote 5), prominence mapping constraints are not the only constraints that can affect the coincidence of strong or weak elements from different scales. Constraints on foot form, for one, can cause stressed syllables to be heavy (e.g. foot binarity) or light (e.g. trochaic shortening), among other adjustments (§2.3.2).

2

Weight scales for stress

2.1 Introduction

The location of stress in a word or phrase is determined by syllable weight in many languages. In describing such cases, a distinction is often made between the CRITERION (or SCALE), which determines how syllables are categorized as heavy or light (etc.), and the RULE, which determines how stress is assigned given a weight template.[1] For example, in Selkup (Uralic), the rule is that stress falls on the rightmost heavy syllable, and otherwise (if no heavy is present) on the leftmost syllable. The criterion is that a syllable is heavy iff it contains a long vowel. Some examples are provided in (1) (Kuznecova et al. 1980, Halle and Clements 1983). Stress is indicated, according to the IPA standard, by ˈ before a syllable with primary stress and by ˌ before one with secondary stress.

(1) a. qumˈmɪː   'our friend'
    b. kanaŋˈmiː   'our dog'
    c. uːˈcɔːmit   'we work'
    d. ˈqoːkitiḻʲ   'deaf'
    e. qumoːqlɪˈlɪː 'your two friends'
    f. uːcikˈkoːqɪ   'they two are working'
    g. ˈamɪrna   'eats'
    h. ˈqoḻʲcimpati 'found'

Kwak'wala (Wakashan) has a stress rule that is the mirror image of Selkup: leftmost heavy, else rightmost. Moreover, its criterion for "heavy" is more inclusive. A syllable is heavy iff it contains a long vowel or nonglottalized sonorant coda (Boas 1947, Zec 1995).

(2) a. an'ˈqa   'to put fire among'
    b. ˈanqa   'to sneeze'
    c. ˈdzəmbətəls 'to bury in hole in ground'
    d. məˈxənχənd   'to strike edge'

---

[1] Such a distinction can be regarded as a descriptive convenience. Depending on the analysis, the rule and criterion might be inextricable (e.g. weight effects induced by FTBIN; §2.3.2).

Prosodic Weight. First edition. Kevin M. Ryan.
© Kevin M. Ryan 2019. First published 2019 by Oxford University Press.

   e. maxʷˈts'a   'to be ashamed'
   f. nəˈpa   'to throw a round thing'
   g. gasˈxa   'to carry on fingers'
   h. ˈdəlxa   'damp'
   i. t'əˈliːdzu   'large board on which fish are cut'
   j. ˈxʷaːxʷəkʷ'əna   'canoes'

The emphasis of this chapter, as of this book, is on weight criteria and their analysis, not on metrical theory per se (Hayes 1995), except insofar as the two coincide. For that reason, and for reasons of space, metrical theory is kept relatively minimal. Most of the case studies below address UNBOUNDED systems, like Selkup and Kwak'wala, in which main stress can occur (nearly) anywhere in the word, as determined by weight.[2] In this chapter, foot structure is shown only when it is relevant to the analysis. Feet and prosodic words are considered in more detail in Chapter 3.

Perhaps 30 per cent to 50 per cent of the world's stress systems are weight-sensitive. In the World Atlas of Language Structures (WALS), 39 per cent of 500 stress systems are weight-sensitive (Goedemans and van der Hulst 2013, based on the StressTyp database). In StressTyp2, the figure is 30 per cent of 742 (Goedemans et al. 2017). In Gordon (2006), it is 44 per cent of 310. Roughly one-third of weight-sensitive stress systems, in turn, are unbounded (Goedemans and van der Hulst 2013). More details on the distribution of metrical types can be found in the three aforementioned surveys, that is, WALS, StressTyp2, and Gordon (2006), online in the first two cases. Additionally, Hayes (1995) remains the most thorough compendium of case studies of stress and accent systems.

Selkup and Kwak'wala possess a binary weight criterion, categorizing syllables exhaustively as heavy or light. Among weight-sensitive stress systems, this is the prevailing arity. For example, 87 per cent of criteria for stress are binary in Gordon (2006). Nevertheless, such a figure likely underestimates the incidence of more complex scales, for a few reasons. First, languages characterized as binary sometimes turn out to exhibit richer weight in some contexts. For example, Gordon (2006) lists Finnish as binary, but more recent work on its secondary stress (e.g. Karvonen 2005, Anttila 2010) and on its metrics (Ryan 2011a) suggests at least ternary weight, with vowel height sensitivity to boot (Yana is another example; §2.3.3 and §2.8.2). Second, languages described as having unpredictable or lexical accent sometimes turn out to exhibit productive regularities, whether as narrow "islands of reliability" (cf. Albright 2002) or as broad tendencies that admit exceptions but are significant nonetheless (§2.8). Third, rules described as categorical sometimes add the caveat that exceptions occur. Exceptions might conceal further generalizations. For example, analyses of Ngalakgan, including the one below (§2.6.7), treat the "core" rule. But Baker (2008:225–8) also suggests that onset and vowel quality affect stress placement in some cases. Descriptions may also exhibit some simplicity bias, in the sense

---

[2] I take this to be the usual sense of "unbounded stress" in the literature (e.g. Hayes 1995, Kager 2007, Goedemans and van der Hulst 2013, Heinz 2014), though some also treat fixed edge-oriented stress as unbounded if rhythmic secondary stress has not been described (e.g. Baković 2008).

that a generalization that is clear and simple is more likely to be reported (and reported accurately) than one that is subtle and complex. Insofar as this holds, simple generalizations will be overrepresented in the primary literature relative to their true incidence. As a salve, experimental and corpus-based research supplement the traditional typology, and are ultimately inseparable from it.

I employ the following notation for criteria/scales. Because onsets are usually irrelevant for weight, only rime structure is indicated. Scales are presented in end-weight order (i.e. from lightest to heaviest), with < indicating "is lighter than." V represents a short vowel, VV a long vowel or (heavy) diphthong, C a consonant, and X any segment. G indicates a geminate or, in VG, the coda portion of a geminate. Finally, criteria are usually stated so as to specify only critical boundaries, rather than attempting to enumerate all of the possible rime shapes in the language. For example, imagine that a language has the rime shapes {V, VC, VV, VVC} and the criterion {V, VC} < {VV, VVC}. This criterion is expressed more succinctly as VC < VV. It goes without saying that V is at least as light as VC and VVC at least as heavy as VV. Thus, even "V(C) < VV(C)" would be extravagant. Similarly, V < {VC, VV, VVC, etc.} criteria are usually simplified to V < VX here.

Figures 2.1 and 2.2 depict the VC < VV and V < VX criteria in terms of a shifting boundary along an implied universal scale. They are sometimes known as the Khalkha and Latin criteria, respectively, after famous exemplars. These two criteria, which are roughly equally frequent, are the most widely attested weight criteria for stress, together accounting for roughly two-thirds of binary criteria. Note that both treat V as light and VV as heavy; it is only VC that varies, being light in Khalkha and heavy in Latin. Put differently, codas contribute to weight in Latin, but not in Khalkha. Languages like Latin that treat codas as heavy are said to exhibit WEIGHT-BY-POSITION, nowadays recognized to be a rankable constraint (§2.5.1).

The layout of the scales in Figures 2.1 and 2.2 implies that VV cannot be treated as lighter than VC; either they are equivalent or VV is heavier (Gordon 2006:21, 126–8; see also §3.1 on prosodic minimality). In other words, VV < VC is implied to be impossible as a (sub)criterion for stress. This is a strong candidate for a universal, but not without controversy. See §2.7.2 for discussion of some potential counterexamples, including Huehuetla Tepehua and Tiberian Hebrew. The rationale for the universal *{VV < VC} is obvious if one considers the (phonological) sonority or (phonetic) energy of the rimes involved. The second timing unit of VV is typically

FIGURE 2.1 The VC < VV ("Khalkha") criterion.

FIGURE 2.2 The V < VX ("Latin") criterion.

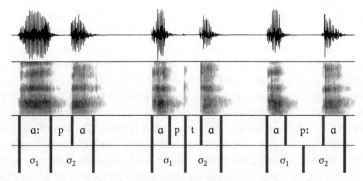

| α: | p | α | | α | p | t | α | | α | p: | α |

| σ₁ | σ₂ | | σ₁ | σ₂ | | σ₁ | σ₂ |

FIGURE 2.3 The energy of the rime like [aː] (VV) greatly exceeds that of [ap] (VC), even as their durations are held constant, and regardless of whether the latter is part of a cluster (VC) or geminate (VG). Prepared in Praat (Boersma and Weenink 2017).

vocalic, and therefore more sonorous than that of VC, which is consonantal. Similarly, as Figure 2.3 illustrates, the overall energy of the rime is greater for VV than for VC, regardless of whether the coda is a singleton or the first part of a geminate.

Aside from VC < VV and V < VX, several less frequent binary criteria are attested. First, vowel quality can be decisive. Some languages treat a syllable as light iff it contains a reduced vowel, or iff it contains a reduced vowel sans coda. These two criteria, as just stated, are essentially translations of VC < VV and V < VX to systems in which "short" is replaced by "reduced" and "long" is replaced by "full." Furthermore, lower vowels can be treated as heavier than higher vowels, or peripheral vowels as heavier than central vowels. Various (combinations of) cutoffs along these two dimensions are attested (de Lacy 2004:193), but the generalization is always that greater sonority correlates with greater weight. Greater vowel sonority usually also correlates with greater duration, but not always (de Lacy 2007:294). These types of criteria are often addressed as SONORITY- or PROMINENCE-DRIVEN STRESS (Kenstowicz 1994b, 1996b, Zec 1995, 2003, Anttila 1997a, 2010, Prince 1999, Gordon 2002b, 2006, de Lacy 2004, 2007, Crowhurst and Michael 2005, Nevins and Plaster 2008, Carpenter 2010, and others). Some of these cases have recently come under fire (cf. de Lacy 2014, Shu-Hao Shih 2016, 2017).

Consonant sonority can also affect weight. The coda behaves like the nucleus, in that greater sonority correlates with, if anything, greater weight. Such a case was presented above: Kwak'wala treats VC as heavy only if C is a (nonglottalized) sonorant. Some other clear or possible cases of a coda sonority rule for stress include Huehuetla Tepehua, Inga Quechua, Lamang, Nuu-chah-nuulth, Orya, Paipai, and Yahi (Zec 1995, Hinton and Luthin 2002, Gordon 2006, Kung 2007).[3] Occasionally, supralaryngeal coda identity affects stress in a way that is not explicable in terms of sonority. For example, in Kayardild, a syllable closed by a trill (but not by a lateral,

---

[3] Beyond stress, heavy sonorant codas are found also in end-weight (§5.5.3), meter (Ryan 2011a), syllable structure (Zec 1995, 2007), and tone licensing (Zhang 2004, Gordon 2006).

rhotic approximant, etc.) is said to bear secondary stress (Evans 1995:79). Compare also Munster Irish [x] (in a coda or onset) in §2.6.1, where [ax] appears to be heavier than other VC (cf. additionally Central Alaskan Yupik [χ, ʁ]; Woodbury 1985). As emphasized by Blum (2018), the Irish case can be explained by the nonreducibility of /a/ before /x/, and need not refer to the weight of /x/ per se. Cases like Kayardild might admit a similar explanation. Tamil, as analyzed in §3.4, is a more convincing case of a violation of the sonority-weight principle, in that coda rhotics (a tap and an approximant) are highly sonorous consonants but consistently do not contribute to weight in weight-sensitive systems, while all other codas, both more and less sonorous, consistently do. As discussed, the Tamil case cannot be explained away by allophony.

Laryngeals such as ʔ and h sometimes receive special treatment relative to other consonants. Vʔ can be either heavier or lighter than other VC. In Hupa (§2.8.1), Ngalakgan (§2.6.7), and Capanahua (Loos 1967, Kager 2012), for instance, Vʔ < VC. But in Cahuilla (§2.6.2) and Huehuetla Tepehua (§2.7.2), VC < Vʔ. Recall also Kwak'wala, in which only nonglottalized sonorant codas are heavy, that is, V͡ʔN < VN. Similarly, geminates sometimes receive special treatment vis-à-vis clusters. VC < VG is attested for stress, as in Sanʼani Arabic (§2.6.4). The reversal, VG < VC, is claimed for Ngalakgan, but see §2.6.7 for a possible counteranalysis. Geminates, it follows, are arguably never lighter than clusters.

Onset sonority can affect weight too, but when it does so, it is in the opposite direction: Less sonority correlates with, if anything, greater weight. Clear or possible cases of obstruent and/or voiceless onsets attracting stress include Arabela (Payne and Rich 1988, Topintzi 2010), English (Nanni 1977, Ryan 2014:314f), Karo (Gabas Jr. 1999, Topintzi 2010; cf. Blumenfeld 2006), Pirahã (Everett and Everett 1984, Daniel Everett 1988, Keren Everett 1998, Gordon 2005), and Tümpisa Shoshone (Dayley 1989).[4] For potential phonetic rationales for this reversal between the onset and coda, see Gordon (2005), Ryan (2014), and §5.9.4. The presence of an onset is also claimed to condition stress placement in several languages (see Ryan 2014:309). Two such cases that Ryan (2014) does not cite include Georgian (Gorgadze 1912:3) and Tsakhur (Ibragimov 1990:50).[5] Furthermore, the presence of a geminate onset conditions stress placement in at least a couple of languages (§2.6.6).

That said, sonority- or place-driven stress is largely set aside in the remainder of this chapter. The emphasis is rather on complex skeletal scales and their analysis. A number of ternary or more complex weight scales have been established for stress. The most common ternary scale is V < VC < VV, as found (as such or as part of a more complex scale) in Abma, Asheninca, Chickasaw, Finnish, Hupa, Kara, Kashmiri, Klamath, Maithili, Mam, Nanti, Pulaar, Sanʼani Arabic, Shipibo, Srinagar Koshur, Tamil, Yahi, and Yapese (§2.6.1). Note that weight scales as characterized in this book never reflect extrametricality effects. In other words, VC is never diagnosed as being intermediately heavy based solely on its being treated specially in final position. All of the languages just mentioned furnish evidence for VC being heavier than V but

---

[4] Beyond stress, heavy voiceless or obstruent onsets are found also in end-weight (§5.5.2) and meter (Ryan 2011a; §4.4).

[5] Lena Borise (p.c.) brought these cases to my attention.

FIGURE 2.4 The V < VC < VV scale, as in Chickasaw.

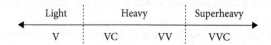

FIGURE 2.5 The V < {VC, VV} < VVC scale, as in Kelkar's Hindi.

lighter than VV in nonfinal positions.[6] Furthermore, some of these languages (e.g. Kashmiri, Nanti, and Pulaar) add a superheavy grade, making for the quaternary scale V < VC < VV < VVC.[7,8]

Ternary V < {VC, VV} < VVC for stress is considerably less common than V < VC < VV. Kelkar's Hindi (§2.3.3) may be the only well-known example, but not all descriptions of Hindi agree with Kelkar on this point (§2.6.3). Gordon (2006) mentions also Eipomek as exhibiting V < {VC, VV} < VVC, but this characterization is hardly established by his source.[9] The canonical ternary scale V < VC < VV combines the two canonical binary criteria, that is, VC < VV and V < VX. Rarer V < {VC, VV} < VVC, by contrast, encapsulates only one of the two canonical criteria, which might explain its markedness (Gordon 2002b). These two ternary scales are visualized in Figures 2.4 and 2.5. In Figure 2.4, I leave the VC category unlabeled because there is no established term for this intermediate grade. In what follows, I refer to rime types directly as V, VC, and VV in such systems to avoid confusion.[10]

2.2 Two theories of complex scales

The bulk of this chapter treats complex quantity for stress, especially V < VC < VV, the most common suprabinary scale. Two theories of such scales are contrasted. The first, COERCED WEIGHT or simply COERCION, proposes that this ostensibly ternary scale reduces to the binary scale $\mu < \mu\mu$, in that V is always monomoraic, VV is

---

[6] Similarly, Classical Arabic is not regarded as exhibiting ternary weight, since it can be analyzed with binary weight and an extrametricality-induced categorial shift in final position.

[7] VCC, for its part, is illicit or infrequent in most of these languages. To the extent that it does occur, it can be categorized anywhere between VC and VVC on the scale. Srinagar Koshur is an example of the former extreme (Munshi and Crowhurst 2012:433), and Kelkar's Hindi an example of the latter (§2.3.3).

[8] See also Woodbury (1985) on a Central Alaskan Yupik dialect that exhibits a scale including V < VC < VV < VVC. Nevertheless, this scale conflates various processes, and Woodbury (1985) suggests that it is not entirely synchronic.

[9] Heeschen (1983:14) writes: "The stress is partially phonemic... The following general rules are to be applied in cases where there are no minimal pairs separated by stress... Two syllable words are stressed on the weighted syllable, i.e. on the one 'having more letters,'" adding that longer words follow the same rule. None of Heeschen's examples of regular stress contains a superheavy.

[10] Light–heavy–superheavy would not be apt for Figure 2.4 because "superheavy" is usually reserved for trimoraic (VXX) syllables.

always bimoraic, and VC varies between monomoraic and bimoraic depending on its context. In particular, VC is only bimoraic in such systems under stress, when VV is unavailable. This has been the prevailing approach to such scales in OT, as advanced by Morén (1997, 1999, 2000, 2001), Rosenthall and van der Hulst (1999), Elias-Ulloa (2004a, 2004b), Hyde (2006), and others. Morén (2001) is followed the most closely here as a representative of the theory, but the same arguments apply to all of its variants.

An alternative approach to such scales, as advanced here, is termed PROMINENCE. On this view, VC and VV can be uniformly bimoraic in $V < VC < VV$ systems, but VV is more optimal for stress because it is more prominent, as encoded here by the constraints MAIN→VV and STRESS→VV, which penalize a short vowel with stress (primary or any, respectively), regardless of the presence and moraicity of the coda.

To be sure, this chapter does not argue against Coercion in general. Indeed, it retains all of the constraints necessary to implement Coercion, so it could not reject it in principle. Rather, it demonstrates inadequacies of Coercion as an explanation for ternary scales. Coercion has uses aside from scale reduction that are not disputed here, including position-specific weight, whereby, for example, VC is heavy only in the initial syllable (e.g. Chugach; Rosenthall and van der Hulst 1999:506) or in the ultima (e.g. Goroa; *ibid.*:510). Contextual moraicity can also serve to optimize foot form, as in Early Latin, where *brevis brevians* renders a coda nonmoraic iff it occupies the weak syllable of a trochee (Mester 1994:12, Hayes 1995:120; see §3.2.1).

Two major arguments are raised against Coercion as an explanation for ternarity. First, secondary stress sometimes reveals VC to be bimoraic even in words in which VV attracts primary stress. Coercion cannot capture this situation, since it needs VC to be monomoraic in order to yield primary stress to VV. The second problem concerns geminates. In ternary $V < VC < VV$ systems (as well as in binary $VC < VV$ systems), VG almost always aligns with VC, not VV, in weight. Coercion therefore requires unstressed geminates in such languages to be long but nonmoraic. This violates a common assumption about geminates, which is that they are defined by their moraicity—the MORAIC THEORY OF GEMINATES. As just stated, this second objection is theoretical, and one could address it by reanalyzing gemination without moraicity. But the second objection has empirical teeth. In many languages with geminates, abundant evidence converges on their weight-bearing status, including stress, metrics, compensatory lengthening, and morphophonology. It is therefore infeasible to analyze them as nonmoraic. Moreover, in many such languages, the *stress system itself* requires geminates to be analyzed as moraic, even when they yield primary stress to heavier VV.

These two problems for Coercion arise not just in a few isolated cases, but in about half of ternary systems. In particular, at least the following eighteen languages are known to exhibit $V < VC < VV$ for stress (as such or as part of a more complex scale): Abma, Asheninca, Chickasaw, Finnish, Hupa, Kara, Kashmiri, Klamath, Maithili, Mam, Nanti, Pulaar, San'ani Arabic, Shipibo, Srinagar Koshur, Tamil, Yahi, and Yapese. Among these, the secondary stress problem for Coercion is evident in Chickasaw, Kara, Klamath, Maithili, Nanti, Pulaar, and Yapese, and the geminate problem for Coercion is evident in Chickasaw, Finnish, Klamath, Maithili, Pulaar, and

Tamil. Insofar as ternary languages do not run afoul of either of these problems, it is usually because they have not been described as having secondary stress or because they lack geminates. In other words, the two problems are nearly ubiquitous insofar as the structures needed to diagnose them are available.

Prominence provides a simple solution to both problems with MAIN→VV. This constraint is natural in the sense that nuclei are more prominent than margins, even if margins need to be analyzed as moraic (note again Figure 2.3). Second, MAIN→VV permits the Moraic Theory of Geminates to be maintained across the board. Previously, languages with binary {VC, VG} < VV, such as Malayalam and Selkup, were often viewed as refuting geminate moraicity (cf. Selkirk 1990, Tranel 1991, Blevins 1995). With MAIN→VV, geminate moraicity can be upheld in these languages. Third, as discussed in §2.6.5, the alternative to MAIN→VV, which is to adopt parametric geminate moraicity, makes erroneous predictions about the typology. Finally, beyond stress, Coercion cannot account for V < VC < VV in other weight-sensitive systems, such as meter or end-weight. Prominence is independently necessary for these systems (§2.5.12).

The remainder of the chapter proceeds as follows. Moraic phonology is introduced in §2.3. Several case studies of ternary systems follow, illustrating deficiencies of Coercion (§§2.4–2.5). Geminate weight is covered in §2.6, where I defend the view that geminates can be treated universally as moraic for stress, thanks to Prominence. An alternative theory of Prominence whereby VC rather than VV attracts stress is critically appraised in §2.7. Finally, §2.8 examines gradient weight for stress, as found in several languages.

2.3 Core apparatus

2.3.1 *Moraic preliminaries*

This book assumes the largely standard view that syllable weight is determined at least in part by moraic quantity (e.g. Hyman 1985, McCarthy and Prince 1986, Hayes 1989, 1995, and numerous others; but cf. Zhang 2002, 2004, Ryan 2016:729f). A short vowel contributes one mora and a long vowel or diphthong contributes two, as depicted in (3). I tentatively take onsets to attach to the syllable node, as in (a–b), which is perhaps the prevailing convention (e.g. McCarthy and Prince 1986, Hayes 1989, 1995, Rosenthall and van der Hulst 1999, Morén 2001). However, some analysts take onsets to attach instead to the first mora, as in (c) (e.g. Hyman 1985). Nothing here hinges on this decision (though an alternative theory of Prominence, as discussed in §2.7.1, crucially assumes (a–b)).

(3)   (a)   σ   (b)   σ   (c)   σ

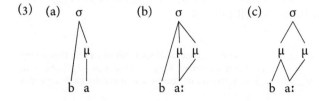

Vowels are here assumed always to be at least monomoraic, though nonmoraic vowels are sometimes invoked elsewhere (e.g. Kager 1990, Crosswhite 2001, Gordon 2002b). There is no need to take a position on this question here. If necessary, a constraint such as σ→μ "a syllable must contain a mora" can be assumed to be undominated below, such that nonmoraic vowels are not in contention. Onsets are typically nonmoraic, though I take them to be moraic when they are geminates (§2.6.6). Otherwise, candidates with moraic onsets are not considered here. If necessary, a constraint against moraic onsets can be assumed to be undominated.

As shown in (4), codas are free to be either (a) moraic or (b) nonmoraic. A coda is referred to as moraic only when it heads its own mora, as in (a). Some analysts take nonmoraic codas to attach to the nearest mora, as in (b) (e.g. Hyman 1985, Hayes 1989, 1995, Crowhurst and Michael 2005), while others take them to attach directly to the syllable node, as in (c) (e.g. McCarthy and Prince 1986, Rosenthall and van der Hulst 1999, Morén 2001). I tentatively assume the former convention, though nothing here rides on this decision (once again, however, an alternative theory of Prominence in §2.7.1 crucially assumes (b)).

(4)   (a)   σ   (b)   σ   (c)   σ

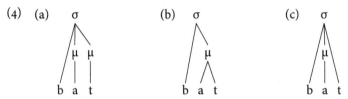

With Hayes (1989), Morén (2001), and many others, I assume that moraicity is DIS-TINCTIVE. That is, segments are specified freely as moraic or nonmoraic in the input, and these differing specifications are sometimes reflected in the output. Faithfulness constraints forbid adding or removing moras vis-à-vis the input. DEP-μ penalizes inserting a mora (e.g. lengthening a segment). MAX-μ penalizes deleting one (e.g. shortening a segment). But moraicity is also COERCED, in the sense that markedness constraints can overrule the input. Most generically, *μ (also known as *STRUC-μ; Crosswhite 1999) favors nonmoraicity, all else being equal. Weight-by-Position (WbyP) penalizes any coda consonant that does not head a mora (Hayes 1989, 1995, Sherer 1994, Morén 1999, Rosenthall and van der Hulst 1999). If undominated, WbyP compels codas to be uniformly moraic. But WbyP might also be dominated by *μ or DEP-μ, in which case nonmoraic codas might arise. In order to permit distinctive vowel length but not consonant length, as in Murik (§2.3.3), the more specific MAX-μ-V can be invoked (Morén 2000).[11] Finally, *3μ penalizes syllables with more than two moras (Prince and Smolensky 1993/2004, Kager 1999). If *3μ is active, any coda consonants that would otherwise exceed the maximum are forced to fuse to the second mora or append directly to the syllable node.

---

[11] If a language lacks geminates and its codas are nonmoraic, one could alternatively employ the ranking *C_μ ≫ MAX-μ ≫ *μ, which nixes moras on consonants altogether. But some languages (e.g. Kashmiri in §2.5.1) possess distinctive vowel length and moraic codas but not geminates, in which case MAX-μ-V is needed.

(5) Some standard constraints for moraification.
   a. DEP-μ   Do not insert moras.
   b. MAX-μ   Do not delete moras.
   c. MAX-μ-V   Do not delete vocalic moras.
   d. *μ   Penalize moras.
   e. WbyP   A coda consonant heads a mora.
   f. *3μ   Syllables are capped at two moras.

2.3.2 Mapping between weight and stress

This section outlines the core weight–stress mapping apparatus; the next will provide some preliminary illustrations. First, the Weight-to-Stress Principle (WSP; Prince 1990, Prince and Smolensky 1993/2004, Anttila 1997a) penalizes each heavy syllable that lacks stress. Second, its transposition, Stress-to-Weight (SWP), requires a stressed syllable to be heavy (Prokosch 1939, Vennemann 1972, Hayes 1980, Hammond 1986, Myers 1987, Prince 1990, Riad 1992, Rice 1992, 2006, Fitzgerald 1997, van de Vijver 1998, Kager 1999, Gouskova 2003, McCarthy 2003, McGarrity 2003). Crowhurst and Michael (2005) express the latter as *P/σ_μ ("no foot peak consists of a light syllable"). I employ the labels σ_μμ→STRESS and STRESS→σ_μμ for WSP and SWP, respectively. For one thing, the proliferation of acronyms can be wearying, particularly given that further variants are forthcoming. Moreover, "weight" and "stress" are both vague. σ_μμ makes explicit what "weight" implies: a bimoraic (or heavier) syllable. As discussed presently, these constraints are available with additional predicates, such as trimoraic syllables. This notation also makes it easy to specify the stress level as STRESS (in general) or MAIN (primary only). The two constraints are recapitulated in (6). In tableaux below, STRESS is abbreviated to S.

(6) a. σ_μμ→S(TRESS)   a.k.a. WSP   Penalize each unstressed heavy.
    b. S(TRESS)→σ_μμ   a.k.a. SWP   Penalize each stressed light.

σ_μμ→STRESS and STRESS→σ_μμ functionally overlap, and are sometimes interchangeable (for example, they are interchangeable for Yana and Murik in the next section). But both are needed. For example, STRESS→σ_μμ can capture a grammar in which stressed light syllables lengthen, such as Tiriyó (Meira 1998). σ_μμ→STRESS is irrelevant for such cases, since it ignores light syllables. Conversely, σ_μμ→STRESS but not STRESS→σ_μμ can capture a grammar in which all heavies are stressed, such as Chickasaw (Gordon 2004a; §2.5.4).

Weight criteria sometimes differ between primary and secondary stress (Parker 1998, McGarrity 2003, Gordon 2004a, 2011, Crowhurst and Michael 2005, Topintzi 2010:171), as exemplified at various points in this chapter (including Chickasaw; §2.5.4). I therefore assume that mapping constraints can be indexed to STRESS or MAIN as necessary. Indeed, Bye and de Lacy (2008) suggest that SWP (i.e. STRESS→σ_μμ) can *only* be indexed to MAIN. All of the case studies in this chapter agree with this suggestion, in that STRESS→σ_μμ is never crucially generic. Nevertheless, since the issue is not critical here, I leave it open. If only primary stress is being analyzed, I use the index STRESS by default. MAIN and STRESS are in a stringency relationship (cf. Prince 1999, de Lacy 2004), in that a constraint indexed to the former incurs a subset of the violations of the same constraint indexed to the latter. There is no need for constraints indexed to secondary stress. Crowhurst and Michael (2005) take the same position with their use of $*\text{Pk}_{Ft}$ and $*\text{Pk}_{PWd}$ constraints, which regulate STRESS and MAIN, respectively.

As mentioned in §2.1, some stress systems exhibit a superheavy grade, which lures stress away even from heavy syllables. One approach to this situation is to posit an analog to $\sigma_{\mu\mu}\rightarrow$ STRESS that applies only to superheavies, for example, the Superheavy-to-Stress Principle (Gussenhoven 2008), abbreviated $\sigma_{\mu\mu\mu}\rightarrow$ STRESS in (7). Because $\sigma_{\mu\mu\mu}\rightarrow$ STRESS incurs a subset of the penalties of $\sigma_{\mu\mu}\rightarrow$ STRESS—once again, the constraints are stringent—the coexistence of $\sigma_{\mu\mu}\rightarrow$ STRESS and $\sigma_{\mu\mu\mu}\rightarrow$ STRESS does not risk generating the (presumably impossible) grammar in which bimoraic syllables are more stress-attracting than trimoraic syllables, all else being equal. Some analysts reject the notion of trimoraic syllables, in which case a different approach to superheavies is needed, such as the one detailed in §2.7.3, which is based on Munshi and Crowhurst (2012). Nevertheless, I adopt a pro-trimoraicity position here, for the reasons elaborated in §§2.7.1–2.7.3. I thus employ (7) when relevant.

(7) $\sigma_{\mu\mu\mu}\rightarrow$ STRESS   Penalize each unstressed superheavy.

A somewhat more traditional, if nowadays less common, approach to multigrade scales is that of PEAK PROMINENCE (PK-PROM) (Prince and Smolensky 1993/2004, based on McCarthy and Prince 1986; see also Kenstowicz 1993), as in (8).

(8)   PK-PROM $\text{Peak}(x) \succ \text{Peak}(y)$ if $|x| > |y|$.

That is, primary stress is more harmonic on syllable x than on syllable y if x is heavier than y. In practice, PK-PROM is usually taken to assign a violation to any candidate in which primary stress falls on a syllable that is not the heaviest syllable type available in the candidate (e.g. Walker 1996, 1997, Morén 2001).[12] As such, one cannot evaluate each syllable locally, as one can with the other constraints in this section. Rather, PK-PROM requires scanning the entire word, saving the maximum, and then comparing the primary stressed syllable to that maximum.

Furthermore, PK-PROM requires the specification of a weight scale. Given that scales ostensibly vary across languages (§2.1), one of two positions must be adopted. The first is to allow PK-PROM to be defined on a language-specific basis (or perhaps to admit many PK-PROMs into CON, promoting the appropriate one as necessary). The alternative, which has been the prevailing stance, is to define a universal scale for PK-PROM in terms of moras: $|\mu| < |\mu\mu| < |\mu\mu\mu|$. Language-specific weight then falls out from independent constraints regulating moraification. For example, Kelkar's Hindi treats VC as equivalent to VV because both are rendered as bimoraic in that language, but Kashmiri renders VC as monomoraic under certain conditions (§2.5.1). This second position—a fixed moraic scale for PK-PROM—shifts the burden of defining weight away from PK-PROM, the comparator, and onto the mora-assigning apparatus (Morén 2000).

---

[12] Kager (2007) has a slightly different interpretation, whereby PK-PROM is equivalent to what is here termed STRESS$\rightarrow\sigma_{\mu\mu}$, since it incurs a violation from an all-light word.

Nevertheless, once the burden of explanation has been so shifted, the comparator can be simplified. For one thing, there is no need for gradience, as Pᴋ-Pʀoᴍ was originally formulated. Gradient constraints are sometimes taken to be deprecated in OT (e.g. McCarthy 2003, Wiltshire 2006, O'Connor 2010). The mapping constraints {WSP, Pᴋ-Pʀoᴍ}, as put forth by Prince and Smolensky (1993/2004), can be replaced by categorical constraints of the $\sigma_{\mu\mu(\mu)} \leftrightarrow$Sᴛʀᴇss family. At any rate, the choice of Pᴋ-Pʀoᴍ vs. $\sigma_{\mu\mu(\mu)} \leftrightarrow$Sᴛʀᴇss does not affect any of the argumentation in this chapter concerning Coercion vs. Prominence. With any combination of the constraints in this section, Coercion is insufficient. One can freely substitute in Pᴋ-Pʀoᴍ for $\sigma_{\mu\mu(\mu)} \leftrightarrow$Sᴛʀᴇss in the case studies below.

All of the constraints introduced thus far directly regulate the coincidence of stress and syllable weight, ignoring foot structure. Constraints enforcing well-formed feet can also affect stress–weight mapping. Some weight effects fall out from binarity in metrical parsing, as enforced by FᴛBɪɴ ("feet are binary in terms of moras or syllables"; §3.2.1). Consider Latin stress, which falls on a heavy penult and otherwise on the antepenult if available. As discussed in §3.2.1, a heavy can be footed by itself, as in (9-a), but a light cannot (b) ("< ... >" indicates extrametricality). In the latter case, if a light antepenult is available, the foot extends to it, as in (c). Other constraints prevent other possible repairs to (b), including lengthening, an iambic foot, footing the ultima, and so forth. The system is more complicated than this, but the point here is just that binarity explains some aspects of weight-sensitivity (Prince 1983).

(9) a. la('tiː)<nus>   'Latin'
     b. *o('pe)<ris>   'of the work'
     c. ('ope)<ris>   'of the work'

Aside from FᴛBɪɴ, other constraints on foot form can affect stress–weight mapping (Baković 1996, Bennett 2012). The most optimal iambs are (H́) and (LH́), where H is heavy, L is light, and parentheses indicate a foot. The most optimal trochees are (H́) and (ĹL) (not the mirror image of optimal iambs; Hayes 1995). As such, iambs are preferably heavy-final, that is, (H́) or (LH́), and sometimes lengthen to achieve this form (ɪᴀᴍʙɪᴄ ʟᴇɴɢᴛʜᴇɴɪɴɢ; Prince 1990, Hayes 1995, Baković 1996, Kager 1999, Bye and de Lacy 2008). Conversely, (H́L) is ill-formed as a trochee, which is resolved in some languages by shortening the head of the foot, yielding (ĹL) (ᴛʀᴏᴄʜᴀɪᴄ sʜᴏʀᴛᴇɴɪɴɢ, as in Boumaa Fijian; Blevins 1994, Hayes 1995, Baković 1996, Zuraw 2018). Trochees of the form (ĹH) can likewise be repaired to (ĹL), confusingly called ɪᴀᴍʙɪᴄ sʜᴏʀᴛᴇɴɪɴɢ ("iambic" referring to the original word shape being quantitatively iambic, that is, light-heavy), as found in Early Latin (Mester 1994). Similarly, de Lacy (2004) analyzes a case in which (Ĺ-nonhigh) trochees are avoided, presumably for the same reason that (ĹH) trochees are avoided: Nonhigh vowels are heavier than high vowels. Kiriwina stress is by default a right-aligned moraic trochee, as in (a–d) in (10); VC and VV count as heavy (c–d). However, the foot retracts from the right edge when it would be (Ĺ-nonhigh), as in (e–f). No retraction occurs in (b) because the foot would be (Ĺ-nonhigh) in either position; thus, retraction is not improving in that context. Although related to iambic shortening, this case cannot be analyzed as (ĹH) avoidance, since $C_0[-high]$ is not a heavy syllable in Kiriwina.

(10) a. imom('koli)   'he tasted (it)'
      b. i('doja)   'it drifts'
      c. iki('um)   'he did secretly'
      d. ivaboda('nim)   'he came last walking'
      e. ('migi)la   'the face'
      f. la('siku)la   'pull canoe'

Kager (1999:174) analyzes trochaic shortening (H́L → ĹL), iambic shortening (LH́ → ĹL), and iambic lengthening (LĹ → LH́) collectively by means of Rh-Contour, which requires that feet of all types end with a strong mora (i.e. head mora of a stressed syllable) followed by a weak mora. At any rate, foot structure is largely irrelevant to the case studies in this chapter, which mainly concern unbounded stress in languages with fixed length, not the sorts of rhythmic adjustments just mentioned.

2.3.3 *Preliminary illustrations: Yana, Murik, Kelkar's Hindi*

Before probing the differences between Coercion and Prominence as explanations of V < VC < VV, it is expedient to introduce some remaining constraints that are shared by both theories and thus not the subject of inquiry here. This standard machinery is illustrated in this section by a few straightforward systems.

In general, analyses of weight-sensitive stress depend on three types of constraints, namely, (1) constraints regulating the moraification of segments, (2) constraints regulating the coincidence of stress and weight, and (3) any remaining metrical apparatus, such as alignment. The first and second groups have already been addressed, in §2.3.1 and §2.3.2, respectively. This section adds some metrical constraints (see Kager 1999:142–93 for a longer overview).

First, GramWd=PWd requires a word to be prosodified, and hence bear stress. This constraint is always undominated in this chapter, such that candidates lacking stress are never in contention. But see the next chapter for further discussion. Second, NonFinality is taken in this chapter to be a simple prohibition on final stress. Once again, the next chapter, which considers foot structure in more detail, provides a more nuanced treatment. Third, Clash penalizes any sequence of two adjacent stressed syllables. Fourth, alignment constraints distinguish between right- and left-oriented systems (McCarthy and Prince 1993, Kager 1999, cf. McCarthy 2003). Align-L pressures for initial stress. If feet are omitted from the tableau, Align-L is interpreted as assigning a penalty for every syllable that intervenes between each stress and the left edge of the word. If feet are shown, the left boundaries of feet are instead reckoned, and Align-L is then the same as All-Feet-L. Align-L-Main is the same as Align-L except specific to primary stress.

(11) Some standard constraints for stress.
      a. GramWd=PWd   Grammatical words are prosodified.
      b. NonFinality   The ultima is not stressed.
      c. Clash   Stressed syllables do not abut.
      d. Align-L (or R)   All stresses are leftmost (or rightmost).
      e. Align-L-Main (or R) Primary stress is leftmost (or rightmost).

Weight–stress mapping is now illustrated for Yana, Murik, and Kelkar's Hindi, in turn. In Yana (Sapir and Swadesh 1960), stress falls on the leftmost heavy syllable if one is available, and otherwise on the leftmost syllable. The criterion is V < VX.[13] To implement this criterion, codas are uniformly moraic, that is, WbyP ≫ {*μ, DEP-μ}. Because $\sigma_{\mu\mu}$→STRESS ≫ ALIGN-L, stress is attracted to a heavy (or the leftmost heavy in case of a tie), but is otherwise leftmost in the word. Tableau (12) shows stress assignment in [hac'aʒidp'aː] "Angelica tomentosa" (Hyde 2006). Codas are annotated by μ if moraic and unannotated if nonmoraic. Vowels are assumed to be moraic throughout and are therefore unannotated. Because codas are moraic, the penult is the leftmost heavy. Shortening the final vowel, as in (f), would save a violation of $\sigma_{\mu\mu}$→STRESS, but MAX-μ rules it out. For another word with no heavies, such as ['irik'i] 'ear ornaments' (not shown), ALIGN-L would yield initial stress.

(12)

hac'aʒidp'aː		WbyP	MAX-μ	$\sigma_{\mu\mu}$→S	ALIGN-L	*μ
a. ☞	hac'a'ʒid$_\mu$p'aː			*	**	******
b.	hac'aʒid'p'aː	*!			***	*****
c.	hac'aʒid$_\mu$'p'aː			*	***!	******
d.	'hac'aʒid$_\mu$p'aː			**!		******
e.	'hac'aʒidp'aː	*!		*		*****
f.	hac'a'ʒid$_\mu$p'a		*!		**	*****

Murik (Abbott 1985) has the same rule as Yana, except with the criterion VC < VV, as in (13). Because *μ now outranks WbyP (and MAX-μ, not shown), codas fail to project moras. The new weight criterion is thus captured without modifying the weight-mapping apparatus per se, that is, $\sigma_{\mu\mu}$→STRESS. Meanwhile, underlying vowel length must be preserved due to MAX-μ-V.

(13)

anənpʰarɛːtʰ		MAX-μ-V	*μ	$\sigma_{\mu\mu}$→S	ALIGN-L	WbyP
a. ☞	anənpʰa'rɛːtʰ		*****		***	**
b.	'anənpʰarɛːtʰ		*****	*!		**
c.	a'nənpʰarɛːtʰ		*****	*!	*	**
d.	a'nən$_\mu$pʰarɛːtʰ$_\mu$		******!*	*	*	
e.	'anənpʰarɛtʰ	*!	*****			**

Turning to the dialect of Hindi described by Kelkar (1968) and analyzed by Prince and Smolensky (1993/2004) and Hayes (1995), three grades of weight are recognized, namely, monomoraic (V), bimoraic (VC or VV), and trimoraic (VVC or VCC). Given this scale, the rule is stated concisely by Hayes (1995) as "stress falls on the heaviest available syllable, and in the event of a tie, the rightmost nonfinal candidate wins." Since a superheavy grade is now relevant, $\sigma_{\mu\mu\mu}$→STRESS is invoked (PK-PROM could be used instead, but see §2.3.2). WbyP compels codas to be moraic, even if

---

[13] This criterion, though widely quoted as such, is likely an oversimplification, since it ignores variation. See §2.8.2 below on the Yahi dialect per Hinton and Luthin (2002).

trimoraicity results (cf. §2.7.3). In (14), the heaviest grade available is superheavy, and it is available nonfinally, so the nonfinal superheavy receives stress. The failure of (b) demonstrates that a superheavy outweighs a heavy.

(14)

a:smã:ja:h	WbyP	$\sigma_{\mu\mu}\rightarrow$S	$\sigma_{\mu\mu\mu}\rightarrow$S	NonFinality	Align-R
a. ☞ $\quad$ $^{\prime}$a:s$_{\mu}$mã:ja:h$_{\mu}$		**	*		**
b. $\quad$ a:s$_{\mu}$$^{\prime}$mã:ja:h$_{\mu}$		**	**!		*
c. $\quad$ a:s$_{\mu}$mã:$^{\prime}$ja:h$_{\mu}$		**	*	*!	
d. $\quad$ a:s$^{\prime}$mã:ja:h$_{\mu}$	*!	**	*		*

In (15), the heaviest grade available is instantiated only in final position. The ultima therefore receives stress, revealing the priority of weight-mapping over NonFinality. This situation is termed QUANTITATIVE NONFINALITY: NonFinality can break ties, as in (14), but if the heaviest available grade is instantiated only finally, NonFinality is effectively suspended, as in (15).

(15)

musalma:n	WbyP	$\sigma_{\mu\mu}\rightarrow$S	$\sigma_{\mu\mu\mu}\rightarrow$S	NonFinality	Align-R
a. ☞ $\quad$ musal$_{\mu}$$^{\prime}$ma:n$_{\mu}$		*		*	
b. $\quad$ mu$^{\prime}$sal$_{\mu}$ma:n$_{\mu}$		*	*!		*
c. $\quad$ mu$^{\prime}$sal$_{\mu}$ma:n	*!	*			*

2.4 MAIN→VV and similar constraints

A further weight–stress mapping constraint is proposed and defended in this chapter, namely, MAIN→VV in (16). The constraint penalizes a short vowel with primary stress.[14] This constraint, like MAIN→$\sigma_{\mu\mu}$, can cause a stressed short vowel to lengthen, but it can also cause stress to shift to an already long vowel or diphthong (e.g. if DEP-µ is highly ranked).

(16)   MAIN→VV   Primary stress falls on a long vowel or diphthong.

---

[14] In all of the languages analyzed here, nuclei contain only vocalic segments. I therefore use "vowel" and "nucleus" interchangeably in descriptions, as do most analysts. As a technicality, one might wish to clarify whether MAIN→VV evaluates [−cons] segments or else nuclear segments for moraic quantity. Empirical evidence is thin, but Pulaar in §2.5.2 favors the nuclear interpretation. VW (where W is an off-glide) is lighter than VV for primary stress, while both rimes are crucially bimoraic. One might therefore analyze W as being a [−cons] moraic coda. MAIN→VV then refers to the quantity of the nucleus, not the total moraic quantity of [−cons] segments in the syllable. Given this stance, MAIN→VV also penalizes stress on a short but not long syllabic consonant.

MAIN→VV is closely related to MAIN→$\sigma_{\mu\mu}$. MAIN→$\sigma_{\mu\mu}$ evaluates the whole syllable for bimoraicity, whereas MAIN→VV evaluates only the nucleus. VV is therefore a subset of $\sigma_{\mu\mu}$. For example, stressed $'V_\mu C_\mu$ satisfies MAIN→$\sigma_{\mu\mu}$ but violates MAIN→VV. {MAIN, STRESS}→VV and {MAIN, STRESS}→$\sigma_{\mu\mu}$ may also be kin in that both tend to be indexed to MAIN rather than STRESS. That said, STRESS→VV (or its transposition) is needed for Finnish secondary stress. Indeed, as discussed in §2.5.8, Karvonen (2005) proposes the constraint *{CV̌V} (VV→STRESS in the present formalism) to deal with Finnish, though STRESS→VV, as in (17), would also work. Given the schema in §1.5, I do not preclude any constraint stating an implication in either direction between the stress levels STRESS or MAIN, on the one hand, and heavy syllable classes such as VV or $\sigma_{\mu\mu}$, on the other.

(17) STRESS→VV   Stress falls on a long vowel or diphthong.
      VV→STRESS   A long vowel or diphthong is stressed.

At first glance, it might appear that MAIN→VV duplicates the work done by Weight-by-Position, which requires codas to be moraic. If WbyP is dominated by, say, *μ, and other factors do not interfere, only nuclei will bear weight. However, as several case studies in this chapter demonstrate, MAIN→VV makes distinct predictions from the combination of WbyP and the weight-mapping constraints in §2.3.2. In particular, it permits vowels to be more stress-attracting than consonants even in contexts in which both must be analyzed as moraic—in brief, $V_\mu C_\mu < VV_{\mu\mu}$.

MAIN→VV has its origin in two lines of research. The first includes proposals to the effect that not all moras are equal. For example, Hayes (1995:299–305; see also Prince 1983, Hyman 1992) posits two-layered moraic grids along the lines of (18). Rules or constraints then refer to strong or weak moras, where strong moras are those that project to the second layer. While I assume a single-layered moraic grid, MAIN→VV and two-layered moraic grids have almost the same explanatory scope. To wit, the strong moras in (18) are associated only with the nucleus. As long as this association holds, MAIN→VV in my formalism is equivalent to MAIN→$\sigma_{\mu\mu}$ contingent on strong moras in the two-layered formalism.

(18) (a) σ (b) σ (c) σ

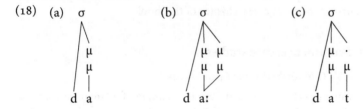

Similarly, Steriade (1991) permits rules to refer to moras according to their sonority levels. MAIN→VV, in this sense, is akin to a constraint on vocalic moras. Another precedent is Levin (1985), which, while not set in moraic theory, permits reference to the nucleus, a constituent rejected by classical moraic theory (cf. Hyman 1985).

Given these affinities, one might wonder whether positing a constraint like MAIN→VV undermines the raison d'être of moras in the first place, harkening back instead to earlier theories of weight based on structured skeletal slots. But mainstream phonology has arguably already traveled inexorably down this road in the last couple of decades with the admission of prominence-driven weight, usually alongside moraic weight. It is this literature on prominence that is the second line of research inspiring MAIN→VV. Munshi and Crowhurst (2012:429) summarize this duality of weight:

It is now well understood that the "mora only" view of weight sensitivity is too rigid. We now know that other phonological distinctions, notably vowel quality, can be primary influences on the distribution of stress in an impressive array of languages (Kenstowicz 1996b, Crowhurst and Michael 2005, Gordon 2002b). Moreover, some of this work has shown that languages do not necessarily fall into one category or the other—it is not uncommon to find languages whose stress pattern is influenced both by the interaction of syllable weight in the moraic sense and by vowel quality (e.g. Kenstowicz 1996b, Crowhurst and Michael 2005).

MAIN→VV (and kin) is in a sense more conservative than accounts of sonority-driven stress, since it invokes only short vowels as a whole, rather than featural subsets of short vowels. The sonority-stress mapping constraints in de Lacy (2004), for instance, simply list the relevant vowels, granting that such lists are constrained by stringency. If constraints such as *HD$_{Ft}$/$i,ə,i\cdot u$ (penalizing stress on i, $ə$, or a high vowel $i\cdot u$; de Lacy 2004) or *Pk$_{PWd}$/DIPH (penalizing primary stress on a short—but not long—diphthong; Crowhurst and Michael 2005) are admitted, it is not much of a stretch to allow also *Pk$_{PWd}$/SHORT (penalizing primary stress on short vowels generally), which is another way of expressing MAIN→VV.

Due to this resemblance, I refer to MAIN→VV as a PROMINENCE-based analysis of rich scales. For other constraint-based analyses of prominential weight, see Kenstowicz (1994b, 1996b), Zec (1995, 2003), Anttila (1997a, 2010), de Lacy (1997, 2004), Prince (1999), Gordon (2002b, 2006), Crowhurst and Michael (2005), Wiltshire (2006), Nevins and Plaster (2008), Munshi and Crowhurst (2012), among others, and heed the cautions of de Lacy (2014) and Shu-Hao Shih (2016, 2017) concerning descriptions. Most of these sources analyze sonority-driven stress, but a few (de Lacy 1997, Wiltshire 2006, Munshi and Crowhurst 2012) analyze certain skeletal weight effects using extramoraic devices, here termed SKELETAL PROMINENCE; see §2.7.1.[15] While weight-mapping under Coercion refers only to the moraic quantity of the syllable, the present proposal adds direct reference to vocalic quantity, irrespective of the coda and its moraicity. Implicit in this proposal is that nuclei are more prominent than margins, a recurring theme of every chapter of this book.

2.5 Coercion vs. Prominence: case studies

2.5.1 *V < VC < VV < VVC in Kashmiri: the Coercion analysis*

Kashmiri (Indo-Aryan) is perhaps the most famous example of a language with the (partial) scale V < VC < VV. Primary stress falls on the leftmost nonfinal syllable of the heaviest available rime class in (19). (As always, monosyllables are a trivial

---

[15] De Lacy (1997) posits a constraint that is nearly equivalent to MAIN→VV, namely, NOTMIN(α, β) "The number of associations between α and nodes of type β is greater than one," where in this case α is "segment" and β is "mora of a primary-stressed syllable." NOTMIN(α, β) effectively requires primary stress to dominate a bimoraic segment, which is typically a long vowel, though tautosyllabic coda geminates would also satisfy it if they can be bimoraic (see §2.6.7). Note also that heavy nuclear diphthongs satisfy MAIN→VV but not NOTMIN(α, β). For de Lacy (1997), NOTMIN(seg, $'μ$) is part of an ensemble of mapping constraints that includes ZERO(α, β), MIN(α, β), NOTMIN(α, β), and EXIST(α, β). The present chapter follows the more restrictive constraint schema in §1.5.

exception to nonfinality, given that GRAMWD=PWD is assumed to be undominated in this chapter.)

(19)   V < VC < VV < VVC

VCC rimes are infrequent at best among nonfinal syllables in Kashmiri, and thus put aside.[16] Geminates are likely absent, or marginal at best (Morén 2001:134), and can therefore also be put aside.[17] The description of Kashmiri stress follows the primary sources Kachru (1969, 1973) and Bhatt (1989) and the secondary sources Kenstowicz (1993, 1994a), Walker (1996), Rosenthall and van der Hulst (1999), Morén (1997, 2000, 2001), Hyde (2006), Wiltshire (2006), and Munshi and Crowhurst (2012). The last of these focuses on Srinagar Koshur, which is a dialect of Kashmiri (note that "Koshur" is the endonym for "Kashmiri"), but with a different stress system. Secondary stress has not been described for Kashmiri, but is posited for Srinagar Koshur (Munshi 2012, Munshi and Crowhurst 2012).

The stress rule stated above entails that monosyllables and disyllables are always initially stressed; it is only in words of three or more syllables that weight matters. Stress is by default leftmost in these longer words too, but is lured away from the initial syllable if a medial syllable is heavier. In that case, stress shifts to the leftmost instance of the heaviest category present among nonfinal syllables. Some examples are given in (20). Although only words of one to three syllables are exemplified, this is not meant to imply a trisyllabic window: As confirmed by longer words, stress is unbounded (DEFAULT-TO-SAME-SIDE UNBOUNDED, as was also the case for Yana, Murik, and Hindi in §2.3.3). Row (i) reveals V < VC, since the latter lures stress away from the former. Row (j) shows VC < VV and (k) shows VV < VVC. Collapsing the distinctions in (i–k) by transitivity yields the total quaternary weight scale: V < VC < VV < VVC.

(20)

	Rime Pattern				
	σ_1	σ_2	σ_3		
a.	X			ˈbal	'strength'
b.	V	X		ˈki.taːb	'book'
c.	V	V	X	ˈpʰi.ki.ri	'understand'
d.	VC	VC	X	ˈjəm.bir.zal	'narcissus'
e.	VV	VV	X	ˈbaː.laː.dər	'balcony'
f.	VC	V	X	ˈin.ti.zaːm	'arrangement'
g.	VV	V	X	ˈkaː.ri.baːr	'business'
h.	V	VV	X	zoˈruː.ratʰ	'necessity'
i.	V	VC	X	ʃoˈkir.vaːr	'Friday'
j.	VC	VV	X	vuʃˈnaː.vun	'to warm'
k.	VV	VVC	X	boːˈdeːs.var	'Lord'

---

[16] Complex codas are found word-finally, where they are irrelevant for the stress rule just stated. Word-medially, they are infrequent. Some potential examples include *saŋgtār* 'orange,' *əndkār* 'darkness,' and *gənzrun* 'to count,' though these may vary by dialect (Koul 2003:903, Munshi and Crowhurst 2012:432). At any rate, I am not aware of examples determining the weight of VCC relative to VC, VV, and VVC. Munshi and Crowhurst (2012) suggest that VCC is lighter than VV and equivalent to VC in Srinagar Koshur.

[17] Morén (2000) analyzes an example with a geminate, but later (2001) suggests that geminates are probably illicit and that the example might have arisen from code-switching.

The remainder of this section presents the Coercion analysis of Kashmiri. The Prominence alternative is taken up in subsequent sections. At its core, the Coercion proposal of Morén (1997, 2000, 2001), Rosenthall and van der Hulst (1999), and Hyde (2006) is that long vowels are always bimoraic, regardless of stress, as in (a–b) in (21) (where 'σ indicates a stressed syllable), while codas are moraic only under stress, as in (c) vs. (d). (Whether [r] in (c) attaches to the mora or syllable is not important here.) This treatment, which emerges from constraint ranking, accounts for the weight distinction between VC and VV in Kashmiri, as described presently.

(21)   (a)   σ   (b)   'σ   (c)   σ   (d)   'σ

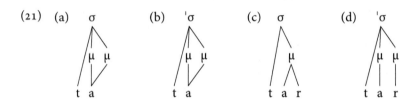

First, vowel length is distinctive (e.g. [bal] 'strength' vs. [baːl] 'forehead'), while consonant length is not (with the caveat in footnote 17). As before, distinctive vowel length arises from the moraic specification of the input being preserved in the output, as in tableau (22), in which MAX-μ-V ≫ *μ entails that long vowels are not shortened.

(22)

	aːni	MAX-μ-V	*μ	MAX-μ
a. ☞	aːni		***	
b.	ani	*!	**	*

Meanwhile, *μ ≫ MAX-μ entails that an input geminate is delinked from its mora, becoming a singleton, as shown in (23), where /n$_\mu$/ in the input can be read as geminate /nː/, as it would surface if its mora were preserved.

(23)

	aːn$_\mu$i	MAX-μ-V	*μ	MAX-μ
a. ☞	aːni		***	*
b.	aːn$_\mu$ni		****!	

Turning to stress, GRAMWD=PWD ≫ NONFINALITY ensures that the ultima is unstressed, unless the word is a monosyllable. When weight is irrelevant, stress is left-most, as guaranteed by ALIGN-L, which outranks ALIGN-R (not shown). But weight-sensitivity must in turn outrank ALIGN-L, since stress is lured away from initial position by a (nonfinal) heavier syllable. To a first approximation (to be augmented below), weight-sensitivity can be implemented by σ$_{\mu\mu}$→STRESS. Some illustrations follow.

First, stress is by default leftmost, and cannot be attracted onto a heavy ultima, as in (24). Furthermore, the ultima cannot shorten, as in (d), to save a violation of σ$_{\mu\mu}$→STRESS. As before, coda consonants are nonmoraic unless annotated by μ.

(24)

mazida:r		NonFinality	Max-μ-V	$\sigma_{\mu\mu}\to$S	Align-L
a. ☞	'mazida:r			*	
b.	ma'zida:r			*	*!
c.	mazi'da:r	*!			**
d.	'mazidar		*!		

In (25), stress is attracted to a heavy syllable at the expense of alignment. Once again, faithfulness constraints proscribe altering vowel length.

(25)

zoru:rat^h		NonFinality	Max-μ-V	$\sigma_{\mu\mu}\to$S	Align-L
a. ☞	zo'ru:rat^h				*
b.	'zoru:rat^h			*!	
c.	'zorurat^h		*!		
d.	zoru:'rat^h	*!		*	**

So far, the only weight distinction implemented is {V, VC} < {VV, VVC}. VC is at this point uniformly monomoraic, given *μ ≫ Max-μ. Furthermore, $\sigma_{\mu\mu}\to$Stress does not distinguish among grades of heavy, so bimoraic syllables are collapsed with trimoraic syllables. To implement V < VC, WbyP can be added.[18] With WbyP ranked as in (26), VC is moraified and attracts stress. The superheavy coda is also compelled, irrelevantly, to be moraic; for simplicity, candidates in which it is not moraic are omitted.

(26)

ʃokɨrva:r		NonFinality	Max-μ-V	$\sigma_{\mu\mu}\to$S	WbyP	*μ	Align-L
a. ☞	ʃo'kɨr$_\mu$va:r$_\mu$			*		*****	*
b.	'ʃokɨrva:r$_\mu$			*	*!	*****	
c.	'ʃokɨr$_\mu$va:r$_\mu$			**!		******	
d.	ʃo'kɨrva:r$_\mu$			*	*!	*****	*
e.	ʃokɨr'va:r$_\mu$	*!		*		*****	**

This ranking elegantly also implements VC < VV without further stipulation, as shown in (27). Because $\sigma_{\mu\mu}\to$Stress ≫ WbyP, the unstressed coda is nonmoraic to

---

[18] Rosenthall and van der Hulst (1999) employ *Append instead of WbyP for this purpose, but the analysis is essentially the same either way. *Append penalizes a consonant that links directly to the syllable node, without μ intervening.

avoid a violation of $\sigma_{\mu\mu}\rightarrow$STRESS. In this way, coda consonants vary in moraicity as depicted in (21), being moraic under stress and in superheavies (regardless of stress) and nonmoraic otherwise.[19]

(27)

vuʃnaːvun	NonFinality	Max-μ-V	$\sigma_{\mu\mu}\rightarrow$S	WbyP	*μ	Align-L
a. ☞ vuʃ'naːvun				**	****	*
b. 'vuʃnaːvun			*!	**	****	
c. 'vuʃ$_\mu$naːvun			*!	*	*****	
d. vuʃ$_\mu$'naːvun			*!	*	*****	*

At this point, the weight hierarchy V < VC < {VV, VVC} is implemented. But nothing yet captures the distinction between heavies and superheavies. To this end, Morén (2001) invokes PK-PROM. But the full power of PK-PROM is not needed, since it is employed only to ensure that superheavies attract stress. Considering also the discussion of PK-PROM in §2.2, one might substitute $\sigma_{\mu\mu\mu}\rightarrow$STRESS for PK-PROM, as in (28).

(28)

boːdeːsvar	NonFinality	Max-μ-V	$\sigma_{\mu\mu}\rightarrow$S	WbyP	*μ	$\sigma_{\mu\mu\mu}\rightarrow$S	Align-L
a. ☞ boː'deːs$_\mu$var			*		******		*
b. 'boːdeːs$_\mu$var			*		******	*!	
c. boː'deːsvar			*	*!	*****		*
d. 'boːdeːsvar			*	*!	*****		

In sum, Coercion reduces an ostensibly quaternary scale (V < VC < VV < VVC) to a ternary one ($\mu < \mu\mu < \mu\mu\mu$), allowing weight-stress mapping in Kashmiri to be analyzed purely in terms of moraic quantity. This analysis works for Kashmiri, but not for cases examined in following sections.

2.5.2 *V < VC < VV < VVC in Pulaar: two problems for Coercion*

Pulaar (Atlantic, Niger-Congo) is analyzed next, as it has the same primary stress rule and scale as Kashmiri. That is, primary stress is assigned to the leftmost nonfinal instance of the heaviest syllable type available on the scale V < VC < VV < VVC. This section assumes the description of Pulaar primary and secondary stress by Niang (1995, 1997) on the dialect of Brakna, Mauritania. See also the analysis of Wiltshire

---

[19] Coercion predicts that in a language like Kashmiri where $\sigma_{\mu\mu}\rightarrow$STRESS ≫ WbyP, unstressed codas are always nonmoraic in VC and always moraic in VVC, a kind of anti-compensatory effect. Intuitively, this seems like a strange prediction, but I cannot furnish an empirical argument against it.

(2006) and the survey of stress across Fula dialects by McLaughlin and Wiltshire (2017), to which I return at the end of this section.

A few points concerning Pulaar phonotactics are relevant. First, VCC is illicit (Niang 1997:32). Second, diphthongs are common in Pulaar, and they are categorized as VC, not VV (Niang 1997:100, 136f). Third, geminates are frequent, and they are also categorized as VC, not VV. A syllable with a short vowel closed by a geminate is notated VG. Thus, {VC, VG} < VV in Pulaar. (As further discussed in §2.6.1, this is the usual treatment of VG in such systems.) Examples are provided in (29).

(29)

	Rime Pattern				
	σ_1	σ_2	σ_3		
a.	X			'ar	'come'
b.	V	X		'pu.laːr	'Pulaar'
c.	V	V	X	'ca.ka.lo	'friendly'
d.	VC	VC	X	'tak.kor.di	'glue'
e.	VV	VV	X	'daː.gaː.de	'walk slowly'
f.	VC	V	X	'hal.ku.de	'kill'
g.	VV	V	X	'piː.la.gol	'tying a scarf'
h.	V	VV	X	da'raː.de	'stand'
i.	V	VC	X	bo'nan.de	'harm'
j.	VC	VV	X	hal'kaː.de	'perish'
k.	VV	VVC	X	naː'naːl.de	'salted area'

Since Pulaar primary stress is exactly the same as that of Kashmiri, it is unnecessary to repeat the analysis of primary stress from §2.5.1. Nevertheless, this section identifies two new issues raised by Pulaar that refute Coercion, namely, geminates and secondary stress. Subsequent sections demonstrate that these same two problems for Coercion recur in several other suprabinary systems.

Consonant length is distinctive in Pulaar (Niang 1997:43–72), with true geminates being extremely common. All consonants except *s, f, h,* and *r* can geminate. Geminates can occur in superheavy syllables and even word-initially (Niang 1997:68–71). As Niang's (1997) exposition and dozens of fully gridded examples make clear, VG is categorized as VC—heavier than V, but lighter than VV. Some examples are given in (30) (glosses are not available). Secondary stress is also shown in (30), but only primary stress is important at the moment. Forms (a–d) demonstrate VG < VV. I could not find a stress-marked example illustrating VG luring stress away from initial V. However, V < VG can still be securely inferred from forms like (f–h), which demonstrate that VG is not light. I follow Niang (1997) in using "y" for a glide and "j" for an affricate.

(30) a. ˌballi'noːwo
      b. jamiran'noːɗo
      c. ʃettiˌnoytu'noːɗo
      d. ˌgoɗɗikino'yiːɗo
      e. 'naːtnaːtˌtondirtuˌnoːɓe
      f. 'joʃʃiˌnoyde
      g. 'takkordi
      h. 'tallorde

The background hierarchy {MAX-μ, DEP-μ} ≫ *μ enables distinctive length in both vowels and consonants. Tableau (31) employs the final ranking from Kashmiri in §2.5.1, except that MAX-μ-V is now replaced by generic MAX-μ in order to allow geminates. Only primary stress is considered for the time being. The should-be winner (b) is bested by (a), as indicated by ☻. Indeed, given that (a) harmonically bounds (b), the should-be winner cannot win under any ranking of these constraints. For simplicity, geminates are henceforth shown as doubled consonants in the input, with the assumption that they are always moraic in the input, just as vowels are treated here.

(31)

ballino:wo	NONFINALITY	MAX-μ	σμμ→S	WbyP	*μ	σμμμ→S	ALIGN-L
a. ☻ 'balμlino:wo			*		******		
b. ☞ balμli'no:wo			*		******		*!*
c. 'balino:wo	*!				*****		
d. bali'no:wo	*!				*****		**

One logically possible (but ultimately unworkable) remedy to the problem in (31) is to admit the possibility of nonmoraic geminates, untethering distinctive length from moraicity (contra Morén 2001 and others, but certainly not without precedent; cf. Selkirk 1990, Tranel 1991, Blevins 1995, Davis 2011, Topintzi and Zimmermann 2014, Topintzi and Davis 2017). For example, in tableaux (32) and (33), hypothetical IDENT(long) (or perhaps simply MAX) preserves the length of geminates, while MAX-μ (not shown) is buried, permitting geminates to be contextually moraic like other codas, yielding their moras—but not their length—when unstressed. While other languages ostensibly violating the Moraic Theory of Geminates have been discussed in the literature (*ibid.*; see §2.6.5), Pulaar would be an especially pernicious case, since it would require true geminates to vary between surface-moraic and surface-nonmoraic within the same language in order to implement V < VG < VV with Coercion. At any rate, nonmoraic geminates are a nonstarter for Pulaar on independent grounds, as explained below the tableaux. Therefore, it is not worth pursuing this possibility further.

(32)

ballino:wo	NONFINALITY	IDENT(long)	MAX-μ-V	σμμ→S	WbyP	*μ	σμμμ→S	ALIGN-L
a. 'ballino:wo				*!	*	*****		
b. ☞ balli'no:wo					*	*****		**
c. 'balμlino:wo				*!		******		
d. balμli'no:wo				*!		*****		**
e. 'balino:wo	*!				*	*****		
f. bali'no:wo	*!					*****		**

(33)

takμkordi		NONFINALITY	IDENT(long)	MAX-μ-V	σμμ→S	WbyP	*μ	σμμ→S	ALIGN-L
a.	'takkordi					*!*	***		
b.	tak'kordi					*!*	***		*
c.	'takkorμdi				*!	*	****		
d.	tak'korμdi					*	****		*!
e.	'takμkorμdi				*!		*****		
f.	takμ'korμdi				*!		*****		*
g. ☞	'takμkordi					*	****		
h.	takμ'kordi				*!	*	****		*

Secondary stress in Pulaar falls on all nonfinal, non-primary-stressed heavies, modulo clash (Niang 1997:81ff, Wiltshire 2006). Geminates count as heavy for secondary stress, meaning that they cannot be monomoraic. As shown in (34), secondary stress can occur on both sides of primary stress, but is suppressed if clash would result.[20]

(34) a. ˌballi'noːwo
       b. 'baːbaˌlaːjo
       c. ˌkaːsa'maːsnaːjo
       d. ˌjolti'noːwo
       e. ˌjoʃʃi'noːwo
       f. naː'naːlde

Lapses of any length are tolerated if no heavy syllables are available to stress, as illustrated in (35).[21]

(35) a. jogoto'noːɗo
       b. leloto'noːɗo
       c. duwa'naːɗo
       d. 'kaːldigelam
       e. 'maːntorgelam
       f. cabobinan'noːɗo
       g. jamiˌroytu'noːɗo

[20] When two resolutions of clash are otherwise tied, the one with leftmost stress wins, suggesting that ALIGN-L is active also for secondary stress. Niang (1997) is not the only description of Pulaar claiming that secondary stress picks out heavies. Prunet and Tellier (1984:81), for one, state that "[l]es autres syllabes lourdes du mot portent des accents secondaires." Indeed, as addressed below, it is common in unbounded systems to apply secondary stress to heavies. Wiltshire (2006) offers an OT analysis of primary and secondary stress in Pulaar, but does not bring up the problem that geminates pose for primary stress under Coercion.

[21] Once again, this generalization is commonplace for unbounded stress. Niang's (1997) presentation of some of these examples requires caution, as he sometimes provides grids only for intermediate representations, leaving certain late rules to prose (e.g. "application of the second stress deletion rule eliminates the incorrectly placed secondary stress on the first syllable").

Comparison of forms such as [ˌballiˈnoːwo], with secondary stress, to those such as [duwaˈnaːɗo], without, supports that VG patterns like VC for secondary stress, as Prunet and Tellier (1984) and Niang (1997) suggest. Moreover, beyond secondary stress, other phonological processes involving geminates in Pulaar corroborate their weight-bearing status, regardless of stress. For example, initial geminates are permitted only if the following vowel is short (Niang 1997:70). Such compensatory relations involving geminates are standardly analyzed as being weight-driven (Hayes 1989, Muller 1999, Davis 1999, 2003, Beltzung 2008, Topintzi 2008, 2010, Kiparsky 2011).

Thus, there is no way out for Coercion. Consider four logical possibilities, namely, (1) geminates are always moraic, (2) geminates are never moraic, (3) geminates are moraic only under stress (of any level), and (4) geminates are moraic only under primary stress. Under (1), VG is always equivalent to VV in weight, and therefore outputs like *[ˈballiˌnoːwo] are predicted. Under (2), VG is always light, and therefore outputs like *[takˈkordi] (with misplaced primary stress) and *[balliˈnoːwo] (without secondary stress) are predicted. To demonstrate the failure of (3), one can work backwards from the should-be winner [ˌballiˈnoːwo]. VG is stressed, and must therefore be a bimoraic syllable according to the premise of (3). But if it is bimoraic, it is erroneously predicted to bear primary stress in that form. (4) is similarly untenable. Once again, [ˌballiˈnoːwo] needs to win. VG receives secondary stress and is therefore light according to the premise of (4). But if VG is light, it cannot receive secondary stress; it is erroneously predicted to be stressed like [duwaˈnaːɗo]. In sum, all four possible analyses of geminates result in contradictions under Coercion. Indeed, Morén (2000) recognizes explicitly that Coercion "makes the strong prediction" that VG must be equivalent to VV. This prediction is neither confirmed nor disconfirmed by Kashmiri, as geminates are absent (with the caveat in footnote 17). But in Pulaar, which has the same rule in a geminate-rich setting, the prediction is revealed to be incorrect.

Aside from $VG_\mu < VV$ for primary stress, a second and independent argument against Coercion, as raised by Wiltshire (2006), is that it cannot account for V < VC for secondary stress. Heavy syllables, that is, all rimes except V, are treated as a uniform class for secondary stress, in that they bear it unless doing so would violate CLASH or NONFINALITY, as in (36). Meanwhile, light syllables never bear secondary stress, regardless of lapse, as (35) demonstrated. Consider [ˌjoltiˈnoːwo]. Under Coercion, VC needs to be a monomoraic rime. If it were bimoraic, it would attract primary stress. But if VC is monomoraic, it cannot bear secondary stress (cf. [duwaˈnaːɗo]).

(36) a. ˌjoltiˈnoːwo
      b. ˌhurtoˈyaːde
      c. ˌgartiˌroytuˈnoːɗo
      d. ˈartiˌroyde
      e. ˈbaːbalˌnaːjo

Thus, Coercion covers neither primary nor secondary stress in Pulaar. Of course, the arguments based on Pulaar only go through if the relevant facts are documented accurately. The two critical phenomena are recapitulated in (37). Note that (a) and (b) are independent objections; neither depends on the other being true.

(37)   Two independent aspects of Pulaar stress that are problematic for Coercion:
    (a)   VG = VC (in a system in which VV is heavier and VG cannot be analyzed as light).
    (b)   V < VC for secondary stress (in a system in which VC < VV for primary stress).

First, there is no reason to doubt (a) or (b) on account of naturalness. Both are amply attested, even normal. First, in languages with VC < VV for stress and geminates, VG almost always aligns with VC as being lighter than VV (see §2.6.1). Second, applying secondary stress to heavy syllables is widespread, especially in unbounded systems (e.g. Walker 1997). Indeed, some analysts assume that heavy syllables always head feet in unbounded systems even when secondary stress has not been explicitly described (cf. McCarthy 2003:155, Gordon 2011). Thus, nothing about Niang's secondary stress rule is unexpected.

Aside from naturalness, it is worth asking whether Niang's rules have any independent support, whether from phonetic analysis, from phonological rules that are conditioned by stress, or from independent descriptions of the language. On these points, the outlook is mixed, as is frequently the case for stress rules found in grammars. Pulaar is part of a dialect chain that spans much of western Africa. Most previous descriptions of Pulaar/Fula stress posit weight-sensitive rules that are broadly reminiscent of, but not identical to, Niang's system. See Niang (1997) and McLaughlin and Wiltshire (2017) for surveys. For example, Prunet and Tellier (1984; not consulted) state that main stress falls on the leftmost heavy, with secondary stress falling on other heavies. For very many words, this agrees with Niang (1997). It differs concerning VC < VV < VVC, which Prunet and Tellier (1984) do not note, though I am not aware of whether they entertained the possibility of these contrasts, which are diagnosed only by words in which a lighter heavy precedes a nonfinal heavier heavy. McIntosh (1984), treating the Kaceccereere dialect of Fula (1,500 miles away in Nigeria), states that nominal stress falls on the rightmost nonfinal heavy, and is otherwise initial. Taylor (1953) suggests that Fula stress "depends on the long vowels," picking out a VC < VV criterion, unlike the previous two sources. Still others find no firm evidence of weight-sensitivity (McLaughlin and Wiltshire 2017). In summary, while Niang's (1997) rule bears a family resemblance to some other descriptions of Fula dialects, it has not been corroborated independently. That said, as subsequent sections show, Pulaar is hardly alone in exhibiting the two problems brought out in this section for Coercion. Both the geminate and secondary stress problems arise in several other languages.

2.5.3   *V < VC < VV < VVC in Pulaar: the Prominence analysis*

An analysis of Pulaar is available with MAIN→VV. MAIN→VV allows syllables with long vowels to be more stress-attracting even when they have moraic codas, which is the situation in Pulaar. At the same time, WbyP can be promoted to undominated, abandoning contextual moraicity. Aside from these adjustments, the analysis of primary stress is the same as in §§2.5.1–2.5.2.

The analysis is now also extended to secondary stress. As described in §2.5.2, secondary stress falls on every nonfinal, non-primary-stressed heavy, unless clash would result. CLASH can therefore be top-ranked, alongside NONFINALITY. Because clash-based ties are broken to the left, ALIGN-L (for stress in general) and ALIGN-L-MAIN (for primary stress) are both active. Tableau (38) shows the effect of alignment on primary stress. Without ALIGN-L-MAIN, (a) and (b) would not be distinguished. But ALIGN-L cannot be dropped, as it is still needed to favor leftmost secondary stress in clash contexts, as in a word such as [ˌdartintuˈnoːɗo].

(38)

baːbalaːjo	CLASH	NONFINALITY	MAIN→VV	σµµµ→MAIN	σµµ→S	ALIGN-L-MAIN	ALIGN-L	ALIGN-R
a. ☞ ˈbaːbaˌlaːjo							**	****
b. ˌbaːbaˈlaːjo						*!*	**	****
c. ˈbaːˌbaˌlaːjo	*!*						***	******
d. ˈbaːbalaːjo					*!			***

VC (including VG) remains lighter than VV for primary stress. But it must still be assigned secondary stress in (39). Here there is no issue for geminates, which trivially fall in with VC given this grammar. (This is not to suggest that VC and VG are predicted always to be equivalent under this approach; see §2.6.4.) The geminate cannot be simplified, given highly ranked MAX-µ, not shown (§2.5.2).

(39)

ballinoːwo	CLASH	NONFINALITY	MAIN→VV	σµµµ→MAIN	σµµ→S	ALIGN-L-MAIN	ALIGN-L	ALIGN-R
a. ☞ ˌbal$_\mu$liˈnoːwo						**	**	****
b. ˈbal$_\mu$liˌnoːwo			*!				**	****
c. ˈbal$_\mu$linoːwo			*!					***
d. bal$_\mu$liˈnoːwo					*!	**	**	*

Superheavies draw primary stress from VV rimes, as in (40). This tableau also illustrates that σµµµ→MAIN cannot be indexed to STRESS, lest (b) win, with secondary stress on the superheavy. Once again, if one prefers PK-PROM, it can be substituted.

(40)

kaːsamaːsnaːjo	CLASH	NONFINALITY	MAIN→VV	σµµµ→MAIN	σµµ→S	ALIGN-L-MAIN	ALIGN-L	ALIGN-R
a. ☞ ˌkaːsaˈmaːs$_\mu$naːjo					*	**	**	******
b. ˈkaːsaˌmaːs$_\mu$naːjo				*!	*		**	******
c. ˌkaːsamaːs$_\mu$ˈnaːjo				*!	*	***	***	*****
d. ˌkaːsaˈmaːs$_\mu$ˌnaːjo	*!				**	**	*****	*******

Finally, stress needs to be suppressed on light syllables, such as the initial syllable of (41), where CLASH is not at stake. Lowly ranked ALIGN-R, for one, effectively favors fewer (nonfinal) stresses. Other constraints would work equally well for this purpose, including STRESS→$\sigma_{\mu\mu}$ (if one allows SWP to apply to secondary stress; §2.3.2) and *GRIDSTRUC (Walker 1996), the latter penalizing each stress.

(41)

duwana:ɗo	CLASH	NONFINALITY	MAIN→VV	$\sigma_{\mu\mu}$→MAIN	$\sigma_{\mu\mu}$→S	ALIGN-L-MAIN	ALIGN-L	ALIGN-R
a. ☞ duwaˈna:ɗo						**	**	*
b. ˌduwaˈna:ɗo						**	**	**!**

In sum, both the geminate problem and secondary stress problem in Pulaar are solved by the addition of MAIN→VV in a uniform moraicity setting. The following sections argue that MAIN→VV is similarly justified for other languages.

2.5.4 V < VC < VV in Chickasaw

Thanks to a detailed phonetic and phonological study by Gordon (2004a), which corroborates earlier descriptions by Munro and Ulrich (1984) and Munro (1996), the empirical situation concerning Chickasaw (Muskogean) stress is relatively secure. Primary stress seeks out a VV rime. If no VV rime occurs, primary stress is final. Secondary stress falls on all non-primary-stressed heavies (V < VX). The ultima, if not primary stressed, also receives secondary stress, regardless of its weight. In words with multiple VV syllables, Gordon (2004a) finds no consistent generalization about which VV is primary. Therefore, only words with zero to one VV syllables are considered here, for which the facts are clear. In (42), (a–d) do not contain long vowels, and primary stress is final. Forms with a long vowel are given in (e–k). Examples like (c–e) confirm that VG syllables are treated as lighter than VV for primary stress, but equivalent to VC and VV for secondary stress.

(42) a. noˌtakˈfa   'jaw'
     b. ˌokˌfokˈkol   'type of snail'
     c. kaˌnanˈnak   'striped lizard'
     d. ˌhattaˈkat   'man'
     e. ʃimmaˈno:ˌliʔ   'Seminole'
     f. faˈla:t   'crow (subject)'
     g. taˈla:ˌnomˌpaʔ   'telephone'
     h. tʃoˈka:ˌno   'fly'
     i. ˈna:ɬtoˌkaʔ   'policeman'
     j. ˈsa:ɬkoˌna   'earthworm'
     k. ˌinˌtikˈba:t   'sibling (subject)'

Given this rule, Chickasaw is like Pulaar in that it exhibits two problems for Coercion: First, VG joins VC in being lighter than VV for primary stress (violating the "strong prediction" of Coercion identified by Morén 2001). Second, VC and VG are heavier than V for secondary stress even when primary stress is lured away by VV, showing that they must retain their coda moras when not primary stressed.

The Prominence analysis runs as follows. For *notakfa* in (43), MAIN→VV is irrelevant, since no long vowel is present. FINALSTRESS is shorthand for ALIGN(PWd, right, stress, right), which requires the ultima to have some degree of stress. $\sigma_{\mu\mu}$→STRESS ensures that heavies receive at least secondary stress, but STRESS→$\sigma_{\mu\mu}$ suppresses stress on lights, modulo FINALSTRESS. Finally, ALIGN-R-MAIN assigns a penalty for every syllable that follows the primary stress. This constraint ensures that primary stress is final when no VV lures it away, even when other heavies are present. As before, coda consonants are uniformly moraic. For simplicity, WbyP and offending candidates are omitted.

(43)

notakfa	FINALSTRESS	MAIN→VV	$\sigma_{\mu\mu}$→S	S→$\sigma_{\mu\mu}$	ALIGN-R-MAIN	ALIGN-R
a. ☞ noˌtak$_\mu$'fa		*		*		*
b. no'tak$_{\mu}$ˌfa		*		*	*!	*
c. notak$_\mu$'fa		*	*!	*		
d. no'tak$_\mu$fa	*!	*			*	*
e. ˌnoˌtak$_\mu$'fa		*		*		**!*

VV attracting primary stress is shown in (44). The stress differs from (43) even though the moraic profile is the same.

(44)

tʃokaːno	FINALSTRESS	MAIN→VV	$\sigma_{\mu\mu}$→S	S→$\sigma_{\mu\mu}$	ALIGN-R-MAIN	ALIGN-R
a. ☞ tʃo'kaːˌno				*	*	*
b. tʃo'kaːno	*!				*	*
c. tʃoˌkaː'no		*!		*		*

Finally, geminates are treated like VC rather than VV, in that they do not attract primary stress away from the ultima, as illustrated in (45). ALIGN-R-MAIN breaks the tie between two equally heavy syllables in (45), favoring final primary stress.

(45)

hattakat	FINALSTRESS	MAIN→VV	$\sigma_{\mu\mu}$→S	S→$\sigma_{\mu\mu}$	ALIGN-R-MAIN	ALIGN-R
a. ☞ ˌhat$_\mu$ta'kat					*	**
b. 'hat$_\mu$taˌkat					*!*	**

Coercion, by contrast, cannot account for these facts, even when one puts aside geminates. The outputs [noˌtak$_\mu$ˈfa] and [tʃoˈkaːˌno] are needed to simultaneously win. No ranking of the "standard" constraints (§§2.3.2–2.5.1) allows this to happen, as the two comparative tableaux in (46) reveal. The two desired winners impose contradictory ranking conditions on Align-R-Main and {$\sigma_{\mu\mu}\to$Main, Main$\to\sigma_{\mu\mu}$}, as shown by mappings (a) and (i). In (a), Align-R-Main must be ranked above both $\sigma_{\mu\mu}\to$Main and Main$\to\sigma_{\mu\mu}$ for [noˌtak$_\mu$ˈfa] to beat *[noˈtak$_\mu$ˌfa]. But for [tʃoˈkaːˌno] to win in (i), either $\sigma_{\mu\mu}\to$Main or Main$\to\sigma_{\mu\mu}$ must be ranked above Align-R-Main. Removing Align-R-Main altogether would not help, as doing so would leave [noˌtak$_\mu$ˈfa] harmonically bounded.

(46)

	Winner ~ Loser	Align-R-Main	$\sigma_{\mu\mu}\to$Main	Main$\to\sigma_{\mu\mu}$	FinalStress	$\sigma_{\mu\mu}\to$S	WbyP	Align-R	S$\to\sigma_{\mu\mu}$
a.	noˌtak$_\mu$ˈfa ~ noˈtak$_\mu$ˌfa	W	L	L					
b.	~ notak$_\mu$ˈfa					W		L	
c.	~ noˈtak$_\mu$fa	W	L	L	W				L
d.	~ noˌtakˈfa		L				W		W
e.	~ noˈtakˌfa	W	L				W		W
f.	~ notakˈfa		L				W	L	
g.	~ noˈtakfa	W	L		W		W		
h.	~ ˌnoˌtakˈfa		L				W	W	W
i.	tʃoˈkaːˌno ~ tʃoˌkaːˈno	L	W	W					

The situation is not improved for Coercion if one takes the homophonous candidate [noˌtakˈfa], with a nonmoraic coda, to be the desired winner. As (47) shows, this candidate is harmonically bounded by *[notakˈfa] in (f).

(47)

	Winner ~ Loser	Align-R	S$\to\sigma_{\mu\mu}$	FinalStress	$\sigma_{\mu\mu}\to$S	$\sigma_{\mu\mu}\to$Main	Align-R-Main	Main$\to\sigma_{\mu\mu}$	WbyP
a.	noˌtakˈfa ~ noˌtak$_\mu$ˈfa		L			W			L
b.	~ noˈtak$_\mu$ˌfa		L				W	L	L
c.	~ notak$_\mu$ˈfa	L	L		W	W			L
d.	~ noˈtak$_\mu$fa		L	W			W	L	L
e.	~ ˌnoˌtak$_\mu$ˈfa	W				W			L
f.	~ notakˈfa	L	L						
g.	~ noˈtakfa		L	W			W		
h.	tʃoˈkaːˌno ~ tʃoˌkaːˈno					W	L	W	

Coercion once again entails a contradiction. In order for VC (unlike V) to receive secondary stress, VC must be bimoraic. But in order for VC to be lighter than VV for primary stress, VC must be monomoraic. As the comparative tableaux demonstrate, this contradiction is evident even when none of the inputs under consideration combines VC and VV in the same form. Their different behavior across forms is sufficient evidence. Moreover, this case study reinforces that the secondary stress problem is independent from the geminate problem, as the comparative tableaux do not contain candidates with geminates. But the geminate problem also applies, with the same logic as in Pulaar. Prominence has no issue with geminates or secondary stress. VC, VG, and VV are all uniformly heavy. VV is more stress-attracting because it contains a long vowel.

2.5.5 *V < VC < VV in Klamath*

Analyses of stress in Klamath (Plateau Penutian), as described by Barker (1964:35–8), include Levin (1985), Hammond (1986), Halle and Vergnaud (1987), and Hayes (1995). If a word contains VV, the rightmost VV receives primary stress. Otherwise, primary stress follows the Latin rule: It is initial in monosyllables and disyllables, and penultimate in words of three or more syllables, unless the penult is light (V), in which case it is antepenultimate. Another minor difference with respect to Latin, not important here, is that Klamath permits degenerate feet as PWds (e.g. *pse* 'daytime').

Barker (1964) also describes secondary stress, which, unlike primary stress, observes purely the V < VX criterion. Secondary stress occurs on the penult if it is heavy and primary stress is earlier (including the immediately preceding syllable). Barker (1964) also suggests that secondary stress applies optionally to certain syllables in the pretonic field (specifically, the initial syllable or the first closed syllable), but is less certain about the pretonic situation. Therefore, like other analysts (see especially Hammond 1986:219–23 for discussion of Klamath secondary stress), I consider only the penultimate secondary stress here, which Barker (1964) states "occurs consistently," and put aside the pretonic field.

Some examples of primary and secondary stress are given in (48) and (49). The forms in (48) are consistent with the Latin rule.

(48) a. 'boc'o   'wild celery'
      b. 'ɢlegatk   'dead?' (sic)
      c. ga:'mo:la   'finishes grinding'
      d. gat'bambli   'returns home'
      e. gankanktk'damna   'used to habitually hunt'
      f. ldaɢalbli'nannwi   'picks a round object right back up'
      g. 'ʔapʔota   'promises'
      h. 'č'aw'iga   'is crazy'

The examples in (49) reveal that long vowels override the Latin rule, such that the rightmost VV attracts stress regardless of where it occurs in the word. Secondary stress, irrelevant in (48), is also illustrated by several of the examples in (49). One of Barker's (1964) examples, (f) below, includes a geminate. He is explicit in this case that primary stress still falls on VV. Thus, VG is equivalent to VC, not VV. Form (e) confirms that a vowel-glide rime [aw] also patterns with VC, not VV. The treatment of both geminates and vowel-glide sequences is the same as in Pulaar (§2.5.2).

(49) a. n'is'q'aːk   'little girl'
      b. ga:'moːla   'finishes grinding'
      c. ča't'aː,wipga   'is sitting in the sun'
      d. ga'w'iːnap,gabli   'is going among them'
      e. sa'n'aː,ẉawli   'wants'
      f. ʔamna'liː,nalla   'goes along the bank crying'

A Prominence analysis of these facts is given by the hierarchy in (50).[22] This analysis essentially amounts to ranking MAIN→VV above a quasi-Latin system. MAIN→VV ensures that VV, if available, takes primary stress. If multiple VV occur, ALIGN-R-MAIN favors the rightmost.[23] The analysis of the quasi-Latin core is a bit more complicated, since foot structure is now relevant. FINALFOOT is short for ALIGN(PWd, right, foot, right), which penalizes every syllable intervening between the final foot boundary and the right edge of the word. NONFINALITY is taken to penalize both final stress and a final foot; if they cooccur, it is violated twice (cf. Prince and Smolensky 1993/2004; this could be split into two constraints if one is so inclined). FTBIN is also assumed to be active here, although it needs to be dominated by faithfulness (not shown) in order to protect subminimal words.

Tableaux (50) and (51) demonstrate that a superheavy ultima does not attract stress unless it contains a long vowel.

(50)

glegatk		FtBin	Main→VV	NonFinality	Align-R-Main	S→σμμ	FinalFoot	Clash
a. ☞	('glegatμkμ)		*	*	*	*		
b.	Gle('gatμkμ)		*	**!				
c.	('Gle)(,gatμkμ)	*!	*	**	*	*		*

---

[22] This analysis incidentally also solves a problem raised by Klamath for extrametricality. As Gordon (2017:40) explains, "The Klamath type of extrametricality is more problematic for moraic theory because it requires that both consonants in CVCC be extrametrical. To allow for two consonants to be extrametrical opens up a theoretical Pandora's box by removing the requirement that extrametricality only affect peripheral elements." Here, there is no problem. Extrametricality need not be invoked in the first place. VCC fails to override NONFINALITY because it does not contain a long vowel.

[23] More precisely, the present analysis predicts that if one of the VV is final, the rightmost nonfinal VV gets primary stress, similar to Kelkar's Hindi. While Barker (1964) does not suggest such an effect, he also does not cite any forms in which final VV and nonfinal VV occupy the same word, leaving one to wonder whether he considered the configuration. I tentatively leave in this nonfinality effect as a prediction, which could be patched if necessary.

(51)

	nisqʼaːk	FTBIN	MAIN→VV	NONFINALITY	ALIGN-R-MAIN	S→σμμ	FINALFOOT	CLASH
a. ☞	nisμ('qʼaːkμ)			**				
b.	('nisμ)qʼaːkμ		*!		*		*	
c.	('nisμ)(ˌqʼaːkμ)		*!	**	*			*

Secondary stress emerges on a penultimate heavy in (52), but not on the antepenultimate heavy.[24]

(52)

	gawʼiːnapgabli	FTBIN	MAIN→VV	NONFINALITY	ALIGN-R-MAIN	S→σμμ	FINALFOOT	CLASH
a. ☞	ga('wʼiː)napμ(ˌgabμ)li			***			*	
b.	ga('wʼiː)(ˌnapμ)(ˌgabμ)li			***			*	*!*
c.	ga(ˌwʼiː)(ˌnapμ)('gabμ)li	*!		*			*	**
d.	ga(ˌwʼiː)napμ('gabμ)li	*!		*			*	
e.	gawʼiːnapμ('gabμ)li	*!		*			*	
f.	ga('wʼiː)napμgabμli			***			**!*	
g.	(ˌgawʼiː)napμ('gabμ)li	*!		*	*		*	

But clash is forced if VV immediately precedes a heavy penult, as in (53). Consistent with Barker (1964), word-initial secondary stress is optional in (53).[25]

(53)

	ʔamnaliːnalla	FTBIN	MAIN→VV	NONFINALITY	ALIGN-R-MAIN	S→σμμ	FINALFOOT	CLASH
a. ☞	(ˌʔamμ)na('liː)(ˌnalμ)la			**			*	*
b. ☞	ʔamμna('liː)(ˌnalμ)la			**			*	*
c.	(ˌʔamμ)na(ˌliː)('nalμ)la		*!	*			*	*
d.	(ˌʔamμ)na('liː)nalμla			**			**!	
e.	(ˌʔamμ)naliː('nalμ)la		*!	*			*	

---

[24] The latter is tentatively attributed to CLASH. Barker (1964) does not give any stress-marked examples with more syllables intervening, such that one could distinguish between CLASH and *GRIDSTRUC.

[25] Other constraints, not shown, would adjudicate between the tied candidates. However, these constraints can be freely ranked with antagonistic constraints, or (in HG) weighted zero. For example, PARSE favors (a), but constraints against feet or stress (such as ALIGNMENT) favor (b).

The final piece of the argument is to show that posttonic secondary stress does not arise when the penult is light. Barker (1964) does not provide a stress-marked example in which VV is antepenultimate or earlier and the penult is light, but he makes explicit that the penult is stressed iff it is heavy, which he exemplifies with positive evidence. The example in (54), *le:mlem'a* 'is dizzy' (Barker 1963), is stressed according to Barker's rule, but Barker does not supply this word with stress. I therefore parenthesize the finger. In (54), the combination of FtBin and NonFinality guarantees that the penult is unstressed. With an arbitrarily longer string of trailing lights, Stress→$\sigma_{\mu\mu}$ would rule out any stressed lights between VV and the ultima.

(54)

le:mlem'a	FtBin	Main→VV	NonFinality	Align-R-Main	S→$\sigma_{\mu\mu}$	FinalFoot	Clash
a. (☞) ('le:m$_\mu$)lem'a				**		**	
b. ('le:m$_\mu$)(ˌlem'a)			*!	**	*		*
c. ('le:m$_\mu$)(ˌle)m'a	*!			**	*	*	*
d. le:m$_\mu$('lem'a)		*!		*	*	*	

An analysis of these facts is unworkable under Coercion. First, under Coercion, for VV to attract stress away from VC, VC must be monomoraic. But then V < VC for secondary stress cannot be captured (in words that contain VV), since V now has the same weight as VC. Second, VV outweighs VG in Klamath. To maintain Coercion, one would have to reject the moraic account of gemination. But that is not an option either, since VG receives secondary stress, confirming that geminates are moraic in such words. Thus, Klamath, like Pulaar and Chickasaw in §§2.5.2–2.5.4, exhibits both the geminate and secondary stress problems for Coercion.

2.5.6   V < VC < VV in Maithili

Maithili (Indo-Aryan) stress is described (among others) by Jha (1940–44, 1958). This section is indebted to Hayes' (1995:149–62) analysis of Jha's account. Primary stress is penultimate unless the word-final sequence is either (...)LH# or (...)HLL#, in which case primary stress falls on the (rightmost) heavy. Secondary stress is assigned uniformly to the word-initial syllable, regardless of weight and clash, unless of course that syllable has primary stress. Tertiary stress (here indicated by ˌˌ) falls on all remaining VC or VV rimes (including the ultima, if not otherwise stressed), and also on certain V rimes to save lapse (e.g. ˌL-V-ˌˌV-'H and ˌL-V-ˌˌV-V-'H, where L is a light syllable, H a heavy syllable, and V a short vowel). The criterion for primary stress is VC < VV; that is, only syllables with long vowels qualify as heavy (H). All remaining, unstressed vowels are reduced, notated by a breve: ŏ, ĭ, and ŭ.

Geminates (VG) clearly pattern as VC in this system, as exemplified in (55). If VG were equivalent to VV, (a) and (b–c) would be treated identically. But only VV, in (a), attracts stress away from the final VV. Similarly, (d–e) show that VV is heavier than VG. VV attracts primary stress to the antepenult in (d), but VG does not do the same in (e).

(55) a. ˈsaː‚‚ɹiː   HH   'sari'
      b. ‚bʰaˈtˈṭiː   LH   'a big oven'
      c. ‚pitˈtiː   LH   'father's brother'
      d. ‚manšˈmoː‚‚hɒnš   LLHLL   (proper name)
      e. ‚čʰu‚‚čʰunˈnɒrĭ   LLLL   (no gloss)

Though VC (including VG) is light for primary stress, there are other respects in which it is heavy. First, otherwise regular patterns of vowel reduction are categorically blocked in closed syllables, which Hayes (1995) argues to be diagnostic of tertiary stress. For instance, in (55-e), the medial syllable, which would otherwise reduce between two stresses, fails to reduce because the rime is VC. Furthermore, in a quadrisyllable of the shape σ-V-V-VV, the third syllable reduces, as in (56-a). But if the third syllable is closed, it cannot reduce, and the second syllable reduces instead, as in (56-b). There is thus twofold evidence for tertiary stress, both in that VC, unlike V, never undergoes reduction and also in that reduction of other syllables can be conditioned by whether or not they are adjacent to VC.

(56) a. ‚a‚‚dinšˈtaː   'misfortune'
      b. ‚ekš‚hatˈtʰaː   'man with one hand'

Second, degemination triggers compensatory lengthening (with stress shift), as in (57).

(57) a. ‚dʰatˈtʰaː   'bamboo fence (long form)'
      b. ˈdʰaːtʰš   'bamboo fence'

Third, Hayes (1995) also points to cases of pretonic shortening triggered by VC, showing that VC can under certain circumstances resist destressing even when an otherwise primary stress-eligible long vowel is (underlyingly) available, as in (58). However, the facts are complicated here (p. 158), and at any rate this issue is not necessarily problematic for Coercion, since the long vowel is eliminated on the surface.

(58) /galaːbɒnna/   →   ‚galšˈbɒnnš   'muffler'
                        *‚gaˈlaː‚‚bɒnnš

Hayes (1995) concludes from the aforementioned observations (especially the first one) that VC is (uniformly) bimoraic in Maithili, even though VV acts as heavier in certain respects, as demonstrated by (55). At this point, he almost cries out for a device like MAIN→VV:

What is odd about the analysis is that only CVː syllables induce this clash-governed extrametricality. One would like to relate this to the typological observation that CVː syllables somehow count as "heavier" than CVC; that is, there are many rules that count CVː as heavy and CVC as light, but no rules that go the other way (chap. 7). I have no concrete suggestions for doing this. (1995:160)

For present purposes, the takeaway is that Maithili is another language in which VV attracts primary stress away from VC, but VC still needs to be bimoraic when that happens. The latter is evident, for one, from the fact that VC behaves differently from V for tertiary stress even while primary stress is on VV elsewhere in the word, as in (55). In (e), for instance, the medial syllable [čʰun] must be lighter than a VV syllables, since it does not lure stress away from the penult as VV would. But it must also be heavier than a V syllable, since it resists reduction between two stresses. Thus, Maithili too exhibits both the secondary stress and geminate problems for Coercion.

2.5.7 *V < VC < VV in Yapese*

Yapese (Austronesian), though it lacks geminates, exhibits the secondary stress problem for Coercion. Native lexical words end with VC or VVC. Additionally, loanwords and grammatical words can end with VV. Primary stress is final unless the penult is VV and the ultima is not VVC, in which case it falls on the penult (Jensen 1977). The penult condition makes it clear that VC < VV. Some examples are provided in (59), where secondary stress is also indicated, following Jensen (1977).

(59) a. ro'gon   'its way'
      b. pa'qag   'my hand'
      c. 'saːlap   'expert'
      d. 'l'oːböṭ   'tangle'
      e. ˌm'ag'paːq   'wedding'
      f. ˌmoe'roes   'savage'
      g. ˌmarnˌgaq'gëːn   'about it'

Jensen (1977) states that secondary stress falls on pretonic heavies, where VX is heavy. Clash is not a consideration. For example, [ro'gon] has no secondary stress, since the penult is light, but [ˌm'ag'paːq] has it, since the penult is heavy. A full analysis need not be developed here, since the logic of the critical point is the same as above. In the penult, {V, VC} < VV for primary stress. Under Coercion, this can only be analyzed as unstressed VC being monomoraic, so as to yield primary stress to the ultima. But if unstressed VC is monomoraic in the penult, then it should not get secondary stress, which is conditioned by bimoraicity. For Prominence, there is no issue, since VC and VV can be differently stressable even while both are bimoraic.

2.5.8 *V < VC < VV in Finnish*

Finnish primary stress is uniformly initial. Secondary stress is largely rhythmic, falling on every other nonfinal syllable thereafter in the basic case, but can also be affected by weight, as described by Anttila (1997b, 2010) and Karvonen (2005). The full structure of this system is complex and gets into probabilistic territory (Anttila 2010). What is relevant here is that it exemplifies the ternary scale V < VC < VV in a setting in which variable moraicity is arguably untenable. The pentasyllables in (60), from Karvonen (2005:44, 76ff), demonstrate V < VC. In particular, secondary stress is penultimate in L̇LLL̀L, as in (a–b), but antepenultimate in L̇LH̀LL, as in (c–d).

(60) a. 'arabiˌkumi   'gum arabic'
      b. 'oligoˌpoli   'oligopoly'
      c. 'heliˌkopteri   'helicopter'
      d. 'alaˌbasteri   'alabaster'

Additionally, VC<VV is demonstrated by words such as (61). In (a–c), the antepenult-penult sequence is VC-VV, and stress is penultimate. In (d–g), it is VV-VC, and stress is antepenultimate. In short, VV attracts stress away from VC (Karvonen 2005:90, Anttila 2010:5, p.c.). As these examples further indicate, VG patterns as VC, not VV.

(61) a. 'horison̩ta:li   'horizontal'
      b. 'instrumen̩ta:li   'instrumental'
      c. 'kotiut̩ta:ko   'send home'
      d. 'ana̩ly:tikko   'analyst'
      e. 'aka̩te:mikko   'Academy member'
      f. 'ko:rdi̩na:tistoja 'coordinate grids (partitive)'
      g. 'ko:rdin̩na:titta   'coordinate (abessive)'

An analysis of these facts invoking Coercion, that is, treating VC as monomoraic when it yields to VV, requires treating Finnish geminates as nonmoraic when they lack stress. However, not only is consonant length distinctive in Finnish, but Finnish is rich with processes that treat VG as heavy (regardless of stress). For example, consonant gradation is conditioned by the following syllable being heavy. *Matto* 'mat,' for instance, degeminates to *matolla* 'on the mat' in the adessive. This suggests that both geminates involved, *tt* and *ll*, are moraic (see Kiparsky 2011 and Spahr 2011 for moraic analyses). Note that the latter is unstressed. With the addition of the single constraint STRESS→VV, the moraicity of geminates can be maintained in Finnish. Karvonen (2005:88) proposes a similar constraint, *{CV̆V} ("no unstressed CVV syllables"), adding in a footnote that Coercion is not well suited to rich scales. Karvonen's constraint is VV→STRESS in the present formalism. Either VV→STRESS or STRESS→VV would work in this case (on this type of interchangeability, recall §2.3.2), but either way, some Prominence constraint is needed.

2.5.9 V<VC<VV<VVC in Nanti

Nanti (Arawakan) is another language whose secondary stress defeats Coercion. (Geminates, for their part, are not permitted.) The full system is presented by Crowhurst and Michael (2005), though the relevant facts highlighted here follow more closely the recapitulation by Munshi and Crowhurst (2012:466–8).

In the most basic case, when weight is neutral, verbs are parsed into disyllabic iambs from left to right, subject to a (presently irrelevant) violable nonfinality condition. If weight is neutral, the rightmost foot is the head foot, as in (a–b) in (62). Weight comes into play in two ways. First, stress within a foot shifts onto the first syllable of the foot if it is heavier than the second syllable of the foot.[26] Twelve grades of weight are recognized, combining the skeletal scale V < VC < VV < VVC with the vowel height scale High < Mid < Low. The question of how exactly these scales are interleaved is

---

[26] Foot inversion can also be triggered—sometimes cascadingly—by CLASH.

put aside as irrelevant here, as are some additional complications.[27] The initial feet of (c–d) illustrate this weight-conditioned inversion.

(62) a. (no'ne)he=ro   'I will see it'
      b. (o₁ko)(wo'go)te=ro   'she harvests it'
      c. (₁piŋka)(mo'soi)gakse 'you (plural) will have visited'
      d. ('noːga)ka=ro   'I consumed it'

Next, primary stress falls on a nonfinal foot if a heavier syllable is available than in the final foot, as in (63).

(63) a. (pi'ka)(bi₁ri)ti   'you get active'
      b. (i'paŋ)(kʃi₁wo)(ha₁ta)kse 'he placed the house support'

Finally, Munshi and Crowhurst (2012) draw attention to the three examples in (64) as sufficing to compactly illustrate the whole skeletal scale $V < VC < VV < VVC$. Primary stress in (a) shows $V < VC$. Primary stress in (b) shows $VC < VV$. Secondary stress in (c) shows $VV < VVC$. For many more examples, see Crowhurst and Michael (2005).

(64) a. (na'mam)(pi₁ja)kse   'I supported (someone)'
      b. (i'roː)(ga₁ksem)pa=ra   'he will consume'
      c. (o₁sa)('raːntai)gakse   'they (feminine) tore it (with a purpose)'

Forms like (64-b) demonstrate the failure of Coercion, as Munshi and Crowhurst (2012) make explicit. Under Coercion, in order for VV (rime [oː]) to attract primary stress away from VC (rime [em]), VV must be bimoraic and VC monomoraic. But if VC is monomoraic in (64-b), then it should yield its secondary stress to [ga], since a low vowel is heavier than a mid vowel, as forms such as (65) reinforce (Crowhurst and Michael 2005:53). One could not instead say that CLASH motivates the stress in (64-b), since weight dominates clash, as exemplified by (64-c).

(65) a. ('name)kse=ro   'I will sharpen it'
      b. (₁piŋ.kʃi)('sa.kse)=ra   'you will have hit'

In conclusion, Nanti is another instance of the secondary stress problem for Coercion, whereby VC yields to VV for primary stress but continues to receive weight-conditioned secondary stress. Crowhurst and Michael (2005) and Munshi and Crowhurst (2012) acknowledge this argument and develop their own kind of Prominence analysis in a uniform moraicity setting. In brief, they treat codas as nonmoraic (fusing to vocalic moras), but use a constraint favoring branching moras under stress to attract stress to syllables with codas. Thus, on their analysis, $V_\mu C$ is heavier than V_μ, even though both are monomoraic. Meanwhile, VV is bimoraic, and

---

[27] In brief, Crowhurst and Michael (2005) actually recognize three scales, namely, Quantity (vowel length), Coda (presence or absence of a coda), and Quality (roughly speaking, vowel height). Ranking these three scales in terms of their priority yields Quantity > Coda > Quality for secondary stress and Quantity > Quality > Coda for primary stress. This is thus another case, like Pulaar, Chickasaw, and Klamath above, in which the treatment of weight differs between primary and secondary stress.

thus heavier than both V and VC. The approach developed here differs in formalism, but the upshot is the same. Here, codas are uniformly moraic, and VV is heavier than VC by virtue of STRESS/MAIN→VV. Meanwhile, V is monomoraic, and thus lighter than both VC and VV. For more details on the distinction between these two approaches to Skeletal Prominence, see §2.7.1. For now, the point is that some kind of Prominence analysis, with uniform weight, is necessary; Coercion does not suffice.

2.5.10 *V < VC < VV in Tamil*

Tamil (Dravidian) is compatible with both Coercion and Prominence, though the former requires geminates to lack moras when unstressed.[28] As described by Christdas (1996) (see also Gordon 2004b), primary stress is initial, unless the initial rime is V and the peninitial rime is VV, in which case it is peninitial.[29] This rule ostensibly diagnoses two criteria, one for each position. Initially, V < VX, as only the former can yield stress. Peninitially, VC < VV, as only the latter can attract stress. Putting these criteria together, ternary V < VC < VV emerges. Some examples follow in (66). VG has the same weight as VC regardless of position. Short vowels are reduced in unstressed syllables. This reduction is a consequence, not a cause, of stress placement, and thus irrelevant here.

(66) a. 'naɾiʋaːluɯ   'fox tail'
    b. 'ʋajəl   'field'
    c. 'saŋgiːdõ   'music'
    d. 'mattaːppɯ   'fire crackers'
    e. 'ʋaːdaːdɯ   'argue'
    f. 'jeɾɯmbɯ   'ant'
    g. 'ʋaɾɯttõ   'worry'
    h. 'naɾɯkkə   'to cut'
    i. pə'laː   'jackfruit'
    j. pɯ'ɾaː   'pigeon'

A possible Coercion analysis runs as follows. FTBIN and ALIGN-L are both undominated, ensuring that a binary foot is flush with the left edge of the word. Candidates violating either of these constraints are not shown in the tableaux below. The heavy lifting is done by three constraints on foot form. First, a foot must not contain two heavies, that is, four moras. Second, ◡̱ is ill-formed as a trochee (Hayes 1995, Kager 1999; §2.3.2). These constraints are labeled *(◻̱◻̱) and *('◡̱◻̱), respectively. Ranked below these constraints is a third constraint on foot form, TROCHEE, which penalizes a foot without initial stress. Finally, WbyP is buried: Codas fluctuate in moraicity as dictated by the other constraints. Gordon (2004b) has a different analysis of these data

---

[28] If it is possible to analyze (unstressed) Tamil geminates as tense rather than geminate, there is no issue for Coercion here. I take no position on whether this is feasible.

[29] This rule is similar to a stress rule that is sometimes posited for other Dravidian languages, including Malayalam (Mohanan 1986, 1989) and Telugu (Sitapati 1936, Pingali 1985; cf. Krishnamurti 2003:59, Kolachina 2016). But it is not exactly the same. In the Malayalam-type rule, only vowel length matters in both initial and peninitial position, thus, VC < VV. In Tamil, by contrast, the weight of the initial syllable depends on whether it has a coda, but the weight of the peninitial syllable does not.

using a position-specific WbyP constraint, WbyP-σ_1. However, this constraint is not needed if foot form constraints are considered.

Tableaux are presented for four critical initial-peninitial configurations. First, V-V receives initial stress thanks to TROCHEE, as in (67).

(67)

puli		*(＿＿)	*('◡＿)	TROCHEE	WbyP
a. ☞	('puli)				
b.	(pu'li)			*!	

Second, V-VC also receives initial stress due to TROCHEE, as in (68). Since the coda is not moraic in (a), (a) does not violate *('◡＿). [ʋa] cannot be a foot by itself because of FTBIN, and [ɾut] cannot be a foot by itself because of ALIGN-L. The tableau also illustrates a nonmoraic geminate, which this analysis requires (unless of course it can be shown that geminates are simplified, in which case the transcription in (68), from Christdas 1996, is incorrect).

(68)

ʋaɾuttam		*(＿＿)	*('◡＿)	TROCHEE	WbyP
a. ☞	('ʋaɾɯt)tõ				*
b.	('ʋaɾɯt_μ)tõ		*!		
c.	(ʋa'ɾut)tõ			*!	*
d.	(ʋa'ɾut_μ)tõ			*!	

Third, VC-X is stressed initially, since VC can be parsed into a moraic trochee by itself, as in (69). An initial coda, unlike a peninitial one, is coerced into moraicity. A second foot on [giː] is not possible here because ALIGN-L is top-ranked.

(69)

saŋkiːtam		*(＿＿)	*('◡＿)	TROCHEE	WbyP
a. ☞	('saŋ_μ)giːdõ				
b.	('saŋgiː)dõ		*!		*
c.	('saŋ_μgiː)dõ	*!			
d.	(saŋ'giː)dõ			*!	*
e.	(saŋ_μ'giː)dõ	*!		*	

Finally, peninitial stress is exemplified by (70). Initial stress would yield an ill-formed light-heavy trochee.

(70)

puɾaː		*(＿＿)	*('◡＿)	TROCHEE	WbyP
a. ☞	(puˈɾaː)			*	
b.	('puɾaː)		*!		

Thus, Coercion can handle Tamil. An alternative analysis, and one that does not require geminates to be nonmoraic, is available in terms of Prominence. WbyP can

be promoted to undominated. Moreover, *('◡—) is no longer needed. FᴛBɪɴ and
Aʟɪɢɴ-L remain undominated, as before (not shown in tableaux). The four tableaux
from above are repeated with these modifications in (71) to (74).

(71)

puli	*(__)	WbyP	Mᴀɪɴ→VV	Tʀᴏᴄʜᴇᴇ
a. ☞ ('puli)			*	
b. (pu'li)			*	*!

(72)

ʋaɾuttam	*(__)	WbyP	Mᴀɪɴ→VV	Tʀᴏᴄʜᴇᴇ
a. ('ʋaɾuɯt)tõ		*!	*	
b. ☞ ('ʋaɾuɯt_μ)tõ			*	
c. (ʋa'ɾut)tõ		*!	*	*
d. (ʋa'ɾut_μ)tõ			*	*!

(73)

saŋki:tam	*(__)	WbyP	Mᴀɪɴ→VV	Tʀᴏᴄʜᴇᴇ
a. ☞ ('saŋ_μ)gi:dõ			*	
b. ('saŋgi:)dõ		*!	*	
c. ('saŋ_μgi:)dõ	*!		*	
d. (saŋ'gi:)dõ		*!		*
e. (saŋ_μ'gi:)dõ	*!			*

(74)

puṛaː	*(__)	WbyP	Mᴀɪɴ→VV	Tʀᴏᴄʜᴇᴇ
a. ☞ (puɯ'ṛaː)				*
b. ('puṛaː)			*!	

2.5.11 V < VC < VV (etc.) in Kara

Kara (Austronesian), like Nanti, has a complex weight scale based on both vowel
height and syllable structure. The source is Schlie and Schlie (1993), but additional
data (Perry Schlie, p.c.) appear in de Lacy (1997). As only the latter is available to
me, this section is brief and tentative. De Lacy (1997) and Gordon (2006) summarize the Kara rime weight scale as (paraphrasing slightly) $V_{nonlow} < \{V_{nonlow}C,$
$V_i V_{k \neq i}\} < a < \{aC, aV\} < V$ː, though the only long vowel is [aː]. If one puts aside
height effects, this hierarchy subsumes the more common rime structure hierarchy
$V < VC < VV$ (e.g. $a < aC < a$ː). De Lacy (1997) implies that primary stress seeks out
the heaviest grade available in the word, and secondary stress also appears. Insofar
as secondary stress exhibits weight effects, he reports that it is sensitive only to the
simpler criterion $V < VX$. See also Pulaar, Chickasaw, Klamath, and Yapese above for
similar simplifications of the criterion for secondary stress vis-à-vis primary stress.

Primary stress can be seen to fall on a long vowel in any position in (75) (all
examples from de Lacy 1997). Secondary stress can appear on both heavies and lights,

but only on the latter under the compulsion of clash or lapse. Comparing (a–b), with secondary stress on final VC, to (c–d), without secondary stress on V in the same environment, reveals that secondary stress is at least partly weight-sensitive, as de Lacy (1997) suggests. However, it is worth emphasizing that the system is complex, and de Lacy (1997) also cites one or two examples in which a final light is stressed.[30]

(75) a. ˈɸaːsiˌlak　　　'sacrifice of abstinence'
　　 b. maˈmaːloˌxan　　'grief'
　　 c. ˈkaːksaxa　　　'one leg'
　　 d. ˈkaːli.u　　　　'around'
　　 e. ˌʔapisaxaˈyaːn　'the sixth'
　　 f. ʔaˌtaːpuˈlaːs　　'keep on doing'

If this characterization holds up to further scrutiny, it is another case of secondary stress defeating Coercion: VV draws stress away from VC in forms like (a–b), but the VC syllables remain bimoraic, as diagnosed by secondary stress.

2.5.12 Coercion vs. Prominence beyond stress

Coercion is also insufficient to explain suprabinary weight in weight-sensitive systems other than stress. As an example from metrics, consider the Homeric hexameter. As described in §4.4.2, each line comprises six metra. Each metron in turn comprises two positions, the LONGUM and the BICEPS. A longum can contain only a heavy syllable. A nonfinal biceps can contain either a heavy or a pair of lights. Thus, every (nonfinal) position, whether longum or biceps, must be filled by two moras. Beyond this bimoraic minimum, poets treat the biceps as being heavier than the longum, in that the heavies that they place in bicipitia tend significantly to be heavier heavies than the heavies that they place in longa (West 1982, Ryan 2011a; see §4.4.2 below). As Ryan (2011a:446f) observes, this situation is incompatible with variable moraicity. A rime like VC has to be uniformly bimoraic, lest it occupy light-requiring positions.[31] But if VC is uniformly bimoraic, its lightness relative to VV cannot be captured by mora count. Prominence must be invoked.

The outlook is the same for end-weight. In end-weight, as in stress and meter, VC is lighter than VV, as seen, for instance, in English binomials such as *lock and key* and *hem and haw* (see §5.5.3 for evidence that such cases are driven by weight rather than by phonotactics). But it is hardly possible to analyze VC words such as *lock* and *hem* as monomoraic: They are stressed, and thus footed, and thus bimoraic (§3.1). Once again, VC < VV has to be captured without moraic quantity. In short, Skeletal Prominence, as advocated in this chapter, appears to be a general property of weight-sensitive systems.

---

[30] In particular, the word "one leg" is cited differently at two different points, first as [ˈkaːksaxa] and then as [ˈqʰaqsaˌyə] (with a different source). Therefore, these generalizations may not be robust.

[31] When C in VC is part of a stop-sonorant cluster, the rime can scan variably as heavy or light, presumably reflecting variable syllabification as VC.CV ~ V.CCV (see §4.2.2). But the argument just stated applies to VC more generally, of which most configurations (e.g. VN, VT.T) do not allow variable scansion.

2.6 Geminates and stress

2.6.1 *Sixty-seven languages with VC < VV for stress: VG almost always aligns with VC*

In languages that distinguish between VC and VV for stress and have geminates, VG almost always joins VC. These {VC, VG} < VV systems are sometimes described as exhibiting "weightless" or "light" geminates, and are sometimes implied to be rare, with a handful of recurrent examples such as Malayalam and Selkup. This section argues for a rather different outlook: {VC, VG} < VV, it is shown, is the nearly universal treatment of VG in VC < VV stress systems. It is VC < {VG, VV}, rather, that is unusual. The reason that {VC, VG} < VV might appear to be rare is that the combination of factors needed to diagnose such a scale is not common; it need not have anything to do with light geminates being marked. This section further maintains, contra the "weightless geminate" perspective, that geminates retain their moras in such systems even when they are not heavy for stress. This analysis, which resolves various problems raised by weightless geminates, is made possible by MAIN→VV, a constraint that was argued to be necessary on independent grounds in §2.5.

A large and diverse sample of languages with VC < VV for stress can be found in Ahn's (2000) and Gordon's (1999, 2006) independent surveys of syllable weight (I also take cues from Kager 2012). I take as my starting point the languages cited in these studies as exhibiting VC < VV, whether by itself or as part of a more complex scale, with some additions and exclusions described presently. Figure 2.6 summarizes the survey, which includes sixty-seven languages with VC < VV for stress, fifty-six of which were checked for gemination. As explained in §2.1, the scales in Figure 2.6 abstract away from certain irrelevant information, showing only the criterial boundaries as opposed to enumerating rime types. Moreover, in some cases, the quoted scale does not represent the full complexity of the system; these scales are prefixed by "incl." For example, in Asheninca, Kara, and others, quality plays a role in addition to syllable structure, but only the latter is relevant here.

Several factors disqualified languages from this survey. First, languages lacking codas or long vowels are excluded. Although a language such as Fijian is commonly referred to as "VV heavy," it lacks codas, and is therefore indeterminate between the Latin (V < VX) and Khalkha (VC < VV) criteria, and thus not useful here. Similarly, Amharic and Ngalakgan, which are relevant concerning the weight of VG, are excluded because they lack long vowels. I return to these two languages in §2.6.4 and §2.6.7. Second, languages are excluded from the present survey if they have major featural riders attached to one or more of the categories. For example, languages in which VC is heavy only if C is a sonorant are put aside (§2.1). But if an otherwise general category such as C has a narrow exclusion, such as glottal stop, the language is retained. Munster Irish, for instance, exhibits VC < VV, but [ax] is special (Doherty 1991, Green 1996, Blum 2018). It is included as VC < VV, ignoring [ax]. Third, some cases depend on the analysis of the inventory. In several languages, reduced vowels pattern as lighter than full vowels. For some such cases, one might entertain that the opposition is really between short and long vowels (§2.1). I follow Gordon (2006) on this point; if he gives the language as Reduced < Full, I exclude it here. Fourth, because the focus of this chapter is stress, I exclude cases of VC < VV that arise only from other domains, such as metrics, or arise only by collapsing distinctions across phenomena.

Furthermore, I add several languages not covered by Ahn (2000) or Gordon (2006), and adjust the scale description in a few cases (e.g. Finnish and Pulaar). I remove a few languages due to insecure or erroneous classification (e.g. Kunama; cf. Connell et al. 2000). Finally, several languages are shaded. These include both cases for which I was unable to obtain the cited references and a few for which complications arise. For example, Telugu, which has geminates, has been characterized as VC < VV, but it may not be secure (cf. Krishnamurti 2003, Kolachina 2016). Koya and Tiberian Hebrew apply secondary stress to syllables with long vowels, which implies {VC, VG} < VV, but rules of the type "all long vowels are stressed" are sometimes susceptible to being low-level perceptual phenomena (§2.6.6). Certain Yupik languages are said to exhibit {VC, VG} < VV (which is the usual alignment), but I tentatively put them aside based on an observation about geminate simplification made by Hayes (1995:302). Ternary V < VC < VV in Abma (Schneider 2010) was brought to my attention by Eleanor Ridge.

The rightmost column, "Geminates," indicates whether geminates are frequent in the language and, if so, how their weight is categorized. For example, "VG=VC" indicates that VG is treated the same as VC and hence lighter than VV. "VG=VC?" notes an ostensible result with caution on my part. For example, geminates are frequent in Wolof, and multiple sources state that stress is initial unless a long vowel follows. This statement, taken at face value, unambiguously identifies VG as light. However, without firsthand examples showing stress *not* being attracted to VG, I am cautious in concluding that VG=VC. The situation is similar for Krongo and Nepali. If this space is blank, it means that I found no evidence to suggest that geminates are frequent in the language. A blank should not be taken to imply that the language forbids geminates in some absolute sense, though in most cases that is so. Even with a grammar in hand, it is often not obvious whether a language permits geminates or not. They can be uncommon, and phonology sections sometimes make no explicit statement, leaving one in the perilous condition of having to infer a negative from an absence of evidence. Perusing materials alone risks both false positives (e.g. if gemination is pseudogemination, nondistinctive, or otherwise idiosyncratic) and false negatives (e.g. if gemination is licit but infrequent or limited constructionally). Therefore, blanks are tentative in many cases. This is not a problem, as no claim is being made that a particular categorization is impossible, nor is there any pretense that this survey is exhaustive. VG is known to pattern both with VC and with VV. The point here is to show that the former is by far the more typical outcome, and underestimated by previous scholarship.

Two cases left blank for "Geminates" in Figure 2.6, namely, Kuuku-Yaʔu and Yaygir, exhibit a kind of nondistinctive gemination that is triggered by initial stress. As analyzed by McGarrity (2003) and O'Connor (2010), such cases can be regarded as "weight-by-position by position" (Rosenthall and van der Hulst 1999), and are therefore not informative regarding the weight of VG relative to VC and VV. In these two languages, all three rime types VC, VG, and VV are bimoraic in the initial syllable, but only VV is bimoraic noninitially. Because VG never occurs noninitially, it is not clear whether VG would pattern with VC or VV in the context in which the two are distinct. Cahuilla is similar: Geminates only occur nondistinctively in the initial syllable, under primary stress. However, the Cahuilla system, unlike Kuuku-Yaʔu and Yaygir, implies that VG is heavier than VC, as discussed below (§2.6.2). Cahuilla is therefore marked in the table.

Of the fifteen languages checked for geminates in Figure 2.6, approximately one-third (nineteen) were identified as possessing geminates, in the sense described above. Of these nineteen languages, VG is equivalent to VC in sixteen (84%) and to VV in the remaining three (16%). Thus, VG tends strongly to align with VC in VC < VV stress systems. In fact, this tendency is likely stronger than the 84 per cent just cited, as only one of the three counterexamples is without significant caveats. The three outliers—in which VG=VV for stress—are Cahuilla, Gupta's Hindi, and San'ani Arabic. The Cahuilla case is highly restricted, as gemination is limited to a single position (initial) and a single morpheme (the intensive), which is commonly associated with iconic lengthening cross-linguistically. Moreover, while this lengthening undoubtedly creates a heavy syllable, the stress-attractingness of that syllable is moot, as primary stress is always initial, as detailed in §2.6.2. Gupta's Hindi, for its part, is anomalous in a few respects, as discussed in §2.6.3. Finally, San'ani Arabic appears to be a robust case of VG=VV for stress, as treated in §2.6.4. In conclusion, if one puts aside Cahuilla and Gupta's Hindi, VG aligns with VC in all but one (94%) of seventeen diverse languages with VC < VV for stress and geminates.

2.6.2 VC < {VG, VV} in Cahuilla

In Cahuilla (Uto-Aztecan), VV and Vʔ are heavy, while V and VC are light (Seiler 1965, 1977, Hayes 1995:132–40). Primary stress is always word-initial. Noninitial heavies receive secondary stress (though may optionally be destressed peninitially). Additionally, every syllable immediately following a heavy receives secondary stress. Any remaining lights are stressed in alternation, heeding CLASH and LAPSE. For example, (a–b) in (76) are light-initial, while (c–d) are heavy-initial. This weight difference is evident from the peninitial secondary stress in (c–d) alone.

(76) a. ˈtaxmuˌʔat   'song'
      b. ˈtakaˌličem   'one-eyed ones'
      c. ˈhaʔˌtisqal   'he is sneezing'
      d. ˈqaːnˌkičem   'palos verdes'

Gemination can arise from the intensive morpheme, whereby the first consonant following the primary stressed vowel is lengthened (Seiler 1977:58, Hayes 1995:139). This is a common means of forming intensives cross-linguistically. For example, the same process is found in Arabic (e.g. *bakā* 'to weep,' *bakkā* 'to weep much'; Watson 2002:84, El Zarka 2005) and Nepali (e.g. *mitʰo* 'delicious,' *mit̪t̪ʰo* 'very delicious'; Bandhu et al. 1971). As discussed in §3.4.3, it is also found in Old Tamil, where it can create supergeminates, which scan metrically as such (e.g. *taṇṇena* 'pleasant,' *taṇṇṇena* 'very pleasant'). A Cahuilla base and its intensive are given in (77). Secondary stress confirms that VG is bimoraic in (b). That is, (b) has the same stress pattern as heavy-initial (c–d) above.

Language	Phylum	Core Scale	Geminates
Abma	Austronesian	V < VC < VV	
Aguatec	Mayan	VC < VV	
Aleut	Eskimo-Aleut	VC < VV	
Asheninca	Arawakan	incl. V < VC < VV	
Aymara	Aymara	VC < VV	
Buriat	Altaic	VC < VV	
Cahuilla	Uto-Aztecan	VC < VV	VG = VV
Cayuga	Iroquoian	VC < VV	
Cherokee	Iroquoian	VC < VV	
Chickasaw	Muskogean	V < VC < VV	VG = VC
Chuvash	Altaic	VC < VV	VG = VC
Comanche	Uto-Aztecan	VC < VV	
Eastern Ojibwa	Algic	VC < VV	VG = VC
Finnish	Uralic	V < VC < VV	VG = VC
Goroa	Cushitic	VC < VV	
Gupta's Hindi	Indo-European	incl. VC < VV < VVC	VG = VV
Huallaga	Quechuan	VC < VV	
Huasteco	Mayan	VC < VV	
Hupa	Na-Dene	incl. V < VC < VV	
Iraqw	Afro-Asiatic	incl. VC < VV	
Junín-Huanca	Quechuan	VC < VV	
Kara	Austronesian	incl. V < VC < VV	
Karok	Hokan	VC < VV	
Kashmiri	Indo-European	V < VC < VV < VVC	
Khalkha	Altaic	VC < VV	
Klamath	Penutian	V < VC < VV	VG = VC
Koasati	Muskogean	VC < VV	VG = VC
Koya	Dravidian	VC < VV	VG
Krongo	Niger-Congo	incl. VC < VV	VG = VC?
Kuuku-Yaʔu	Australian	VC < VV	
Lenakel	Austronesian	VC < VV	
Leti	Austronesian	VC < VV	VG = VC
Luiseño	Uto-Aztecan	VC < VV	
Maithili	Indo-European	V < VC < VV	VG = VC
Malayalam	Dravidian	VC < VV	VG = VC
Malto	Dravidian	VC < VV	
Mam	Mayan	incl. V < VC < VV	
Menominee	Algic	VC < VV	
Mojave	Hokan	VC < VV	
Munster Irish	Indo-European	incl. VC < VV	
Murik	Trans-New Guinea	VC < VV	
Nanti	Arawakan	incl. V < VC < VV < VVC	
Nepali	Indo-European	VC < VV	VG = VC?
Nganasan	Uralic	incl. VC < VV	
Ngarinyin	Australian	VC < VV	
Nyawaygi	Australian	VC < VV	
Ossetic	Indo-European	VC < VV	VG = VC
Pulaar	Niger-Congo	V < VC < VV < VVC	
San'ani Arabic	Afro-Asiatic	V < VC < VV	VG = VV
Selkup	Uralic	VC < VV	VG = VC
Shipibo	Panoan	V < VC < VV	
Southwest Tanna	Austronesian	VC < VV	
Srinagar Koshur	Indo-European	V < VC < VV < VVC	
Tamil	Dravidian	V < VC < VV	VG = VC
Telugu	Dravidian	VC < VV?	VG
Tibetan	Sino-Tibetan	VC < VV	
Tiberian Hebrew	Afro-Asiatic	incl. VC < VV	VG
Tidore	West Papuan	VC < VV	
Tübatulabal	Uto-Aztecan	VC < VV	VG = VC
Wargamay	Australian	VC < VV	
Winnebago	Siouan	VC < VV	
Wintu	Penutian	VC < VV	
Wolof	Niger-Congo	VC < VV	VG = VC?
Yahi	Hokan	incl. V < VC < VV	VG
Yapese	Austronesian	V < VC < VV	
Yaygir	Australian	VC < VV	
Yupik languages	Eskimo-Aleut	VC < VV	VG

FIGURE 2.6 VC < VV stress systems and the categorization of VG if it is present and discernible. The "Geminates" column is left blank if the language lacks frequent geminates; see the text for caveats. Shaded languages were not checked.

(77)   a. 'čexi,wen   'it is clear'
       b. 'čex,xiwen   'it is very clear'

Cahuilla is thus a clear case of VG being bimoraic in a context in which VC is monomoraic. However, it is not a case of VG being heavier than VC for purposes of stress location. Primary stress is initial regardless of the weight of the initial syllable. Thus, while VG is heavier than VC for foot construction, there is no evidence from Cahuilla that VG is more prominent than VC for stress assignment. This case is therefore rather unlike the (mostly unbounded) stress systems analyzed in §2.5, where VV is more stress-attracting than VC_μ, as analyzed by attributing greater prominence to VV. A second caveat about Cahuilla is that geminates are not, as far as I can determine, part of the core phonology; they arise only through iconic lengthening.

Assuming that geminates are otherwise forbidden, Cahuilla moraification can be implemented by {Max-μ-V, Dep-μ-V} ≫ *μ ≫ {WbyP, Max-μ, Dep-μ}. With this ranking, codas are never moraic. A special provision has to be made for glottal stop, which is heavy, perhaps WbyP-ʔ. Finally, the intensive can be analyzed as the prefixation of a mora, that is, /μ-/. This mora cannot dock on the onset, since moraic onsets are marked. It also cannot dock on the vowel, since vowel moraicity is more faithful than consonant moraicity on this ranking. Finally, a constraint would have to ensure that the mora is not deleted altogether. REALIZEMORPHEME can ensure that the prefix has some phonological exponent (Kurisu 2001, Ryan 2010:768). This constraint allows spurious Richness-of-the-Base geminates to be simplified while protecting gemination that arises from a morpheme that can only be expressed as such.

2.6.3 *VC<{VG, VV} in Gupta's Hindi?*

In Gupta's (1987) description of Hindi stress, primary stress is said to fall on the leftmost instance of the heaviest syllable in {V, VC} < VV < VVC < {VCC, VVCC}. This scale is surprising in two respects. First, V and VC are conflated as light in an unbounded system in which codas otherwise count for weight (e.g. VV < VVC). This situation, which may be unattested elsewhere (see, for instance, Figure 2.6),[32] seems to call for WbyP conditional on vowel length. Nevertheless, as Curtis (2003) observes, Gupta (1987) omits critical evidence bearing on whether V and VC are in fact conflated, controlling for finality. Second, the contrast VVC < VCC is likely also unattested. Indeed, even VV alone is almost always *heavier* than VCC cross-linguistically in non-extrametricality contexts (Gordon 2006:127). Curtis (2003: 152–6) notes other oddities about the description.

The question here is whether there is evidence for VC < {VG, VV}. Gupta (1987) cites only the three examples (a–c) in (78) with geminates. (a) is uninformative, as both syllables are superheavy (NB. the "h" is not aspiration, but a full consonant: Sanskrit *aṭṭahāsa*). Comparing (b–c) to (d–f) suggests that VG is treated like VV, not VC. However, (b), at least, is a compound (*sáttā* 'power' and *ārūṛʰ* 'mounted'), and the

---

[32] This statement ignores extrametricality, which can create the appearance of {V, VC} < {VCC, VVC} in some languages, but only finally (e.g. Classical Arabic and Stoney; McCarthy 1979a, Hayes 1982, Shaw 1985). The proposed scale is not limited to final position, so extrametricality is moot.

left members of compounds are prosodically stronger than the right members. This leaves only (c), which seems not to be a compound, though it has the same *aṭṭa* "lofty" morpheme as (a).

(78) a. 'aṭṭhās   'guffaw'
     b. 'sattārūr^h 'in power'
     c. 'aṭṭālikāyē   'attics'
     d. 'āvārā   'vagabond'
     e. sil'vāne   'to stitch'
     f. bah'lāne   'to entice'

In sum, VC < {VG, VV} is not reliably in evidence from Gupta (1987). The description is problematic in several ways (Curtis 2003) and somewhat isolated among descriptions of Hindi (on which, see Hayes 1995:162ff), on top of which perhaps only one example is given which sheds light on this question. It would be worth returning to Hindi to investigate the stress-attracting status of geminates more carefully.

2.6.4 *VC < {VG, VV} in Saṇani Arabic (and VC < VG in Amharic)*

San'ani is a conservative dialect of Arabic with c. 100,000 speakers around San'a, Yemen (Watson 2002:10). Watson (2002:81–4) describes primary stress assignment (see also Davis 2011). In some ways, it is reminiscent of Klamath in §2.5.5, where a commonplace final-window rule is subject to an unbounded "override" condition involving VV. Putting aside morphological conditioning, Watson (2002) gives essentially the following algorithm:

(79) a. Stress the rightmost nonfinal {VV, VG}. ("Override Condition")
     b. Otherwise stress a final superheavy.
     c. Otherwise stress VC in the penult.
     d. Otherwise stress VC in the antepenult.
     e. Otherwise stress the leftmost V rime.[33]

Recall that Klamath essentially combines the Latin rule with the override condition to the effect that the rightmost VV attracts stress. The San'ani override condition differs from Klamath's in that it is limited to nonfinal positions and VV is joined by VG. Beyond the override condition, the San'ani basic rule differs from that of Klamath/Latin in that a final superheavy attracts stress and default leftmost stress is not confined to the trisyllabic window (though it oddly favors V over VC; footnote 33).

For present purposes, the critical issue is the categorization of VG by the override condition. As shown in (80), VV and VG take priority over a final superheavy (a–b), but V and VC do not (c–d).

---

[33] This last rule implies a kind of anti-weight-to-stress effect: An initial VC syllable rejects stress (e.g. *maktábati* 'my library') while an initial V syllable does not (e.g. *rágabatih* 'his neck'). Such an effect could conceivably arise due to a preference for disyllabic trochees, all else being equal, though this is conjecture. This analysis assumes that trochees of the form (H́X) are unavailable (see also §2.3.2).

(80) a. 'saːfart   'I/you (masc. sg.) traveled'
      b. 'darrast   'I/you (masc. sg.) taught'
      c. da'rast   'I/you (masc. sg.) learned'
      d. gam'bart   'I/you (masc. sg.) sat'

Furthermore, VV and VG lure stress outside of the final trisyllabic window, as in (81) (a–b), but VC does not, as in (c). (Given the formulation of rule (e) in (79), initial stress in (81-a) cannot be treated as a case of default leftmost stress.)

(81) a. 'haːkaḏahaː   'like this'
      b. mu'sajjilatiː   'my recorder'
      c. mak'tabatiː   'my library'

Thus, San'ani appears to be a robust case of VG being grouped with VV to the exclusion of VC. This categorization can arise from the ranking Max-μ ≫ *μ. Tableaux (82) and (83) provide a simple illustration. In (82), the input consonants are nonmoraic (i.e. not geminates), and *μ penalizes adding moras to them in the output. This results in VC being light. In (83), the input contains a moraic (i.e. would-be geminate) consonant (Hayes 1989:257ff; §2.5.1). Preserving the moraicity of this consonant entails gemination, since *[bat$_μ$.a] violates Onset and *[ba.t$_μ$a] violates a highly ranked prohibition on moraic onsets. This results in VG being heavy.[34]

(82)

bakta		Max-μ ¦ Onset	*μ
a. ☞	bak.ta	¦	**
b.	bak$_μ$.ta	¦	***!

(83)

bat$_μ$a		Max-μ ¦ Onset	*μ
a. ☞	bat$_μ$.ta	¦	***
b.	ba.ta	*! ¦	**
c.	bat$_μ$.a	¦ *!	***
d.	bat.a	*! ¦ *	**

This approach to San'ani thus far predicts that VG and VV(C)—that is, rimes with distinctive length—are heavy, while V and VC(C) are light. But this is not the whole story. If no VG or VV(C) is available, VC(C) then attracts stress (within the trisyllabic window). Coercion provides a solution: If no obligatorily bimoraic rime is available, VC(C) can be coerced into bimoraicity under stress, as with Kashmiri in §2.5.1. In this manner, V < VC(C) < {VG, VV(C)} emerges.[35] Although many of the case studies above argued against Coercion, the argument was always that Coercion is insufficient,

---

[34] If geminate codas are forbidden, one can assume that they are ruled out by a highly ranked constraint that is not shown here, rendering Richness-of-the-Base /bak$_μ$ta/ as [bakta].

[35] Extrametricality complicates this picture slightly, but not in a way that is outside of the norm for Arabic. Consonant extrametricality can be enforced by a constraint against a final moraic consonant (WeakEdge or *Final-C$_μ$; Kager 1999:268).

not that it is unavailable. As long as WbyP is rankable with weight mapping, Coercion is a possible analysis. In many cases, it is not viable for other reasons, but the two most common problems in §2.5, namely, secondary stress and nonmoraic geminates, do not arise in San'ani as described.

That said, San'ani remains unusual: It is the only robust case in this chapter of VC < {VG, VV} for stress attraction and, as just analyzed, the only case of stress attraction for which Coercion is crucially invoked. Given this situation, further study, especially phonetic, is a desideratum. For example, if it were found that vowels gradiently lengthen before geminates, that would provide a simple way out (Donca Steriade, p.c.): VG would then be V·G, distinct from VC by virtue of vowel length. While most languages with geminates compress vowels preceding them (Ridouane 2010), cases of vowel lengthening preceding a geminate have been documented, as in Japanese (Campbell 1999, Idemaru and Guion 2008); see Ridouane (2010) for additional examples.

Although San'ani is the only language in the survey in Figure 2.6, if one sets aside Cahuilla and Gupta's Hindi, that contrasts the weights of VC and VG, another case of VC < VG for stress is found in Amharic. The survey omitted Amharic because it lacks long vowels and therefore lacks the requisite VC < VV criterion. Amharic stress exhibits the scale {V, VC} < VG. That is, only geminates are heavy. This fact is evident both from the stress system (Sande and Hedding 2017) and from affix placement (Sande 2014). An infixing CV reduplicant seeks out a geminate if one is available. If none is available, another construction must be employed. Sande (2014) therefore argues that the reduplicant is attracted to weight rather than stress. All bases have stress, but only some bases have geminates. The moraicity of geminates but not codas in Amharic can be analyzed along the same lines as San'ani.

A few other cases of VG being heavier than VC appear in the literature, but these concern syllable structure rather than stress. For example, in Koya, VVC is a possible rime, but VVG is not (Tyler 1969, Sherer 1994; cf. Fula, Seto, and West Swedish; Davis 2011, Topintzi and Davis 2017). This is attributed to *3μ, assuming that G contributes a mora and C does not. Alternatively, however, it might be analyzed as a quantitative complementarity effect, such that two long segments cannot occupy the same syllable. Under this latter approach, the illicitness of VVG would not be due to its being heavier than VVC.

2.6.5 {VC, VG} < VV in Koasati and as the typological norm
for VG in VC < VV systems

Aside from San'ani Arabic (and with the caveats for Cahuilla and Gupta's Hindi), the fifteen remaining languages with diagnosable VG and VC < VV in Figure 2.6 categorize VG as VC. These include Chuvash, Eastern Ojibwa, Finnish, Klamath, Koasati, Krongo, Leti, Maithili, Malayalam, Nepali, Ossetic, Selkup (including Taz Selkup; Ringen and Vago 2011:158), Tamil, Tübatulabal, and Wolof. Even if the survey is allowed a substantial margin of error, there is no doubt that this outcome is the typological norm.

As mentioned in §2.6.1, this result undermines the conventional wisdom that VG being light for stress is uncommon. It rather suggests that the Principle of Equal Weight for Codas (Tranel 1991), though not exceptionless, holds up rather well for geminates. If VC is heavy for stress, VG is arguably always heavy (see §2.6.7 regarding one putative exception in Ngalakgan). If VC is light for stress, VG is light over 90 per cent of the time. San'ani Arabic is a clear exception, but for the most part, VG is not special vis-à-vis VC. In particular, there is no tendency for VG to be heavier than VC.

Several cases of VG = VC in the context of suprabinary scales were analyzed in §2.5 (viz. Pulaar, Chickasaw, Klamath, Maithili, Finnish, and Tamil). To exemplify {VC, VG} < VV in a binary setting, consider Koasati (Muskogean; Kimball 1991, 1994), which has not to my knowledge been previously discussed as a case of "VG light." In root nouns, primary stress (or perhaps culminative pitch accent) is final, unless the penult is VV. Examples of final stress are given in (84), showing that VC in the penult and VV in any pre-penult position fail to attract stress away from the ultima.

(84) a. lak'ca   'crow'
      b. ittapa'hi   'grassland'
      c. oːlan'wi   'a winter celebration'
      d. tohnaclaːna'si   'a variety of melon'
      e. waksah'li   'corn tassle'

A VV penult attracts stress from the ultima, as shown in (85).

(85) a. 'noːbi   'throat'
      b. tofoh'liːci   'ball player'
      c. ta'moːka   'night'
      d. taholloso'baːli   'Friday'
      e. takkolin'saːwa   'peach branch'

Finally, a VG penult fails to attract stress, as in (86). Therefore, VG = VC, both being lighter than VV.

(86) a. isbak'ki   'head'
      b. nok'ko   'beaver'
      c. tiskom'ma   'cardinal'
      d. paːsat'ta   'armadillo'
      e. tikbiɬ'ɬi   'thrush'

To analyze this case with Coercion, one must once again abandon the tenet that geminates are moraic, or at least relegate their moraicity to underlying forms alone. With Prominence, however, the Moraic Theory of Geminates can be maintained. VG and VV are both bimoraic, but the latter attracts stress because it contains a long vowel, which is more prominent than a short vowel, as encoded by MAIN→VV. A possible Prominence analysis is given in the following tableaux. WbyP is assumed to be undominated. The final two-syllable window is implemented here by foot structure (one could alternatively employ a constraint proscribing a lapse at the right edge; cf. Gordon 2002a, Kager 2012). Undominated ALIGN-R requires a foot to be rightmost in the word. This analysis leaves open whether the final foot is degenerate, as in (a), or oversize, as in (b), which are homophonous candidates. The important thing in (87) is that stress cannot be lured outside of the disyllabic window by an earlier VV. In this respect, the rule is almost a mirror image of Tamil in §2.5.10.

(87)

o:lanwi		ALIGN-R	MAIN→VV	IAMB
a. ☞	o:lan$_\mu$('wi)		*	
b. ☞	o:(lan$_\mu$'wi)		*	
c.	('o:)lan$_\mu$wi	*!*		
d.	o:('lan$_\mu$)wi	*!	*	
e.	('o:lan$_\mu$)wi	*!		*

In (88), VG is shown to be treated like any other VC, in that it fails to bear stress in the penult. VC, VG, and VV are all bimoraic rimes.

(88)

nokko		ALIGN-R	MAIN→VV	IAMB
a. ☞	nok$_\mu$('ko)		*	
b. ☞	(nok$_\mu$'ko)		*	
c.	('nok$_\mu$ko)		*	*!
d.	('nok$_\mu$)ko	*!	*	

Finally, VV attracts stress in the penult. Ideal foot structure is sacrificed in the name of higher-ranked ALIGN-R and MAIN→VV.

(89)

no:bi		ALIGN-R	MAIN→VV	IAMB
a. ☞	('no:bi)			*
b.	(no:'bi)		*!	
c.	no:('bi)		*!	
d.	('no:)bi	*!		

Koasati joins at least fifteen other languages in treating VG < VV. This list is not only growing, but includes languages that one might dub "canonical moraic geminate" languages—languages in which true geminates abound and are by all other indications weight-bearing—including Finnish, Malayalam, and Pulaar.[36] Rejecting moraic geminates for such languages is tantamount to rejecting moraic geminates tout court: If one can analyze consonant length in Finnish, Malayalam, and Pulaar without moras, one can presumably do the same for any language. But a simple alternative is available with MAIN→VV, which is at any rate needed independently for secondary stress in several languages in §2.5.

Another problem with taking geminates to be nonmoraic in just the languages with VG < VV is that an unexpected gap then arises. If languages could vary parametrically in whether geminates are moraic or not, one would expect geminate moraicity to be

---

[36] The possibility of reanalyzing geminates as tense consonants is sometimes raised, and may be viable for some of the languages among the fifteen. But it is not viable for all of them (as Hayes 1995:299 also notes). See, for instance, Mohanan (1989:620) on why a reanalysis in terms of tensity would fail for Malayalam.

(at least largely) independent from the selection of a weight criterion for stress (the latter being determined by the sorts of considerations enumerated in Broselow et al. 1997, Gordon 1999, 2002b, Ahn 2000, and others).[37] Say that x per cent of languages have moraic geminates under the "parametric geminate moraicity" approach. One would then expect about x per cent of VC < VV systems with VG to treat VG as heavy. One would expect the same rate among V < VX systems with VG. The reality is strikingly different: In VC < VV systems, VG is heavy roughly 6 per cent of the time. In V < VX systems, VG is heavy nearly (if not entirely) 100 per cent of the time (§2.6.7). Rather than approximately the same rate of VG heavy in both systems, the opposite is found—almost total complementarity. This is another reason to reject the notion of variable geminate moraicity that is entailed by theories lacking Vowel Prominence.

The Prominence approach addresses the absence of light VG accompanying a V < VX criterion as follows. Geminates are moraic regardless of the criterion for stress. Three situations are then possible. First, codas are moraic and weight-mapping is driven by syllable-level weight (e.g. $\sigma_{\mu\mu} \rightarrow$ STRESS). In this case, VG = VC as heavy in a V < VX system (e.g. Latin). Second, codas are not moraic and weight-mapping is driven by syllable-level constraints. In this case, VG = VV as heavy in a VC < VV system (e.g. San'ani Arabic; an uncommon type, but one that needs to be generable). Third, weight-mapping is driven by vowel prominence, regardless of coda moraicity. In this case, VG = VC as light in a VC < VV system (e.g. Koasati). But no language is generated in which VG is light in a V < VX system (on which, see §2.6.7): Such a criterion is sensitive to codas, and therefore sensitive to geminates.

In summary, MAIN→VV permits the surface-moraic analysis of geminates to be maintained. Without MAIN→VV or a similar Prominence constraint, one must allow geminate moraicity to vary parametrically (at least on the surface), such that languages like Finnish, Malayalam, and Pulaar permit surface-nonmoraic geminates. However, such languages exhibit independent evidence for the surface moraicity of (both underlying and derived) geminates, including compensatory processes (e.g. Hayes 1989, Beltzung 2008, Kiparsky 2011; see §2.5.6 for a relevant example), metrics (e.g. Mohanan 1989; Chapter 4), and morphophonology (e.g. reduplication, or affixes that are realized wholly or in part by moras, which trigger gemination; Niang 1997, Zimmermann 2017). More importantly, in a number of cases, the stress system itself compels the analysis of geminates as being moraic even while the same system treats VG as lighter than VV (§2.5). Admitting that stress can favor VV per se avoids all of the complications raised by the alternative of parametric geminate moraicity.

2.6.6 *The weight of GV for stress*

Also related to the weight of geminates for stress but not applicable to Figure 2.6 are languages with weight-sensitive stress and GV, where G in this case represents a geminate parsed wholly into the onset (e.g. [a.pːa] as opposed to [ap.pa]). This section provides a brief survey and a new analysis of Leti; see Davis (1999), Topintzi

---

[37] One could not reply that geminate moraicity follows from coda moraicity, such that both reflect WbyP, as this position would be incompatible with VC < VG systems such as Amharic.

(2010), and Topintzi and Davis (2017) for more discussion. In Pattani Malay, primary stress is final, unless GV occurs earlier in the word, in which case GV takes primary stress (Yupho 1989, Hajek and Goedemans 2003, Topintzi 2010). GV is possible only word-initially. All remaining syllables with full vowels receive secondary stress. Codas are evidently weightless for primary stress: They neither attract primary stress when nonfinal nor prevent primary stress from shifting when final. Pattani can be analyzed like the "Override Condition" just described for San'ani Arabic (§2.6.4): G, being distinctively moraic, projects a mora. Moras are suppressed on other consonants. Stress then falls on the (rightmost) heavy, else rightmost. A simple example of GV attracting stress is provided in (90) (Yupho 1989:133). As Topintzi (2010) notes, GV attracts stress in (b) even though it contains a reduced vowel that otherwise eschews stress. She also notes that (b) is derived from /ki-kida/. I note that opacity (§6.2) cannot motivate this case: /ki-kida/ would be stressed on the ultima if stress were applied before prefix reduction. The presence of the geminate is crucial.

(90)   a. kiˈda   'shop'
        b. ˈkːiˌda   'to the shop'

The foregoing description of Pattani Malay stress has been challenged. Abrahamson (2003) and Pittayaporn and Iamdanush (2014) observe that f_0 and intensity are significantly higher after a geminate than after a singleton, consistent with this description, though they argue that these are reflexes of gemination rather than stress (but see Topintzi 2010:176f). Duration is a wash: The vowel is shorter after a geminate, but this is compensatory (§1.2) and does not preclude stress. Finally, a contrastive pitch accent *HL falls on the ultima even in GV-initial words (Pittayaporn and Iamdanush 2014), perhaps the most damning fact for the analysis of GV as attracting stress. If it were possible to analyze this accent as a boundary tone, stress might yet have a way out, though I am unaware of how encliticized structures behave.

Marshallese is another potential case of heavy GV. As described by Zewen (1977) and analyzed by Topintzi (2010), stress falls on the leftmost heavy within the final trisyllabic window. VV and GV count as heavy; V is light (and VC is light finally, but otherwise unclear). That G is parsed wholly as an onset is suggested by the fact that it attracts stress to the following as opposed to preceding vowel (e.g. [jiˈbbuŋ] 'morning'), though this is not clinching evidence. Perhaps relatedly, pretonic gemination is widely attested, as in Tiberian Hebrew (McCarthy 1981), Lezgian (Yu 2004), Ndjébbana (Wolf 2008), and Eastern Popoloca (Topintzi 2010). Furthermore, tone or pitch suggests that GV bears onset weight in Luganda (Muller 2001; also allomorphy) and Tedumuni Okinawan (Shinohara and Fujimoto 2011). The latter suggest that GV can be parsed as such even word-medially.

Onset geminates do not always appear to bear weight. For stress, the case of "light GV" in Leti is analyzed presently, where it is suggested that G can still be treated as moraic, despite its not attracting stress.[38] Moreover, two alleged cases of GV not

---

[38] Topintzi and Davis (2017) mention Baghdadi Arabic as another possible case, in that "a word-initial syllable that begins with a geminate does not attract stress," but do not offer further details. The question is whether GV fails to attract stress to a position where another bimoraic syllable would do so.

contributing to prosodic minimality, namely, Leti and Thurgovian Swiss German, are addressed in §3.1.

In Leti (Austronesian), primary stress always falls on the penult. Secondary stress also occurs, on all long vowels and otherwise on alternating syllables (van Engelenhoven 1994, Hume 1997, Hume et al. 1997, Curtis 2003). Only the former is relevant here, as illustrated by the initial syllables of trisyllables, as in (91) (Hume et al. 1997). Secondary stress occurs only on VV, as in (f–g). It does not occur on V (a), VC (b–c), VG (d), or GV (e).

(91) a. riˈmɔta   'kind of turtle'
      b. nvalˈtʲani   'he digs'
      c. matˈruma   'master of the house'
      d. pɛpˈpɛrta   'heavy'
      e. pːuˈnarta   'nest's edge'
      f. ˌrɔːˈnenu   'they eat turtle'
      g. ˌmaːˈnʷaːna   'chick'

This stress pattern is easily analyzed if one assumes that geminates, like other consonants, are nonmoraic in Leti (Hume et al. 1997). However, it is just as easily analyzed *with* moraic geminates using STRESS→VV. For example, a tableau for initial VG is given in (92). The geminate keeps its mora, but resists stress, thanks to the short vowel. The short vowel cannot lengthen, nor the geminate simplify, due to various faithfulness constraints, indicated by the placeholder "(Faith)." I tentatively assume that WbyP is buried and that the head foot is a right-aligned moraic trochee. PARSE penalizes unfooted syllables.

(92)

			(Faith)	S→VV	PARSE
a.	☞	pɛp$_\mu$(ˈpɛr.ta)		*	*
b.		(ˌpɛp$_\mu$)(ˈpɛr.ta)		**!	
c.		pɛ(ˈpɛr.ta)	*!	*	*
d.		(ˌpɛːp$_\mu$)(ˈpɛr.ta)	*!	*	

Meanwhile, VV is free to take stress, as in (93).

(93)

			(Faith)	S→VV	PARSE
a.	☞	(ˌrɔː)(ˈne.nu)		*	
b.		rɔː(ˈne.nu)		*	*!

Thus, Leti does not entail nonmoraic geminates. It can be analyzed with STRESS→VV, like several other languages in this chapter. That said, the descriptive generalizations are not secure to begin with. Hume et al. (1997) is critiqued by Curtis (2003:208–230). For example, Hume et al. (1997:399) claim that duration is the only reliable phonetic correlate of stress, which makes it circular to claim also that all long vowels bear stress. See Curtis (2003) for other arguments.

Aside from stress, Hume et al. (1997) provide other support for the nonmoraicity of geminates, including minimality. C_0V, C_0VC, and GV are subminimal as words, while C_0VV and GVV are licit. This suggests that G in GV is nonmoraic. Nevertheless, as Curtis (2003) observes (agreeing with van Engelenhoven 1994 and Hume 1997), VV in these words (e.g. *ai* 'wood') is actually disyllabic, [a.i]. Therefore, the minimum is arguably not bimoraic, but disyllabic. C_0V, C_0VC, and GV are subminimal by virtue of being monosyllables, regardless of mora count. There is additional evidence on both sides, but no reason to pursue the issues further here.

2.6.7 VG is arguably always heavy in V < VX systems (with special attention to Ngalakgan and Tashlhiyt Berber)

Whereas the previous sections considered languages with the Khalkha criterion (VC < VV), this section briefly addresses languages with the Latin criterion (V < VX). In virtually all languages with geminates and V < VX for stress, VG is equivalent to VC. This includes Latin, Italian, Arabic, Hindi, and numerous others. I am aware of one case of apparent VG < VC for stress, namely, Ngalakgan, and likely neighboring languages (Baker 1997, 2008; see also Davis 2011, Ringen and Vago 2011). As this section argues, however, Ngalakgan is plausibly not a case of weight-driven stress in the first place.[39]

In Ngalakgan, stress is described as regularly falling on the leftmost nonfinal heavy, else leftmost (with some exceptions; Baker 2008:225–8). A heavy syllable is one ending with a coda possessing its own place node, as opposed to sharing its place with the following onset. A vowel followed by a geminate (TT), homorganic nasal (NT), or glottal stop (ʔ) is light, as shown in (94), which employs Baker's broad as opposed to narrow transcription. Baker (2008) interprets TT and NT as being syllabified as onsets (with the caveat that they cannot occur initially), but the syllabification question is not critical here. Whether TT is syllabified as an onset or as straddling syllables, the moraic theory of geminates requires it to bear a mora. As (a–b) illustrate, consonant length is distinctive. Moreover, phonetically, geminates are substantially longer than the corresponding singletons, on the order of three to four times as long (Baker 2008:38 finds means of 203 ms and 56 ms for posttonic geminate and singleton stops, respectively).

(94) a. 'calapir   'red ant species'
      b. 'moḷoppoḷ   'shovelhead catfish'
      c. 'ŋoloŋkoʔ   'eucalyptus'
      d. 'calpurkic   'jewfish'
      e. 'ɲaɲaʔpaj   'and moreover'
      f. pu'ṭolkoʔ   'brolga'
      g. pu'ruṭci   'water python'
      h. ˌmaca'purka   'plant species'
      i. ki'piḷkuluc   'tawny frogmouth'

---

[39] Ngalakgan was excluded from the survey in §2.6.1 because it lacks long vowels, leaving the weight of VG relative to VV indeterminate. It would also fail to qualify for that survey on the grounds that it applies major exclusions to C.

Various analyses are conceivable. The first, and perhaps most obvious—though not the analysis pursued here—is to analyze geminates (as well as NT and ?) as being nonmoraic in Ngalakgan, at least on the surface (cf. Davis 2011, Ringen and Vago 2011, Topintzi and Zimmermann 2014, Topintzi and Davis 2017). The remaining details depend on the assumptions about syllabification. On the one hand, if NT and TT are parsed into onsets, as Baker (2008) assumes, then one can posit WbyP for the remaining codas. Glottal stop is nonmoraic either because it is placeless, because it is realized as creakiness on the vowel (Baker 2008:219–24), or because a principle against moraic glottal stops (e.g. *$?_\mu$) is available. Furthermore, such an approach would need to account for distinctive consonant length without moras, for instance, by treating them as double root nodes. On the other hand, if NT and TT are heterosyllabified, as Baker (1997) and Davis (2011) suggest, one would need to condition coda moraicity on the presence of an unshared supralaryngeal [place] node.

However, there are also ways to analyze Ngalakgan stress without abandoning the moraicity of geminates. I outline two independent possibilities here. The first is the licensing approach, according to which coda place is licensed by stress. Baker (1999) dismisses this approach on the grounds that stress is mobile and that independent coda place is possible in unstressed syllables, as seen in (d) above. Thus, one has to say that stress seeks out [place], not vice versa. But this dismissal may be premature. Thanks to violable constraints, a grammar can exert a preference for stress and coda place to coincide without going so far as to nix coda place whenever that coincidence cannot be achieved.

In many languages, more place contrasts are licensed in stressed than unstressed syllables (Beckman 1998, 2013). This arguably applies to coda place: For example, Tamil, treated in §2.5.10, may be one language in which coda assimilation is conditioned by the absence of stress.[40] In principle, this could reflect either faithfulness under strength or markedness under weakness (*ibid.*). The latter is more expedient for Ngalakgan. CODACOND penalizes a coda with its own place node (Itô 1986, 1989, McCarthy 2008). I thus take CODACOND-ŏ to penalize unassimilated coda place in unstressed syllables. But unassimilated coda place always surfaces faithfully among both stressed and unstressed syllables in Ngalakgan, as ensured by MAX(place) ≫ CODACOND-ŏ. These two constraints are repeated in (95).

(95) a. MAX(place)   Penalize the deletion of a [place] node.
      b. CODACOND-ŏ   Penalize an unstressed coda with its own [place].

---

[40] Beckman (1998) treats Tamil as a case of initial privilege, but it might just as well be accentual privilege. Her source, Christdas (1988), implies the latter, and all of the cited heterorganic codas occupy stressed syllables, which also happen to be initial. To distinguish between the positional and accentual hypotheses, assuming the stress rule in §2.5.10, one would have to determine whether assimilation is required in words of the shape V-'VVC-(...). Such words are uncommon, given root and word formation constraints, but I find at least one example in *ilāṇkaṇ* 'in one who lacks' (*Tirukkuṟaḷ* 135). It contains a suffix (-*kaṇ*), but so do Christdas' examples (-*pu*). Another point in favor of stress is that it is not clear what would motivate initial coda faithfulness perceptually, if not for stress. Initial strengthening, unlike accentual lengthening, is not a whole-syllable effect (Fougeron and Keating 1997, et seq.).

The rest of the analysis is trivial. Align-L handles default placement and breaks ties, and NonFinality is undominated. I also assume that WbyP is undominated. A word with no nonfinal heavies is shown in (96).

(96)

calapir		NonFinality	Max(place)	CodaCond-ŏ	Align-L
a. ☞	'calapir$_\mu$			*	
b.	cala'pir$_\mu$	*!			**
c.	'calapiʔ$_\mu$		*!		

Unstressed [place] nodes remain intact in (97). Conversion to glottal stop illustrates just one possible outcome of deleting [place] (see McCarthy 2008). Because [place] is never actually deleted in Ngalakgan, the issue is moot.

(97)

calpurkic		NonFinality	Max(place)	CodaCond-ŏ	Align-L
a. ☞	'cal$_\mu$pur$_\mu$kic$_\mu$			**	
b.	cal$_\mu$'pur$_\mu$kic$_\mu$			**	*!
c.	'cal$_\mu$puʔ$_\mu$kiʔ$_\mu$		*!*		

If the initial syllable does not have an independent coda but a subsequent (nonfinal) syllable does, stress shifts, as in (98). This is the situation in which CodaCond-ŏ is decisive.

(98)

puruʈci		NonFinality	Max(place)	CodaCond-ŏ	Align-L
a. ☞	pu'rut$_\mu$ci				*
b.	'purut$_\mu$ci			*!	
c.	'puruʔ$_\mu$ci		*!		

Finally, VG (similarly homorganic VN and Vʔ) does not attract stress in (99), despite being a bimoraic rime. CodaCond is not violated by a geminate, homorganic cluster, or laryngeal, as none of these codas possesses independent [place]. Note that this analysis covers the lightness of glottal stop without further stipulation, since laryngeals lack [place].

(99)

	moloppoḷ	NonFinality	Max(place)	CodaCond-ð	Align-L
a. ☞	'moḷopμpoḷμ			*	
b.	mo'ḷopμpoḷμ			*	*!
c.	moḷopμ'poḷμ	*!			**

In sum, a straightforward analysis of Ngalakgan is available that does not require any unorthodox assumptions about weight, moraicity, syllabification, or glottal stop.

A second possible analysis of Ngalakgan stress that preserves geminate moraicity may also be available, particularly if (stressed) heterorganic codas are significantly longer than (stressed) homorganic codas (or if stressed vowels are significantly longer before heterorganic codas). Some languages have distinctive consonant length in codas. Estonian is one example, permitting minimal pairs such as (100) (Prince 1980, Hayes 1989; see also Hajek 2000, Hall 2002; for surveys of ternary length contrasts, see Bye et al. 2009 and Türk et al. 2018). Some analysts, including Hayes (1989), take these length differences to reflect moraic differences, as in $[tɑ_μn_μ.ki_μ]$ vs. $[tɑ_μn_{μμ}.ki_μ]$ (p. 296).

(100)   a. 'tɑnki   'tongs (genitive singular)'
        b. 'tɑnːki   'tongs (partitive singular)'

Geminates wholly contained within codas, while not frequent typologically, are not rare. They can be found also in Arabic and Hindi. The Hindi example of ['aṭṭ.haːs] 'guffaw' came up in (78). The initial syllable has to be parsed as $['a_μṭ_{μμ}.ha_{μμ}s_μ]$, with a bimoraic coda geminate, lest it yield stress to the final superheavy, as in $[baː'zaːr_μ]$. Returning to Ngalakgan, the idea is that it may be possible to analyze heterorganic codas (or perhaps the vowels preceding them) as being bimoraic, at least under the coercion of stress. Stress would then be attracted to (coercible) superheavies. Several stress systems invoke a superheavy grade, even if one puts aside cases like Arabic where it is relevant only word-finally (e.g. Hindi, Kashmiri, Nanti, Pulaar). Gussenhoven (2008) posits SUPERHEAVY-TO-STRESS for Dutch. As the final step, homorganic codas would need to be prevented from lengthening under the compulsion of stress. This can be accomplished by invoking a constraint against triply linked place nodes, as would result if a geminate or homorganic cluster were further lengthened. In other words, supergeminates are forbidden, a common restriction in languages otherwise admitting geminates and superheavy syllables. Glottal stop would also have to be prevented from lengthening, but that is a common restriction cross-linguistically (Windsor 2016), and may also follow from its realization as creakiness in Ngalakgan.

This second possibility is pure speculation without a phonetic study, and may well be inviable. At any rate, the first analysis strikes me as being more straightforward. Either way, Ngalakgan may not be a strong case for abandoning a typological generalization that is otherwise universal. As analyzed, Ngalakgan is no longer a case of "VG light" in a V < VX stress system. VC and VG are both uniformly bimoraic. Stress shifts to *certain* VC not because VC is heavier than VG, but because stress licenses place. In short, Ngalakgan is arguably not a language with weight-sensitive stress.

Tashlhiyt Berber is another language that is sometimes cited for VG < VC in a V < VX system. The evidence comes from meter, not stress, and is therefore not directly relevant to the foregoing survey. The meter contains certain positions that require heavies and others that require lights. Normally, V is light and VC (including VG) is heavy. But VG, unlike VC, can optionally scan as light (Dell 2011, Dell and Elmedlaoui 2017), diagnosing apparent VG $\lesssim$ VC. The phonetics furnishes a possible solution: V is significantly shorter before G than before C (Ridouane 2010). Therefore, the contrast might be restated as V̆G $\lesssim$ V·C, and the generalization that VG cannot be lighter than VC *ceteris paribus* is salvaged. The compression of V before G in Tashlhiyt Berber is modest, but then VG only sometimes scans as light. Another approach, albeit more stipulative, would be to invoke the paraphonology, which determines how phonological material is interpreted in poetry (Kiparsky 1977). In this case, one could posit that geminates are optionally simplified in the paraphonology. Dell (2011) illustrates the paraphonology with French *violettes*. In the normal phonology—"conversational Parisian French"—it is disyllabic: [vjɔˈlɛt]. But for text-setting purposes, it can be rendered with up to four syllables, [v(i)jɔˈlɛt(ə)], reverting to a more conservative pronunciation that is characteristic of verse and song. In this case, epenthesis is said to be paraphonological.

2.7 Alternative approaches to Skeletal Prominence

2.7.1 *Vowel vs. Coda Prominence*

Prominence-stress mapping constraints most familiarly refer to vowel sonority (Kenstowicz 1994b, 1996b, Gordon 2002b, Crowhurst and Michael 2005, de Lacy 2002a, 2004, 2007, Nevins and Plaster 2008). Analysis of such systems in terms of mora count is untenable (de Lacy 2004:175–7): While some cases might be amenable to analyzing reduced vowels as nonmoraic, or analyzing light short vowels as monomoraic and heavy short vowels as bimoraic, these tacks do not generalize. For example, in some languages, such as Nanti in §2.5.9, short vowels exhibit three or more grades of weight, all in a system that additionally exhibits phonemic length. Thus, constraints regulating the association of sonority and stress are admitted. This set of nonmoraic stress–weight mapping constraints is referred to as the theory of Prominence.

MAIN→VV, as supported in this chapter, is akin to a Prominence constraint in the sense that it penalizes a primary stressed short vowel regardless of the moraic quantity of the syllable that it occupies. As mentioned in §2.4, it joins the family of other Prominence constraints such as *P/i,u (Kenstowicz 1994b), *HD$_{Ft}$/$i,ə,i·u$ (de Lacy 2004), and *P$_{Ft}$/DIPH (Crowhurst and Michael 2005). To be sure, MAIN→VV invokes moraic quantity in some form, since it does not penalize long vowels, but so do the other constraints just mentioned. *P$_{Ft}$/DIPH, for instance, evaluates only short (i.e. monomoraic) diphthongs in Nanti; *P/i,u does not penalize long high vowels; and so forth. If a constraint like *P/i,u were to penalize high vowels while ignoring length, unattested systems would be generated, such as one in which long high vowels are lighter than short mid vowels.

Main→VV effectively treats syllables with long vowels as being heavier than those with short vowels, and as such is a theory of Vowel Prominence. This allows $V_\mu < V_\mu C_\mu < VV_{\mu\mu}$ to be analyzed in a uniform moraicity setting. But there is another logically possible way to analyze $V < VC < VV$ with uniform moraicity that is not pursued in this book, namely, to treat syllables with codas as heavier than those without, regardless of mora count (Coda Prominence). For this latter proposal to work, one must take codas to be uniformly nonmoraic, such that the scale is $V_\mu < V_\mu C < VV_{\mu\mu}$. $VV_{\mu\mu}$ is then heavier than V_μ by virtue of mora count, while $V_\mu C$ is heavier than moraically equivalent V_μ by virtue of its coda.

To implement Coda Prominence, one could employ a constraint such as Main→Coda, which penalizes primary stress on an open syllable, regardless of moraic considerations. The schematic competitions in (101) and (102) illustrate $V < VC < VV$ emerging from this system. When Stress→$\sigma_{\mu\mu}$ ≫ Main→Coda, VV beats out VC for stress, as in (101). But when no VV is available, as in (102), VC beats out V. Here I assume that codas are uniformly nonmoraic (e.g. $^*\mu$ ≫ WbyP, not shown). For the sake of exposition, no positional constraints are in play; stress is free to seek out the heaviest syllable.

(101)

V-VC-VV		S→$\sigma_{\mu\mu}$	Main→Coda
a. ☞ V_μ-$V_\mu C$-$'VV_{\mu\mu}$			*
b. V_μ-$'V_\mu C$-$VV_{\mu\mu}$		*!	
c. $'V_\mu$-$V_\mu C$-$VV_{\mu\mu}$		*!	*

(102)

V-VC		S→$\sigma_{\mu\mu}$	Main→Coda
a. ☞ V_μ-$'V_\mu C$		*	
b. $'V_\mu$-$V_\mu C$		*	*!

Thus, Main→Coda allows $V < VC < VV$ to be analyzed in a uniform moraicity setting. Although Main→Coda has not been proposed as such, two similar constraint proposals are found in Exist($'\sigma$, seg) (de Lacy 1997, Wiltshire 2006) and in $^*P_{PWd}$/NoBranch(μ) (Munshi and Crowhurst 2012; cf. nearly equivalent $^*P_{PWd}$/Mon in Crowhurst and Michael 2005). Exist($'\sigma$, seg) requires a stressed syllable to have a nonmoraic coda. In a non-WbyP setting, as immediately above, this constraint does the same work as Main→Coda: Both favor stress on closed syllables, even though codas are nonmoraic. $^*P_{PWd}$/NoBranch(μ) requires every mora in a primary stressed syllable to be branching, under the assumption that nonmoraic codas link to the previous mora, not to the syllable node. In practice, this also favors stress on syllables with nonmoraic codas. The violations of these constraints for various stressed rime shapes are summarized in (103).

(103)   Three approaches to Coda Prominence.

	$'V_\mu$	$'V_\mu C$	$'V_\mu C_\mu$	$'VV_{\mu\mu}$	$'VV_{\mu\mu}C$	$'VV_{\mu\mu}C_\mu$
Main→Coda	*	✓	✓	*	✓	✓
Exist($'\sigma$, seg)	*	✓	*	*	✓	*
$^*P_{PWd}$/NoBranch(μ)	*	✓	**	**	*	***

Coda Prominence faces at least four problems that Vowel Prominence does not. First, it generates languages in which VC is heavier than VV. For example, if MAIN→CODA or either of the other constraints in (103) is the only active weight-mapping constraint, stress will be favored on VC over VV in a non-WbyP setting. This prediction is acknowledged by de Lacy (1997), Wiltshire (2006), Crowhurst and Michael (2005), and Munshi and Crowhurst (2012), but not viewed as a problem; see the next section. MAIN→VV, for its part, cannot implement VV < VC. VV always contains at least as many moras as VC and nothing else favors stress on closed syllables. Second, Coda Prominence requires analyzing geminates as being nonmoraic when VG yields stress to VV in V < VC < VV systems. As shown in §2.5, this position is untenable for some systems. Third, Coda Prominence fails to address the secondary stress problem in §2.5, whereby VV is heavier than VC_μ (whose bimoraicity is diagnosed by secondary stress). Coda Prominence has no way of favoring primary stress on $VV_{\mu\mu}$ over $V_\mu C_\mu$ in this situation.[41] Fourth, evidence from beyond stress sometimes supports the bimoraicity of VC even when VC yields stress to heavier VV. For example, Koasati observes VC < VV for stress (§2.6.5). But syllable structure suggests that codas are moraic in Koasati: VVC is illicit, as is usually analyzed by invoking a mora population limit (*3μ) along with the assumption of moraic codas. For similar cases, see §2.5.12. It should be noted, however, that one claimed advantage of Coda Prominence is that it permits systems with superheavies to be analyzed without invoking trimoraic syllables, as I discuss further in §2.7.3.

2.7.2 The questionable existence of VV < VC for stress

The previous section established that Coda Prominence predicts the possibility of VV < VC for stress, while Vowel Prominence, as favored in this chapter, does not. The question is then an empirical one: Is VV < VC a possible (sub)criterion for stress? It is rare at best, arguably unattested. Gordon's (2006) survey of 408 genealogically diverse languages yielded 136 weight-sensitive stress systems. Among these, VV < VC is found zero times, while the converse, VC < VV, is found over forty times. Gordon (2006:21) does, however, acknowledge that VV < VC is apparent for the pitch accent systems of Seneca, (closely related) Oneida, and Kashaya Pomo, and also for stress in Tiberian Hebrew, which was not in his survey (see immediately below). Similarly, WALS (Goedemans and van der Hulst 2013) identifies at least 118 languages with weight-sensitive stress, but mentions only Dutch as a possible case of VV < VC, allowing that there are alternative analyses. These include treating VV as tense (van Oostendorp 2000) or as a reflex of STRESS→$\sigma_{\mu\mu}$ (Gussenhoven 2008), among others. Hayes (1995:160) observes that "there are many rules that count CV: as heavy and CVC as light, but no rules that go the other way." Morén (1999) also takes VV < VC to be unattested, highlighting as a virtue of his theory that it cannot be generated, and Topintzi (2010) expresses the same sentiment about an analysis

---

[41] Wiltshire (2006) avoids this problem by invoking both Coda and Vowel Prominence constraints for Pulaar. She assumes that codas are moraic in VC but not in VVC. Vowel Prominence then handles $V_\mu C_\mu < VV_{\mu\mu}$, while Coda Prominence handles $VV_{\mu\mu} < VV_{\mu\mu}C$. If Coda Prominence alone were employed, VC would have to be monomoraic in order to be lighter than VV, and the present objection would apply.

(p. 175f). Moreover, in other weight systems, VV < VC is comparably rare-to-unattested, including minimality, metrics, tone licensing, and end-weight. In short, it is a strong candidate for a phonological universal. The explanation for such a universal is clear (§2.1): Descriptively, VV and VC possess the same number of timing slots, but the second slot is more sonorous (or, perceptually speaking, loud) in VV. Two apparent counterexamples are now addressed.

First, primary stress in Tiberian Hebrew falls on the ultima if it has a coda, and otherwise on the penult (McCarthy 1979a). Stress avoids a final long vowel, ostensibly diagnosing VV < VC. However, as Balcaen (1995) and Dresher (2009) observe, final vowel length is not contrastive; only VV occurs (with the caveat in Dresher 2009:222). Moreover, final position is special cross-linguistically in that it is susceptible to final lengthening. They therefore suggest that Tiberian Hebrew final vowels are underlyingly short. Weight is then treated naturally for stress assignment, as V < VX in this case, but opacified by a late rule of final lengthening. For example, oversimplifying from the aforementioned sources, consider [hɔːˈrɔːɣuː] 'they slew' (prepausal form), for which Dresher (2009) posits underlying /harag-u/. The synchronic derivation then constructs a right-aligned moraic trochee before final lengthening applies: /haragu/ → [ha(ˈragu)] → [ha(ˈraguː)]. On this approach, there is no need for a rule or constraint that treats VC as heavier than VV. Indeed, as Dresher (2009:214) observes, other aspects of Tiberian Hebrew stress treat VC as lighter than VV, so this approach has the added benefit of rendering weight coherent. This type of opacity is well attested cross-linguistically. For example, final, unstressed /i/ in English patterns as phonologically short, though it is realized as long in many dialects (Chomsky and Halle 1968:45). Tiberian Hebrew stress is otherwise highly opaque (see §6.2). Finally, philological issues must be carefully navigated for an ancient language, particularly when a universal is on the line.[42]

A second possible case of VV < VC comes from Huehuetla Tepehua (Kung 2007), though I suggest a reanalysis. Like Tiberian Hebrew, it involves VV and VC in final position. Primary stress is final if the ultima contains a sonorant coda, specifically, /m, n, l, h, ʔ, w, j, ɾ, r/, and otherwise penultimate. Kung (2007) takes /h/ and /ʔ/ to be [+son]. Thus, the rule is the same as in Tiberian Hebrew, except confined to sonorant codas. VV < VN holds of final position, in apparent violation of the universal that VC cannot exceed VV in weight. Unlike Tiberian Hebrew, V and Vː clearly contrast phonemically in word-final position. Kung (2007) proposes that only [+son] codas project moras (citing also compensatory lengthening), which, as far as it goes, is natural (§2.1). But she has no explanation for bimoraic VN being treated as heavier than presumably bimoraic VV.

Some examples of final stress are provided in (104). In (e–f), what is transcribed in the surface forms as final VV counts as VN because it is underlyingly a diphthong /uw/ or /ij/. This reflects opacity in the system, as does morphology (e.g. underived [luːˈluː] 'soft' vs. derived [ˈluːluː] 'submerged'), a merger of /q/ and /ʔ/ (e.g. [ɬʔapaʔ] 'phasmid,' where [ʔ] is light because its source is /q/, not /ʔ/), and various other processes: I have noted from Kung's grammar seven types of opacity in the stress

---

[42] As Dresher (2009:223) notes, "Khan (1987) argues that Hebrew vowels at the time of completion of the Tiberian notation system were no longer distinguished by quantity. Thus, the transcriptions and grammar presented here refer to an earlier stage of the language."

system; see §6.2 for details. Furthermore, certain lexical classes have a separate stress pattern; loanwords do not follow the rule; and some other exceptions are found. On the whole, the rule appears to be systematic (Kung 2007:104–23), but given these points, its productivity is not a foregone conclusion.

(104)　a.　/huːmpaj/　　[huːmˈpai]　　'dragonfly'
　　　　b.　/kiɬih/　　　[kiˈɬih]　　　'lace'
　　　　c.　/tukulun/　　[ˌtukuˈlun]　　'rheumatism'
　　　　d.　/tsʼaʔam/　　[tsʼaˈʔam]　　'dried corn stalk'
　　　　e.　/skʼiːk-luw/　[skʼiːkˈluː]　　'eel'
　　　　f.　/awij/　　　[ʔaˈβiː]　　　'mouse'

With a V_1T_0 ultima, stress is penultimate, as in (105). This includes VT_1 (a–b), VV (c–d), VVT_1 (e–g), and V (h–i).

(105)　a.　/lapanak/　　[laˈpanak]　　'person'
　　　　b.　/mutsaqs/　　[ˈmutsaqs]　　'camote'
　　　　c.　/kuːkuː/　　　[ˈkuːkuː]　　　'sand'
　　　　d.　/kukwiːtiː/　　[kukˈβiːtiː]　　'horsetail'
　　　　e.　/ʔaːlaːʃuːʃ/　　[ʔaːˈlaːʃuːʃ]　　'orange'
　　　　f.　/qesiːt/　　　[ˈqɛsiːt]　　　'nail (finger, toe)'
　　　　g.　(not given)　　[ˈtamauɬtʃ]　　's/he already bought it'
　　　　h.　/puʃlimti/　　[puʃˈlimtι̥]　　'nephew'
　　　　i.　/palata/　　　[paˈlatạ]　　　'more'

The V-final forms (h–i) raise an issue that may be important. Phrase-finally, short vowels are "always voiceless" and optionally delete (Kung 2007:124–6). This raises the possibility of a chain shift, whereby final VV is phonologically short, as argued for Tiberian Hebrew above. As further support of such a shift, short final vowels in Spanish loanwords are invariably borrowed as long, regardless of stress, as in (106). Stressed syllables are boldface in the Spanish sources.

(106)　a.　atole　　[ʔaˈtoːliː]　　　'corn drink'
　　　　b.　docena　　[duˈseːnaː]　　'dozen'
　　　　c.　espírito　　[ʔɛsˈpiːɾituː]　　'spirit'
　　　　d.　borrego　　[boˈreːguː]　　'sheep'
　　　　e.　abonar　　[ʔaβoˈnalaː]　　'fertilize'
　　　　f.　ensayar　　[ˌʔɛnsaˈjaːlaː]　　'he rehearsed'

I therefore suggest that Kung's VV in the ultima can be analyzed as V, that is, a full vowel, and Kung's V can be analyzed as a reduced vowel, which I notate V̆ here. V̆ devoices in phrase-final position. Unnatural {V, VT, VV, VVT} < {VN, VVN} is then reinterpreted as natural {V̆, V̆T, V, VT} < {V̆N, VN}.[43] With Kung (2007), I take N but not T to be moraic. Thus, {V̆, V̆T, V, VT} are all monomoraic rimes, while {V̆N, VN} are bimoraic. (As discussed in §2.7.1, the distinction between full and reduced vowels

---

[43] Only the light syllable types need to be reinterpreted for this proposal to work. The heavy rimes could remain VN and VVN, as Kung (2007) takes them. Moreover, the proposed reinterpretation can be confined to the ultima if necessary.

need not be implemented in terms of moras, even when they contrast in weight.) Nowhere in this reinterpreted system does VC outweigh VV.

Word-final V̌ is devoiced only phrase-finally, but my proposal suggests that it is reduced across the board, even when not devoiced. On this point, a phonetic study is a desideratum. Kung (2007) does not suggest that V̌ is voiceless before T, where I also take it to be reduced, but she gives an independent hint that V̌ might be reduced in this position: High vowels are lax in VT but tense in VN. As I stated in footnote 43, the present analysis does not require any vowels to be reduced before sonorants, as sonorant-final syllables are always heavy.

Concluding this section, VC < VV is one of the most frequent criteria for stress. Figure 2.6 enumerated sixty-seven languages with VC < VV for stress, many of them unbounded. By contrast, the reversal, VV < VC, is between marginal and unattested for stress. Moreover, insofar as it is attested, it is found only in final position, which is subject to various confounds. VV < VC for stress is therefore reminiscent of other unnatural processes in phonology that are attested in only a handful of controversial cases (e.g. final voicing; Yu 2004, Kiparsky 2006a, 2008, Beguš 2018). In this chapter, I tentatively favor the more restrictive approach of MAIN→VV, which, coupled with the other weight-mapping apparatus but excluding Coda Prominence, cannot implement VV < VC for stress.

2.7.3 Coda Prominence as an antidote to trimoraicity

One advantage of Coda Prominence is that it permits superheavy-sensitive systems such as Hindi and Kashmiri to be analyzed without invoking trimoraic syllables (Crowhurst and Michael 2005, Munshi and Crowhurst 2012). I here confirm this advantage for NoBranch (short for *P_{PWd}/NoBranch(μ) in Munshi and Crowhurst 2012), which was defined above in (103).

Consider once again Kelkar's Hindi (§2.3.3). Stress falls on the heaviest available syllable on the scale V < {VC, VV} < {VCC, VVC}. If more than one syllable instantiates the heaviest grade, the rightmost nonfinal instance wins. To analyze this system without trimoraic syllables, one must take superheavy VVC to possess a nonmoraic coda. But other codas must still be moraic, since VC and VV are equivalent. This situation is achieved by *3μ ≫ WbyP ≫ *μ. In other words, weight-by-position applies, unless it would engender a trimoraic syllable. In (107), BRANCH breaks ties between {VC$_\mu$, VV} and VVC, all of which are bimoraic, in favor of VVC. Recall that only moraic codas violate BRANCH. Candidates with trimoraic VVC$_\mu$ are not shown in (107), as *3μ is assumed to rule them out.

(107)

aːsmãːjaːh	σ$_\mu$→S	BRANCH	NONFINALITY	ALIGN-R
a. ☞ 'aːsmãːjaːh	**	*		**
b. aːs'mãːjaːh	**	**!		*
c. aːsmãː'jaːh	**	*	*!	

Ties are broken rightwards (but not as far as the ultima), as in (108). $V_\mu C_\mu$ and VV are equivalent on BRANCH because both contain two non-branching moras. $V_\mu C$ is not considered in the tableau given the assumption of $^*3\mu \gg$ WbyP $\gg {}^*\mu$.

(108)

darvaːze	$\sigma_{\mu\mu} \to S$	BRANCH	NONFINALITY	ALIGN-R
a. ☞ dar$_\mu$'vaːze		**		*
b. 'dar$_\mu$vaːze		**		**!

This analysis also handles $\{VC_\mu, VV\} < VC_\mu C$ properly. The three are equivalent on $\sigma_{\mu\mu} \to$ STRESS. $V_\mu C_\mu C$ has one non-branching mora, while the others have two. $V_\mu C_\mu C$ is therefore favored for stress. However, a potential drawback of this analysis—see the next paragraph for others—is that it requires rejecting the moraic theory of geminates. For example, Hindi permits geminates in codas, which contrast with singletons (§2.6.3, §2.6.7). This contrast cannot be implemented in terms of moras under the BRANCH analysis, since syllables are capped at two moras. One could not take Hindi singleton codas to be nonmoraic on this analysis, since BRANCH would then cause $V_\mu C$ to draw stress away from VV.

In sum, BRANCH permits stress systems with superheavies to be analyzed without trimoraicity, which is a virtue of that approach. MAIN→VV, by contrast, requires trimoraicity. Nevertheless, this chapter opts for the latter, given its net advantages (§2.7.1). First, MAIN→VV does not generate the pathological VV < VC criterion for stress. More generally, coda prominence is incompatible with the stringent approach to weight pursued here. The predicate "coda" (or VC) is not a superset of heavier VV, while $\sigma_{\mu\mu}$, on the present approach, is a superset of heavier VV. Second, MAIN→VV allows geminates to be moraic, as in systems with VG < VV for primary stress but V < VG for secondary stress. Third, MAIN→VV alone can handle systems in which $V_\mu C_\mu < VV_{\mu\mu}$. Fourth, eliminating trimoraicity from certain stress systems is only an advantage if trimoraicity can be eliminated in general. But trimoraic syllables are independently supported by various other systems, including ternary length contrasts (as in Estonian; see §2.6.7), syllable structure constraints, and compensatory lengthening (Hayes 1989:291–3, Baković 1996, Hajek 2000, Hall 2002). See Bye et al. (2009) and Türk et al. (2018) for surveys of ternary length distinctions in vowels and consonants. Both focus on Inari Sami, which exhibits a ternary consonant length contrast that is realized in terms of duration and not pitch or intensity. Trimoraic syllables are also necessary in metrics, as argued in §4.1 for Persian, where superheavies scan differently from heavies and cannot be analyzed as disyllabic, and independently in §4.3 for archaic Indo-European, where superheavy syllables are avoided in cadences. Furthermore, many languages permit long vowels and geminates to cooccur in arguably trimoraic syllables, as with Japanese words such as *tootta* 'went through' (Kubozono 1999). Eliminating trimoraic syllables from stress systems such as Kelkar's Hindi only results in greater parsimony if trimoraic syllables can be eliminated from all of these other systems. If they are generable at all, the factorial typology will generate them in stress systems.

It should be emphasized, however, that BRANCH and MAIN→VV are both Prominence solutions to deficiencies of Coercion. The bigger question is whether Coercion alone suffices to analyze rich scales, or whether it must be augmented or replaced by Skeletal Prominence. This chapter joins Wiltshire (2006), Crowhurst and Michael (2005), and Munshi and Crowhurst (2012) in supporting the latter position.

2.8 Gradient weight for stress

Most of the stress systems treated thus far have been CATEGORICAL, which is to say that (1) stress placement is fully determined by the distribution of weight and (2) weight instantiates an ordinal scale. The remainder of the chapter treats stress systems in which weight sensitivity is GRADIENT, in the sense that (1) weight effects emerge as significant tendencies in a system exhibiting variation and (2) weight instantiates a ratio scale. An ORDINAL SCALE is discrete and non-quantifiable. For example, for a language like Kashmiri (§2.5.1), it would not make sense to say that VV is x times heavier than VC. In terms of the phonology, one can only conclude that VV is strictly heavier than VC: Whenever the two cooccur nonfinally, the former takes stress. With a RATIO SCALE, weight differences are quantifiable, and can be arrayed meaningfully along a continuum. One might conclude, for instance, that the difference between V and VC is greater than that between VC and VV, even though both contrasts are significant. I begin with Hupa.

2.8.1 VH $\lesssim$ V $\lesssim$ VC $\lesssim$ VV in Hupa

Gordon and Luna (2004) quantify the distribution of stress in Hupa (Athabaskan) based on eighteen (of seventy-seven) stress-marked texts transcribed originally by Edward Sapir in 1927 and reissued in Sapir and Golla (2001). Based on 2,230 words, they find that stress tends strongly (>90%) to be confined to the first two syllables of the word. Sporadic occurrences of stress outside of this window appear not to be conditioned by weight. Within the disyllabic window, at least four grades of weight are evident, namely, VH $\lesssim$ V $\lesssim$ VC $\lesssim$ VV, where H refers to a laryngeal (ʔ or h) and $\lesssim$ indicates that the difference is significant, but not categorical. Gordon and Luna (2004) do not test for further gradations (such as vowel quality), so it is possible that the scale is even more fine-grained.

Gordon and Luna (2004) present a four-by-four cross-tabulation of counts of initial vs. peninitial stress for all sixteen combinations of {VH, V, VC, VV} in the disyllabic window. I plot their counts in Figure 2.7.[44] The scale VH $\lesssim$ V $\lesssim$ VC $\lesssim$ VV is revealed independently by both the first and second syllable (σ_1 and σ_2). The effect of σ_1 is apparent from the rising lines in Figure 2.7. As σ_1 gains weight on the x-axis, it is increasingly likely to be stressed (height on the y-axis). The effect of σ_2 is apparent

---

[44] These counts do not control for morphology, but Gordon and Luna (2004) suggest that "stress in Hupa was largely blind to morphological structure at the time of Sapir's work." It is not clear whether they imposed a minimum word size for inclusion in the cross-tabulation.

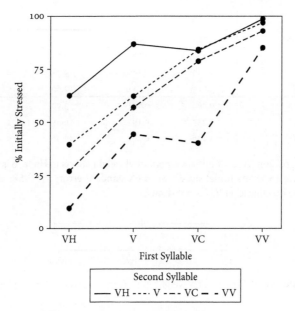

FIGURE 2.7 Percentage of Hupa words that are initially (as opposed to peninitially) stressed as a function of the weights of the initial and peninitial syllables, based on data from Gordon and Luna (2004).

from the vertical stacking of the lines. If one holds σ_1 constant, initial stress (height on the y-axis) decreases as the weight of σ_2 increases.

Weight criteria sometimes differ between initial and peninitial position (as in Tamil in §2.5.10, and other cases in Rosenthall and van der Hulst 1999). Although the scales appear to be similar for σ_1 and σ_2 in Hupa, this correlation can be established more precisely using logistic regression, as in Figure 2.8, simultaneously regressing on the weights of both positions.[45] First, note that the absolute magnitudes of the coefficients are greater for σ_1 than for σ_2. This indicates that Hupa speakers are gradiently more sensitive to σ_1 than to σ_2, a case of what might be called EDGE-BASED DECAY. Edge-based decay is documented also for Portuguese, which has a final trisyllabic window, but with weight sensitivity decreasing gradiently from the ultima to the antepenult (Garcia 2017b); see also English in §2.8.3. In Hupa, once one corrects for the greater sensitivity to σ_1, the scales for σ_1 and σ_2 are almost identical. Figure 2.9 depicts the inferred ratio scales for both positions. The two continua are rescaled so as to have the same breadth.[46]

Gordon and Luna (2004) do not provide a generative analysis of these results, but one can be developed along the following lines. The disyllabic window can be

---

[45] This model was also tested including interactions, but none was near significant. The simpler interaction-free model is therefore presented.

[46] In the continua, the proximity of V to VC is due in part to the plateaus in Figure 2.7 where $\sigma_1 \in \{V, VC\}$ and $\sigma_2 \in \{VH, VV\}$. I return to this discrepancy at the end of the section.

	β	SE	z	p
(Intercept)	0.292	0.219	1.34	0.18
σ_1 = V	1.364	0.165	8.29	< .0001
σ_1 = VC	1.819	0.189	9.61	< .0001
σ_1 = VV	3.715	0.211	17.60	< .0001
σ_2 = V	− 0.864	0.221	− 3.90	< .0001
σ_2 = VC	− 1.257	0.195	− 6.45	< .0001
σ_2 = VV	− 2.236	0.204	− 10.96	< .0001

FIGURE 2.8 Regression table for initial vs. peninitial weight effects in Hupa. β is the coefficient estimate (positive ⇒ favors initial stress); SE is β's standard error; z is β/SE; and p indicates significance. The baseline level VH is not shown.

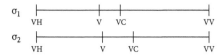

FIGURE 2.9 Ratio scales for weight in σ_1 (top) and σ_2 (bottom) in Hupa.

implemented by positing a rigidly left-aligned foot. WbyP is undominated, such that codas are always moraic. V $\lesssim$ VC$_\mu$ is due to MAIN→$\sigma_{\mu\mu}$, and VC$_\mu$ $\lesssim$ VV is due to MAIN→VV. One approach to the extra-light weight of VH is to analyze pre-laryngeal vowels as being "checked" and reduced. A constraint such as MAIN→FULL (vel sim.), which eschews stress on reduced vowels, is needed independently for reduced vs. full criteria (§2.1). I therefore provisionally employ MAIN→FULL to penalize stress on VH. This analysis does not predict that vowels are reduced pre-laryngeally in all languages (recall, for instance, Huehuetla Tepehua, in which VH is heavier than VT; §2.7.2). As noted since §1.3, laryngeals vary widely in their effects on weight. But the constraint set developed in this chapter otherwise guarantees that V $\lesssim$ VC $\lesssim$ VV if those three categories are distinguished (once again, see §2.7.2). Finally, when weight is tied between the first two syllables, stress tends to be initial, as favored by TROCHEE.

Gradient systems can be analyzed with numerically weighted constraints. In this book, I use maximum entropy (maxent) Harmonic Grammar for this purpose (Goldwater and Johnson 2003, Wilson 2006, Hayes and Wilson 2008), along with weight-learning software by Wilson and George (2008). The constraints for Hupa were assigned the weights in (109). Undominated constraints were not weighted, as they can be assigned arbitrarily high weights.

(109) WbyP   (undominated)
       ALL-FEET-L   (undominated)
       FTBIN   (undominated)
       MAIN→VV   1.519
       MAIN→FULL   1.107
       TROCHEE   1.006
       MAIN→$\sigma_{\mu\mu}$ 0.676

Weighted constraints define a probability distribution over candidates, as exemplified in (110) for the schematic input V-VC. Constraint weights are given under their labels. For convenience, asterisks are replaced by nonpositive integers. These violations are multiplied by their constraints' weights and the resulting products are summed, giving the candidate's harmony $\mathscr{H}$. Finally, a candidate's probability p is given by $\exp(\mathscr{H}_0)/\sum_i \exp(\mathscr{H}_i)$, where $\mathscr{H}_0$ is the candidate's harmony and $\mathscr{H}_i$ ranges over all candidates. Thus, the grammar generates initial stress on V-VC 58 per cent of the time (cf. the real rate of 57%). For more background on this framework, see Hayes and Wilson (2008).

(110)

V-VC	p	$\mathscr{H}$	MAIN→VV 1.519	MAIN→FULL 1.107	TROCHEE 1.006	MAIN→σμμ 0.676
a.	'V-VC$_\mu$	.58	−2.195	−1	0	0	−1
b.	V-'VC$_\mu$	.42	−2.525	−1	0	−1	0

The generated proportions for all initial–peninitial combinations of {VH, V, VC, VV} are depicted in Figure 2.10 alongside the real rates, which are repeated from Figure 2.7. The grammar smooths out two notable plateaus in the real data, but otherwise the fit is relatively good ($r^2 = .91$). The plateaus can be characterized as follows. Iff the peninitial is VH or VV, increasing the initial from V to VC has no effect on stress. I cannot explain this idiosyncrasy, and put it aside. In general, however, this section illustrates that a few independently motivated stress–weight mapping

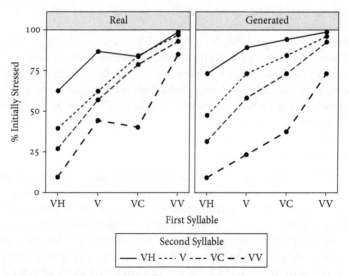

FIGURE 2.10 Real (left) and generated (right) rates of initial stress in Hupa. Generated rates reflect the grammar in (109).

constraints, assigned weights, achieve a reasonably good fit to sixteen rates of initial stress (four syllable types in first position × four syllable types in second position) in Hupa.

2.8.2 $V \lesssim VC \lesssim VV$ (etc.) in Yahi (Yana)

In addition to Hupa, Sapir worked on Yana, whose stress rule is analyzed in §2.3.3 above: Leftmost VX, else leftmost. Sapir and Swadesh (1960) note that this rule is only a tendency. Hinton and Luthin (2002) analyze stress more systematically for the Yahi dialect, as spoken by Ishi, based on Sapir's field notes from 1915. Their corpus is 256 words, comprising all trisyllables (and quadrisyllables in quotative -*ti*) in the first forty-four pages. They find that stress follows the aforementioned rule 71 per cent of the time in these materials. Many of the exceptions involve skipping VC to stress a subsequent VV. Indeed, they suggest that the rule would have better (albeit still imperfect) coverage if it were amended to "leftmost VV, else leftmost VC, else leftmost."

Hinton and Luthin (2002) present the summary table in (111), adapted slightly, which suggests that weight is likely also to be sensitive to the sonority of the coda (N = nasal, L = lateral, W = glide). The rightmost column refers to the fact that -*si* (present tense) tends to be prestressing, but pre-penultimate stressed syllables increasingly resist yielding stress to -*si* as their weight increases. As Hinton and Luthin (2002) is only slides from a talk, I cannot provide further empirical details.

(111)	Rime Type	% Stressed	% Resistant to -*si*
	VN	40	35
	VL	60	50
	VW	60	60
	VV	70	70

Assuming, however, that $VN \lesssim VL \lesssim VW \lesssim VV$ holds up to further scrutiny, extensions of MAIN→VV can implement the sonority scale. For example, MAIN→V[+*son*] and MAIN→V[+*approx*] can implement $VN \lesssim VL$. Because these constraints are stated stringently, approximants being a subset of sonorants, no ranking or weighting of them generates a grammar in which VN outweighs VL. See §5.5.3 and §5.9.1 for further discussion.

2.8.3 Skeletal structure in English

The topic of English stress has spawned several books, including the most cited book in the history of phonology (Chomsky and Halle 1968). This section makes no attempt to summarize the system, as metrical phonology is not the focus here. Rather, I briefly illustrate that syllable weight is treated as highly complex under certain conditions.

Take monomorphemic (SIMPLEX) disyllables. Though there are some strong tendencies, such as initial stress in nouns and final stress in non-light-final verbs, stress placement is hardly deterministic, as the near-minimal pairs of nouns in (112) exemplify (see also Moore-Cantwell 2016 for discussion of exceptions in English stress).[47] Only primary stress is marked; secondary stress is put aside in this section. Some of these examples vary by dialect, which only reinforces their arbitrariness.

(112) a. Mérlin   Berlín
       b. Dúrex   duréss
       c. própane   cocáine
       d. córal   corrál
       e. tútu   tattóo
       f. sítar   guitár

Nevertheless, regressing on the weights of the two syllables yields significant and phonologically sensible trends that go far beyond binary weight (Kelly 2004, Ryan 2011b, 2014; cf. also Olejarczuk and Kapatsinski 2016). As a representative corpus, I take the 8,323 simplex disyllabic nouns, verbs, and adjectives from CELEX (Baayen et al. 1993), the same corpus employed by Ryan (2014). The present logistic regression takes each word as a datum, the dependent variable being whether the word is initially stressed (1) or not (0). The skeletal rime shapes of σ_1 and σ_2 are included as predictors, as are the onset sizes of σ_1 and σ_2 (see below) and the part of speech (three levels). The latter corrects for the different propensities of nouns, verbs, and adjectives to take initial stress. The resulting coefficients for rime shape are depicted in Figure 2.11. In regressions, one level of each factor is normally taken as the baseline level, which is not assigned an error (as distinct from the general intercept, which is not factor-specific). For σ_1, the baseline is V, and for σ_2, it is VC. The latter is not taken to be V because no forms in the data have stress on final V. From this fact, final V can be inferred to be strictly lighter than final VC, which sometimes takes stress, as in *omít*.

The trends in Figure 2.11 are summarized as hierarchies in (113). VCC is not shown for σ_1 because its range encompasses both VC and VV. Other uncommon rimes shapes are omitted from both Figure 2.11 and (113) if their standard errors exceed one.

(113) σ_1: V $\lesssim$ VC $\lesssim$ VV $\lesssim$ {VVC, VVCC}
       σ_2: V $<$ VC $\lesssim$ VV $\lesssim$ VCC $\lesssim$ {VVC, VCCC} $\lesssim$ VVCC

These two hierarchies agree not only with each other, but with the typology. Even on points where the English hierarchies are ambivalent, such as the insecure weight of VCC in σ_1 relative to VC and VV, the typology evinces the same ambivalence (see footnote 7 on VCC). Moreover, edge-based decay is once again in evidence, just as

---

[47] Chomsky and Halle (1968) seek to reduce some of the irregularity (though they cannot eliminate it altogether) by positing highly abstract and opaque underlying forms. For example, *Néptune* is stressed differently from *cartóon* because the former ends with an underlying /e/, which is never pronounced, and the two words also differ in the underlying length of [u], which again is always neutralized: /kartUn/, /neptune/. Similarly, *banána* is stressed differently from *cínema* because the former is said to have an underlying geminate: /bananna/. In short, their approach replaces (transparent) accentual diacritics with (opaque) segmental diacritics. In a constraint-based setting, transparency is favored: /kartún/, /néptun/. A drawback of Chomsky and Halle's (1968) approach is that without an explicit theory of how underlying forms are derived from surface data, that is, a theory of learnability, its predictive success cannot be judged. For instance, one cannot say what percentage of a (sub)lexicon is regular. With a surface-oriented analysis, assessing coverage is straightforward, permitting models to be compared and falsified.

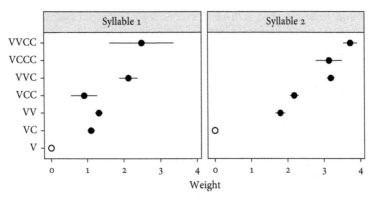

FIGURE 2.11 Weight coefficients of seven rime types in English simplex disyllables, paneled by position. Standard errors are shown by bars. Circles represent baseline levels, which are zero by fiat.

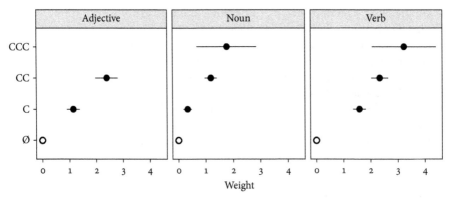

FIGURE 2.12 Weight coefficients of four word-initial onset types in English simplex disyllables, paneled by part of speech.

with Hupa (§2.8.1) and Portuguese (§2.8.4). Consistent with the rightward orientation of primary stress in English, weight sensitivity is greatest for the ultima, both in detail and in degree. Furthermore, most aspects of the hierarchies in (113) have been shown to be productive in nonce probe experiments (WUG TESTS; Berko 1958). Guion et al. (2003) find that VC $\lesssim$ VV is significant for the initial syllables of disyllables, as are VCC $\lesssim$ VVC and VC $\lesssim$ VVC for final syllables. Ryan (2011b) wug-tests V $\lesssim$ VC $\lesssim$ VV $\lesssim$ VVC in the initial syllables of disyllables, finding every pairwise link to be a significant.

Onset structure also significantly affects stress placement in English disyllables, as demonstrated by Kelly (2004) and Ryan (2014). Figure 2.12 reveals that for word-initial onsets of disyllables, the hierarchy Ø $\lesssim$ C $\lesssim$ CC is observed across parts of speech, with every link significant in every part of speech. In the aggregate (not shown), CC $\lesssim$ CCC is also significant, hence the quaternary scale in (114).

The coefficients in Figure 2.12 are from the regression above, meaning that rime structure is controlled. Other possible confounds are addressed by Kelly (2004) and Ryan (2014), including frequency and etymological origin. They further demonstrate the productivity of the effect under various experimental protocols, both production- and perception-based. Ryan (2014) argues that the effect cannot be attributed to analogy, as it applies even in neighborhoods in which analogy predicts its reversal.

(114) $\emptyset \lesssim C \lesssim CC \lesssim CCC$

These onset and rime effects combine to form a highly complex scale. Sonority effects are not considered here, but may also be relevant. Carpenter (2010) demonstrates experimentally that English (and French) speakers favor stress on low as opposed to high vowels, in the sense that they learn a low=heavy rule more effectively than a high=heavy rule given equal evidence and controlling for phonetic cues such as duration. Carpenter (2010) does not address whether such a generalization receives any support from the English lexicon—the assumption being that it does not—but even if it does not, if it were applied to wugs, it would be part of English grammar. This question invites further investigation. Furthermore, an auditory wug test in Garcia (2017a) finds that coda sonorants significantly outweigh coda obstruents in English penults and antepenults.

2.8.4 Other cases of gradient weight: Russian, Finnish, Italian, Spanish, and Portuguese

Gradient weight-sensitive stress has been described for several other familiar languages, as briefly surveyed here. First, Ryan (2014) demonstrates that Russian, like English, exhibits a strong correlation between stress and onset size in simplex words, controlling for part of speech, frequency, word length, rime structure, and vowel quality. For example, in trisyllables, as the size of the word-initial onset increases, the propensity for initial accent increases with it, revealing quaternary $\emptyset \lesssim C \lesssim CC \lesssim CCC$ (every link significant).

Second, Finnish secondary stress is conditioned by many factors, including skeletal structure and vowel sonority (Anttila 1997a, 1997b, 2010, Karvonen 2005). In some contexts, these factors are gradient. Anttila (*ibid.*) analyzes weight and stress largely through the lens of suffix allomorphy, which is sensitive to both. As an example of a gradient sonority effect, consider (115). The genitive plural suffix has a weak variant *-(j)en* and a strong variant *-den* or *-ten*. The strong variant, unlike the weak variant, is preceded immediately by a stressed, heavy syllable. In (a–b), the stem is low vowel-final *kamera*, which favors the strong suffix. In (c–d), the stem is high vowel-final *naapuri*, which (weakly) favors the weak suffix. This effect is gradient, but highly systematic.

(115)	a.	ˈka.me.ro.jen	1%	'cameras (genitive)'
	b.	ˈka.meˌroi.den	99%	'cameras (genitive)'
	c.	ˈnaa.pu.ri.en	63%	'neighbors (genitive)'
	d.	ˈnaa.puˌrei.den	37%	'neighbors (genitive)'

Third, Cei and Hayes (2012) and Hayes (2012) analyze Italian stress. They put aside final stress, which is fairly well circumscribed, and focus on predicting whether stress is penultimate or antepenultimate in words of three or more syllables with a light penult. They find that a low vowel in the penult significantly favors stress, as does onset complexity in the penult. Fourth, Shelton (2007) presents four experiments on Spanish stress, finding that rising diphthongs pattern as intermediate between light and heavy. In this respect, Spanish resembles Nanti (§2.5.9), except in a gradient setting.

Finally, Garcia (2016, 2017a, 2017b, 2017c) analyzes Portuguese stress from the perspectives of both the lexicon and experiments, identifying a number of significant gradient generalizations. First, although stress is confined categorically to a final trisyllabic window, within that window, edge-based decay is observed (as in Hupa and English above): Speakers are most sensitive to the structure of the ultima, followed by that of the penult and antepenult, respectively. Garcia (2016, 2017b, 2017c) focuses on speakers' treatment of margin complexity. Broadly speaking, consonant count correlates monotonically with stress propensity, as in English (§2.8.3). However, syllabification complicates the picture. In particular, increasing the size of the penult onset from zero to two consonants increases the stress propensity of the antepenult, not that of the penult. This suggests that weight is based on total vowel-to-vowel intervals, such as VC.V and VCC.V, as in Interval Theory (Steriade 2008, 2012; see §4.6). However, increasing onset complexity in the antepenult correlates weakly with increasing antepenult stress (perhaps because some of the antepenults are word-initial), and results for the final onset are mixed. Garcia (2017c) demonstrates that some of these effects are replicated in wugs.

2.9 Conclusion

Weight criteria for stress are most often binary, but ternary and more complex scales are also well established. This chapter focuses on suprabinary skeletal scales, the most common one being V < VC < VV, as found in at least twenty languages (here, seventeen categorical and three gradient). Two analyses of such scales are contrasted, namely, Coercion and Prominence. Coercion maintains that VC is intermediate in weight because it varies in moraicity in the relevant languages, being bimoraic under stress and monomoraic otherwise. Prominence is compatible with fixed moraicity (language-internally), such that VC and VV are both bimoraic in the relevant languages, while the greater weight of VV is attributed to a principle that favors stress on long vowels. As argued in §2.5, the majority of ternary systems are incompatible with Coercion, due to two issues. First, secondary stress sometimes requires VC to be heavy even when it yields primary stress to VV. Second, because geminates usually align with VC in such systems, Coercion requires unstressed geminates to be analyzed as nonmoraic. This contradicts other evidence for their moraicity in the relevant languages, which is sometimes furnished by the stress system itself. To be sure, I do not argue against Coercion in general in this chapter. I just argue that it is insufficient to analyze V < VC < VV systems, and must be augmented by a theory of Prominence.

A further advantage of introducing a constraint that favors stress on long vowels is that it permits geminate moraicity to be maintained across the board for stress systems. In particular, among sixty-seven languages with a VC < VV criterion, VG aligns with VC over 90 per cent of the time. Without a constraint like Main→VV, geminates have to be treated as nonmoraic in such languages, which include languages like Finnish, Malayalam, and Pulaar, in which evidence abounds for the moraicity of geminates. With Main→VV, there is no need to adopt "parametric geminate moraicity" with its ensuing problems (§2.6.5). Indeed, this chapter argues that there are no strong cases of G being lighter than C for stress (see §§2.6.6–2.6.7 regarding putative cases such as Ngalakgan and Tashlhiyt Berber).

An alternative to Main→VV, namely, Coda Prominence, is treated in §2.7. Coda Prominence figures in some previous analyses of complex scales (e.g. Crowhurst and Michael 2005, Wiltshire 2006, Munshi and Crowhurst 2012) and has the advantage of allowing systems with superheavy grades to be analyzed without invoking trimoraic syllables. Nevertheless, Vowel Prominence, as supported here, is argued to be superior to Coda Prominence on typological grounds. For one thing, Coda Prominence predicts VV < VC criteria, which arguably do not exist for stress (§2.7.2). Coda Prominence also runs afoul of the secondary stress and nonmoraic geminate problems just described for Coercion, among other issues (§2.7.3).

Finally, I discuss gradient weight for stress, as documented for languages such as English, Finnish, Hupa, Italian, Portuguese, Russian, Spanish, and Yahi. Gradient weight is often associated with highly complex scales, potentially involving the interaction of vowel length, coda size, onset size, and sonority. For example, gradient effects of onset structure have been established for English, Finnish, Italian, Portuguese, and Russian. I turn next to prosodic minimality, which, as discussed in the next chapter, is often treated as an epiphenomenon of stress.

3

Prosodic minimality in isolation and in context

3.1 Introduction

Prosodic minimality refers to the minimum size requirements that languages impose on prosodic words (PWds). For example, in Pitta-Pitta, Yidiɲ, and many other languages, a PWd must be at least two syllables, as exemplified for Yidiɲ in (1) (Dixon 1977, Hayes 1995, Garrett 1999, Gordon 2006). In Latin, English, and many other languages, by contrast, a PWd can be a monosyllable, but that monosyllable must have a rime that is VC, VV, or larger (Mester 1994, Morén 1997, Blumenfeld 2011). This is illustrated for Latin in (2) (see also §3.2). As a third example of a minimum, in Bella Coola, a PWd need not contain any vowel at all if it has at least two consonants, as shown in (3) (Topintzi 2010).

(1) Yidiɲ   a. digir   'nose'
                  b. dirɡul   'fat'
                  c. *dir   (illicit)

(2) Latin   a. ter   'thrice'
                  b. deː   'of'
                  c. *de   (illicit)

(3) Bella Coola a. sps   'northeast wind'
                  b. sx   'bad'
                  c. *s   (illicit)

Prosodic minimality applies to PWds, but not necessarily to words in general in a language. For example, the possessive clitic 's in English and the conjunctive clitic *que* in Latin are by all rights grammatical words. But they are not individually subject to prosodic minimality, because they are clitics. As such, they adjoin to some other word, which serves as their host, and that cliticized complex as a whole is evaluated on the surface for minimality.

Since Prince (1980) and McCarthy and Prince (1986), the general insight concerning the motivation for prosodic minimality has been that it follows from the structure of stress feet in the language. If a PWd must bear stress, it must contain a stress foot, and therefore must be at least as large as a foot. A strong hypothesis,

Prosodic Weight. First edition. Kevin M. Ryan.
© Kevin M. Ryan 2019. First published 2019 by Oxford University Press.

then, is that all prosodic word minima can be explained by the same machinery that is independently motivated by the analysis of stress systems. In Latin, for example, even if one were to look only at words of three or more syllables, it is apparent that the foot type is a moraic trochee and that any syllable with a long vowel and/or coda counts as heavy (see §3.2). From these facts, one could predict, correctly in this case, that a monosyllabic word would also be a moraic trochee, that is, a heavy syllable, and that the criterion for heaviness in this context would be the same as it is elsewhere for stress.

Nevertheless, the parallelism between prosodic minimality and foot shape or syllable weight in other contexts is not always as straightforward as it is in Latin. In many languages, for instance, VC is a light rime for stress, but counts as heavy for prosodic minimality (e.g. Hupa and Buriat; Gordon 2006, Blumenfeld 2011). In some cases, the minimal word is arguably larger than the maximal foot (e.g. Carib and Hixkaryana). Similarly, in at least one case (Cahuilla), a foot can be V for main stress, but V is subminimal as a word. (As in the previous chapter, unless onset structure is critical, criteria are stated in terms of rime structure, omitting onset C_0.) These sorts of mismatches are amply documented by Garrett (1999), Downing (2005), and Gordon (2006) (cf. also Dresher and van der Hulst 1998). Indeed, Gordon (2006) finds that mismatched syllable weight criteria between stress and minimality are more frequent than matched criteria. Different systems appear to define "heavy" differently.

That said, these superficial mismatches do not necessarily defeat the prosodic hierarchy approach to minimality sketched above. As Blumenfeld (2011) argues, in the context of Optimality Theory (Prince and Smolensky 1993/2004), we expect "elsewhere" conditions to emerge because constraints can be dominated. For example, in a language that treats VC as light for stress but heavy for minimality, one can argue that the coda is being COERCED into bearing a mora in just the case that it occupies a monosyllable. In other words, the constraint requiring codas to be nonmoraic is compelled to be violated in certain contexts by a higher-ranked constraint. Moreover, coercion is not confined to prosodic minimality, but may be supported by other systems as well (§2.2, §2.6.4). Although the last chapter was largely devoted to showing that Coercion undergenerates, it did not reject Coercion in general. The point was that Coercion is insufficient, not that it is unavailable.

On this prosodic approach, minimality is enforced only on the surface. A subminimal input is repaired by increasing its size (usually through epenthesis or lengthening), and PWds can be protected against reductive processes (such as apocope) if they threaten minimality (see Kager 2007 for examples of both). Minimality, on this approach, is not a property of roots.[1] Indeed, in Optimality Theory, the input cannot be constrained (Richness of the Base). That said, it remains an open question to what extent root or other presurface minimality might be defended empirically. See Downing (2005), Ketner (2006), and Blumenfeld (2011) for discussion of this issue. Blumenfeld (2011) observes that minima are sometimes opacified on the surface.

---

[1] Roots might nevertheless come to reflect it indirectly via Lexicon Optimization, which favors symmetry between underlying and surface forms, all else being equal (Prince and Smolensky 1993/2004).

For example, in Diyari and Pintupi, words are minimally disyllabic underlyingly, but glide deletion can render them monosyllabic on the surface (leaving Pintupi with perhaps only one monosyllable, according to Garrett 1999: [tʲaː] 'mouth'). See also Hayes (1995:217) on Eastern Ojibwa. In Anguthimri, minimality-driven lengthening appears to be counterbled by prothesis (Crowley 1981, Blumenfeld 2011). Finally, another side of this problem is languages in which roots are more regularly minimal than one would expect, given the availability of repairs. In Latin, for instance, perhaps only one extant word necessitates repair, namely /da/ → [daː] 'give'; cf. [dăre] 'to give,' [dăte] 'give! (PL),' etc. (§3.2). Lexicon optimization cannot explain why this alternation is rare, though analogy may be relevant (see §3.2.6).

Beyond any requirements imposed by prosodification, certain phonetic tendencies also conspire to make short words such as monosyllables longer in duration (cf. also Mori 2002, Braver and Kawahara 2012, 2014). First, syllable duration is inversely correlated with the number of syllables in the word, all else being equal (Lehiste 1970, 1972, Lindblom and Rapp 1973). Thus, a syllable is typically longer as a monosyllable than that same syllable would be in any position of a longer word. Second, syllables tend to be protracted at the ends of words, all else being equal (Delattre 1966, Lindblom 1968, Wightman et al. 1992, Turk and Shattuck-Hufnagel 2000, 2007, Lunden 2006). Finally, assuming that monosyllables are stressed, stressed syllables tend to be longer than their unstressed counterparts (Turk and Sawusch 1997, Turk and White 1999, Turk and Shattuck-Hufnagel 2000). These phonetic universals are not mutually exclusive with the prosodic account of minimality, but augment it: For example, they are possible phonetic precursors for its phonologization.

The most extensive survey of prosodic minima is Gordon (1999, 2006:210–225), who reports on 144 languages exhibiting minimality restrictions. The three most common criteria are VX (i.e. both VC and VV are allowed), as in Latin (eighty-three languages), VV, as in Chickasaw (thirty languages), and VC_0V, that is, disyllabic, as in Yidiɲ above (twenty-two languages). Nevertheless, as Gordon (2006) points out, such figures should be tempered by consideration of phonotactics. For instance, a language without codas could not possibly exhibit a VX criterion. To that end, if one considers only the 108 languages in the sample in which both VC and VV are licit syllable types and the minimum is not disyllabic, seventy-three (68%) possess the VX criterion and eighteen (17%) possess the VV criterion. In short, VX might be regarded as the unmarked minimality criterion. In languages in which the criterion could just as well be VV or VC_0V on purely phonotactic grounds, VX is attested approximately four times as frequently as each of the two other criteria.

The weight hierarchy in (4) emerges by transitivity from this typology (cf. Garrett 1999, Gordon and Applebaum 2010:70). If a language permits a minimal word of some category in (4), it also permits words of every category to the right of that category, assuming that the category (e.g. long vowels) is otherwise available in the language. By the same token, perhaps no language with final long vowels counts VC as minimal, but not VV. This hierarchy, including rime VC being (if anything) lighter than rime VV, agrees with the weight hierarchies treated throughout this book.

(4) $C < CC < V < VC < VV < VC_0V$

Beyond VC, VV, and VC_0V, rarer criteria for minimality are also attested. For example, in Menominee, a monosyllable must be VVC (apparently because historical VC lengthened; Blumenfeld 2011). In Estonian, a monosyllable must contain either an overlong vowel or an overlong coda (which Gordon 2006:222 notates CVVV, CVCCC). A VX criterion in which only certain consonants qualify for X (due to minimality per se, as opposed to independent phonotactics) is not suggested by Gordon's (2006) survey, but see Tamil in §3.4 below for such a case.

Furthermore, onsets are sometimes relevant. Gordon (2006) mentions three cases in which CCV and CVC but not CV is minimal, namely, Czech, Kashuyana, and Tsou. Topintzi (2005, 2010) extensively treats a fourth case, that of Bella Coola. CC, CV, VC, and VV are all licit words, while V and C are not (p. 146). Thus, among other things, the presence vs. absence of an onset can be decisive: V < CV. As a fifth case, geminate onsets contribute to minimality in Trukese, in that CV is subminimal, but CːV is not (Hart 1991).

Conversely, there are cases in which the onset might be expected to contribute to minimality, but does not. In particular, a common view of geminates is that they necessarily bear a mora (Chapter 2). But some languages have onset geminates that apparently do not contribute to minimality. One case is Leti (Hume et al. 1997), though it has been reanalyzed as a disyllabic minimum (Curtis 2003), in which case mora count is irrelevant (see §2.6.6). Another case is Thurgovian Swiss German, in which a geminate-initial word such as [ttaːk] 'day' is said to undergo vowel lengthening contingent on bimoraic minimality (cf. [ttake] 'days'), despite the onset geminate (Kraehenmann 2001, 2003, Muller 2001, Ringen and Vago 2011, Topintzi and Zimmermann 2014). Nevertheless, Thurgovian onset geminates neutralize with singletons phrase-initially and in some other contexts (Kraehenmann 2001:136–8). If gemination is imperceptible absolute-initially, as Kraehenmann (2001) maintains, it is perhaps not surprising that gemination in that position does not contribute to prosodic minimality.

Some of the more extravagant weight hierarchies that arise in systems like stress and meter are moot for minimality, which is usually assumed to be an exclusively categorical and binary phenomenon. Nevertheless, it is possible that future research will reveal gradience and/or suprabinary sensitivities in minimality. Gradience certainly occurs in the sense that reported minima sometimes exhibit exceptions. Italian, for one, observes a disyllabic minimum, but a handful of otherwise normal, native words (well under 1%) are monosyllables, for example, *don* 'don' and *re* 'king' (Thornton 1996). The situation is similar for Modern Hebrew (where Ussishkin 2000 estimates that about 3% of monosyllables are CV), for Telugu content words (Kolachina 2016), and perhaps also to a lesser extent for Mandarin (Chen 2000) and other Asian languages, where prevailing disyllabic (or sesquisyllabic) minima sometimes admit exceptions. See also the case of Māhārāṣṭrī Prakrit in §3.3, where a contextual minimum is enforced almost rigidly, but with exceptions.

One open question concerning ostensibly exceptionful minima is whether the exceptions reveal anything about gradience in weight. Consider English, which has VC minimality, that is, only VC, VV, and larger words are licit (Morén 1997, Gordon 2006). This criterion rules out a monosyllable ending with a short/lax vowel, but such words are common as slang or ideophones (e.g. *yeah, nah, waah, wha, duh, meh, bleh*; cf. *a, the* in isolation). Nevertheless, even in slang, there seems to be an effect of length. Words with low vowels (e.g. *yeah*) are the most felicitous, followed by words with mid vowels, which are much less frequent (e.g. *meh*), followed by words with high vowels (such as hypothetical *[ˈmɪ] or *[ˈmʊ]), which are excluded altogether in my judgment. It is therefore plausible that English slang evinces gradient minimality effects, including High $\lesssim$ Mid $\lesssim$ Low. For further discussion of this example and the prospect of gradience for minimality, see the conclusion (§6.4).

The remainder of this chapter presents three case studies, on Latin (§3.2), Māhārāṣṭrī Prakrit (§3.3), and Tamil (§3.4), respectively. All three languages enforce a bimoraic minimum for isolated PWds, but each differs in its response to (potential) breaches of PWd minimality that arise from resyllabification in the configuration #C₀V́C#V(...). In LaTeX: $\#C_0\acute{V}C\#V(\ldots)$. Latin permits the resulting degenerate foot ($C_0\acute{V}$) to surface as such, though Virgil almost categorically avoids that configuration in his verse, owing, I argue, to such syllables qualifying as neither heavy nor light. Māhārāṣṭrī Prakrit, by contrast, blocks resyllabification when it would render a C_0VC word subminimal. Finally, Tamil minimality is of interest in two respects. First, all coda consonants except rhotics make position, flouting the sonority principle. Second, Tamil repairs violations of minimality that are induced by resyllabification by lengthening a consonant or vowel. Crucially, in all three languages, the relevant repair or avoidance strategy applies only to minimal C_0VC, not to all PWds ending in (...)VC. Thus, the repairs are driven by prosodic minimality rather than by general phonotactics.

3.2 Latin

3.2.1 *Minimality as it applies to words in isolation*

An isolated PWd cannot be a light syllable in Latin. A PWd may end with a long vowel (e.g. *dē* 'of') or consonant (e.g. *et* 'and'), or comprise multiple syllables (e.g. *tibi* 'to you'). But short-vowel-final monosyllables such as hypothetical **pre* and **ta* do not meet the minimum, and are thus illicit as PWds.[2] This restriction does not concern word-final syllables in general: Minimality aside, length is contrastive absolute-finally (e.g. *fēmina* 'woman' vs. *fēminā* 'from [the] woman'). There is no general prohibition on final short vowels.

A monosyllable must therefore be bimoraic. As always, a short vowel contributes one mora and a long vowel or diphthong contributes two, as in (5) (a–b). Moreover, in Latin, codas are moraic, as in (c).[3] This reflects the constraint WEIGHT-BY-POSITION (WbyP), which requires a coda consonant to head a mora (§§2.3.1–2.5.1). By standard assumptions, a Latin syllable is maximally bimoraic, which can be enforced by *3µ

---

[2] In traditional Latin orthography, macrons are usually omitted. In this book, however, vowel length is indicated in all examples, meaning that any vowel lacking a macron is short.

[3] In Early Latin, codas can be rendered nonmoraic in certain contexts due to iambic shortening (Mester 1994:12, Hayes 1995:120; see §2.3). But this process is uncommon in the Classical language, and at any rate irrelevant for present purposes.

(§2.3.1). Any consonants in excess of this maximum fuse to the second mora, as shown in (6). Thus, *3μ can be taken to dominate WbyP, but this pair of constraints is otherwise undominated in Latin (see Tamil in §3.4 for a more nuanced treatment of WbyP). Given these assumptions, WbyP-violating candidates such as (5-d) are not shown in the tableaux below. Codas are assumed to be moraic throughout. If they are not already moraic in the input, WbyP coerces them into moraicity in the output (Morén 2001, Blumenfeld 2011).

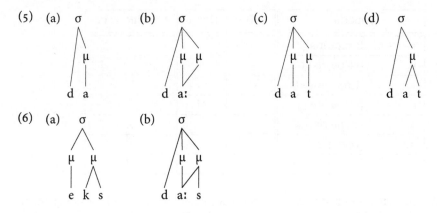

The standard analysis of Latin prosodic minimality runs as follows (Mester 1994, Prince and Smolensky 1993/2004, Blumenfeld 2011). First, FᴛBɪɴ requires a foot (*f*) to be binary in terms of moras (μ) or syllables (σ), as with, for instance, (a–d) in (7) (Prince 1980, Broselow 1982, McCarthy and Prince 1986, Prince and Smolensky 1993/2004, Hayes 1995). This constraint is usually taken to be a disjunction. That is, if one level, whether syllables or moras, has two elements, the other level can be ignored. A foot comprising a single light syllable, as in (7-e), violates FᴛBɪɴ, and is termed DEGENERATE.

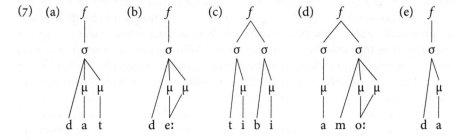

FᴛBɪɴ is motivated not just by minimality, but is independently needed for other systems, such as stress placement (it is sometimes also invoked in metrics; e.g. Ryan 2017b). For example, tableau (8) illustrates antepenultimate stress in *operis* 'of the work.' Parentheses indicate feet and brackets (subscripted with ω) indicate the PWd. FᴛBɪɴ is required to rule out certain forms with penultimate stress, such as (b–c)

in the tableau. Some other active constraints include DEP-μ, which penalizes lengthening (also known as IDENT-μ or WT-IDENTITY, which penalize lengthening or shortening), and NONFINALITY, which (on one interpretation; Kager 1999:151, Jacobs 2003, McCarthy 2003:117) penalizes a word-final foot. This brief analysis of Latin stress is incomplete (for one thing, it does not account for the rightward orientation of primary stress), but additional considerations are not important for the present discussion of minimality. See Jacobs (2003) for a more detailed account.

(8)

/operis/		FTBIN	DEP-μ	NONFINALITY
a. ☞	[('o.pe)ris]ω			
b.	[o('pe)ris]ω	*!		
c.	[(ˌo)('pe)ris]ω	*!*		
d.	[o('peː)ris]ω		*!	
e.	[o('pe.ris)]ω			*!
f.	[ope('ris)]ω			*!
g.	[(ˌo.pe)('ris)]ω			*!

A candidate is omitted from (8) that usually comes up in this discussion, namely, the candidate lacking prosodic structure altogether. This candidate is sometimes taken to be ruled out by GRAMWD=PWD, which requires a grammatical word to be a PWd (e.g. Kager 1999, Blumenfeld 2011). GRAMWD=PWD is based on Lx≈Pr in Prince and Smolensky (1993/2004), which requires any word assigned to a morphosyntactic category ("MCAT") to be a PWd. Gordon and Applebaum (2010) make it more explicit that GRAMWD=PWD requires a one-to-one mapping between grammatical words and PWds, such that each grammatical word must head its own PWd. For example, they take GRAMWD=PWD to be violated by a candidate in which two grammatical words are fused into a single PWd, even though both grammatical words are exhaustively dominated by a PWd node in such a candidate. Given this interpretation of GRAMWD=PWD, a more precise definition would be that for any grammatical word *w* such that *w* corresponds to at least one segment, a segment corresponding to *w* must be the head of a PWd. More succinctly, every grammatical word must culminate in a word stress. Given the existence of processes such as fusion and cliticization, however, GRAMWD=PWD is violable. Indeed, it must be violated in Latin by cliticized structures such as *operisque* 'and of the work,' where *que* is by every right a grammatical word (cf. *et*), but cannot be stressed. Latin cliticization is discussed further below, at which point constraints other than GRAMWD=PWD are invoked to guarantee stress on content words like *operis*.

Returning to minimality, the ranking just posited for stress also motivates the bimoraic minimum. Consider the input /da/ 'give!,' as in (9). That *da* rather than *dā* is the stem here is evident from the rest of the paradigm, including the infinitive *dare* 'to give,' the imperative plural *date*, and other forms (Mester 1994:22, Blumenfeld 2011:210, Weiss 2011:406). Compare, for instance, *stā* 'stand,' with a long stem vowel, as seen in *stāre* and *stāte*.[4] FtBin compels lengthening at the expense of Dep-μ. Other conceivable repairs, such as epenthesis, are ruled out by additional faithfulness constraints, not shown.

(9)

/da/		FtBin	Dep-μ	NonFinality
a. ☞	[(ˈdaː)]_ω		*	*
b.	[(ˈda)]_ω	*!		*

If, by contrast, the input is sufficiently heavy, as with *dor* 'I am given' in (10), lengthening does not occur. (Note that C_0Vː*r* is otherwise a licit shape for a monosyllable, as in *cūr* 'why' and *pār* 'equal.') More generally, minimality-driven lengthening never occurs in a monosyllable that ends with a consonant. The coda of such a monosyllable projects a mora.

(10)

/dor/		FtBin	Dep-μ	NonFinality
a. ☞	[(ˈdor)]_ω			*
b.	[(ˈdoːr)]_ω		*!	*

3.2.2 Minimality as it applies within cliticized structures

Prosodic minimality in Latin is a constraint on the surface forms of PWds, not on roots. Blumenfeld (2011) offers other examples of plausibly subminimal roots in Latin, including verbs like *n-ā-* 'swim,' in which the root is arguably just the consonant, and the noun *ex-ta* 'entrails,' which "appears synchronically not to have any root at all" (p. 210). Moreover, some grammatical words remain subminimal on the surface by virtue of cliticization, which I take to be adjunction to the PWd. Enclitics include *que* 'and,' *ve* 'or,' *ne* (negation, used as a question particle), and some less frequent items (Bennett 1918, Plank 2005). Additionally, the present analysis recognizes that function words such as *ab* 'from' are normally proclitics, akin to English *from* (Probert 2002). Clitic adjunction is illustrated for *que* in (11-a). Structure (b), in which *que*

---

[4] The paradigm for *dō* 'give' exhibits an additional irregularity that is beyond the scope of this discussion. In particular, the second-person singular indicative is *dās* (e.g. *dās epulīs* in *Aeneid* 1.79). This form suggests that either (1) the root is instead /daː-/ or (2) would-be *das* undergoes lengthening. (1) contradicts other forms of the paradigm, as mentioned. (2) is at first glance difficult to reconcile with words such as *bis*, *quis*, *is*, and *es*, which do not lengthen. Nevertheless, (2) is conceivably driven by analogy, either within the paradigm (e.g. 2sg. imperative *dā* influences 2sg. indicative *dās*) or with other first conjugation verbs (e.g. type *amās* influences *dās*). It may be relevant that *dās* is a content word, unlike other monosyllables in V*s*, including the copula *es*. Dieter Gunkel (p.c.) raises the possibility that *dās* might have been lengthened due to FtBin at a time that word-final *s* was not moraic, and then lexicalized as such. In Old Latin inscriptions, word-final *s* is often omitted, and in Old Latin non-dramatic verse, word-final *s* does not make position in weak positions (see Weiss 2011:60). The fact that function words such as *es* were not lexicalized with lengthening would jibe with their being cliticized and therefore not subject to FtBin on the present account. I note in closing that even if the input for *dā* were /daː/, it would not alter the general point being made here, which is that Latin enforces a bimoraic minimum. If one wished to argue that the input for 'give!' is /daː/, then /da/ in tableau (9) can be considered a richness-of-the-base input, and the analysis stands.

is prosodified as a separate PWd, and hence lengthened (as required by FᴛBɪɴ), is not found. Moreover, (c), with fusion instead of adjunction, is incorrect for Classical Latin on the grounds that cliticized structures are not treated as simple words for stress assignment (Plank 2005). For example, *ab avō* 'from the ancestor' (with broad focus) is stressed *ab ávō* in Classical Latin.[5] If it were treated as a simple PWd, with fusion, one would expect **áb avō*.[6] See also Probert (2002) on the lack of stress in Latin function words, including proclitics, enclitics, and non-emphatic pronouns. A second argument against the fusion analysis of cliticization is that lengthening applies under cliticization but not under suffixation (cf. e.g. *dā=que* 'and give! [sg]' vs. *da-te* 'give! [pl]'), as analyzed presently.

(11)   (a)   (b)   (c)

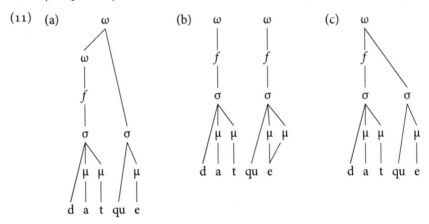

The prosodic structures in (11) are evaluated in tableau (12). Candidate (a), with adjunction of *que*, bests (b), without adjunction, because (a) avoids a violation of Dᴇᴘ-μ (and also saves one violation of NᴏɴFɪɴᴀʟɪᴛʏ). Furthermore, two constraints are added in (12) to ensure that clitics adjoin rather than fuse, as illustrated by (c). This candidate incurs critical violations from an alignment constraint (McCarthy and Prince 1993) that forces the right edge of a lexical word to coincide with the right edge of a PWd: Aʟɪɢɴ(LexWd, Right, PWd, Right), abbreviated Aʟɪɢɴ-R in tableaux.[7] In (c), this constraint receives two violations from the two segments that separate the

---

[5] This stress pattern is confirmed, for one, by stress requirements of metrical cadences in verse (e.g. Ryan 2017b on the hexameter). Early Latin, however, may have stressed leading function words under some circumstances (Radford 1903).

[6] The situation is more complicated for stress in encliticized words. On the one hand, they cannot be treated as simple words. For example, *scélera* 'crimes' with an enclitic was likely stressed *scéleraque* or *scéleráque*, not **sceléraque*, as would be expected if the word were simplex (Newcomer 1908, Bennett 1918, Jacobs 1997, Plank 2005). Thus, recursion is justified. On the other hand, *que* is not simply excluded from consideration for stress assignment. If the stem ends with a heavy syllable, stress shifts to that syllable, as in *amátque* (cf. *ámat*). Because the stress system is not the interest of this section, these complications are put aside. All that is relevant here is that cliticization in Classical Latin can be treated generally as adjunction.

[7] Other schemes for enforcing the homology between grammatical and prosodic words would likely also work. Aɴᴄʜᴏʀ (McCarthy and Prince 1995), for one, is not used here because surface grammatical words are sometimes reshaped in context by deletion.

right edge of *dat* from the nearest PWd boundary. Similarly, Align-L requires the left edge of a lexical word to coincide with the left edge of a PWd, though this constraint is not active in (12).

(12)

/dat kʷe/		Align-L	Align-R	FtBin	Dep-μ	NonFinality
a. ☞	[[(ˈdat)]ω kʷe]ω					*
b.	[(ˈdat)]ω [(ˈkʷe:)]ω				*!	**
c.	[(ˈdat) kʷe]ω		*!*			

Tableau (13) illustrates procliticization in *ab virō* 'from the man.' Given the lexical word alignment constraints, *virō* cannot cliticize to *ab*, as in (c).

(13)

/ab wiro:/		Align-L	Align-R	FtBin	Dep-μ	NonFinality
a. ☞	[ab [(ˈwiro:)]ω]ω					*
b.	[(ˈab)]ω [(ˈwiro:)]ω					**!
c.	[(ˈab) wiro:]ω	*!*				
d.	[ab (ˈwiro:)]ω	*!*				*

The analysis as it stands correctly predicts that *dā* should lengthen under cliticization, as with *dāque* 'and give!' in (14).[8] (Lengthening does not occur in *neque* ~ *nec* 'and not,' but this form is plausibly lexicalized.)

(14)

/da kʷe/		Align-L	Align-R	FtBin	Dep-μ	NonFinality
a. ☞	[[(ˈda:)]ω kʷe]ω				*	*
b.	[(ˈda:) kʷe]ω		*!*		*	
c.	[(ˈda kʷe)]ω		*!*			*

Thus, on the present analysis, minimality is not enforced for clitics, where clitics include both obligatory enclitics such as *que* and function words such as *ab* when

---

[8] A reader inquires whether an output-output constraint such as Max-μ-OO "penalize shortening in a derived form relative to its base" might instead be used to ensure that lengthening is preserved in *dāque*. This is unnecessary, as all of the constraints that achieve this end in (14) are independently motivated. Max-μ-OO would be redundant. Moreover, one would have to restrict Max-μ-OO to clitic derivatives (e.g. *dāque*) as opposed to morphological derivatives (e.g. *dáte*).

they are prosodified as clitics, and hence unstressed. If minimality is driven by stress (FTBIN), it goes without saying that it passes over unstressed words. At any rate, even if one puts aside their lack of stress, it is independently clear that minimality cannot apply to proclitics. A phrase such as *ab avō* 'from the ancestor' undergoes resyllabification (as confirmed by the meter), such that the *b* is rendered as an onset rather than as a coda: [a('b a.woː)]. Therefore, *ab* is associated with only one mora on the surface, and would violate minimality if minimality applied to it. Of course, if *ab* is pronounced in isolation or is otherwise stressed, as is always an option for function words (except obligatory enclitics), then minimality applies as normal (no lengthening necessary: [('a$_\mu$b$_\mu$)]$_\omega$). On the absence of underlyingly subminimal function words such as hypothetical /de/, see the end of this section.

3.2.3 *The interaction of minimality and resyllabification*

Resyllabification is the requirement that the final consonant of a word is parsed as the onset of the following word, assuming that the two words occupy the same intonation group (Selkirk 1982, Steriade 1982, Harris 1983, Peperkamp 1997, Hall 1999, Tranel and Del Gobbo 2002). It is the rule in Latin and most of its descendants. An example from Italian, *snob orrendo* 'horrendous snob,' is given in (15-a), omitting for simplicity the mora and foot layers (Peperkamp 1997). The *b* of *snob* is syllabified as the first onset of *orrendo*. (Although the term "resyllabification" implies that it was initially parsed as a coda and then reaffiliated, in a nonderivational framework like classic OT, it is only ever syllabified as an onset.) Although resyllabification in some languages is associated with PWd fusion (cf. Booij 1983, Ọla Orie and Pulleyblank 2002, Gordon and Applebaum 2010, Mudzingwa 2010), resyllabification clearly does not require PWd fusion in the general case in Latin and Romance. For example, parse (15-b) is incorrect for Italian. As Peperkamp (1997) observes, both words retain their word stresses, as confirmed by the open-mid qualities of the vowels, which is diagnostic of stress in Italian. In the diagrams, σ_s indicates a stressed syllable.

(15) (a)

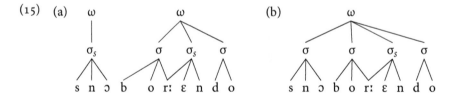

Resyllabification is also the norm in Latin intonation groups, and does not in general implicate fusion (Allen 1973, 1978, Boldrini 1999, Ryan 2013b). This is evident, for one, from verse, where resyllabification throughout the line—even across caesura—is necessary to assign weight correctly. For example, a line of hexameter from Virgil is given in (16). Tie bars indicate C#V junctures, across which resyllabification applies (orthographic *h* is ignored in the last case). The scansion is provided in (17), using solid vertical lines to indicate the boundaries between metra (metrical feet) and the dashed line to indicate caesura. Each one of the six metra must have the form __ (i.e. two heavy syllables) or _◡◡ (i.e. a heavy followed by two lights). A light syllable is one ending with a short vowel, that is, rime V. Thus, in order to metrify such a line, word-final consonants must be assumed to be syllabified with following vowels whenever possible. If a consonant follows, as in *et pater*, resyllabification is blocked, and the syllable is heavy. Therefore, one cannot simply say that word-final consonants are ignored for mora assignment. Metrics is not the only evidence for resyllabification. It is also evident from sandhi, comparative reconstruction, and grammatical treatises.

(16)   et pater Aenēās ‖ et avunculus excitat Hector?

(17)   et   pa   te │ r Ae   nē │ ā ┊ se   ta │ vun   cu   lu │ s ex   ci   ta │ t Hec   tor
        _   ◡   ◡ │ _   _ │ _ ┊ ◡   ◡ │ _   ◡   ◡ │ _   ◡   ◡ │ _   _

If resyllabification always implicated fusion, the entire line in (17) (except *et*) would comprise a single PWd. Aside from the prima facie implausibility of such a parse, the whole-line PWd would violate caesura, which is an obligatory word break (i.e. PWd or higher boundary) in the third or fourth metron. It would also violate the metrical mandate that the initial syllables of the fifth and sixth feet bear word stress (Sturtevant 1919, 1923a, 1923b, Knight 1931, 1950, Allen 1973, Ross 2007, Ryan 2017b). In this case, the fifth and sixth feet are *excitat Hector*, which must be parsed as in (18) (putting aside the foot layer and the resyllabified *s* from the third-last word, *avunculus*).

(18)

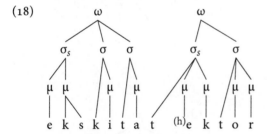

Resyllabification is driven by the constraint Onset, which penalizes a syllable with an empty onset, as in (19). This constraint must dominate any competing constraint that pressures for PWds to align with grammatical words, such as Align-L/R above (McCarthy and Prince 1993, Shih and Zuraw 2016) or CrispEdge (Ito and Mester 1999, Selkirk 2011). Standard assumptions about prosodic phonology also forbid splitting a syllable between two PWds, not shown (e.g. Selkirk 1984, Nespor and Vogel 1986, 2007). Onset is violated also by the absolute-initial vowels in (19); presumably higher-ranked (segmental) Dep, not shown, forbids prothesizing a consonant to prevent this infraction.

(19)

/ekskitat ektor/		Onset	Align-L ┊ Align-R
a. ☞	[eks.ki.ta]ω[t ek.tor]ω	*	* ┊ *
b.	[eks.ki.tat]ω [ek.tor]ω	**!	┊

Consider now a VC word, such as *ab* 'from,' before a vowel-initial word, such as *ōrīs* 'shores.' Four logically possible structures are depicted in (20), of which (a) is arguably correct empirically. Structure (c), without resyllabification, can be ruled out on the grounds that *ab* always scans as light prevocalically (as in the opening line of Virgil's *Aeneid*, from which this phrase is taken). Structure (b) is excluded both because it violates FtBin and because *ab* must be unstressed in this context, as one might expect for a preposition (cf. English *frŏm shóres*). Indeed, in the hexameter cadence (i.e. final two metra), a weak position cannot be filled by a stressed syllable (on the independent evidence for this restriction, see Ryan 2017b and references therein). *Ab ōrīs*, in this case, occupies the cadence, and therefore must possess the amphibrachic stress configuration in (a) or (d). Structure (a) involves adjunction of the preposition to the PWd, forming a recursive PWd, while (d) involves fusion into a single PWd. Here, it is assumed that recursion is the appropriate analysis of cliticization (e.g. Ladd 1986, Wagner 2005, Itô and Mester 2009, Selkirk 2011), as was motivated for Latin above based on stress and lengthening.

(20)

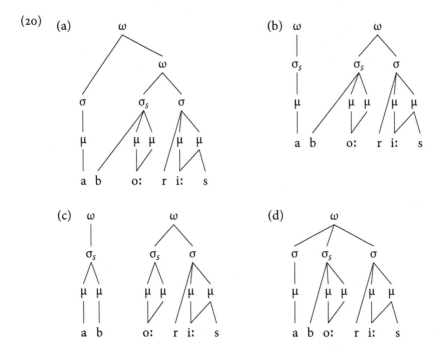

Tableau (21) shows how these same four candidates are evaluated given the constraint ranking established above, now adding Onset to the top.

(21)

/ab oːriːs/	ONSET	ALIGN-L	ALIGN-R	FTBIN	DEP-μ	NONFINALITY
a. ☞ [a[('b oː)riːs]ω]ω	*	*				
b. [('a)]ω[('b oː)riːs]ω	*	*		*!		*
c. [('ab)]ω [('oː)riːs]ω	**!					*
d. [a('b oː)riːs]ω	*	**!				

Resyllabification affects not only function words, but can also render a stressed, lexical word such as *dat* 'gives' subminimal on the surface, as in *dat ōrās* 'gives [the] shores' in (22). Resyllabification never feeds lengthening, as in candidate (b). Lengthening is suppressed in (22) by the output-output (OO) correspondence constraint DEP-μ-OO, which requires that a vowel in a derived form not lengthen relative to its correspondent in its base form (cf. Benua 1995, 1997, Kenstowicz 1996a, Kager 1999, Ussishkin 1999, Steriade 2000, McCarthy 2005, Zuraw 2013, Ryan 2017a). In this case, the derived form is the phrase (*dat ōrās*), and the base form is the free-standing word (*dat*). (*Ōrās* also corresponds vacuously to its isolation form.)

(22)

/dat oːraːs/	DEP-μ-OO	ONSET	ALIGN-L	ALIGN-R	FTBIN	DEP-μ	NONFINALITY
a. ☞ [('da)]ω[('t oː)raːs]ω			*	*	*		*
b. [('daː)]ω[('t oː)raːs]ω	*!		*	*		*	*
c. [('dat)]ω [('oː)raːs]ω		*!					*
d. [da('t oː)raːs]ω			**!*	****			
e. [da[('t oː)raːs]ω]ω			*	**!**			
f. [[('da)]ωt oː.raːs]ω			**!*	*	*		*

3.2.4 *Evidence for degenerate feet*

The evidence that (a) is the empirically correct winner in (22) can be divided into three parts, each supported in turn: (1) lengthening does not occur (as in (b)); (2) resyllabification is not suppressed (as in (c)); and (3) stress on *dat* is not suppressed (as in (d–e)). First, prevocalic *dat* is not repaired by lengthening. Prevocalic VC words are never indicated as long, and metrical scansion confirms the same: The first syllable of VC#V virtually always scans as light.

Second, one cannot maintain that resyllabification is suppressed in cases like *dat ōrās*. As discussed, resyllabification is ubiquitous in Latin and its descendants, applying even across high-level boundaries such as caesura in verse. As more direct evidence against suppression, *dat* in (c), in which resyllabification is suppressed, is a heavy (i.e. bimoraic) syllable. Therefore, one would expect prevocalic *dat* (etc.) to occur freely in metrical positions that require a heavy syllable. But prevocalic VC#V, regardless of whether it is lexical or grammatical, is actively forbidden from such positions, meaning that it cannot be bimoraic. Rather, it must resyllabify.[9]

Third, one cannot maintain that a lexical word like *dat* cliticizes and thereby loses its stress, as was proposed above for function words like *ab*. In general, cliticization does not accompany resyllabification for lexical words; see (15) above and the discussion immediately following it. Furthermore, lexical VC#V (type *dat ōrās*) is actively avoided in verse (in all positions), as demonstrated presently, while grammatical VC#V (type *ab ōrīs*) is not. Meanwhile, both configurations are common in prose. The avoidance of specifically lexical VC#V in verse can be explained if VC#V retains its stress, distinguishing it from grammatical VC#V, which is unstressed. In brief, $[('V)]_\omega$, despite being monomoraic, is too long for a light position by virtue of its stress and monosyllabicity. Meanwhile, all other monomoraic syllables, including unstressed lights and stressed lights in polysyllables, are felicitous in light positions. The remainder of this section elaborates on this analysis.

The metrical corpus employed here is the first six books of Virgil's *Aeneid*, with macrons following Pharr (1964). The meter is the dactylic hexameter, which can be characterized descriptively by the template in (23) (Raven 1965, Duckworth 1969, Halle 1970, Halporn et al. 1980, Prince 1989, Boldrini 1999). An example of a scanned line can be found above in (17). All that is relevant here is that the meter diagnoses whether a syllable is heavy or light. If a syllable is found in positions labeled _ in (23) (here termed HEAVY POSITIONS), it is heavy. If it is found in ⏑ (LIGHT POSITIONS), it is light. This is not the standard metrical terminology, but it is descriptively straightforward and employed in this chapter for simplicity.[10]

(23)

Foot 1		Foot 2		Foot 3		Foot 4		Foot 5		Foot 6	
S	W	S	W	S	W	S	W	S	W	S	W

$$-\left\{ \begin{array}{c} - \\ \cup\cup \end{array} \right\} - \left\{ \begin{array}{c} - \\ \cup\cup \end{array} \right\} - \left\{ \begin{array}{c} - \\ \cup\cup \end{array} \right\} - \left\{ \begin{array}{c} - \\ \cup\cup \end{array} \right\} - \left\{ \begin{array}{c} (-) \\ \cup\cup \end{array} \right\} - \left\{ \begin{array}{c} - \\ \cup \end{array} \right\}$$

In Virgil, VC words such as *ab* and *dat* scan as light prevocalically, indicating that resyllabification applies as normal. That said, however, a closer look at prevocalic VC words in Virgil reveals that they are almost never lexical. Lexical VC words, some of which are otherwise frequent in the corpus, are actively avoided prevocalically. The complete list of VC nouns and verbs in this corpus is provided in (24). Verbs

[9] Ambisyllabicity—the sharing of a consonant between two syllables (Kahn 1976, Gussenhoven 1986, Rubach 1996, Kessler 1998)—would be of no aid here, even if one puts aside various independent objections to ambisyllabicity, especially in a geminate-rich language like Latin (Jensen 2000). If the ambisyllabic consonant were moraic, the syllable is then bimoraic, and incorrectly predicted to be admitted in heavy positions in meter. If, on the other hand, the ambisyllabic consonant were nonmoraic, nothing is gained, since the first syllable would then still constitute a degenerate foot.

[10] The more standard terms from generative metrics (strong vs. weak positions) or traditional metrics (e.g. longum vs. biceps) would require more explanation, since heavy syllables can occupy both position types. It is therefore simpler here to be able to refer directly to a syllable-sized slot in the meter that requires a light syllable, that is, a light position.

here exclude any form of the copula *esse* (e.g. *sum, es*). Of fifty-five such content word tokens, only two occur prevocalically. The lines in which the two cases are found are given in (25). In both, the VC word (*vir* and *fer*, respectively) scans as light prevocalically. Overall, the prevocalic rate for VC lexical words, judging by nouns and noncopular verbs, is 3.6 per cent.

(24)

Word	Pre-C	Pre-V
dat	16	0
det	2	0
fac	1	0
fer	0	1
fit	5	0
it	11	0
rem	2	0
spem	3	0
stat	8	0
stet	1	0
vim	4	0
vir	0	1
Totals	53	2

(25) a. *Hic **vir**, hic est, tibi quem prōmittī saepius audīs*
      b. *Vāde age, et ingentem factīs **fer** ad aethera Trōiam*

The situation is very different for VC function words and for VVC words of any category. Consider first VC function words. The five most common VC prepositions are exemplified in (26). (*Ab* is omitted because it is usually realized as *ā* before a consonant.) In this set, 39.3 per cent of tokens are prevocalic, a starkly different rate from the 3.6 per cent rate for lexical words (Fisher's exact test odds ratio = 17.1, $p < .0001$).

(26)

Word	Pre-C	Pre-V
ad	105	51
in	226	109
ob	5	4
per	74	92
sub	45	38
Totals	455	294

VVC monosyllables are likewise frequently prevocalic regardless of whether they are function or content words. Virgil's aggregate prevocalic rate for VVC function words is 40 per cent (242 of 609) and for VVC content words is 51 per cent (69 of 135). Even when the VVC content word is a paradigmatic counterpart of one of the VC content words in (24), it is not avoided prevocalically. For example, *dat* and *det* are prevocalic zero of eighteen times, while *dās* is prevocalic one of two times. Similarly, *rem* is prevocalic zero of two times, while *rēs* is prevocalic eight of fourteen times.

Spem is prevocalic zero of three times, while *spēs* is prevocalic seven of thirteen times. Though each individual example is not frequent in these illustrations, the aggregate picture emerges clearly that they abide by the general distributions of VC content words (close to 0% prevocalic) vs. VVC content words (roughly 50% prevocalic). Thus, the avoidance of VC content words before vowels cannot be attributed to individual lexical items, nor can it be attributed to a more general avoidance of consonant-final content monosyllables before vowels.

Polysyllables ending with VC are of course not difficult to metrify prevocalically. Their aggregate prevocalic rate is 52 per cent (61% if *m*-final words, which are subject to elision, are excluded). This rate appears not to be substantially affected by functional status.

Finally, as VC function words demonstrate, a VC#V sequence is not difficult to metrify even when VC is a monosyllable. Its near-categorical avoidance for monosyllabic content words like *dat* must have some other cause. Here, it is proposed that this cause is stress. Specifically, the prepositions in (26) normally cliticize, while the nouns and verbs in (24) normally do not. This distinction is illustrated in (27) and (28). These tableaux introduce nothing new, but rather highlight four relevant candidates, two per input. *Dat* does not cliticize in (27-a), but remains a stressed PWd. This is ensured by ALIGN, which, as defined above, requires the edges of lexical words to coincide (as nearly as possible) with the edges of PWds. But because this version of ALIGN does not evaluate function words, *ab* is free to cliticize in (28). Indeed, once ALIGN is out of the picture, cliticization is favored in (28) by both FTBIN and NONFINALITY.

(27)

/dat oːraːs/	DEP-μ-OO	ONSET	ALIGN-L	ALIGN-R	FTBIN	DEP-μ	NONFINALITY
a. ☞ [('da)]ω[('t oː)raːs]ω			*	*	*		*
b. [da[('t oː)raːs]ω]ω			*	**!**			

(28)

/ab oːriːs/	DEP-μ-OO	ONSET	ALIGN-L	ALIGN-R	FTBIN	DEP-μ	NONFINALITY
a. [('a)]ω[('b oː)riːs]ω		*	*		*!		*
b. ☞ [a[('b oː)riːs]ω]ω		*	*				

Unlike in verse, lexical VC words are not avoided prevocalically in prose. As a roughly contemporary (if two or three decades older) prose sample, I take Julius Caesar's *Commentaries on the Gallic War*. Lexical VC is prevocalic 28 per cent of the time, essentially the same rate as functional VC, which is 32 per cent (odds ratio 1.2, $p = .51$). Frequency tables are given in (29) and (30), omitting any all-zero rows.

(29)

Word	Pre-C	Pre-V
dat	7	2
fit	9	4
rem	30	13
spem	14	4
vim	11	4
vir	1	1
Totals	72	28

(30)

Word	Pre-C	Pre-V
ad	520	243
in	816	358
ob	3	13
per	71	35
sub	24	15
Totals	1,434	664

It follows that lexical VC#V is avoided in Virgil's verse for a specifically metrical reason, not for a phonological reason that would apply also to regular speech. The proposal here is that Virgil avoids lexical VC#V because it is neither heavy nor light. Rather, it is intermediate in weight, and therefore excluded from both position types. The proposed constraint *Foot⊂Light penalizes a light position in the meter that contains a foot. In the hexameter, "light position" refers to a light subposition of the BICEPS, that is, one of the syllabic positions in a ∪∪ sequence in (23).[11] Clitic monosyllables such as *ab*#V are not penalized in light positions, presumably because their vowels are not footed. Furthermore, outside of the cadence, stressed light syllables are not penalized in light positions.[12]

For example, Virgil fills one ∪∪ sequence with *brévis*#V, prosodified [('bre.wi)] [s V...], as in (31). The phonological structure is depicted above the segmental tier and the verse structure (∪∪) below it. This form does not violate *Foot⊂Light because neither light position contains a foot. In other words, *Foot⊂Light penalizes

---

[11] Virgil observes this constraint almost categorically, but other poets may not. Brief examination of Ovid, for one, suggests that he observes the constraint as a preference, but not nearly as rigidly as Virgil does. Any poet differences do not undermine the analysis here: It is well known that some poets' versification is sensitive to phonological criteria that others' is not (cf. Milton vs. Shakespeare; Kiparsky 1977, Hayes et al. 2012). In most cases, these differences are not due to differences of dialect, but rather indicate that the poets have internalized subtly different versions of the same meter. For example, some poets happen to be stricter than others, regardless of dialect.

[12] As mentioned above, the hexameter cadence imposes special restrictions on stress, such that weak positions (whether _ or ∪∪) cannot bear stress. These restrictions are orthogonal to the present discussion; see Ryan (2017b) on their analysis.

only degenerate feet in light positions, as in (31-b), which is (nearly) illicit in Virgil, save for a handful of exceptions.

(31)   (a)   (b)

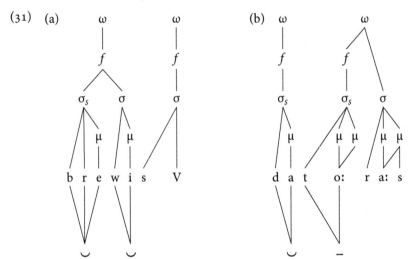

3.2.5 Varying cliticizability

For expositional purposes, the foregoing analysis has oversimplified in assuming a rigid distinction between lexical and functional words. In reality, while it remains the case that nouns and (noncopular) verbs almost never cliticize, some other types of words, such as pronouns, are intermediate in their propensities to cliticize; they are somewhat avoided prevocalically, but not as stringently as content words. The table in (32) shows all VC words with a frequency of five or greater in the metrical corpus.[13] Corpus totals, prevocalic rates, and (necessarily rough) glosses are provided. Rows for Vm words are shaded, as their prevocalic avoidance is possibly influenced by an independent factor. In particular, Vm is realized as a nasalized vowel Ṽ in Classical Latin, as evident in part from the fact that final Vm is normally elided before a vowel (Allen 1978). The poets may have preferentially avoided placing monosyllables in contexts in which they would have to undergo elision, independently motivating the low prevocalic rates of Vm words.

---

[13] I note the following additional exclusions. *Ab, ac,* and *nec* are omitted due to allomorphy (e.g. *ac* is usually *atque* before a vowel). The text is annotated for vowel length, so otherwise identical pairs such as *es* 'are' and *ēs* 'eat' are distinguished, such that the long-voweled forms are excluded. Finally, some VC words plausibly end underlyingly with CC (e.g. *os* 'bone'; cf. *ossa* 'bones'). Such words are excluded. This exclusion applies also to *hic* and *hoc,* which Virgil usually treats as heavy prevocalically (i.e. as implicit VCC), despite their ostensible short vowels. Other exclusions, such as *is,* follow from the frequency cutoff.

(32)

Word	Gloss	N	% Prevocalic
an	'or whether'	10	0
bis	'twice'	14	0
dat	'gives'	16	0
dum	'while'	38	0
fit	'becomes'	5	0
it	'goes'	11	0
stat	'stands'	8	0
ter	'thrice'	15	0
tum	'then'	104	0
cum	'with, when'	115	1
at	'yet'	50	2
quam	'how'	51	2
quem	'what'	43	2
nam	'thus'	24	4
tam	'so'	12	8
sit	'is'	11	9
quod	'what, which'	30	10
ut	'that'	51	10
sed	'but'	74	11
iam	'already'	103	13
vel	'or'	14	14
et	'and'	1,047	16
quid	'what'	43	19
id	'it'	5	20
tot	'that many'	19	21
quis	'who'	38	24
ad	'to'	156	33
in	'in'	335	33
ob	'towards'	9	44
sub	'under'	83	46
per	'through'	166	55
es	'are'	5	80

Some general trends are evident from (32). Prepositions (viz. *per, sub, ob, in,* and *ad*) collectively exhibit the highest prevocalic rates. The one outlier is *cum*, but it is special in at least two respects: First, it ends with *m*, and therefore might be avoided prevocalically due to elision avoidance.[14] Second, it is often conjunctive in

---

[14] As mentioned above, even *m*-final polysyllables are avoided somewhat before vowels relative to those ending in other consonants.

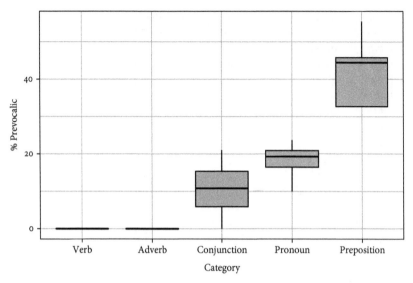

FIGURE 3.1 Prevocalic rates and hence inferred cliticizabilities of five approximate part-of-speech categories of monosyllables in Virgil's *Aeneid* I–VI. Verbs and adverbs (and nouns, not shown) are the least cliticizable, while prepositions are the most cliticizable.

force, introducing clauses. Nouns, adverbs, and noncopular verbs all exhibit zero or near-zero prevocalic rates, arguably because they resist cliticization, being lexical words. Note that *tot* is more connective in force ('so many...that many'), and therefore treated not as an adverb but as a conjunction. The remaining words, which might be termed loosely pronouns and conjunctions, are intermediate between prepositions and lexical words. All of these categories are summarized as a box plot in Figure 3.1. The box plot excludes Vm words.

Recall that lexical words are prevented from cliticizing by ALIGN constraints, specifically ALIGN(LexWd, Right, PWd, Right) and its left-left equivalent, which can be together abbreviated as ALIGN-L/R(LexWd). To implement intermediately cliticizable categories such as pronouns, additional ALIGN-L/R constraints can be posited for other categories, for example ALIGN-L/R(Pro). (It is also conceivable that contentfulness is stringent, for example LexWord, LexWord+Conjunction, LexWord+Conjunction+Pronoun, etc.) These constraints can then be numerically weighted in a framework such as maxent HG (§2.8.1). The precise weights are not important here, as the goal of this discussion has been only to argue that resyllabification of a VC content word yields a degenerate PWd. The fact that some lexical categories pattern as intermediate between content words and function words is both orthogonal to this argument and straightforwardly implemented by tailoring weighted alignment constraints to more fine-grained lexical categories.

3.2.6 *Latin minimality: conclusion*

In conclusion, this section maintains, with previous scholarship, that prosodic minimality in Latin is driven in part by foot binarity. A new argument here is that subminimal prosodic words regularly do surface in Classical Latin, once one considers whole phrases and not just isolated words. In particular, VC content words retain their stress while simultaneously undergoing resyllabification, resulting in a degenerate foot and hence subminimal PWd on the surface. The syllable created when a stressed VC word undergoes resyllabification is neither heavy nor light, but intermediate in weight, and therefore cannot (except rarely) be employed in regulated verse, at least for Virgil. Virgil, it is proposed, observes *FOOT⊂LIGHT, which forbids a light position from containing an entire foot, ruling out degenerate feet in light positions even though they are monomoraic. Proclitics such as *ab* are not footed and are therefore free, if prevocalic, to occupy light positions in verse.

A short vowel in a stressed monosyllable is typically longer than both (1) an unstressed short vowel and (2) a stressed short vowel in a polysyllable. As such, a short vowel in a stressed monosyllable is too long for a light position in verse, unlike (1) and (2). A similar situation has been demonstrated for Japanese, where an underlyingly short-voweled monosyllable such as *ki* 'tree' is significantly longer than a light syllable in a polysyllabic PWd (e.g. *ki ga* 'tree NOM'), but at the same time significantly shorter than an underlyingly bimoraic monosyllable such as *ki:* 'key' (Mori 2002, Braver and Kawahara 2012, 2014). More generally, a stressed monosyllable reflects the culmination of three independent dimensions of lengthening: First, stressed syllables are longer than unstressed syllables, all else being equal (ACCENTUAL LENGTHENING; Turk and Sawusch 1997, Turk and White 1999, Turk and Shattuck-Hufnagel 2000). Second, final syllables are longer than nonfinal syllables, all else equal (FINAL LENGTHENING; Delattre 1966, Lindblom 1968, Wightman et al. 1992, Turk and Shattuck-Hufnagel 2000, 2007, Lunden 2006). Finally, syllable duration is inversely correlated with the number of syllables in the word, all else equal (polysyllabic shortening; §1.2). In short, if a stressed monosyllable is forced to be monomoraic, it is expected to be longer than all other monomoraic syllables. It is perhaps not surprising, then, that some poets might eschew such a syllable in metrically light positions.

As one final issue, this analysis recognizes explicitly that function words are not always required to be minimal, since they are not always footed. (In cases when they are footed, I maintain, they are required to be minimal.) Minimality only applies to words when they are stressed. Therefore, if a word is realized in a context in which it lacks stress, nothing forces it to be minimal. The present analysis thus predicts, potentially incorrectly (but see the next paragraph), the possibility of V function words that alternate on the surface between short and long depending on whether they are cliticized in the particular utterance (a situation that has been documented for Northern Sami; Neilsen 1926, Gordon and Applebaum 2010). For example, a hypothetical preposition such as /de/ is predicted to be possible, which would generally be short before its object, but sometimes long in other contexts. This is at first glance not the case: Function words (except enclitics) are generally minimal in their underlying forms, which means that they are realized as minimal whether cliticized or not. In other words, they are minimal through concurrence (Ketner 2006), not repairs.

One response to this concern is that any such alternating forms might tend to be leveled historically in favor of their nonalternating, that is, long, allomorphs. For example, *prō* 'for' was historically **pro*, and is indeed still *pro* in many Classical forms (e.g. *profugiō* 'I flee,' *profundus* 'deep'; cf. *prōpōnō* 'I put,' *prōmittō* 'I promise'). It is conceivable that at some point *prō* was in flux, lengthening when footed but not necessarily otherwise. At any rate, by Classical Latin, any such fluctuations were leveled by positing the long vowel as underlying, such that the unstressed form would match its stressed form and abide by minimality regardless of stress.[15] Second, the proclitics of Classical Latin may have been stressed in earlier stages of Latin (see Radford 1903 on Terence). If this was the case, they would have come to acquire long vowels via FtBin, and there would then be no reason to undo the length after the language shifted away from phrase-initial stress. Finally, at least one V function word arguably does alternate in length depending on whether it is realized as a clitic or not. *Nē* 'not' is realized as *ne* as an enclitic (e.g. *estne* 'is it?') or prefix (e.g. *nescio* 'I do not know'), but when it appears as an independent word, for example as an interjection or conjunction, it is long. Thus, the premise that function words never alternate might itself be challenged.

3.3 Māhārāṣṭrī Prakrit: gradient contextual prosodic minimality

Māhārāṣṭrī Prakrit (Middle Indo-Aryan) has a bimoraic minimum (Ollett 2012:256).[16] Similar to Japanese, the only consonant that is permitted word-finally is a kind of placeless, moraic nasal, called *anusvāra* and transcribed *ṃ*. Resyllabification of *anusvāra* is optional. That is, VN#V can scan either as heavy, without resyllabification (Vṃ .V), or as light, with resyllabification (V.m V). When the nasal resyllabifies, it is recorded as plain *m*; when it does not, it is recorded as *ṃ*. Superheavy syllables are not permitted; thus, if a word ends with a consonant, it ends with -Vṃ ~ -Vm.

Some Māhārāṣṭrī verses are given in (33), from the *Sattasaī*. In every case, the first N-final word shows N resyllabifying (as *m*) and the second N-final word shows N failing to resyllabify before a vowel (remaining *ṃ*). This distinction is crucial for scansion: Metra, indicated by bars, are required to comprise four moras (excepting the antepenultimate and ultimate metra in (33), which comprise single syllables). For more on the meter, which is the *āryā*, see §4.1.

---

[15] Aside from analogy, phonotactics often also conspire to favor long vowels in V words. For example, short *o*, *u*, and *i* generally do not occur word-finally in Latin, except due to iambic shortening (e.g. *ego* alongside *egō*), which is irrelevant for monosyllables. Thus, even putting minimality aside, *prō* arguably could not be short in Classical Latin anyway. Additional possible confounds favoring length in some V words include case (as in *quā*, an inflected form of *quī* or *quis*) and compensatory lengthening (as in *ē* for *ex*). However, phonotactics, case, and compensatory lengthening cannot motivate the long vowels of *dē*, *sē*, *tē*, *mē*, and *nē*. Therefore, it remains clear that minimality is active for V function words, as this analysis maintains, though the set of words for which it is crucially invoked is small.

[16] Māhārāṣṭrī is sometimes spelled Mahārāṣṭrī, but the former, with *vṛddhi*, is more correct (Ollett 2012:243).

(33)   a. diṭṭam a|ṇukkhit|tamuhaṃ |ēsō |maggō |ku|lavahū|ṇaṃ   (526cd)
      b. ṇivvara|ṇam aṇiv|vūḍhē |ṇivvū|ḍhē jaṃ |a|ṇivvara|ṇaṃ   (255cd)
      c. pikkaṃ|vaṭṭhivi|ṇiggaa|kōmala|m aṃvaṃ|ku|raṃ ua|ha   (62cd)

Resyllabification can affect both monosyllables and polysyllables, though it is significantly more frequent for the latter, as summarized for the *Sattasaī* in (34). Consonant-final monosyllables (which are always C_0Vm) resyllabify 6 per cent of the time, while consonant-final polysyllables (which always end with -Vm) resyllabify 33 per cent of the time (Fisher's exact test $p = .025$).[17] Monosyllables are also somewhat less likely to be prevocalic than polysyllables (6.1% vs. 8.2%, respectively), though this difference is not significant.

(34)

	Monosyllable	Polysyllable
Pre-V, resyllabifies	1	55
Pre-V, does not resyllabify	16	114
Pre-C	262	1,880

The different behavior of monosyllables and polysyllables can be explained by prosodic minimality. Resyllabification threatens the minimality of monosyllables, but not of polysyllables. Therefore, it is more likely to be suppressed for monosyllables. Assuming that ONSET drives resyllabification and FTBIN drives minimality (along with a requirement that words not lose their footing altogether), FTBIN > ONSET achieves this state of affairs: Resyllabification occurs (satisfying ONSET) except when doing so impinges on FTBIN by stealing the second mora of a word. However, because there is some variation, the ranking is not strict.

3.4 Tamil

While Māhārāṣṭrī Prakrit suppresses the resyllabification of a VC monosyllable, Tamil repairs it: When a VC monosyllable immediately precedes a vowel in Tamil, the consonant is geminated, allowing it to serve simultaneously as an onset (satisfying ONSET) and coda (satisfying FTBIN). The full analysis is presented in §3.4.6. Tamil thus exemplifies the third logically possible response to a prosodically minimal VC word being placed in prevocalic position. Latin permits resyllabification but does not repair the word; Māhārāṣṭrī suppresses resyllabification, meaning that the word does not need to be repaired; and Tamil permits resyllabification, but repairs the word to bring it back up to size.

---

[17] The one token of a monosyllable resyllabifying appears to be legitimate. A second apparent case involving *taṃ taṃ* was not counted, since *taṃ taṃ* appears about half the time as a single word *taṃtaṃ*, and was plausibly prosodified as a disyllable rather than as a sequence of two monosyllables.

3.4.1 *Overview of prosodic minimality in Tamil*

Standard Tamil, like Latin, observes a strict bimoraic minimum for words of all types (Christdas 1988, 1996, Gordon 2006, Ryan 2013b). VC (with the caveats in the next two paragraphs) and VV both count as minimal rimes, while V does not. Like Latin, the vast majority of Tamil roots are underlyingly minimal, and as such do not need to be repaired (cf. concurrence; Ketner 2006). But some subminimal roots are found, confirming that the grammar actively enforces minimality, among other evidence below. For example, the infinitives [ʋaɾa] 'to come' and [ʈaɾa] 'to give' correspond to the 2sg. imperatives [ʋaː] and [ʈaː], respectively. The vowel lengthening in these cases can only be explained by minimality, as vowels do not otherwise lengthen in imperatives (e.g. [naɖa] 'walk!') or shorten in infinitives (e.g. [poːɣa] 'to go' in (35)). The parallelism with Latin is striking, though the two languages are unrelated; (35) summarizes the pattern for both languages.[18]

(35)

Language	Root	Gloss	Infinitive	2SG Imperative
Latin	/staː/	'stand'	[staːre]	[staː]
Latin	/da/	'give'	[dare]	[daː]
Tamil	/po:/	'go'	[poːɣa]	[poː]
Tamil	/ʋa(ɾ)/	'come'	[ʋaɾa]	[ʋaː]
Tamil	/ʈa(ɾ)/	'give'	[ʈaɾa]	[ʈaː]

Tamil differs from Latin in that (traditionally, at least) an isolated PWd cannot end with an obstruent.[19] Thus, isolated VT is illicit as a PWd in Tamil. But this gap is motivated by general phonotactics, not by minimality. Even when minimality is not at stake, a PWd cannot end with an obstruent. VT is a licit syllable nonfinally, where its coda is clearly moraic; but it is illicit absolute-finally, regardless of the size of the word. Moreover, even while the bimoraic minimum remains in force in the modern language, obstruent-final loanwords are becoming more common (see §3.4.2 below), corroborating that this gap is unrelated to minimality.

There is, however, an exception to the minimality of VC that cannot be attributed to phonotactics: VC is minimal only if the coda is nonrhotic. If the coda is one of the two rhotics (namely, [ɾ] or [ɻ]; McDonough and Johnson 1997, Narayanan et al. 1999, Keane 2004), the word is subminimal. VR (R being any rhotic) occurs neither as a root nor as a PWd. Some monosyllabic words are exemplified in (36) (University of Madras *Tamil lexicon*, 1924–1936).

---

[18] It is not obvious whether the rhotic should be posited in the underlying forms of these two Tamil roots. Infinitives always end with [-a], but the preceding consonantism varies according to verb class (Hart 1999, Schiffman 1999, Asher and Annamalai 2002). With either option, the pair is irregular: If the rhotic is part of the root, its loss in the 2sg imperative is irregular (cf. *uʈkāra* 'to sit'; *uʈkār* 'sit!'). If the rhotic is not part of the root, its appearance in the infinitive is irregular. However, the question is irrelevant here, since vowel lengthening in either case can be explained only by minimality.

[19] In the context of a phrase, however, a Tamil word can end with an obstruent due to sandhi with the following word (see (46) below for some examples).

(36)

	Short Vowel		Long Vowel	
	pon	'gold'	poːn	'trap'
	poj	'lie'	poːj	'went (converb)'
	*po	(subminimal)	poː	'go'
	*poɾ	(subminimal)	poːɾ	'wear'
	*poɻ	(subminimal)	poːɻ	'be cleft'
	kal	'stone'	kaːl	'leg'
	kaj	'hand'	kaːj	'unripe fruit'
	kaɳ	'eye'	kaːɳ	'sight'
	*ka	(subminimal)	kaː	'protect'
	*kaɾ	(subminimal)	kaːɾ	'be pungent'
	*kaɻ	(subminimal)	kaːɻ	'solidity'

This gap is entirely systematic. For instance, (37) and (38) show frequencies of the two rhotics in various phonological contexts in the *Rāmāyaṇa* of Kamban, a medieval Tamil epic (Hart and Heifetz 1988, critical edition Kamban 1956). Token counts are given first, followed by type counts in parentheses.[20] The absence of VR words is also suggested by the earliest (c. 200 AD) Tamil grammar, the *Tolkāppiyam* (1.2.14ff; Murugan 2000).

(37)

	Rime type:			
	Vɾ		Vɻ	
Final in Monosyllable	0	(0)	0	(0)
Final in Polysyllable	10,617	(2,549)	345	(71)
Word-Medial	35,344	(14,199)	9,877	(4,195)

(38)

	Rime type:			
	VVɾ		VVɻ	
Final in Monosyllable	2,356	(41)	269	(16)
Final in Polysyllable	4,954	(2,165)	43	(39)
Word-Medial	6,595	(3,043)	2,159	(838)

As these frequencies also clarify, rhotic codas are felicitous after short vowels when minimality is not at stake; consider frequent words such as [aʋaɾ] 'he (polite),' [tamiɻ] 'Tamil,' and [kaɾʋam] 'pride.' Furthermore, when minimality is unthreatened, vowel length is contrastive before rhotics; consider [aʋaɾ] 'he (polite)' vs. [kiɻaːɾ] 'water lift,' or [kaɾmam] 'karma' vs. [aːɾmai] 'sharpness.' Recordings (from the CD

---

[20] In some editions of Kamban, the three words *a* 'that,' *i* 'this,' and *or* 'one' (one of a few forms of 'one' for Kamban, alongside the more usual *oru* and *ōr*) are written as separate orthographic words, but there is no doubt that these items are proclitics when they appear in these forms.

accompanying Hart 1999) were checked for rime [aɾ] vs. [aːɾ], confirming that the orthographic vowel length contrast is indeed realized as expected phonetically. Thus, prerhotic length in Tamil cannot be attributed to a more general prerhotic lengthening process, as in, for instance, Dutch (e.g. *giro* [ˈxiːro] 'gyro'; Gussenhoven 1993, 2008).

3.4.2 *Loanwords support the subminimality of VR*

Loanword phonology also supports VR failing to achieve minimality. Loanwords in Tamil of the shape VR invariably have a long vowel (as (38) would suggest), even when the corresponding vowel in the donor language is short.[21] For example, Sanskrit words such as *sphira* 'abundant flow', *dharā* 'house', and *dur-* 'bad' correspond to Tamil [piːɾ], [ʈaːɾ], and [ʈuːɾ], respectively. Greek *árēs* 'Ares' was borrowed into early Tamil as [aːɾ] 'Mars'. In nonminimality contexts, comparable lengthening is not found (e.g. [kaɾmam], [kaɾumam], or [kam] < Sanskrit *karman* or Prakrit *kamma* 'karma'). The Sanskrit prefix *dur-* 'bad' is only long in Tamil in its isolation form, *tūr* [ʈuːɾ]. When employed as a prefix (or first part of a compound) in Tamil, it remains short, even when the stem to which it is attached is of Dravidian origin, for example *turmaṇam* [ʈuɾmaɳam] 'bad smell'.

Although English loanwords are numerous in contemporary Tamil, they are arguably not diagnostic of minimality. To be sure, they are consistent with VR being subminimal. English words such as *sir* and *car* are invariably borrowed with long vowels—[saːɾ] and [kaːɾ], respectively—while other consonant-final monosyllables with lax vowels are borrowed with short vowels, e.g. [kap] 'cup', [cek] 'check', [mes] 'mess', and [pen] 'pen' (Hart 1999; as in Japanese, lax vowels tend to map to short vowels; Takagi and Mann 1994, Dupoux et al. 1998). On the one hand, this discrepancy is consistent with hypothetical words such as *[saɾ] and *[kaɾ] being subminimal and therefore repaired by lengthening. On the other hand, the vowels in *sir* and *car* are long in English (e.g. [sɜː] and [kʰɑː], though the dialect from which these words were originally borrowed might have been rhotic). As further support for this second possibility, Japanese has borrowed these same two words with long vowels ([saː] and [kaː]). The loanword [paːɾk] 'park' in Tamil further supports that stressed English *-ar-* is rendered as [aːɾ] regardless of minimality, since [paɾk] would be minimal. Thus, English loanword phonology is mute on the question of whether VR is subminimal or not, while loanwords from other languages, such as Sanskrit, support the conclusion.

3.4.3 *Rhotics are nongeminable in Tamil*

As just established, VC is minimal in Tamil except when C is a rhotic. An analysis of this situation is that rhotics are not moraic in the language. This conclusion is supported not only by minimality, but also by geminability. A standard analysis of the

---

[21] The one exception that I have encountered is the brief entry *ṭar* in the Madras *Tamil lexicon* for Hindi *ḍar* 'fear', though this word has no entry (with a long or short vowel) in the extensive Tamil dictionary, *Kariyāviṉ taṟkālat Tamiḻ akarāti* (University of Madras 1992) and was absent from my poetic corpora.

difference between a singleton and geminate is that the latter alone projects a mora, as in [ama] vs. [amma] in (39) (e.g. Hyman 1985, McCarthy and Prince 1986, Zec 1988, Hayes 1989, Morén 2001).

(39)   (a)   (b)

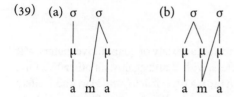

The rhotics are the only consonants in Tamil that cannot geminate. All other consonants, including the glides and laterals, are frequent as geminates and actively susceptible to gemination by phonological rules (e.g. Christdas 1988, Rajam 1992, Lehmann 1994, Nagarajan 1995, Murugan 2000). Indeed, since length is also contrastive for all Tamil vowels, it can be said that the two rhotics are the only segments in the language that do not admit a length distinction.[22] Although one might expect that a tap per se cannot admit a length distinction on phonetic grounds, many languages exhibit distinctive phonological length in the rhotics, sometimes with the singleton being a tap and the geminate being a trill (Bradley 2001). Moreover, only one of the two rhotics in Tamil is a tap (McDonough and Johnson 1997, Narayanan et al. 1999, Keane 2004; §3.4.7).

Beyond their nongeminability, the rhotics are also the only sonorants in Tamil that cannot undergo onomatopoetic overlengthening. Overlengthening is indicated in the script by multiplying a character, for example, *taṉṉṉeṉa* 'pleasant' in *Malaipaṭukaṭām* §352. This process, known in Tamil as *aḷapeṭai*, is employed for purposes of onomatopoeia, emphasis, or metrical exigency (Thinnappan 1976, Rajam 1992).

The nonmoraicity of rhotics is one possible cause for their nongeminability. Nevertheless, some languages forbid the geminate rhotics even when rhotics are otherwise moraic, so nongeminability does not entail nonmoraicity. Sanskrit and Prakrit, for instance, permit all consonants that can be both onsets and codas to geminate except the rhotic *r*, which is repaired when it occurs in the input (across a juncture; e.g. Sanskrit /punaɾ ɾaːmas/ → /punaː ɾaːmah/; Whitney 1889:§179). Biblical Hebrew and Wolof are also reported to permit geminate obstruents, laterals, and glides, but not rhotics (Podesva 2002). The same holds of Pulaar, except that the voiceless continuants (*s*, *f*, and *h*) join *r* in being nongeminable (Niang 1997:48). In Hindi, the retroflex rhotics are among only a handful of segments unable to geminate (Ohala 1983). In West Germanic gemination (e.g. Gothic *saljan* vs. Old English *sellan*), the rhotic is the only consonant not subject to gemination (though Old English acquired geminate *rr* through assimilations such as **ster-la > steorra* 'star') (Donka Minkova, p.c.).

---

[22] The Old Tamil letter called *āytam* independently cannot be an onset, and is therefore not geminable for that reason. But it is moraic and can also undergo overlengthening, as described in the next paragraph, unlike the rhotics.

In at least some of these languages, coda rhotics are moraic. In Sanskrit and Prakrit, for instance, VR scans as heavy in verse. In Pulaar, VR counts as heavy for stress. Thus, the nongeminability of rhotics in Tamil, while consistent with their being nonmoraic, does not entail their nonmoraicity.

3.4.4 VR is light in Tamil meter

Kamban's *Rāmāyaṇa* epic, cited above, comprises a variety of quantitative meters. VR syllables normally scan as light in these meters, with V and against all other VC. One frequent meter in Kamban is schematized in (40) (a type of *āciriyam*; Hart and Heifetz 1988, Niklas 1988, Zvelebil 1989, Parthasarathy 1992, Rajam 1992, Ryan 2017b). As before, a position labeled _ must be filled by a heavy, while ∪ must be filled by a light; additionally, × is anceps, accepting a syllable of any weight. Also like Latin, resyllabification applies throughout the line, and a vowel usually elides immediately preceding another vowel. Various sandhi rules apply; one important rule, revisited below, is that the final consonant of a VC word geminates before a vowel.

(40)   _ × / _ ∪ × / _ ∪ × / _ ∪ ×

Three of Kamban's quatrains in this meter are given in (41) through (43) (verses 55, 402, and 700). Standard romanization is given first, IPA second, the latter annotated for syllables (periods) and metra (slashes).[23] VR rimes in non-anceps positions are boldface in the IPA. In every case, they occupy light positions.

(41)   a. *vāṇakam taṇil, maṇṇiṇiṇ, maṇ uyir*
       b. *pōṇakam taṇakku eṇṟu eṇum puntiyaḷ,*
       c. *tāṇavaḷ, kumatip peyarāḷ taṇai*
       d. *ūṇ ozittaṇaṇ vaccirattu umpar kōṇ.*

       a. [ʋaː.na/ɣaɳ .ʈa.nin /maɳ.ɳi.nin /man.n u.jiɾ]
       b. [poː.na/ɣaɳ .ʈa.nak/k en.d e.ɳũ /puɳ.ɖi.jaɭ]
       c. [ʈaː.na/ʋaʈ .ku.ma/ɖip .pe.ja/ɾaːʈ .ʈa.nǎj]
       d. [uː.n o/ɹiʈ.ʈa.nan /ʋac.ci.ɾaʈ/ʈ um**baɾ** koːn]

(42)   a. *vēḷai veṇṟa mukattiyar vem mulai,*
       b. *āḷai, niṇṟu muṇintiṭum, aṅku orpāl;*
       c. *pāḷai tanta matupparuki, paru*
       d. *vāḷai niṇṟu matarkkum maruṅku elām.*

       a. [ʋeː.ɭǎj /ʋen.da .mu/ɣaʈ.ʈi.jaɾ /ʋem .mu.lǎj]
       b. [aː.ɭǎj /nin.du .mu/niɳ.ɖi.ɖum /aŋ**g** oɾpaːl]
       c. [paː.ɭǎj /ʈaɳ.ɖa .ma/ɖup.pa.ɾu/ɣi .pa.ɾu]
       d. [ʋaː.ɭǎj /nin.du .ma/ɖaɾk.kũ .ma/ɾuŋ.g e.laːm]

---

[23] In Tamil romanization, underlined coronals are alveolar, dotted coronals are retroflex, and unmarked coronals are dental. Z represents the retroflex rhotic [ɻ] and *r* represents an alveolar plosive (which would become a postalveolar tap in later Tamil).

(43)   a. *ītu muṉṉar nikazntatu; ivaṉ tuṉai*
       b. *mā tavattu uyar māṉpu uṭaiyār ilai;*
       c. *nīti vittakaṉ taṉ aruḷ nērntaṉir,*
       d. *yātu umakku aritu? eṉṟaṉaṉ īṟu ilāṉ.*

       a. [iː.ḍu /munnaɾ ni/ɣaɪn.ḍa.ḍ i/ʋan .tu.ŋǎj]
       b. [maː .ṭa/ʋaṭ.ṭ u.jaɾ /maːŋ.p u.ṱǎj/jaː.ɾ i.lǎj]
       c. [ṉiː.ḍi /ʋiṭ.ṭa.ɣan /tan.n a.ɾuɳ /ŋeːɾn.ḍa.niɾ]
       d. [jaː.ḍ u/mak.k a.ɾi/ḍ en.da.na/n iː.d i.laːn]

To demonstrate that these examples are representative, particularly since exceptions to the meter occasionally occur even for securely heavy or light syllables (Ryan
2017b), Figure 3.2 depicts the aggregate heavy (i.e. metrically strong) vs. light (i.e.
metrically weak) rates of seven rime types in 908 hand-parsed lines of Kamban. V is
any short vowel; R is rhotics; N is nasals; L is laterals; T is plosives; W is glides; and
VV is long vowels. VR is grouped empirically with V, supporting the nonmoraicity of
rhotic codas. However, a possible confound in Figure 3.2 is that VR is not distributed
in words like the other rime types: It is rarely initial, whereas all of the other rime
types are frequently initial.[24]

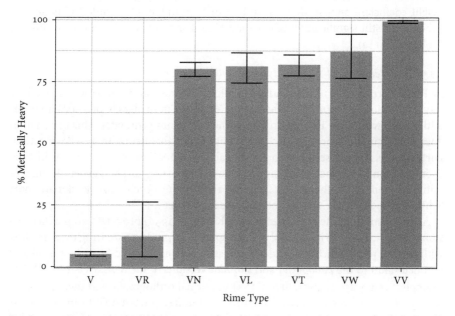

FIGURE 3.2 Rates with which rime types are found in heavy (strong) as opposed to light (weak)
positions in a Middle Tamil poem.

---

[24] The explanation for this gap is the prosodic subminimality of VR. Roots ending with rhotics are
typically either VVR or VRV, and longer words are created by adding suffixes to these roots.

	β	SE	z	p
(Intercept)	8.250	1.117	7.4	< .0001
Rime = VC	− 6.488	0.856	− 7.6	< .0001
Rime = VR	− 13.674	3.507	− 3.9	< .0001
Rime = V	− 13.541	0.968	− 14.0	< .0001

FIGURE 3.3 Regression table for rime placement in 908 lines of Kamban. β is the coefficient estimate (greater ⇒ heavier); SE is β's standard error; z is β/SE; and p indicates significance. The baseline rime level is VV. Random intercepts are not shown.

That said, if one controls for position in the word, the conclusion that VR is light remains unaltered. One means of controlling for word shape is through regression, in this case, a mixed-effects logistic regression. The dependent variable is whether each token is placed in a metrically heavy (coded 1) or light (coded 0) position. The single fixed effect is rime shape, here with levels VV, VC, VR, and V. VV is the baseline level against which the others are compared in Figure 3.3. Rimes of other shapes are excluded. The model includes random intercepts for word shape, that is, the binary template of the syllable with the syllable's position in that template X-ed out (e.g. HXH for a rime in a trisyllabic word between two heavies). As Figure 3.3 shows, VR has a weight coefficient almost identical to that of V in this model, while VC is heavier (albeit itself still significantly lighter than VV). For more details on this technique, see Ryan (2011a).

3.4.5 *The interaction of minimality and resyllabification*

In Premodern Tamil, unlike Latin, violations of prosodic minimality induced by resyllabification are repaired. Whenever a VC word immediately precedes a vowel-initial word within the intonation group, the consonant geminates. This gemination does not occur for words whose minimality is not threatened by resyllabification. Furthermore, it is not sensitive to the lexicality of the VC word, as Latin was in §3.2. Even function words such as *eṉ* 'my' are repaired. Note that accent is generally phrase-initial in Premodern Tamil (cf. Christdas 1988, 1996, Bosch 1991, Beckman 1998, Schiffman 1999, Krishnamurti 2003, Keane 2003, 2006).

As an illustration, the critical edition of Kamban (1956) provides two parallel versions of the text, one in its normal orthographic form, and one showing the same text with sandhi, resyllabification, and metron structure, as it would be pronounced and scanned (akin to the *padapāṭha* and *saṃhitā* versions of the Sanskrit Ṛg-Veda). For example, verse 1,050 is given first in (44) in normal orthography and then in (45) in its *saṃhitā* form. Both are romanized from the Tamil script, but no information is lost or altered in the transliteration. Note that the first word of lines (a) and (c), undoubled in (44), geminates before a vowel in (45). Other examples of this phenomenon can be found in the verses parsed above, such as at the end of the first line of (41).

(44) எள் அரும் திசைகளோடு, யாரும், யாவையும்,
கொள்ளை வெண்ணிலவினால் கோலம் கோடலால்,
வள் உறை வயிர வாள் மகரகேதனன்
வெள்ளணி ஒத்தது வேலை ஞாலமே

   a. *eḷ arum ticaikaḷōṭu, yārum, yāvaiyum,*
   b. *koḷḷai veṇṇilaviṉāl kōlam kōṭalāl,*
   c. *vaḷ urai vayira vāḷ makarakētaṉaṉ*
   d. *veḷḷaṇi ottatu vēlai ñālamē.*

(45) எள்ளருந் திசைகளோ டியாரும் யாவையும்
    கொள்ளைவெண் ணிலவினாற் கோலங் கோடலால்
    வள்ளுறை வயிரவாண் மகர கேதனன்
    வெள்ளணி யொத்தது வேலை ஞாலமே

   a. *eḷḷarun ticaikaḷō ṭiyārum yāvaiyum*
   b. *koḷḷaiveṇ ṇilaviṉār kōlaṅ kōṭalāl*
   c. *vaḷḷurai vayiravāṇ makara kētaṉaṉ*
   d. *veḷḷaṇi yottatu vēlai ñālamē.*

Such doubling does not occur for larger words, such as the line-initial VCVC words at the beginning of every line in (46) and (47) (verse 1,056, in a longer meter). Other examples of non-doubling include *nōkkiṉ* in (a), the second token of *okkum* in (a), and so forth.[25]

(46) a. *viṭaṉ okkum neṭiya nōkkiṉ amiztu okkum iṉ colār tam*
   b. *maṭaṉ okkum maṭaṉum uṇṭē! vāḷ nutal orutti, kāṇāt*
   c. *taṭaṉ okkum nizalaip poṉ cey taṉ naṟum tēral vaḷḷattu*
   d. *uṭaṉ okka uvantu nīyē uṇṇāti tōzi! eṉṟāḷ.*

(47) a. *viṭaṉokku neṭiya nōkki ṉamiztokku miṉco lārtam*
   b. *maṭaṉokku maṭaṉu muṇṭē vāṇuta lorutti kāṇāt*
   c. *taṭaṉokku nizalaip poṉcey taṉṉaṟun tēral vaḷḷat*
   d. *tuṭaṉokka vuvantu nīyē yuṇṇāti tōzi yeṉṟāḷ.*

Similarly, VVC monosyllables never undergo gemination prevocalically. For example, *ūṉ ozittaṉaṉ* stands as such in verse 55, cited in (41) above.

Prevocalic gemination applies even to VCV words that become VC words due to elision. In Old Tamil, several adjectives have the form VCV, for example, *putu* 'new,' *neṭu* 'long,' *kuṟu* 'short' (Lehmann 1994).[26] Before a vowel-initial word, the final *u* is elided, as is normal (see the verses above), and the consonant must then geminate. For example, *ezuttu* means 'letter.' The Old Tamil word for 'long letter' (geminate or long vowel) is *neṭṭezuttu*, not *neṭezuttu. Similarly, a short (*kuṟu*) letter is a *kuṟṟezuttu* (recall that *ṟ* transliterates a plosive, not a rhotic). The interest of such adjectives for the present discussion is that some have the form VRV, with a medial rhotic, for instance *paza* 'old' (*z* being the romanization of [ɻ]), *iru* 'big,' *peru* 'big,' *aru* 'difficult,' *oru* 'one,' and *iru* 'two' (*ibid.*). Before a vowel, the rhotic cannot geminate (§3.4.3). Rather, the vowel lengthens in these cases. For example, 'one' (*oru*) 'letter' (*ezuttu*) is *ōr ezuttu*,

---

[25] The word *kāṇāt* at the end of (b) does not contradict the claim above that isolated PWds cannot be obstruent-final, since it has acquired its *t* via gemination of the following initial in (c).

[26] Kamban, for his part, who represents Middle rather than Old Tamil, has moved away from this type of adjective, using instead derivative forms such as *putiya* 'new,' *neṭiya* 'long,' and *kuṟiya* 'short.'

and 'two letters' is *īr ezuttu*. Before a consonant, all of these adjectives assume their isolation forms (e.g. *oru mozi* 'one word', *iru mozi* 'two words').

3.4.6 Analysis

To summarize the section so far, Standard Tamil has two rhotics, [ɾ] and [ɻ], notated R here. They are unique among consonants in that they are never moraic. First, they do not contribute to prosodic minimality. VC is minimal except when the coda is a rhotic. Second, the rhotics are the only consonants that cannot geminate, even when gemination is otherwise compelled. Third, VR is treated as light in quantitative meter, against all other VC. Available evidence is therefore unanimous on their nonmoraicity. Finally, words are required to be minimal feet not only in isolation, but also in the context of the phrase. Because resyllabification is also obligatory within phrases, minimality forces the final consonant of a VC(u) word to geminate prevocalically, except when gemination is impossible, as with R, in which case the vowel lengthens instead.

The nonmoraicity of rhotics is implemented here by the constraint $*\mu/R$. On the phonetic motivation for this constraint, see §3.4.7 below. $*\mu/R$ dominates WbyP, which requires codas to be moraic. Both $*\mu/R$ and WbyP must dominate MAX-μ in order to rule out richness-of-the-base inputs with geminate rhotics, as in tableau (48). Shortening the input geminate incurs a violation of MAX-μ, on the assumption that input gemination is represented moraically (§2.3.1, §2.6.4). In the following tableaux, the moraicity of every coda is indicated. If the consonant has subscript μ, it is moraic; if it does not, it is nonmoraic.

(48)

/aɻ_µa/		$*\mu/R$	WbyP	MAX-µ
a. ☞	[(a.ɻa)]_ω			*
b.	[(aɻ.ɻa)]_ω		*!	
c.	[(aɻ_µ)ɻa]_ω	*!		

As before, minimality is enforced by FTBIN, as shown in (49) for a hypothetical richness-of-the-base input /aɻ/ (cf. loanwords such as Sanskrit *dur-* > Tamil *tūr*).

(49)

/aɻ/		$*\mu/R$	FTBIN	DEP	WbyP	MAX-µ	DEP-µ
a. ☞	[(aːɻ)]_ω				*		*
b.	[(aɻu)]_ω			*!			*
c.	[(aɻ_µ)]_ω	*!					*
d.	[(aɻ)]_ω		*!		*		

An input such as *eṇ* [en] 'my' in (50), by contrast, is already minimal in isolation, and need not be repaired. With $*\mu/R$ being irrelevant, nothing stops coda /n/ from being parsed as moraic, regardless of its input moraicity. /n/ is not moraic in the input in this tableau, but if it were, the winner would be the same; the winner would just lack the violation of DEP-μ in that case.

(50)

	/en/	*μ/R	FtBin	Dep	WbyP	Max-μ	Dep-μ
a.	[(eːn)]_ω				*!		*
b.	[(enu)]_ω			*!			*
c. ☞	[(en_μ)]_ω						*
d.	[(en)]_ω		*!			*	

As discussed, a word like *en* geminates when prevocalic. In (51), *en ūr* /en uːɾ/ 'my city' is realized as [en.n uːɾ]. Resyllabification is compelled by Onset, as in Latin; it cannot be obviated by epenthesis, given highly ranked Dep. Unlike Latin, the degenerate foot created by resyllabification is not left to stand: FtBin is now undominated. Fusion of the two words into a single word is not optimal, given Align-L and Align-R, which in this case stand for Align(GramWd, L/R, PWd, L/R). Alignment is not sensitive to lexical status, as it was in Latin; it applies to all grammatical words. Therefore, fusion of the two words into a single PWd, as in candidate (c), or cliticization of the first word without footing it, as in (d), are unavailable. As an alternative to Align-L/R, one could employ GramWd=PWd to require that every grammatical word head a PWd, as in Gordon and Applebaum (2010). Dep-μ above is now split into two constraints, Dep-μ/V and Dep-μ/C, the former dominating the latter. This ranking ensures that lengthening the consonant, as in (a), is favored over lengthening the vowel, as in (g), as a response to FtBin. The constant violation for WbyP arises from the final rhotic, while the constant violation of Onset is due to the phrase-initial vowel, which is left to stand.[27]

(51)

	/en uːɾ/	*V.V	*μ/R	FtBin	Dep	WbyP	Onset	Max-μ	Align-L	Align-R	Dep-μ/V	Dep-μ/C
a. ☞	[(en_μ)]_ω[(n uːɾ)]_ω					*	*		*	*		*
b.	[(en_μ)]_ω [(uːɾ)]_ω					*	**!					*
c.	[(e.n uːɾ)]_ω					*	*		**!	**		
d.	[e[(n uːɾ)]_ω]_ω					*	*		*	**!		
e.	[(e)]_ω[(n uːɾ)]_ω			*!		*	*		*	*		
f.	[(en_μ)]_ω [(ʋuːɾ)]_ω				*!	*	*					*
g.	[(eː)]_ω[(n uːɾ)]_ω					*	*		*	*	*!	

Finally, an input like /oɾu uːɾ/ 'one city' in (52) is realized as [oːɾ uːɾ]. *V.V prevents the underlying vowel hiatus from surfacing as such. Hiatus is resolved in this case by deletion rather than insertion, given Dep ≫ Max-μ.[28] The rhotic then must resyllabify, but it cannot geminate, given *μ/R and WbyP. Vowel lengthening is therefore employed as a last resort.

---

[27] This analysis refers to standard, premodern Tamil. In present-day spoken Tamil, phrase-initial /e/ is usually accompanied by prothesis, as [ʲe] (Keane 2004), which would require a somewhat different ranking.

[28] It is debatable whether the underlying form of "one" is in fact /oɾu/ or /oɾ/, though lexicon optimization favors the former. At any rate, even if it were analyzed as /oɾ/, hiatus resolution would then be irrelevant in this case (but not in general), and the proposals here would not be materially affected. Resyllabification-triggered lengthening occurs either way.

(52)

/oɾu uːɾ/	*V.V	*μ/R	FtBin	Dep	WbyP	Onset	Max-μ	Align-L	Align-R	Dep-μ/V	Dep-μ/C
a. ☞ [(oː)]ω[(ɾ uːɾ)]ω					*	*	*	*	*	*	
b. [(oɾμ)]ω [(uːɾ)]ω		*!			*	**	*				*
c. [(oɾμ)]ω[(ɾ uːɾ)]ω		*!			*	*	*	*	*		*
d. [(oːɾ)]ω[(ɾ uːɾ)]ω					**!	*	*	*	*	*	
e. [(oːɾ)]ω [(uːɾ)]ω					**!	**	*			*	
f. [(o.ɾu)]ω [(uːɾ)]ω	*!				*	**					
g. [(o.ɾu)]ω [(ʋuːɾ)]ω				*!	*	*					
h. [(o.ɾ uːɾ)]ω					*	*	*	**!	**!		
i. [o[(ɾ uːɾ)]ω]ω					*	*	*	*	**!		
j. [(oɾ)]ω [(uːɾ)]ω			*!		**	**	*		**		
k. [(oɾ)]ω[(ɾ uːɾ)]ω			*!		**	*	*	*	*		

3.4.7 The realization and sonority of Tamil coda rhotics

This section seeks to clarify two points, first, that the Tamil coda rhotics are in fact true consonants, as they are transcribed above (as opposed to being deleted or realized as vowel colorations), and second, that they are highly sonorous consonants, intermediate between the laterals and glides in sonority, as is normal typologically. This will set the scene for discussion of the naturalness of *μ/R.

As mentioned above, conservative Tamil, like closely related Malayalam (Asher and Kumari 1997) and arguably Proto-Dravidian (Krishnamurti 2003), distinguishes between two rhotics, namely, the (pre)alveolar tap [ɾ] and the palatal rhotic

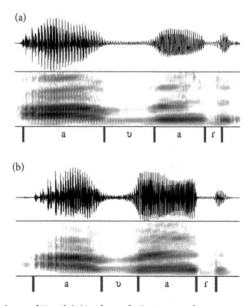

FIGURE 3.4 Two tokens of Tamil /ɾ/ in the coda (408 ms and 314 ms windows, respectively).

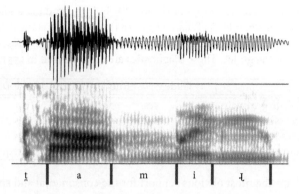

FIGURE 3.5 Tamil /ɻ/ in the coda (372 ms window).

approximant [ɻ] (McDonough and Johnson 1997, Narayanan et al. 1999, Keane 2004). Segmented waveforms and spectrograms of the two rhotics are provided in Figure 3.4 (two tokens of [aʋaɾ] 'he (polite)') and Figure 3.5 (one token of [ṱamiɻ] 'Tamil'). The recordings are from the CD accompanying Hart (1999) and the graphics were made in Praat (Boersma and Weenink 2017).[29]

Phonotactically, the rhotics pattern as a highly sonorous natural class. For instance, only a vowel, glide, or rhotic—but not a lateral or any other consonant—can precede a geminate or cluster (Murugan 2000:1.2.14). This constraint is an active factor in allomorphy. For example, the dative suffix surfaces as *-ku* after a stem ending in an obstruent, nasal, or lateral, and as geminated *-kku* elsewhere, including after vowels, glides, and rhotics, and regardless of the weight of the stem-final syllable. The plural suffix *-(k)kaḷ* exhibits similar allomorphy.

Second, only the nasals, laterals, and obstruents trigger progressive place assimilation across coronals (e.g. /ṱaːn/ 'indeed' in [ṱamiɻ ṱaːn] 'Tamil indeed' vs. [kaṇ ṭaːn] 'eye indeed'; cf. Murugan 2000:1.5ff). Third, nasals and laterals often alternate with homorganic stops in Premodern Tamil sandhi, whereas glides and rhotics never undergo such alternations. For example, a lateral typically becomes the homorganic obstruent when it immediately precedes obstruent, assimilating in (non)sonorancy, as in /kal-pu/ → [katpu] 'chastity' (cf. /caːr-pu/ → [caːrpu] 'place'); these rules also operate across word boundaries, as can be seen in the *saṃhitā* versions of the verses in §§3.4.4–3.4.5. Fourth, poetic rhyme provides some evidence for sonority. In Tamil half-rhyme, the span of melodic correspondence normally begins with the first post-vocalic consonant (Rajam 1992, Ryan 2007). But poets sometimes skip over the first post-vocalic consonant in assessing rhyme (e.g. [oːjnṱa] ∼ [eːnṱu] in Kamban

[29] Some contemporary Tamil dialects have innovated a third rhotic, the postalveolar tap [ɾ] (romanized *r*; Christdas 1988:131, Narayanan et al. 1999, Keane 2004), making for up to five contrastive liquids in total— [r], [ɾ], [ɻ], [l], [ɭ]—though [ɻ] often nowadays merges with [ɭ] and [ɾ] with [r]. But [ɾ] is clearly derived from an alveolar stop [t ∼ d] in earlier Tamil and is still pronounced as such in some conservative dialects. Thus, for present purposes, I consider only conservative Tamil with its two-rhotic system.

§6,852). As in this example, skipping is most likely if the coda is a glide, the most vowel-like of the consonants. As Rajam (1992:193) observes, it is the next most likely with the rhotics [ɾ] and [ɻ], again suggesting that they are more vowel-like than all consonants except the glides. These diagnostics are summarized in (53).

(53)

	Glide	Rhotic	Lateral Nasal Obstruent
Can precede geminate	yes		no
Triggers assimilation	no		yes
Alternates with plosive	no		yes
Skippable in rhyme	most frequent	next most	very infrequent

Finally, perhaps the most obvious support for the consonantal and sonorant qualities of the rhotics comes from their phonetic characteristics (cf. Parker 2002), including the fact that both are spontaneously voiced liquids, being a tap and an approximant, respectively, and were likely such throughout their reconstructible history (Krishnamurti 2003). In both cases, the rhotic is not just a coloration of the vowel (as in the Dravidian language Badaga, with its rhotacized vowels; Emeneau 1939:43, Ladefoged and Maddieson 1996:313), but a distinct constriction following the vowel, as can be seen clearly in Figures 3.4–3.5. While these acoustic snapshots of course represent a present-day speaker, coda /ɾ/ and /ɻ/ were present as such throughout the history of Tamil and must have been realized as sonorant consonants in that position also in Old and Middle Tamil, judging by their phonological behavior, by their internal reconstruction, and by the descriptions of them in early grammatical treatises. Thus, the nonmoraicity of the rhotics cannot be dismissed on the grounds that the rhotics were simply deleted or absorbed as rhotacized vowels.

3.4.8 *μ/R: discussion

*μ/R "a rhotic must not head a mora" is at first glance an unnatural constraint. Moraicity is putatively tied to sonority, such that if a phenomenon assigns moras to only a subset of segments, that subset is uniformly more sonorous than the nonmoraic subset (Zec 1988, 1995, 2003, Prince 1999, Gordon 2001, 2002b, 2006, de Lacy 2004, Crowhurst and Michael 2005, Gordon et al. 2008, Nevins and Plaster 2008). For example, in many languages, only vowels are moraic; vowels are more sonorous than consonants. If a cutoff divides the vowels, it is typically lower and/or longer vowels that are heavier, again consistent with their greater sonority. Similarly, if a cutoff is drawn among the consonants, it is typically the sonorants that are moraic and the obstruents that are not. Contour tone or pitch accent licensing, for instance, often bifurcates coda consonants in this manner (e.g. Steriade 1982, Zec 1995, Zhang 2002, 2004, Gordon 2006). Moreover, if stress placement is sensitive to the sonority of the coda, the sonorants are normally heavier as a class (as in Kwak'wala, Nuu-chah-nulth, Lamang, Inga Quechua, Paipai, and Huehuetla Tepehua; Zec 1995, Gordon 2001, 2006, Kung 2007).

Standard Tamil violates this putative universal. Phonological and phonetic diagnostics unanimously agree that its rhotics [ɾ] and [ɻ] are highly sonorous consonants (§3.4.7). Indeed, they pattern as intermediate in sonority between the glides and the laterals, as is typical cross-linguistically (Wiese 2001, Parker 2002). The (Tamil and typical) sonority hierarchy is given in (54); only the rhotic class, boldface, cannot project moras.

(54)   Obstruent < Nasal < Lateral < **Rhotic** < Glide < Vowel

And yet the evidence from phonological weight in at least three independent systems converges on the rhotics being nonmoraic. First, they uniquely do not contribute to prosodic minimality (§§3.4.1–3.4.2). Second, they are uniquely light in quantitative meter (§3.4.4). Third, they are uniquely nongeminable; all other phonemes exhibit distinctive length (§3.4.3; although, as discussed, nongeminability does not entail nonmoraicity). Additional potentially relevant systems, such as weight-sensitive stress, are not diagnostic.[30] Meanwhile, all nonrhotic codas, whether greater or less in sonority than rhotics, contribute to weight. For example, all nonrhotic consonants (including glides) geminate, contribute to minimality, and so forth.

We are forced to conclude that weight distinctions do not necessarily follow from sonority. Nevertheless, if one considers the phonetic realization of the Tamil rhotics, their nonmoraicity is arguably natural in a different sense. The tap, for its part, is much shorter than other consonants. Preliminary examination of six tokens of word-final [ɾ] in isolated words of the shape VVR revealed [ɾ] to have a mean duration of 32 ms. To compare another, nonrhotic sonorant, take the alveolar nasal [n]. In six tokens of the same frame (VVN), its mean duration was 88 ms, over twice as long as the tap. Given these stark differences, the lighter weight of the tap is hardly surprising.

This account does not extend straightforwardly to Tamil's other rhotic, [ɻ], which clearly patterns as nonmoraic phonologically, but is harder to pin down phonetically, for a few reasons. First, as an approximant, it is more difficult to delimit from the vowel. Second, the realization of [ɻ] varies by dialect and register. Perhaps most contemporary speakers merge /ɻ/ and /l̪/ to /l̪/ (which is why English received the name of the language, which ends with this sound, as *Tamil* rather than *Tamir*). In Old and Middle Tamil, it must have been a retroflex rhotic of some kind, but it is uncertain whether its manner was more flap-like or approximant-like (present-day pronunciation favors the latter, but could have shifted from a millennium ago). Even today it is sometimes described as a flap, as in Hart (1999), who dubs it a "lateral flap," perhaps in consideration of the rhotic-lateral merger. Finally, regardless of how /ɻ/ is realized, it is considerably less common than /ɾ/, perhaps one tenth as frequent (see (37) above). Thus, it is conceivable that even if not particularly short in its own right, it might have piggybacked on /ɾ/ phonologically, given that the rhotics are a natural class (cf. Hayes 1997, 1999 and Gordon 2002b on this notion of phonological symmetry at the expense of phonetic uniformity).

---

[30] Stress in Premodern Tamil is nondistinctive and usually claimed to fall on the initial syllable, the conservative Dravidian pattern (Zvelebil 1970, Christdas 1988, Hart and Heifetz 1988, Beckman 1998, Schiffman 1999, Krishnamurti 2003, Keane 2003, 2004, 2006). However, in some dialects, a VV peninitial attracts stress away from a V, but not VC, initial (Christdas 1996, Gordon 2004b). In such dialects, a word like [kaɾmaː] would be diagnostic of the weight of VR for stress. However, VRCV: words are uncommon, and I am not aware of where the evidence stands on this question.

In conclusion, weight classes usually correspond to sonority cutoffs, but not always. In Tamil, the rhotics are nonmoraic, and hence light, despite being highly sonorous consonants in codas. Phonologically, the behavior of the two phonemic rhotics is identical. Phonetically, they diverge, in that one is a short tap, while the other is a longer approximant. The short duration of the tap conceivably motivates its treatment as nonmoraic, but the same explanation is problematic for /ɻ/, as just discussed. At any rate, the tap is by far the more frequent rhotic.

A final question concerns why this special treatment of rhotics is not more frequent typologically. In the vast majority of languages with weight-by-position and (realized) rhotic codas, rhotics are moraic. Phonetic detail is likely to be part of the explanation. Even in languages in which rhotics are taps intervocalically, they are often realized otherwise (as trills, approximants, or fricatives) in coda position, effectively lengthening (cf. e.g. Willis and Bradley 2008 on Spanish). On the other hand, some language-specificity in minimality is likely even when one controls for rhotic allophony; for example, Murik contrasts [ˈsaɾ] 'stomach' with [ˈsaːɾ] 'type of shark' (Abbott 1985). It remains for future research to test how far phonetic differences between Tamil and languages with moraic coda rhotics can motivate their divergent phonology.

3.5 Conclusion

Latin, Tamil, and Māhārāṣṭrī Prakrit all exhibit resyllabification. In Latin, resyllabification can render PWds surface-subminimal, that is, degenerate feet, where evidence supports that they remain stressed as opposed to cliticizing. These degenerate PWds are frequent in prose, but Virgil avoids them almost categorically in verse. The proposal here is that they are avoided in verse because, descriptively, they are neither heavy nor light, but an intermediate category. Specifically, Virgil cannot put degenerate PWds in heavy positions because they are not bimoraic, and he cannot put them in light positions because they are too long phonetically, violating a constraint against filling a light position with a foot. Thus, while degenerate PWds are felicitous in normal speech, they are resisted in meter.

In Tamil, by contrast, PWds that would be subminimal due to resyllabification are repaired, either by gemination or by lengthening. Moreover, Tamil furnishes a case of minimality being sensitive to the type of consonant that occupies the coda. Because rhotics cannot project moras in Tamil, as independent evidence corroborates, they cannot contribute to minimality. The nonmoraicity of Tamil rhotics can be explained by their phonetics. The more common of the two rhotics is substantially shorter than other consonants. But rhotic nonmoraicity cannot be explained by sonority, as all diagnostics point to the rhotics being highly sonorous consonants, intermediate between the laterals and glides, their usual place in the sonority scale typologically. Therefore, weight classes do not always align with sonority cutoffs (contra conventional wisdom; e.g. Zec 1995). Finally, Māhārāṣṭrī Prakrit is intermediate between Latin and Tamil, in that it (preferentially) suppresses the resyllabification of VC monosyllables, thereby preserving the minimum in context.

4

Quantitative meter
Categorical and gradient weight

4.1 Introduction

At first glance, the subject of syllable weight for poetic meter may appear trivial. Nearly all of the world's quantitative meters are described as exhibiting the same arity and criterion, namely, binary weight with the so-called LATIN CRITERION (i.e. light iff C_0V). To the extent that languages ostensibly vary in the scansion of weight, it is usually attributed to differences in syllabification rather than to weight per se. For example, VtrV is heavy in Sanskrit but (usually) light in Latin. This difference is conventionally ascribed to syllabification, that is, Vt.rV in Sanskrit vs. V.trV ($\sim$ Vt.rV) in Latin (cf. Steriade 1982, Devine and Stephens 1994). In this sense, Sanskrit and Latin treat weight identically, but diverge in terms of syllable structure.

As this chapter argues, even if one puts aside issues related to syllabification, weight is richly complex in quantitative meter. Indeed, some of the most fine-grained weight scales yet documented for any phonological phenomenon derive from meter (Ryan 2011a, 2011b). In perhaps all such cases, the complexity coexists with a binary criterion. Thus, the conventional analysis of weight as dichotomous is not incorrect; it is just not a complete description of the meter. To give one example, in the Ancient Greek hexameter, heavy syllables are permitted both initially and finally in the METRON (metrical foot). But metron-final heavies tend significantly to be heavier heavies than metron-initial heavies, all else being equal. From this discrepancy, a continuum of intra-heavy weight is diagnosed, which includes VT $\lesssim$ VN $\lesssim$ VV $\lesssim$ VVC, and appears ultimately to dissolve into a continuum of weight (§4.4.2).

As background, a meter is termed QUANTITATIVE if it relates syllable weight or mora count to metrical strength.[1] Quantitative meter is often opposed to accentual meter, which regulates stress, but in fact a single meter can be simultaneously quantitative and accentual (Ryan 2017b). Quantitative meters vary along a continuum typologically in terms of the importance that they ascribe to syllables vs. moras, as

---

[1] A definition such as "a quantitative meter is any meter that regulates weight" would belie the standard usage of the term, as even the English iambic pentameter would then be identified as quantitative. For example, for some English poets, a metrical position may be filled by two syllables, but only if the first is light. This is a quantitative restriction, but it concerns position size rather than metrical strength (see Hanson and Kiparsky 1996:299).

Prosodic Weight. First edition. Kevin M. Ryan.
© Kevin M. Ryan 2019. First published 2019 by Oxford University Press.

Syllabic	Syllabo-Moraic	Moraic
(as in Tocharian)	(as in Sanskrit)	(as in Japanese)

FIGURE 4.1 The typological range of quantity sensitivity in meter, from purely syllabic to purely moraic.

schematized in Figure 4.1. At one extreme are SYLLABLE-COUNTING meters, which fix the number of syllables per line but neglect their weights, as in, for instance, French (Biggs 1996), Georgian (Silagadze 2009), and Tocharian (Bross et al. 2013, 2014)—usually, though not always, languages lacking phonemic vowel length. This label is an oversimplification in two respects. First, "counting" should not be taken literally. If a line requires, say, eight syllables, it need not be because the poet counts to eight; rather, it presumably reflects nested structure with simple constraints such as, "a line/hemistich/foot must be binary" (see §4.6 on the *haiku*). Second, these meters sometimes turn out to exhibit subtle sensitivities to weight and/or stress, even though they do not enforce them rigidly (e.g. Bross et al. 2013 on Tocharian B, Kümmel 2018 on Gathic Avestan). Thus, the true extremes of the continuum in Figure 4.1—a truly pure syllabic or moraic meter—may not exist. A Tocharian B verse is exemplified in (1) (THT 5 a4–6). Every line of this meter must be fourteen syllables, reflecting the colometry 4$^|$3$^{||}$4$^|$3 (where $^{||}$ is a major caesura and $^|$ a minor caesura).

(1) a. wñā-neś (po)yśi $^|$ karuntsa $^{||}$ mā tañ ñyātstse $^|$ śolantse :
     b. mā r= asānmeṃ $^|$ laitalñe $^{||}$ cem sklok ptārka $^|$ pälskomeṃ :
     c. kos tne ñakta $^|$ pelaikni $^{||}$ (po) śaiṣṣents= ā$^|$naiwacci :
     d. tary= akṣā-ne $^|$ pudñäkte $^{||}$ teki ktsaitsñe $^|$ srukalñe 68

At the other extreme are MORA-COUNTING meters, in which each line must contain a fixed number of moras. In the most extreme cases, syllable structure is ignored (again with the caveat that subtle tendencies might obtain). Japanese *haiku*, with its 5-7-5 tercets, is the most famous example. Moraic meter is also found in the *karintaa* chants of the Arawakan language Nanti (Michael 2004). A refrain couplet is followed by verse couplets. The mora counts of the two lines of the refrain are normally duplicated in each verse. Two illustrations are provided in (2). In (a), the moraic pattern is 7-6, and in (b), it is 7-7. Unlike Japanese, nasal codas do not count as moraic in Nanti meter, despite being true codas (Crowhurst and Michael 2005). It can also be seen in (2) that syllable count is not regulated, nor is the distribution of heavies and lights.

(2)	a.	Refrain	iinkiro iinki	7 moras	(5 syllables)
			iinkiro bee	6 moras	(5 syllables)
		Verse	birorityo tyamparo	7 moras	(7 syllables)
			kogapage pini	6 moras	(6 syllables)
	b.	Refrain	kee kage kakega	7 moras	(6 syllables)
			kee kage kakega	7 moras	(6 syllables)
		Verse	pairo nopuhoo-	7 moras	(5 syllables)
			nopuhonkatakera	7 moras	(7 syllables)

Most of the world's quantitative meters fall somewhere between these two extremes. Within this range, meters vary widely in how sensitive they are to moras vs. syllables. Vedic Sanskrit meters, for instance, come close to being syllabic, in that lines have fixed syllable counts, but certain positions are regulated for weight (Oldenberg 1888, Arnold 1905, Kiparsky 2018). For example, Vedic meters of the DIMETER type comprise lines of eight syllables each, of which the fifth position is light, the sixth heavy, and the seventh light, as in (3). Positions in the first half of the line—and the ultima—are largely free (notated ×), though they might exhibit a weak tendency towards the iambic pattern implied by the specified positions (Ryan 2014).

(3)   × × × × ◡ ⏤ ◡ ×

The licenses in (3) reflect two putative universals of quantitative meter. First, line-final position is typically indifferent to weight (FINAL INDIFFERENCE). This may be due to final lengthening, which prolongs a final light; it might also be attributed to extrametricality, such that the ultima is essentially in fermata (Ryan 2013a). Second, endings tend to be stricter than beginnings (FINAL STRICTNESS). These two principles might seem at first blush to be at odds with each other, but the term "final" has different scopes. Final indifference affects only the ultima, whereas final strictness applies more generally across metrical constituents (but never overrides final indifference). Thus, metrical strictness tends to increase up to the penult, inclusive. Final strictness may follow from prosodic headedness, in that constituents above the metron are head-final (cf. Hayes 1983 on English). For example, if the second hemistich is the head hemistich, mapping constraints can be indexed to the head (cf. Ryan 2017b on Latin and Old Norse). This analysis would comport with natural prosody, where there is a tendency across languages for prosodic constituents above the p-phrase to be right-headed, even in verb-final languages (see §5.12.1). Note also that final indifference, as defined, applies only to quantitative as opposed to accentual meters, but final strictness applies to all meters.

Closer to the mora-counting end of the spectrum, some meters exhibit lines of fixed mora count, but impose restrictions on how those moras are distributed in syllables. Take the Sanskrit/Prakrit *āryā* meter (Ollett 2012; cf. also Deo 2007). Each line comprises eight metra (*gaṇas*). Each metron normally comprises four moras, with two exceptions: First, the line-final metron comprises only a single syllable, of any weight (though it is traditionally scanned as bimoraic even if light; cf. final indifference above). Second, the sixth metron of even lines must be a light syllable. Thus, odd lines have thirty moras, even lines twenty-seven. The grouping into four-mora blocks is not merely a descriptive convenience. For one, it rules out certain syllabic configurations a priori. For example, both lines in (4) contain thirty moras. But only (a) is a possible odd-parity *āryā*, since (b) splits a syllable between metra.

(4)   a.   ⏤◡◡|⏤◡◡|⏤◡◡|⏤◡◡|⏤◡◡|◡◡◡◡|⏤◡◡|⏤   (30 moras)
         b. *⏤◡⏤◡◡◡|⏤◡◡|⏤◡◡|⏤◡◡|◡◡◡◡|⏤◡◡|⏤   (30 moras)

Moreover, certain metra are internally constrained syllabically. In particular, an odd-parity metron must not be ◡⏤◡, while the sixth metron of an odd-parity line must be ◡⏔◡. (◡⏤◡ is special in that it is the only grouping of four moras that cannot be divided into two positions of two moras each.) A descriptive syllabic template for the *āryā* is given in (5) (ignoring boundary requirements), and exemplified by a couplet in Māhārāṣṭrī Prakrit in (6) (*Sattasaī* 148).

(5)

(6) a. ṇiddā|lasapari|ghummira|taṃsava|laṃtad|dhatāra|ālō|ā
     b. kāmas|sa vi duv|visahā |diṭṭhiṇi|vāā |sa|simuhī|ē

As mentioned at the outset of this chapter, nearly all quantitative meters observe the Latin criterion (light iff C_0V), whereby codas count for weight. The Khalkha criterion (light iff C_0VC_0), which ignores codas, is considerably less common for metrics than it is for stress (where the two criteria are roughly equally frequent). For example, in his survey of syllable weight across phenomena, Gordon (2006) notes eighteen languages with weight-sensitive meter in his sample.[2] Every one employs the Latin criterion. Nevertheless, he offers three caveats. First, Fijian lacks codas, and is therefore actually indeterminate between the Latin and Khalkha criteria. Second, the sample is not genealogically diverse, in that almost all of the meters derive, either by inheritance or borrowing, from two broad metrical traditions, namely, Indo-European and Semitic. For example, Malayalam and Thai are not Indo-European languages, but their meters ultimately descend from Sanskrit. Third, he mentions Kayardild (Evans 1995) as being one case of the Khalkha criterion for metrics, though the language was not included in his core survey.

Nevertheless, this conclusion about Kayardild is not secure from Evans (1995). The relevant passage appears to be a spell for raising the dead, quoted in (7) (p. 597). This is part of a twelve-line text, but the remainder of the text, as with Evans' other texts, is prose.

(7)   7. dangka=tha=ka   raba-nharra   dangka=tha=ka   raba-nharra
      8. riin-ki=ka   mawurru-wa   riin-ki=ka   mawurru-wa
      9. dangka=tha=ka   raba-nharra   dangka=tha=ka   raba-nharra
     10. riin-ki=ka   mawurru-wa   riin-ki=ka   mawurru-wa
         riin-ki=ka   mawurru (sic)

Evans (1995) notes the "strict 4/4 metre" of this fragment, adding that "the long vowel in *riinki* is metrically equivalent to two short vowels." Thus, the meter is

---

[2] These are Arabic, English, Estonian, Fijian, Finnish, Ancient Greek, Hausa, Hindi, Hungarian, Old Icelandic, Japanese, Latin, Luganda, Malayalam, Persian, Tamazight Berber, Telugu, and Thai.

not syllable-counting, since long vowels count for double. But codas are evidently irrelevant, as in *dangka=tha=ka*, where *tha* and *ka* are "syllabic fillers" used to bring the metron up to size, coda [ŋ] being inert. That said, the passage contains only four words, repeated, of which *riinki=ka* is one. It is therefore not strong evidence for an established meter that ignores codas.

Nanti, however, is a strong case for the Khalkha criterion in metrics. As treated above, long vowels count as bimoraic for the meter, but coda nasals (the only codas) are ignored. Michael (2004) quotes several lines in which nasals appear not to count towards the moraic total. He notes that the mora count requirement is not entirely rigid (p. 252f), which means that one should approach isolated examples with caution, but the Khalkha criterion appears to be systematic.

A third case that might be mentioned in this connection is Gathic Avestan meter. Avestan is traditionally taken to be syllable-counting, but Kümmel (2018) argues that it exhibits weight sensitivity. As he suggests, these tendencies largely, though not entirely, ignore consonants. On his account, this is because clusters are usually parsed into onsets, often at the expense of sonority sequencing (e.g. "ə$_\mu$.rš may$_{\mu\mu}$"). One might entertain the alternative that codas are parsed normally, but vary in their moraicity (cf. Kwak'wala in §2.1). In other words, whether the Latin or Khalkha criterion is appropriate hinges on the analysis of syllabification. However, the question of weight-sensitivity in Avestan meter is rife with subtleties, and I leave it here (cf. also Bross et al. 2013 on the question of weight-sensitivity in Tocharian B syllable-counting meters, though Tocharian lacks long vowels).

Weight criteria for metrics are usually binary, but Persian adds to the Latin criterion sensitivity to a superheavy (i.e. trimoraic) grade, yielding the scale $V < VX < VXX$ (Hayes 1979b, 1988). Superheavies scan as $\smile\cup$ line-internally and as $\smile$ line-finally. Because of this line-final treatment, one cannot simply say that they are de facto disyllabic.

4.2 Variable weight due to optional processes

In many quantitative meters, certain syllable types are free to scan as heavy or light. As this section describes, such syllables need not be regarded as being intermediate in weight. They are traditionally analyzed in terms of optional rule/process application (which is not to imply that they can only be analyzed that way, as discussed below). Four examples are presented, namely, optional resyllabification, variable syllabification of clusters, optional shortening in hiatus, and variable final vowel length.

4.2.1 Optional resyllabification

First, as treated in §3.3, a Māhārāṣṭrī Prakrit word may end with either a vowel (long or short) or a short vowel followed by the nasal *anusvāra*, transcribed *ṃ*. When an *ṃ*-final word immediately precedes a vowel-initial word, *ṃ* optionally resyllabifies as its onset, becoming *m*. With resyllabification, the ultima scans as light; otherwise, it remains heavy. Thus, while one might speak loosely of final VN being intermediate in weight, or acategorial, as standardly analyzed, it evinces an optional process in binary weight setting.

4.2.2 *Optional cluster or geminate compression*

Second, the best-known case of variable weight concerns *muta cum liquida* (MCL) clusters, as in Latin and Ancient Greek. I consider Virgil's Latin here. MCL-eligible clusters in Latin include any nonstrident obstruent plus liquid, that is, {p, b, t, d, k, g, f} plus {r, l} (though one might exclude *tl* and *dl*). As traditionally analyzed, MCL clusters are optionally COMPRESSED into onsets (*a.kra*) or SPLIT across syllables (*ak.ra*). Clusters straddling a word or morpheme boundary are normally split (*ab .lī.to.ra, ab.lā.ta*), and those in word onsets are normally compressed (*da.re .brac.chia*), such that syllable boundaries tend to coincide with morpheme boundaries. MCL clusters are also assumed to be compressed after a long vowel or consonant, though their status in this context is irrelevant for scansion, since weight is not affected (*crē.bra*). Variation is found after a short vowel when the vowel and cluster are tautomorphemic. In (8), for instance, *suprēmum* is compressed in (a), scanning as ⏑‒‒, but split in (b), scanning as ‒‒‒.

(8) a. vul.ne.ri|bus .dō|nec $^{||}$ .pau|lā.t$_{im}$ ē|vic.ta .su|prē.mum   (*Aeneid* 2.630)
     b. con.di.mu|s et .mag|nā $^{||}$ .sup|rē.mum |vō.ce .ci|ē.mus   (*Aeneid* 3.68)

Some MCL clusters are more likely to be compressed than others. Figure 4.2 shows the approximate compression rates for Virgil based on books I–VI of the *Aeneid* (with macrons from Pharr 1964). Only clusters immediately following a short vowel within the word are considered, excluding the prefixes *ab-*, *ob-*, and *sub-*. An automated parser collected all lines containing each cluster in this context and attempted parsing the line with and without compression, tallying which (if any) treatment was successful. (In some cases, due to extraneous factors, neither treatment succeeds, in which case the line is ignored; but it is never the case that both succeed.) The error bars in Figure 4.2 are 95 per cent confidence intervals based on the binomial. Clusters attested fewer than ten times in the relevant context are excluded (viz. *dr, fl, fr, tl, dl*, and *gl*).

One trend that is clear from Figure 4.2 is that voiceless MCL clusters (TR) are more compressible than voiced ones (DR). Steriade (2008) notes a similar generalization for Ancient Greek, connecting it to the greater likelihood of intrusive vowels for DC than TC in modern languages (e.g. Colantoni and Steele 2005, Davidson 2006). Vowel duration may also be relevant, in that vowels tend to be longer before voiced than voiceless consonants cross-linguistically. For example, in English, DR is shorter than TR, but vowels are longer before DR.[3] If vowel duration matters for Latin, it would be difficult to reconcile with the analysis in terms of variable syllabification of the cluster. At any rate, the phonetic facts are unclear for Latin. Variable syllabification

---

[3] This was confirmed using the Buckeye corpus (Pitt et al. 2007). I collected all words with V{T,D}RV straddling the first and second syllables, excluding the suffix *-ly*. In a mixed model with the identity of the first vowel as a random intercept, the voicing of the cluster contributes positively and significantly to the duration of the first vowel. But the voiced clusters themselves are significantly shorter.

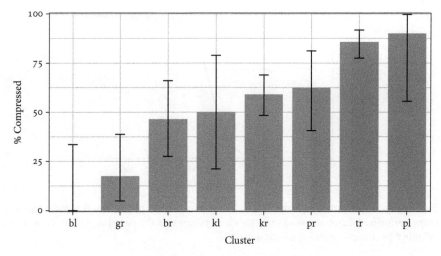

FIGURE 4.2 Estimated compression rates for V__V(V) clusters in Latin.

remains viable prima facie.[4] On the treatment of MCL clusters in Ancient Greek, see Devine and Stephens (1994). Recall also the case of Tashlhiyt Berber meter (Dell and Elmedlaoui 2017), in which geminates are optionally parsed as light. This possibility was connected in §2.6.7 to the shorter durations of vowels before geminates than before clusters in that language, though I also mentioned the possibility of geminate compression in the paraphonology, which would be more akin to the treatment of MCL clusters in Latin. Compare also the variable syllabicity of words with certain phonological characteristics in English meter, such as *flower*, which can scan as one or two syllables. For example, in (9), from Shakespeare's Sonnet 124, *flowers* scans as monosyllabic in the first instance and disyllabic in the second (Kiparsky 1977:244).

(9)   Weeds a/mong weeds, / or flowers / with flow/ers gath<er'd>

4.2.3 *Optional correption in hiatus*

Third, in Vedic Sanskrit, as in many other languages, a long vowel in HIATUS (i.e. immediately preceding another vowel) is free to scan as long or short, though the latter predominates (Gunkel and Ryan 2011).[5] This shortening is known as CORREPTION ("vocalis ante vocalem corripitur"). As Gunkel and Ryan (2011) observe, a priori, one might approach variable weight in one of two ways.[6] The first approach is BINARY WEIGHT WITH BIMODAL PHONOLOGY. On this approach, weight is strictly binary,

---

[4] Another possible approach to MCL variation assumes that MCL clusters are parsed uniformly, but their different weight propensities follow from their different durations (cf. Steriade 2008; §4.6).

[5] This assumes that the two vowels surface as disyllabic. In Vedic, it is more common for underlying /VV#V/ to fuse into a single vowel [VV], in which case correption is moot.

[6] While I assume a syllable-based framework here, this discussion applies equally to an interval-based framework (§4.6). Either must contend with the variable weight of VV#V, for which the parse is invariant.

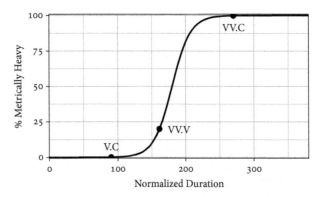

FIGURE 4.3 Illustration of intermediate weight with unimodal phonology. A logistic function maps normalized duration onto p(heavy), where p(heavy) is the percentage of the time that a syllable type occupies a strong metrical position.

and the relevant phonological rule applies optionally as an all-or-nothing Bernoulli process. For correption, one would say that a long vowel optionally shortens in hiatus (with high odds, say, 80%). On this analysis, the phonology generates a bimodal distribution: Some hiatus vowels shorten completely, and others do not shorten at all; there is no partial shortening.

Another conceivable approach is INTERMEDIATE WEIGHT WITH UNIMODAL PHONOLOGY (cf. West 1970 on intermediately heavy positions in meter). On this approach, long vowels in hiatus are intermediate in duration between long and short. Due to this intermediacy, they can be shoehorned into either strong or weak positions, but will be more felicitous in one than the other as a function of their phonetic proximity to the target category. A hypothetical schema is illustrated in Figure 4.3, which assumes a logistic function from normalized duration to binary positional strength (as could be implemented in maxent HG). V.C is aggregately short enough that it is virtually always mapped onto weakness, and VV.C onto strength.[7] The normalized duration of VV in VV.V, however, falls in zone of variation, such that it is felicitously mapped onto both strong and weak positions. While this second approach is likely closer to the phonetic reality, I tentatively assume the former, discrete approach here, which conforms better to traditional metrics. (In subsequent sections, I argue for gradient weight on independent grounds.)

4.2.4 Variable final vowel length

As a final example of variable weight, certain word-final vowels in Vedic vary freely in length even before simple onsets (Wackernagel 1896:311, Oldenberg 1906, Macdonell 1910:62, Kuiper 1955, Krisch 2009). Oldenberg (1906) refers to such vowels as possessing "middle quantity" (*Mittelzeitigkeit*). For example, *ádha* 'then' is realized

---

[7] I refer to the aggregate duration here because a phonetics–phonology model of this sort requires normalization (cf. Flemming 2001, Steriade 2009).

as *ádha* thirty-six times and as *ádhā* seventy-two times before a following CV-initial word in the R̥g-Veda. One might take this variation to be metri causa (*sāmavaśa*), in that the final vowel of *ádha* takes on whichever length best suits its position. But it is not always so. In (10), for instance, the two variants occupy the same metrical context.

(10)   a.   ádha yác cárathe gaṇé   (R̥g-Veda 8.46.31a)
         b.   ádhā víśvāsu háviyo   (R̥g-Veda 5.17.4c)

Moreover, only certain (albeit many) words and endings are permitted to vary. For example, *iva* 'like' and *utá* 'also' have the same metrical shape as *ádha*, but cannot lengthen.[8] Further, *ihá* 'here' is of the same semantic field as *ádha*, but lengthens only rarely (2%). Nor would it simplify the analysis to assume that *ádha* is underlyingly long-final. Long-final words of the same shape, such as *máyā* 'by me,' cannot shorten. Thus, the variation is at least partly lexically conditioned, though not randomly so; for one thing, it does not afflict nonfinal vowels. It might reflect prosodic phrasing in a way that has not yet been articulated. This complicates the lexicon and phonology, but does not complicate weight on the view just adopted. Weight remains binary on this view; it is rather the conditioning of lengthening that is problematic.

4.3 Superheavy avoidance

Conventional wisdom holds weight to be binary in archaic Indo-European meters such as in Vedic Sanskrit and Ancient Greek. Nevertheless, these meters also exhibit a clear sensitivity to a superheavy (or "overlong") grade of weight, in that superheavies are significantly avoided in cadences (Hoenigswald 1989, 1991). The cadence is no doubt singled out because it is the strictest part of the line (cf. final strictness in §4.1).

Consider the R̥g-Veda. Figure 4.4 shows that the incidence of superheavies sharply declines in the cadences of three meters. The meters are labeled 8, 11, and 12 based on the number of syllables per line (*pāda*).[9] The eight-syllable meter is the dimeter described in §4.1; it has the cadence ◡‒◡×. The eleven- and twelve-syllable meters are TRIMETER; they have the cadences ‒◡‒× and ◡‒◡×, respectively. Final position is omitted from the figure, as is any position that is filled by lights over two-thirds of the time. For example, only the first ten positions of the twelve are shown because the eleventh is ◡ and the twelfth is ×. The ninth of the twelve is also ◡, but it is interpolated in the figure. A superheavy is taken to be any short vowel followed by at least three consonants (VCCCV) or long vowel followed by at least two consonants (VVCCV).[10]

---

[8] Acute accents indicate pitch accents, which are irrelevant for length and metrification in Vedic.

[9] The tradition takes each *pāda* type to be further subdivided into meters according to stanzaic structure. But since stanzaic structure is irrelevant here, *pāda* size alone suffices. Moreover, I omit "special" meters and sections here, such as the epic *anuṣṭubh*, trochaic *gāyatrī*, the Vālakhilya, repeated *pāda*s, and so forth, taking only "normal" dimeter and trimeter, as in Gunkel and Ryan (2011).

[10] These parses need not be consistently accurate for syllabification, and at any rate their accuracy for individual items is moot: It is hard to say whether a word like *saṃskr̥tam* 'Sanskrit' should be *saṃ.skr̥.tam* or *saṃs.kr̥.tam*; either way it scans as a cretic. But the aggregate effect of superheavies is clear, which means that at least some of the time, VCCCV is parsed as VCC.CV.

Thus, regardless of the meter, the final two strong positions of the line strongly eschew superheavies. In this zone, ∼2 per cent of heavies are superheavy.[11] In earlier parts of the line, the rate is roughly three times as great. Though it is not shown in the figure, ultraheavies are avoided even more stringently in the cadence, being four times as frequent in the pre-cadence (though given their rarity, this difference is not significant). Superheavies are also eschewed in verse relative to prose. In a (later) Vedic prose corpus of four Brāhmaṇas (240,272 words), superheavies account for 12.7 per cent of heavies, treating resyllabification the same as in verse. This prose result suggests that superheavies are avoided even in the pre-cadence, though their avoidance in the cadence is much stronger.

At first glance, superheavy avoidance might appear paradoxical, in that it is strongest in the positions that are the "heaviest" (i.e. filled with heavies the greatest proportion of the time). For example, in the 8 and 12, the penult is filled by a heavy over 98 per cent of the time, the highest rate anywhere in the line. Yet it is precisely in this position that superheavies are the most avoided. Nevertheless, the paradox is resolved if it is recognized that superheavy avoidance is independent of prominence mapping. Prominence mapping instantiates the rhythm of the meter, and can be implemented by STRONG→$\sigma_{\mu\mu}$ (Hanson and Kiparsky 1996, Ryan 2017b).

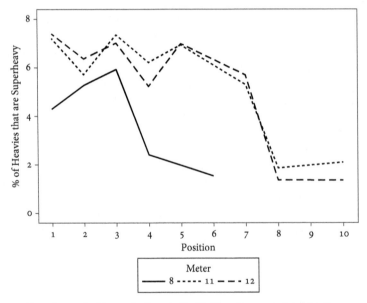

FIGURE 4.4 Superheavy incidence declines in Ṛg-Vedic cadences, judging by the proportion of heavies in each position that are superheavy. Weak positions are skipped and interpolated in the plot.

---

[11] This zone corresponds loosely to the traditional notion of the cadence, but overreaches it by one position in the case of the 8 and 12 (though at least the latter could be reasonably said to possess a five-syllable cadence, in which case there is no overreaching).

Since this constraint is strictest in the cadence in Vedic, it can be so indexed: STRONG$_{cadence}$→$\sigma_{\mu\mu}$. Meanwhile, a constraint penalizing superheavies came up in Chapters 2 and 3, namely, *3μ. This constraint can likewise be indexed to the cadence: *3$\mu_{cadence}$ (and weighted, as exceptions occur).[12] In short, as a hypothesis, cadences are strict for both prominence and prosodic phonology more generally, though it remains to be explored how generally markedness asserts itself in cadences.

The case studies thus far in this chapter have involved VARIABLE WEIGHT due to optional processes. The remaining case studies in §4.4 and §4.5 illustrate GRADIENT WEIGHT in meter, in which phonological structure (including syllabification) is fixed, but syllables of different types vary in their propensities to occupy certain metrical positions.

4.4 Gradient weight in meter I: positional discrepancies

4.4.1 Kalevala Finnish

As the remaining case studies in this chapter illustrate, even in ostensibly binary meters, poets are sensitive to detailed continua of syllable weight in choosing how to metrify syllables. I begin with the *Kalevala*, a Finnish/Karelian epic of 22,795 lines (Lönnrot 1849). Each line normally contains eight syllables, though this total can be increased by resolution or decreased by late phonological rules (Kiparsky 1968). As the descriptive template in (11) suggests, a line comprises four disyllabic trochaic metra. The mapping rule is then that stressed syllables must be heavy in strong positions (S) and light in weak ones (W) (Sadeniemi 1951, Kiparsky 1968, Leino 1994). To a first approximation (cf. Ryan 2017b), "stress" here refers to primary stress, which is always word-initial in Finnish. Consistent with final strictness, the rigidity of the mapping rule increases over the course of the line. The first foot is largely if not entirely unregulated. The following three feet are stricter, but exceptions are not uncommon.

(11)	Foot 1	Foot 2	Foot 3	Foot 4
	S W	S W	S W	S W

In this case, it is the ostensible exceptions that reveal weight gradience, in that violations of the mapping rule tend to be minimal. For example, if a poet places a stressed heavy in a weak position, it tends to be on the lighter side of heavies (e.g. VC as opposed to VV or VVC). Of course, to make such an argument, it is necessary to have a control condition, demonstrating that VC is not just chosen frequently, but chosen more frequently than one would otherwise expect. To this end, one can compare stressed heavies in strong positions to stressed heavies in weak positions, showing that the former are aggregately heavier (Ryan 2011a). Indeed, not only are they heavier in

---

[12] Donca Steriade (p.c.) notes that superheavies might also be avoided due to their similarity to heavy–light sequences. Recall the treatment of superheavies in Persian (§4.1), though note that they cannot actually scan as heavy–light in Vedic as they can in Persian.

the aggregate, but as weight increases, the skew towards strong positions increases, revealing an intra-heavy continuum of weight.

I employ mixed-effects logistic regression to demonstrate the significance of these effects.[13] The fixed effects are factors involving syllable shape, as summarized in Figure 4.5. The random effects are intercepts for word shape, defined as the word's heavy–light template with the syllable in question X-ed out (e.g. X‿◡◡◡ for *ajat-televi*). On the motivation for including shape as a random effect, see Ryan (2011a). In brief, syllable types are often distributed differently in words of different shapes, and words of different shapes are distributed differently in meter. For example, in the present corpus, word-initial X is over twice as likely to be heavy in a disyllable than in a trisyllable (87% vs. 34%). Disyllables and trisyllables are also distributed somewhat differently within the line, to some extent *metri causa*, but also due to irrelevant factors such as end-weight. Random effects for shape control for these potential confounds by absorbing any skewness in weight that can be attributed to shape.

As data, I take all (30,122) primary stressed syllables in the *Kalevala* falling within the final three feet, excluding monosyllables. The dependent variable is whether the syllable occupies a strong (1) or weak (0) position. Factor levels are forward-difference coded in Figure 4.5, meaning that each is interpreted relative to the specified comparandum rather than the general intercept. This coding characterizes the significance of each step of a scale. Onset and rime structure are treated separately in Figure 4.5.[14] The resulting scales are given in (12).

(12)   Rime scale: $V \lesssim VT \lesssim \{VN, VV\} \lesssim VVC$
       Onset scale: $\emptyset \lesssim N \lesssim T$

	β	SE	z	p
(Intercept)	15.007	1.842	8.2	< .0001
Rime VT (vs. V)	8.217	0.217	37.9	< .0001
Rime VN (vs. VT)	3.388	0.650	6.0	< .0001
Rime VV (vs. VN)	1.261	1.173	1.1	= .282
Rime VVC (vs. VN)	40.887	5.493	7.4	< .0001
Onset N (vs. T)	−0.737	0.176	−4.2	< .0001
Onset Ø (vs. N)	−0.540	0.221	−2.4	= .015

FIGURE 4.5 Regression table for syllable weight in the *Kalevala*. Factor levels are forward-difference coded, and thus interpretable only with respect to the specified level of comparison (positive ⇒ heavier than the comparandum).

---

[13] The purpose of using regression as opposed to merely computing the optimal weights of the constraints is to test contrasts for significance while controlling for potential confounds such as word shape, as discussed. The factors in regression tables in this chapter could be recast as constraints on the model of §1.5 by reformulating the predicate stringently and relating it to STRONG. For example, "Rime VN (vs. VT)" being significant implies that STRONG→$V_\mu[+son]_\mu$ is active. All codas are moraic in the languages analyzed by regression in this chapter.

[14] They could in principle be combined into a single fifteen-level factor, but the results are then harder to interpret, since (1) some levels are sparsely populated and (2) typological expectations are less clear (e.g. is TVT expected to be heavier or lighter than ØVN? —see §1.3 and §1.5 on the issue of noncontainment).

All of these results agree with the universal phonology of weight. First, the skeletal rime scale is $V \lesssim VC \lesssim VV \lesssim VVC$, as in Kashmiri and Pulaar stress, except now gradiently. Second, sonority is further overlaid on this scale, such that $VT \lesssim VN$, as in, say, Kwak'wala stress. Finally, onset presence and voicing matter. Filled onsets are heavier than empty onsets, and among filled onsets, voiceless/obstruent onsets are heavier than voiced/sonorant onsets, just as in Pirahã stress, which also observes $\emptyset < N < T$ for onsets.

4.4.2 Homeric Greek

The basic weight template for the Homeric hexameter is given in (13) (Maas 1962, Raven 1962, Halle 1970, West 1982, Prince 1989, Ryan 2011a). Each metron is divided into two parts, namely, after West (1982), the PRINCEPS, also known as the LONGUM (obligatory _) and (except finally) the BICEPS (_ or ∪∪).

(13)

Metron 1	Metron 2	Metron 3	Metron 4	Metron 5	Metron 6
$- \left\{ {- \atop \cup\cup} \right\}$	$- \left\{ {- \atop \cup\cup} \right\}$	$- \left\{ {- \atop \cup\cup} \right\}$	$- \left\{ {- \atop \cup\cup} \right\}$	$- \left\{ {- \atop \cup\cup} \right\}$	$- \left\{ {- \atop \cup} \right\}$

Heavies in bicipitia tend to be heavier than heavies in longa. West (1982:39) notes that lighter heavies—including V: in hiatus, V preceding an MCL cluster, and so forth (cf. §4.2)—are avoided in bicipitia relative to longa: "the biceps, being of greater duration, requires more stuffing." Indeed, this sentiment finds an ancient precedent among the Greek rhythmicians (Allen 1973:255, West 1982:18; but cf. Devine and Stephens 1994).[15]

As Ryan (2011a) argues, this discrepancy between biceps and longum diagnoses a continuum of intra-heavy weight. Figure 4.6 is based on 24,677 parsed lines from the *Iliad* and the *Odyssey*. Note that $VV \lesssim VVC$ is highly significant, though this contrast is not made explicit in the table. VCC, for its part, falls in the range of VV, being marginally heavier than VN (not shown) and marginally lighter than VVC. Ryan (2011b) also reports that $\emptyset < C < CC_1$ for onsets in this corpus, though he does not test voicing.

---

[15] Given that the longum is usually analyzed as the strong position of the metron (Halle 1970, Prince 1989, Ryan 2017b), one might expect to find heavier heavies in the longum rather than in the biceps. There are several possible explanations for the biceps' greater target weight. First, a pair of lights is typically longer than a single heavy. Thus, when substituting a heavy for a pair of lights, poets might prefer heavier heavies, or heavies whose two moras more resemble the rimes of two lights by virtue of their sonority (e.g. VV is more like V:V than VT; Dieter Gunkel, p.c.). Second, the metron as a whole might be akin to a "resolved moraic trochee" (Hanson and Kiparsky 1996), in which length is permitted only in the second position of a two-position trochee: $'\cup\cup$, $'\cup\_$, $*'\_\cup$, $*'\_\_$. For the hexameter, one would have to add that the position of the metron that corresponds to $'\cup$ in this foot schema must still contain a heavy, thanks to FtBin (Ryan 2017b). In other words, the short–long $'\cup\_$ "foot" would now be implemented in terms of two binary metrical positions rather than two syllables. Finally, one might consider analyzing the biceps as being the strong position of the metron, though this would mean that constraints such as STRONG→HEAVY, which Ryan (2017b) employs to eschew (pairs of) lights in longa, would have to find some other analysis.

	β	SE	z	p
(Intercept)	−3.357	1.452	−2.3	= .021
Rime VN (vs. VT)	0.265	0.034	7.8	< .0001
Rime VV (vs. VN)	0.217	0.026	8.3	< .0001
Rime VCC (vs. VV)	0.005	0.101	0.1	= .958
Rime VVC (vs. VCC)	0.208	0.105	2.0	= .049

FIGURE 4.6 Regression table for syllable weight in the *Iliad* and the *Odyssey*. Factor levels are forward-difference coded, as in Figure 4.5. Interactions are omitted.

The Homeric Greek scales are summarized in (14).

(14)   Rime scale: $V \lesssim VT \lesssim VN \lesssim \{VV, VCC\} \lesssim VVC$
         Onset scale: $\emptyset \lesssim C \lesssim CC_1$

4.4.3 Tamil and other languages

See also Ryan (2011a, 2011b) for similar analyses of meters in Latin, Old Norse, Sanskrit, and Tamil. The Tamil study, for instance, reveals at least nine statistically significant grades of weight as well as a tight correlation with the phonetics. Figure 4.7 plots rime duration (measured from a conservative Modern Tamil speaker) against inferred metrical weight in Kamban's epic (as in §3.4.4). Each dot is a measured syllable. The overall phonetics–phonology correlation is high (Spearman's $\rho = .85$), as suggested by the proximity of points to the solid diagonal. Nevertheless, there is some stratification into heavy vs. light (perhaps among other categories), as suggested

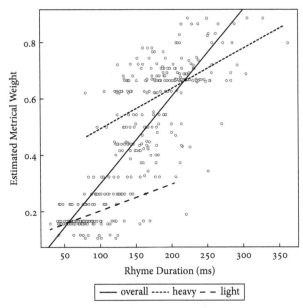

FIGURE 4.7 Rime duration vs. strength propensity in Kamban's Tamil meter.

Source: Ryan (2011a:438f).

by the two flatter regression lines, which were calculated separately for heavy vs. light syllables. If binary weight played no role, these intracategorial lines would approximate the grand diagonal.

4.5 Gradient weight in meter II: final indifference

As discussed in §4.1, one way in which weight in quantitative meter differs from weight for stress is that meters overwhelmingly favor the Latin criterion, while stress systems are more evenly divided between the Latin and Khalkha criteria. Another difference is that syllabo-moraic quantitative meters virtually always exhibit final indifference,[16] whereas stress systems often do not. Recall from §4.1 that final indifference refers to the suspension of weight sensitivity in line-final position.[17] Stress systems can exhibit a similar property with final syllable extrametricality, as in Latin, but many lack this property. This section argues that despite exhibiting final indifference, syllabo-moraic meters can (and perhaps always do) show weight tendencies in final position. Thus, final indifference should be interpreted as a suspension of *categorical* weight restrictions in final position, not as a lack of weight sensitivity altogether.

4.5.1 Homeric Greek

Consider once again the Ancient Greek hexameter. Line-final position accepts a syllable of any weight, as implied by the template in (13), and is thus said to be indifferent (*adiáphoros*). However, closer examination reveals that Homer is not wholly indifferent to weight line-finally, but rather significantly prefers a heavy there. For example, words of the shape ∪_× are light-final 42 per cent of the time nonfinally. Line-finally, they are light-final 18 per cent of the time (Fisher's exact test odds ratio = 3.35, $p < .0001$). As the mixed model in the next paragraph demonstrates, the same bias applies more generally across word shapes.

Indeed, the heavier the heavy, the more skewed it is towards final position, suggesting (once again) that Homer is sensitive to a continuum of weight. A logistic regression predicts whether a word token is line-final (1) or not (0). The fixed effect is ultima rime shape $\in$ {V, VC, VV, VVC}. Word shape is a random effect, as in §4.4.2. A word is included only if it has more than one syllable and its ultima contains a mid vowel or diphthong, as vowel length in these cases is encoded orthographically. The resulting data comprise 13,280 line-final words and 30,580 nonfinal words.

Figure 4.8 summarizes the results of this model separately for the *Iliad* and the *Odyssey*. In both, V $\lesssim$ VC $\lesssim$ VV $\lesssim$ VVC is observed, with every link significant. Rime V is given as zero with no error because it is the baseline level. (Against another interpretation of these results whereby lighter syllables are avoided line-medially, see the next section.)

---

[16] "Mora-counting" meters such as the *haiku* appear not to exhibit this license.
[17] The context is sometimes also given as period-final or prepausal. Indifference is occasionally encountered line-internally, as before caesura.

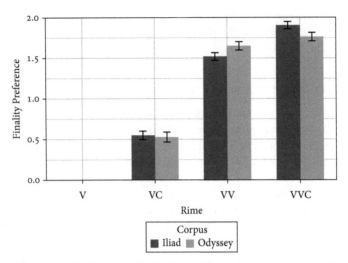

FIGURE 4.8 The heavier the rime type, the higher its bias towards line-final position, based on the two Homeric corpora. "Finality Preferences" are coefficients in a logistic model and error bars are their standard errors.

4.5.2 *Classical Latin*

The Latin hexameter, as in Virgil, shows the same line-final tendency as the Greek. While Virgil permits both lights and heavies line-finally, he prefers heavies there (Allen 1973). Indeed, the magnitude of his preference generally scales with the weight of the syllable along the typologically expected scale, as Figure 4.9 illustrates. The model is set up as in §4.5.1, except that V and VC are now subdivided by vowel height, with Mid V being the baseline. High V is omitted because a line cannot end with a short high vowel for independent reasons.

Figure 4.9 suggests the scale Mid ≲ Low ≲ VC ≲ VV. This height effect agrees with the typology, where lower vowels are if anything heavier than higher vowels. VC ≲ VV is clearly significant if VC is pooled; it is only Low VC whose error overlaps with that

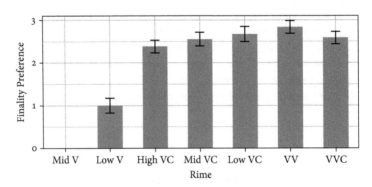

FIGURE 4.9 A graded heaviness preference for line-final position in Virgil's *Aeneid*.

of VV. One seeming anomaly in Figure 4.9 is that VVC appears to be lighter than VV, albeit not significantly. This trend might reflect superheavy avoidance in the cadence, as described in §4.3. Indeed, Ryan (2013a) finds a significant contrast of VV $\lesssim$ VVC for final position in Latin using a different, prose comparison model. The prose model also addresses a possible objection to the foregoing model to the effect that Virgil might not be avoiding line-final lights, but rather favoring line-medial lights (though one would still have a weight continuum to explain). By comparing Virgil's line-final words of a given shape to words of the same shape sampled from prose, I corroborate Virgil's preference for progressively heavier ultimas. The poet-to-poet test in the next paragraph similarly avoids this objection.

Additionally, Ryan (2013a) argues that some other quantitative meters, such as Catullus' hendecasyllables and the Old Norse *dróttkvætt*, exhibit a gradient pro-light rather than pro-heavy preference in final position. For example, comparing Catullus' line-final words to Virgil's line-final words for a particular word shape reveals a graded discrepancy, such that Catullus prefers lighter endings and Virgil heavier endings, the degree of discrepancy between the two scaling with weight. The same trend was demonstrated independently for _× and ∪_× words, the two most typical hexameter endings. Moreover, it is not the case that Virgil prefers heavies while Catullus ignores final weight: A prose test confirms that Catullus independently favors progressively lighter syllables in final position.

In summary, final indifference is potentially viable as a universal in the sense that quantitative meters do not rigidly enforce a criterion line-finally. But quantitative preferences still leak through. In the Homeric and Virgilian hexameters, final position skews heavy, presumably because the second halves of metra are normally bimoraic in that meter.[18] In the Phalaecian hendecasyllable, by contrast, final position skews light, since the cadence is otherwise trochaic in that meter, as schematized in (15). In short, final position shadows the expected polarity of the meter, just not categorically.

(15)   × ×_∪∪_∪_∪_×

4.6 Interval Theory

As set out in the opening paragraphs of this book, while I assume, with most of the literature, that weight is a property of syllables, an alternative approach is that of INTERVAL THEORY (Steriade 2008, 2011, 2012). I describe this theory in a chapter on meter, but it applies to nearly all weight-sensitive phenomena, including stress. The INTERVAL, short for total vowel-to-vowel interval, extends from the left edge of each vowel to that of the following vowel. If no vowel follows, it extends to the end of the relevant prosodic group. A group-initial onset is extraprosodic. For example, two lines of Latin hexameter are parsed in (16) and (17) using syllables and intervals, respectively. Bars separate intervals. The meter is the same either way; it is only the

---

[18] The preference for final heavies is perhaps unexpected, by contrast, under the common view that the final metron is a catalectic dactyl _∪<∪> accompanied by final indifference (Dieter Gunkel, p.c.).

criterion that is adjusted. An interval is light in Latin iff it is V or VC (I return to this criterion and the issue of optional processes below).

(16) Syllables:
  a. .ar.ma .vi.rum.que .ca.nō .trō.iae .quī .prī.mu.s a.b ō.rīs. (Aeneid 1.1)
  b. .prī.a.mi.dē.n ^{h}e.le.num .grā.iās .rēg.nā.re .pe.r ur.bīs. (Aeneid 3.295)
  –⏑⏑/–⏑⏑/––/––/–⏑⏑/––

(17) Intervals:
  a. |arm|a v|ir|umqu|e c|an|ō tr|ōi|ae qu|ī pr|īm|us |ab |ōr|īs| (Aeneid 1.1)
  b. <pr>|ī|am|id|ēn ^{h}|el|en|um gr|āi|ās r|ēgn|ār|e p|er| urb|īs| (Aeneid 3.295)
  –⏑⏑/–⏑⏑/––/––/–⏑⏑/––

Interval Theory has pregenerative precedents. For example, Ryan (2016) points out that it is widespread in Norse philology, quoting Pipping (1903): "The morae of a syllable are counted from its vowel to (but not including) the vowel of the following syllable." On this scheme, a syllable is heavy iff it contains three or more moras. What follows is a compact description of some (but not all) of the arguments that have been put forth for intervals, based loosely on handouts by Steriade (2008, 2011, 2012).

First, vowels in hiatus sometimes pattern as lighter than vowels before consonants. For long vowels, one could say that they shorten in hiatus (§4.2), but short vowels also show signs of being lighter in hiatus. For example, in Finnish, they reject secondary stress (e.g. *tánanarìve* vs. *érgonòmi.a*; Karvonen 2008).

Second, intervals arguably better capture the typology of the treatment of final position for stress. With intervals, final VC is equivalent to medial VCV. There is thus no need to invoke final consonant extrametricality; it is "built in" to the parse. Intervals, as Steriade (2008) notes, can also capture systems in which VC# is heavier than V#, as long as they do not require VC# to be equivalent to VC.CV. For example, intervals can handle a language in which stress is final unless the ultima is V.[19] Intervals would be refuted by an unbounded system in which VC# is equivalent to VC.CV, but it is not obvious that such a system exists. Insofar as such a system is unattested, it is another point in favor of intervals.

As a sample of potentially relevant cases, I consider the eighteen unbounded systems enumerated by Hayes (1995:296f). Fourteen are disqualified because they do not have the necessary "VC heavy" criterion. Further, Classical Arabic is disqualified because it has extrametricality, and thus does not treat VC# as equivalent to VC.CV. Amele, Kwak'wala, and Yana remain. The latter two were discussed in Chapter 2. Kwak'wala turns out not to be diagnostic because of its leftmost-heavy-else-rightmost orientation.[20] Yana is also not diagnostic, at least pending further research, since

[19] In Manam, for instance, stress falls on the rightmost heavy within the final three syllable window (Hayes 1995). With intervals, this case could be analyzed with ternary $V < VX < VXX$.

[20] Consider two schematic disyllables, *amán* and *ámpan*. With syllables, both contain heavies, and stress falls on the leftmost heavy. With intervals, VC|VC is light–light and therefore receives default rightmost stress, while VCC|VC is heavy–light and therefore receives stress on its only heavy. The two theories are therefore indistinguishable, since one cannot tell pretheoretically whether VCVC receives final stress due to weight attraction or to default rightmostness.

its rule is only a tendency (§2.8.2), and the treatment of VC# is not secure. Amele is ostensibly the strongest case in the list for VC# = VC.CV, though it is arguably also not secure. Roberts (1987) describes the rule as leftmost heavy, else leftmost (modulo morphology). Amele has diphthongs (VW) but not phonemic vowel length. On Roberts' analysis, VC is always heavy, but VW is heavy only finally (but see below). Nonfinal VC (where C ≠ W) is rare within morphemes; Roberts (1987:347) notes that "clustering can occur word medially with certain lexical items (often names which may be some kind of reduced or composite form)." It is clear from Roberts' examples that stress is final unless the ultima is light, in which case stress is initial. What is less clear is that the system is unbounded. Roberts (1987) offers only one example of an implied simplex form with medial stress, namely, [jæ'wælti] 'wind from north' (pp. 347, 358). (A handful of other examples showing nonfinal VC taking stress, such as ['hænse] 'left hand,' are compatible with default initial stress when the ultima is light.) If [jæ'wælti] turned out to be a compound, as is plausible a priori given its semantics and its rare internal coda, its stress might be explained otherwise. Finally, note that under Roberts' analysis, Amele breaks a near-universal: Word-internally, VW is lighter than VC. With the reanalysis that I suggest, the universal is restored: VW is always heavy in Amele. If the ultima is light, medial VW is passed over not because it is light, but because stress is not weight-sensitive in that situation; it is default leftmost.

The last couple of paragraphs should at least convey that teasing apart the predictions of interval and syllable theory is not as straightforward as it might first seem. Indeed, this is equally true for the experimental literature: As it stands, results appear to be mixed for syllables vs. intervals, with Hirsch (2014) supporting intervals, Garcia (2016, 2017b) largely supporting intervals, but not in every respect, and certain results in Ryan (2014) and Olejarczuk and Kapatsinski (2016) challenging intervals; see Ryan (2016:726) for a somewhat more detailed overview of this literature. For example, Garcia (2017b) finds that increasing the size of the penult onset increases the odds of antepenultimate stress in Portuguese, favoring intervals. But he also finds a tauto-augmenting effect of onset size for the antepenult, favoring syllables, or at least the incorporation of initial onsets.

A third argument for intervals is that syllable division judgments are sometimes ambiguous, even while the treatment of the same configuration in meter is invariant. This situation is expected if metrical systems rely on intervals rather than syllables. Fourth, intervals arguably better capture the typology of rhyme. In particular, for rhyme systems in which spans are not required to extend to the end of the line, the interval, but not syllable or rime, is attested as a minimum domain of correspondence. For example, Virgil has rhyming sets such as *Diōrēs, ōra, clāmōribus, honōrem, decōrae*, and so forth, in which the stressed interval of each word (here, *ōr*) rhymes. Finally, intervals are more restrictive than syllables concerning the relation of duration to weight. Because intervals are always parsed out to the vowel, if one cluster is heavier than another, it can only be because the heavier cluster is longer. With syllables, this correlation does not necessarily obtain; clusters might be syllabified differently for reasons not connected to duration.

Returning to the Latin criterion, a V or VC interval is light, while a VCC or longer interval is heavy (e.g. |arm|a v|ir|umqu|e| = $\_\cup \cup\_\cup$). A VV interval, as found when a long vowel stands in hiatus, is also normally heavy in Latin (e.g. <pr>|ī|am|id|ēn| = _◡◡_).[21] Thus, the criterial boundary for intervals is VC < VV. This criterion cannot be defined in terms of timing slots (as both sides have two) or moras (as Interval Theory rejects moras for the phenomena it purports to explain). Rather, it necessitates some type of vowel prominence constraint (cf. §2.4) or other reference to the total energy of the interval. A further complication is the treatment of clusters, which vary in their scansion (§4.2). Unlike with syllables, variable parsing is not an option for intervals. |Vkr|V| must be parsed as such regardless of whether |Vkr| scans as heavy or light. Steriade (2008) implies a short vs. long parse, perhaps associated with the optional realization of the rhotic (in this case) as a tap vs. trill.

Similarly, consider optional resyllabification, as in Māhārāṣṭrī Prakrit (§3.3, §4.2). A word-final consonant, which can only be the nasal *anusvāra*, optionally resyllabifies with a following vowel-initial word. Iff it does so, the ultima scans as light. With syllables, the analysis is obvious: Variable weight reflects variable syllabification. Indeed, such discrete variation is implied by the orthography, which renders the nasal with an entirely different symbol depending on whether it is an onset or coda. With intervals, however, |VN| must be parsed as such regardless of whether it scans as heavy or light. One would have to assume either that N substantially lengthens in its coda variant (enough to fall in with heavy |VCC| as opposed to light |VC|) or that |VN#| (but not medial |VN|) is uniformly intermediate in duration and therefore free to occupy strong or weak positions (cf. Figure 4.3).

Interval Theory as defined above cannot account for tauto-augmenting onset effects, as described for meter in §§4.4–4.5 and for stress in §2.8.3 (see Ryan 2014 for additional cases of both). As will be discussed in §6.3, the weight percept, even if defined as total energy, cannot accommodate all such onset effects if its domain begins with the vowel (though it can accommodate some of them). One possible amendment to Interval Theory that would accommodate absolute-initial onset effects would be to parse the group-initial onset with the first interval instead of treating it as extraprosodic. Nevertheless, onset effects also obtain group-internally. Another possible amendment, raised by Ryan (2014), would be to treat intervals as spanning successive p-centers rather than successive vowel edges. The p-center is, roughly speaking, the perceptual beat of the syllable (Morton et al. 1976). These tend to approximate the left edge of the vowel, but can anticipate it slightly with longer onsets. As such, p-center intervals predict that a longer onset should make the following domain slightly heavier (even while it increases the length of the preceding domain as well). See Ryan (2014), Mai (2018), and §6.3 for further discussion.

Finally, consider so-called mora-counting meters, such as the *haiku* (e.g. McCawley 1965, 1968). Each line has a fixed number of moras, but no hard constraints on their distribution into syllables nor on the distribution of word boundaries. A stipulative constraint of the type LINE=7μ is undesirable, and indeed precluded with intervals. But if one assumes structure, fixed counts can fall out from binarity. For the

---

[21] To be sure, many historical cases of VV.V within the word underwent correption, now being recorded as V.V in the text. Moreover, across a boundary, VV#V usually undergoes elision.

seven-mora line, one can invoke three binary levels ($2^3 = 8$), plus catalexis of a mora (Hanson and Kiparsky 1996, Ryan 2017b), as in (18). The empty final position might also be enforced by SALIENCY, as in Hayes and MacEachern (1998) and Blumenfeld (2016a), which requires a metrical cadence to be distinct (e.g. by leaving a position empty that is otherwise required to be filled). The labels in (18) are immaterial (metra might just as well be called positions). The structure in (18) splits syllables between metra (or even hemistichs), but this is arguably not a problem, since metrical constituents generally do not align with phonological constituents. For example, PWds and feet are regularly split across metra and (abstract) hemistichs cross-linguistically. The hemistichs in (18) are abstract, not meant to imply a caesura. Not all traditions require hemistichs to align with word breaks.

(18)

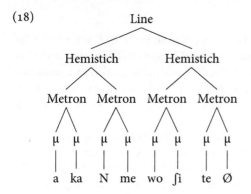

naku neko ni ‖ akanme wo shite ‖ temari kana (Issa)

In a mora-free setting, as with Interval Theory, analyzing such a meter is less straightforward. One might begin by positing a line consisting of seven light intervals (or eight, with catalexis), as above, with the additional license that a heavy interval can substitute for two light intervals in any position. But it is not obvious how to implement such a context-free license in a constraint-based framework. The standard approach to ⏑⏑ = — licenses in metrics is to require some constituent to contain two moras. For example, the hexameter biceps can be ⏑⏑ or —. If each position is required to be bimoraic, say, due to FTBIN, the license emerges (in bicipitia; it is quashed in the longum due to STRONG→HEAVY; Ryan 2017b). But with the *haiku*, there are no fixed positions, analogous to the biceps, to analyze as bimoraic or bicipital in any sense. Substitutions can span odd–even pairs or even–odd pairs. With a structure like (18), substitution can occur even across hemistichs. One might permit multiple line structures, but then the analysis of the meter is complicated. One might also entertain treating moraic consonants as initiating intervals (e.g. |ak|a|Nm|e|), but this would lead to implausible intervals such as silence (e.g. the silent closure of |pː| in *teppō* 'gun,' which would be <t>|e|pː|o|o|).

This section is meant only to outline Interval Theory and to raise some issues with which it would have to contend. After all, this book assumes Syllable Theory, and Interval Theory is yet to be promulgated in a generative publication. But a book about weight would be remiss to overlook the topic. If nothing else, I hope to have conveyed that the two approaches are less easily distinguished than one might expect. At first glance, they might appear to be radically different approaches to weight, but one might also regard intervals as being a kind of syllabification algorithm, namely, strict coda maximization.[22] Indeed, when scholars such as Pipping (1903) above talk about intervals, they refer to them as "syllables." On such a view, the syllables that the grammar manipulates are not necessarily the same entities that speakers utter when asked to syllabify a word, which is a language game constrained by extraneous desiderata, including the desire to shoehorn each chunk into a well-formed PWd (Steriade 1999).

4.7 Conclusion

Almost all quantitative meters exhibit the Latin criterion for weight, whereby codas "make position." But the Khalkha criterion (vowel length only, ignoring codas) is also attested, at least in Nanti, if not in Kayardild, and perhaps also as a tendency in Avestan. Indeed, once one includes tendencies, the Khalkha criterion is found as a tendency (VC $\lesssim$ VV) in several meters that select the Latin criterion for categorical weight (V < VX).

Ternary weight is attested in metrics in at least three independent ways. First, some meters scan superheavies differently from heavies (e.g. as $\_\cup$ line-internally). However, as suggested at the end of §4.1, superheavies cannot be analyzed as being literally disyllabic in such cases. Second, other meters categorize heavies and superheavies identically (as $\_$), but avoid superheavies in cadences, revealing that the poets are still sensitive to their extra weight (§4.3). Third, gradient weight systems sometimes diagnose a superheavy grade, among other distinctions (§4.4).

A distinction is drawn between VARIABLE WEIGHT and GRADIENT WEIGHT. Variable weight reflects optional processes, such as optional resyllabification, variable syllabification of certain clusters, optional shortening in hiatus, and variable final vowel length (§4.2). As such, weight is strictly binary, but syllables vary in their affiliations depending on whether the rule applies. Gradient weight describes the rather different situation in which syllable types fit better or worse in strong vs. weak positions in a way that cannot be analyzed as reflecting a discrete process of lengthening or shortening. For example, in various meters, VC is gradiently lighter than VV, even when both must be parsed as categorically heavy. Gradient weight in metrics sometimes reveals highly articulated continua of weight, comprising several significant gradations with quantifiable separations. It is documented for Finnish, Ancient Greek, Latin, Old Norse, Sanskrit, and Tamil (§4.4).

Gradient weight is also revealed by final position in quantitative meters, which is putatively indifferent cross-linguistically (FINAL INDIFFERENCE). As I have argued (§4.5), indifference should be interpreted as the suspension of categorical weight

---

[22] This would render the domain the same, though the availability of moraic devices might still leave the resulting theory rather different from the one envisaged by Steriade (2012).

restrictions, not as the suspension of weight sensitivity altogether. In meters such as the hexameter, final position still exhibits a tendency to be heavy. Indeed, the effect is gradient: The lighter the syllable, the more it is avoided line-finally. But the position may be light or heavy.

The final section (§4.6) introduced Interval Theory, according to which the domain for weight (in meter and elsewhere) reflects not syllable structure, but the total interval between the left edges of successive vowels. Some advantages, problems, and theoretical variants were briefly outlined, but the primary aim was to illustrate that Syllable Theory and Interval Theory are surprisingly convergent in their predictions, inviting further research into the specific phenomena for which they differ.

5

Prosodic end-weight and the stress–weight interface

5.1 Introduction

In the preceding chapters, WEIGHT was synonymous with SYLLABLE WEIGHT, being treated solely as a property of the syllable. This chapter turns to phenomena in which larger constituents—prosodic words and phrases—bear prosodic weight. This higher-level weight is argued to interact with phrasal stress, such that heavier constituents are attracted to positions of greater sentential prominence (NUCLEAR STRESS). In this sense, it is proposed, the stress–weight interface is operative not only within words, as treated in Chapter 2, but also in sentence-level prosody. A constraint-based formalization of this interface is put forth in §5.9.

The relevant phenomena are collectively known as END-WEIGHT (as termed by Quirk et al. 1972), which refers to the tendency of speakers to localize heavier constituents later in sentences, all else being equal (e.g. Wasow 1997, 2002).[1] End-weight has been recognized since antiquity (e.g. Pāṇini 2.2.32ff, Quintilian 9.4.22ff), and is famously formulated as the GESETZ DER WACHSENDEN GLIEDER ("law of increasing members") by Behaghel (1909). This tendency can be evident when two or more constructional options compete for (approximately) the same meaning, as with the phenomena enumerated in §5.2. For example, a conjunction *X and Y* is usually (but not always) synonymous with its transposition *Y and X*, and is usually (but not always) grammatical in both orders. In such cases, end-weight affects ordering preferences (e.g. *wit and humor* is preferred to *humor and wit*).[2] To be sure, many factors aside from phonological weight also influence such ordering decisions, including frequency, rhythm, semantics, and syntactic complexity, among others (§§5.3–5.4). But when these other factors are controlled, phonological weight is confirmed to contribute independently (§§5.5–5.6).

---

[1] As treated in §5.12, BEGINNING-WEIGHT, that is, a heavy-first tendency, also exists in some languages (*ibid.*, Hawkins 1994, 2004).

[2] The former is roughly an order of magnitude more frequent than the latter in the Google Books Ngram corpus of American English from 1900 to 2000 (Michel et al. 2011), despite *humo(u)r* being roughly twice as frequent as *wit* in the same material.

Prosodic Weight. First edition. Kevin M. Ryan.
© Kevin M. Ryan 2019. First published 2019 by Oxford University Press.

It is this phonological aspect of end-weight, or PROSODIC END-WEIGHT, that is the focus of this chapter. A long line of previous research has established several phonological properties that consistently correlate with end-weight, at least for binomials and echo reduplication, which are the best-studied end-weight phenomena phonologically. But these properties have not previously received a unified treatment. For example, one consistent finding is that for syllable codas, greater sonority correlates with greater weight (e.g. *thick and thin, push and pull, pots and pans*), but for onsets, the generalization is reversed, such that less sonority favors finality (e.g. *wear and tear, huff and puff, wheel and deal*). It is proposed in §5.9 that this sonority reversal is consistent with the treatment of weight in other domains and is therefore subsumed, along with the other phonological properties of end-weight, by the general theory of phonological weight.

The explanation for prosodic end-weight is argued here to be phrasal (or nuclear) stress, in the sense that phrasal stress motivates all of its core properties, which are summarized in §5.7. Other explanations that have been suggested for prosodic end-weight, including final lengthening, rhythm, phonotactics, and complexity deferral, are argued either to be orthogonal to the phenomenon or too provincial to motivate its core properties (§5.8). A constraint-based mechanism for the computation of the weight of phonological words and phrases based on phrasal stress is defined in §5.9. This mechanism broadly involves integrating over syllable weight, but, as argued, this integration is not simply additive: For one thing, stressed syllables contribute more to the percept of phrasal weight than unstressed syllables do, though the latter cannot be ignored. In short, weight integration over syllables is stress-weighted.

One major prediction of this analysis is that in prosodically head-initial contexts, one should find prosodic beginning-weight rather than end-weight. This prediction is supported, as treated in §5.12. For example, in Turkish, in which prosodic phrases are head-initial, binomials favor the long-first order, judging by conjoined color terms. Similarly, the stereotyped vocalism in Turkish places low (heavier) before high (lighter), the mirror image of languages with end-weight such as English.

5.2 Constructions exhibiting end-weight

This section reviews a range of word order phenomena for which end-weight is relevant. The list is not exhaustive. Indeed, for languages such as English, end-weight is such a pervasive principle of grammar that any constructional choice involving word order might be expected to exhibit it. Moreover, some cases of phrasal weight do not involve word order alternation at all; a few examples are provided at the end of this section. The range of phenomena enumerated here is more extensive than previous surveys of end-weight, in part because it covers phenomena that tend to feature in phonologically oriented discussions (e.g. coordination and compounds) as well as phenomena that tend to be confined to research conceiving of weight in syntactic terms (e.g. heavy NP shift), and it is an open question how much crossover there is between these phenomena. Nevertheless, insofar as phonological factors have been investigated across them, the results are largely convergent, justifying at least programmatically a unified approach to the phonological aspect of end-weight, as developed in §5.9 and §5.14.

First, in coordination, conjuncts tend to be organized from lightest to heaviest, all else being equal, as illustrated in (1) (Jespersen 1905, 1938, 1961, Abraham 1950, Malkiel 1959, Jakobson 1960, Bolinger 1962, Gustafsson 1974, 1975, Cooper and Ross 1975, Pinker and Birdsong 1979, Oden and Lopes 1981, Ross 1982, Oakeshott-Taylor 1984, Kelly 1986, Allan 1987, Fenk-Oczlon 1989, McDonald et al. 1993, Wright and Hay 2002, Wright et al. 2005, Benor and Levy 2006, Wolf 2008, Copestake and Herbelot 2011, Lohmann 2012, Mollin 2012, 2013, Lohmann and Takada 2014, Morgan and Levy 2016; cf. also Volkmann 1885 and Behaghel 1909 for early general statements of end-weight, including cases from coordination). Conjuncts are shown increasing in syllable count in (a–e) and in vowel length in (f–h). The broader question of how exactly "heavier" is operationalized for words or phrases is postponed until §5.9.

(1)　a.　kit and caboodle
　　　b.　trials and tribulations
　　　c.　friends, Romans, countrymen
　　　d.　lock, stock, and barrel
　　　e.　Joan and Margery
　　　f.　trick or treat
　　　g.　slip and slide
　　　h.　tit for tat

As the body of work just cited makes clear, end-weight applies as a significant tendency both to idiomatically frozen binomials or multinomials (e.g. *kit and caboodle*) and to relatively free or novel ones (e.g. *Joan and Margery*).[3] In what follows, the terms BINOMIAL and MULTINOMIAL refer to coordinate (or similar; cf. (1–h)) pairs and lists, respectively, regardless of fixity. Furthermore, end-weight is found in both speech and written corpora, is widely attested cross-linguistically, and is productive in experiments, including nonce-word ordering tasks (§§5.5–5.6).

Second, echo-reduplicative and dvandva compounds favor end-weight, as in (2). Echo reduplication involves copying a word with some minor alteration, such as a change in vocalism (ABLAUT), as in (a–b), or in onset consonantism, as in (c–d), in which case the elements rhyme. Elements tend to be organized such that the differing vowels or consonants increase in weight, in a sense to be clarified in §5.5.1 (Wheatley 1866, Jespersen 1938, 1961, Biese 1939, Malkiel 1959, Thun 1963, Marchand 1969, Wescott 1970, Cooper and Ross 1975, Campbell and Anderson 1976, Dienhart 1999, Minkova 2002, Parker 2002, Mortensen 2006, Wolf 2008).

---

[3] "'Why do you always say *Joan and Margery*, yet never *Margery and Joan*?...' In a sequence of two coordinate names, as far as no rank problems interfere, the precedence of the shorter name suits the speaker" (Jakobson 1960:356).

(2) a. pitter-patter
     b. tic-tac-toe
     c. itsy-bitsy
     d. helter-skelter
     e. devamanuṣyāḥ   'gods (*deva-*) and humans (*manuṣya-*)'
     f. mitrā́váruṇā   (Mitra and Varuṇa, two deities)
     g. kuśakāśam   (*kuśa-* and *kāśa-*, two kinds of grass)

A DVANDVA is a type of compound whose force is conjunctive. As such, the order of its members is not syntactically determined, but left to other factors, including end-weight. Such compounds are rare in English, but well established in certain other languages, such as Sanskrit in (2) (e–g), where they tend to exhibit end-weight (Wackernagel 1905:165, 1938, Kiparsky 2010; see also Müller 1997 on German and Kiparsky 2009 on Modern Greek). For example, in (2-f), Varuṇa is both more frequent and more important than Mitra in the Ṛg-Veda, and yet Mitra must go first in the compound, as his name has fewer syllables. The earliest accounts of end-weight come from the ancient Sanskrit grammarians regarding dvandva order. Pāṇini (c. 500–350 BC) treats dvandva order in the three rules 2.2.32–4 of his grammar, the *Aṣṭādhyāyī* (Cardona 1988:262; cf. Böhtlingk 1887, Vasu 1898). The first rule states that an *i*- or *u*-final stem precedes an *a*-stem, the second that a vowel-initial stem precedes a consonant-initial stem, and the third that the shorter element goes first. In the last case, Pāṇini operationalizes length in terms of vowel (i.e. syllable) count, but Kātyāyana, a later commentator, extends Pāṇini's rule to moras, such that a short-voweled stem precedes a long-voweled stem, all else being equal, as illustrated in (2-g).

Third, extraposition of a relative clause to the end of the sentence becomes more likely as the relative clause becomes heavier (Ross 1967, Hawkins 1990, 1994, 2004, Wasow 2002, Francis 2010, Ingason and MacKenzie 2011, MacKenzie 2012, Büring 2013, Francis and Michaelis 2014, Rasekh-Mahand et al. 2016). For example, extraposed constructions like (b) in (3) are increasingly favored over (a) as the relative clause, in brackets, increases in weight. While this and the remaining phenomena have mostly been considered in terms of word count and/or syntactic complexity, there are also indications that phonology (e.g. syllable count and/or number of main stresses) matters independent of syntax, though evidently as a weaker effect than syntax (e.g. Ingason and MacKenzie 2011, MacKenzie 2012, Shih et al. 2015, Stephanie S. Shih 2016; see §5.14).

(3) a. a bus [that advertised the store on its window] passed
     b. a bus passed [that advertised the store on its window]

Fourth, heavy NP (or DP) shift, also known as complex NP shift in earlier research,[4] is often propelled by end-weight, as is scrambling more generally in applicable languages (Chomsky 1958/1962:228, 1961:fn. 18, 1975:477, Ross 1967:51ff, 1986:32f, 47–50, Bever 1970, Kimball 1973, Larson 1988, Zec and Inkelas 1990, Wasow 1997,

---

[4] In what follows, N(P) stands for "noun (phrase)," DP for "determiner phrase," V(P) for "verb (phrase)," P(P) for "preposition (phrase)," and A(P) for "adjective (phrase)."

2002, Arnold et al. 2000, Yamashita and Chang 2001, Choi 2007, Chang 2009, Francis 2010, Stallings and MacDonald 2011, Thuilier 2012, Büring 2013, Faghiri and Samvelian 2014, Stephanie S. Shih 2016).[5] For example, Zec and Inkelas (1990) argue that heavy NP shift in English is conditioned by the shifted argument comprising two or more prosodic words (PWds), as in (4) (their judgments), where ω here indicates a PWd. Hetzron (1972:253f) asserts that pronominal object clitics in Modern Hebrew are ordered in terms of increasing syllable count (cf. also Friedman 1971 on end-weight in Mishnaic Hebrew).

(4) a.   Mark showed some letters to John.
     b.   [??]Mark showed to John [some letters]$_\omega$.
     c.   Mark showed to John [some letters]$_\omega$ [from Paris]$_\omega$.

Fifth, the dative alternation involves the choice between V NP NP and V NP PP for certain ditransitive verbs, as in (5). Unlike heavy NP shift, this choice implicates not only word order but also realization of the indirect object as an NP vs. PP. The preferred construction is affected by the relative weights of the direct and indirect objects (Wasow 1997, 2002, Zubizarreta 1998, Arnold et al. 2000, Bresnan and Nikitina 2003, 2009, Bresnan 2007, Bresnan et al. 2007, Anttila 2008, Bresnan and Hay 2008, Anttila et al. 2010, Bresnan and Ford 2010, Grafmiller and Shih 2011, Kendall et al. 2011, de Marneffe et al. 2012, Wolk et al. 2013, MacDonald 2015). Sixth, and similarly, Wasow (2002) describes a locative alternation in which the location and theme can be reordered, sensitive in part to end-weight, as in (6).

(5) a.   give her the book
     b.   give the book to her

(6) a.   spray paint on the wall
     b.   spray the wall with paint

Seventh, the genitive alternation involves the choice between a prenominal possessor (*X's Y*) and a postnominal one (*Y of X*), as in (7), the latter being favored by a heavier possessor relative to the possessum, as with (c–d) (Rosenbach 2002, 2005, Hinrichs and Szmrecsányi 2007, Grafmiller and Shih 2011, Wolk et al. 2013, Ehret et al. 2014, Shih 2014, Shih and Zuraw 2016, Shih et al. 2015).

(7) a.   [the story]'s ending
     b.   the ending of [the story]
     c.   [the shortest story I've ever read]'s ending
     d.   the ending of [the shortest story I've ever read]

Eighth, particle verbs such as *pick up* are increasingly likely to realize the object after the particle as the object becomes heavier, as in (8) (Sankoff 1980, Wasow 1997, 2002, Lohse et al. 2004).

---

[5] The studies in this list addressing Japanese, Korean, and Persian argue for weight-based effects on word order, but such that the directionality is reversed, being beginning-weight (§5.12) rather than end-weight.

(8) a.   pick her up ~ *pick up her
     b.   pick the child up ~ pick up the child
     c.   ?pick the child, his dog, and several of his classmates up
          ~ pick up the child, his dog, and several of his classmates

Several additional constructions that are sensitive to phrasal weight have been treated less extensively in the literature. Stacked adjuncts, such as adjectives or prepositional phrases, evince end-weight effects (e.g. Hawkins 2000 on stacked PPs; Vendler 1968, Eichinger 1992, and Rijkhoff 2002 on stacked adjectives, though cf. Kotowski 2016 and Kotowski and Härtl 2016 for a null result for phonology). Adjective–noun ordering can be subject to end-weight (e.g. Thuilier 2012 on French; cf. mixed results for Tagalog in Shih and Zuraw 2016). Likelihood of clefting is also affected by weight (Erdmann 1988, Wasow 2002). Furthermore, some weight-sensitive constructions do not involve word order variants at all. For instance, optional complementizers (*which* and *that*) are favored by heavier (at least in the sense of more complex) relative clauses and/or heads (Fox and Thompson 2007). Auxiliary verb or copula contraction is favored by a heavier immediately preceding phrase, where weight appears to be a function of both syntactic and prosodic considerations (Walker and Meechan 1999, Ingason and MacKenzie 2011, MacKenzie 2012, Anttila 2016). The raising to second position of unaccented verbs has been suggested to correlate with the length of the verb, as in Vedic Sanskrit (Wackernagel 1955, Rothstein-Dowden 2018). Finally, *as far as* clauses in English have an optional verbal coda (usually *goes* or *is concerned*) which becomes less likely as the syntactic and/or prosodic complexity of the clause increases (Rickford et al. 1995, Wasow 2002).

5.3 Non-phonological factors in end-weight

In constructions exhibiting flexibility in word order, such as binomial conjunctions *X and Y*, numerous factors affect ordering, including information-theoretic, semantic, syntactic, and phonological considerations. Before going on to isolate the contribution of phonology in §§5.4–5.5, non-phonological factors are surveyed in this section.

First, items tend to decrease in frequency, presumably reflecting the priority of more accessible items (Bock 1982, Kelly 1986, Kelly et al. 1986, Allan 1987, Fenk-Oczlon 1989, McDonald et al. 1993, Griffin and Bock 1998, Golenbock 2000, Wright et al. 2005, Benor and Levy 2006, Shih and Zuraw 2016). For example, in *kit and caboodle*, while *kit* is the lighter conjunct phonologically, it is also the more frequent. In general, frequency and weight are negatively correlated (Zipf 1936), meaning that much of the observed tendency for end-weight could in principle reflect frequency rather than weight. Most studies deconfounding the two factors support an independent contribution of frequency (e.g. Fenk-Oczlon 1989, Benor and Levy 2006, Mollin 2012, Shih and Zuraw 2016; but cf. Lohmann and Takada 2014 and Shih et al. 2015 for null results for frequency). However, when frequency is controlled, either through holding it constant[6] or through regression modeling, weight remains a clear effect, as further discussed in §§5.5–5.6. Indeed, in corpus studies with large sets of predictors, frequency is usually either nonsignificant or relatively weak relative to structural predictors (e.g. Benor and Levy 2006, Mollin 2012, Lohmann and Takada 2014, Shih et al. 2015).

Furthermore, semantics and pragmatics influence ordering, as studied extensively for coordinated pairs. One influential early treatment of semantic factors is Cooper and Ross's (1975) article "World order" (sic), which attempts to subsume several semantic predictors of priority under a principle termed ME FIRST, according to which initial position favors properties associated with the prototypical speaker. See also Allan (1987), Benor and Levy (2006), and Lohmann and Takada (2014) for more recent surveys of semantic and pragmatic predictors. Some notable factors include animacy (more animate first; Byrne and Davidson 1985, McDonald et al. 1993, Shih et al. 2015), proximity (nearer in time or space first; Jespersen 1961, Cooper and Ross 1975, Ross 1982; cf. also an OWN BEFORE OTHER tendency, *ibid.*), iconicity (reflecting temporal or other scales; Malkiel 1959, Benor and Levy 2006, Lohmann and Takada 2014), gender (male before female; Malkiel 1959, Cooper and Ross 1975, Wright and Hay 2002, Wright et al. 2005), concreteness (Bock and Warren 1985), specificity (Karimi 2003, Faghiri and Samvelian 2014), and prototypicality or unmarkedness (Benor and Levy 2006). Priority also tends to favor more active, agentive, positive, powerful, or culturally important elements (Malkiel 1959, Cooper and Ross 1975, Allan 1987). A further pragmatic principle is OLD BEFORE NEW, that is, given information tends to precede new information (Bock 1977, Fenk-Oczlon 1989, Wasow 2002, Ferreira and Yoshita 2003, Wasow and Arnold 2003, Benor and Levy 2006, Lohmann and Takada 2014). Focus can also affect word order (Quirk et al. 1985, Zubizarreta 1998, Büring and Gutiérrez-Bravo 2001, Szendroi 2001, Arregi 2002, Samek-Lodovici 2005, Vogel 2006, Selkirk 2011, Büring 2013).

As a final factor to consider before turning to phonology, end-weight is often analyzed in terms of syntactic complexity. Indeed, for higher-level end-weight phenomena such as extraposition and heavy NP shift, many studies reckon weight in terms of word count or syntactic complexity, without considering phonological form (though of course syntactic and phonological complexity are highly correlated). Syntactic weight is usually operationalized gradiently in terms of word count, node count, or phrase (maximal projection) count; see especially Wasow (2002:§2), Szmrecsányi (2004), and Shih et al. (2015) for comparisons of different measures (Ross 1986 suggests "a quasi-continuous function of length and complexity"; cf. also Chomsky 1961:fn. 18, 1958/1962:228, 1975:477). Accounts of end-weight (or beginning-weight) from the processing literature typically rely on syntactic complexity as it affects the cost of integration (Hawkins 1990, 1994, 2004, Gibson 1998, 2000,

---

[6] Holding frequency constant can be accomplished either by selecting approximately equally frequent attested items or by examining the behavior of unattested (i.e. constructed) items, whose frequencies are zero. Moreover, the frequency factor is largely moot for the cases of end-weight in §5.2 involving multiword phrases, since most such phrases (e.g., in the first such case above, "that advertised the store on its window") have corpus frequencies of zero.

Temperley 2007), though specifically phonological processing has also been considered in the context of binomials (Cutler and Cooper 1978). Most studies directly comparing phonological to syntactic criteria for higher-level end-weight suggest that syntactic and semantic considerations dominate phonological ones, at least at that scope of complexity (e.g. Shih and Grafmiller 2013; see §5.14). Finally, Malkiel (1959) suggests that greater morphological complexity favors final position in binomials, though this conclusion has not been tested in controlled models.

5.4 Phonological factors not involving weight

When the syntactic, semantic, and pragmatic factors in §5.3 are factored out, phonology remains as a significant contributor to end-weight. Non-phonological factors can be controlled either by wug-testing or by multivariate modeling. A WUG is a constructed nonce probe (Berko 1958). As such, a wug does not necessarily have properties such as frequency or meaning. Moreover, if the wug is a single, unanalyzable word, morphosyntactic complexity is irrelevant. Several wug tests have been conducted for binomial ordering and similar tasks (Bolinger 1962, Pinker and Birdsong 1979, Oden and Lopes 1981, Oakeshott-Taylor 1984, Parker 2002). For example, a wug test might determine speakers' ordering preferences for nonce pairs such as {*glip*, *badooza*} to gauge the degree to which the heavy-last order is preferred when syntax, semantics, and frequency are moot.

Beyond wug-testing, several corpus studies of end-weight phenomena such as binomials have been conducted, often analyzing the data with regression models including a range of potentially relevant factors in an attempt to assess their independent contributions (e.g. Wright and Hay 2002, Wright et al. 2005, Benor and Levy 2006, Grafmiller and Shih 2011, Lohmann and Takada 2014, Shih et al. 2015; cf. also Kelly 1986 for a non-regression multifactorial approach). As these wug tests and corpus studies collectively make clear, phonology affects ordering in at least three independent ways, namely, EURYTHMY (i.e. stress patterns), EUTAXY (i.e. segmental phonotactics), and prosodic weight per se (syllable count, vowel length, coda sonority, etc.). Raw phonological complexity may also be relevant, but, as argued below in §5.8, cannot substitute for weight. For instance, in end-weight, as in phonological weight more generally, V: is heavier than VC, despite the former being less complex (§2.7.2).

Among non-weight-related phonological factors, phonotactics can affect ordering, in that marked sequences are sometimes avoided. This avoidance is best documented for adjacent identical consonants, which violate Obligatory Contour Principle (OCP) constraints. For example, the English genitive alternation favors orders that avoid adjacent sibilants (e.g. *seats of the bus* ≻ *the bus's seats*; *of the analysis* ≻ *the analysis's(s)*; cf. Zwicky 1987, Hinrichs and Szmrecsányi 2007, Ehret et al. 2014, Shih et al. 2015). Shih and Zuraw (2016) also find a significant avoidance of adjacent nasals in Tagalog noun-adjective ordering (e.g. *na itím* 'LINK black' ≻ *itím na*). This effect is strongest for immediately adjacent nasals but obtains weakly even across a vowel. Hiatus avoidance, that is, avoiding placing a vowel-final word immediately before a vowel-initial word, such that the vowels abut, can also affect word order (Gunkel and Ryan 2011, Stephanie S. Shih 2014, 2016). These phonotactic factors do not necessarily favor end-weight; they are cited here only as a type of general phonological factor in word order.

A couple of additional phonological factors in binomial ordering that have been claimed in the literature to be due to phonotactics are reanalyzed here as being due to weight. First, Parker (2002) claims that echo reduplications such as *roshy-toshy*, with the more obstruent onset in second position, are favored over their reversals (in this case, *toshy-roshy*) due to a SYLLABLE CONTACT LAW that favors a low sonority onset immediately following a nucleus, which is invariably high in sonority. See §5.5.3 and §5.8.3, however, for arguments that such orderings are driven by weight, not by the OCP. Second, Wright et al. (2005) suggest that an increasingly complex onset should be increasingly favored in the initial position of a binomial, since if it were in the second position (e.g. after *and*), it would abut a coda, creating a highly complex cluster. But they find no significant effect of onset complexity, and in other studies that do, complexity is favored in second position, consistent with weight but not phonotactics (§5.5.2).

A second non-weight-based phonological factor in word order that can sometimes create the appearance of end-weight is metrical optimization (Schlüter 2005, Shih 2014), both in the avoidance of CLASH (i.e. adjacent stressed syllables) and of LAPSE (i.e., descriptively, two or more unstressed syllables in a row, especially between stresses; cf. Gordon 2002a), and perhaps also in NONFINALITY, that is, the avoidance of a phrase-final stressed syllable (on the latter in binomials, see Bolinger 1962, Müller 1997, Benor and Levy 2006, Mollin 2012).[7] Indeed, rhythm is perhaps the earliest proposed explanation for the syllable-count effect in English binomials. Jespersen (1905) observes that ó and óσ (e.g. *bread and butter*) induces an evenly alternating rhythm of two trochees, violating neither CLASH nor LAPSE (nor NONFINALITY). The alternative order, *butter and bread*, violates LAPSE (and NONFINALITY). Thus, in some cases, ostensible phonological end-weight might actually reflect eurythmic tendencies. Ehret et al. (2014) and Shih (2014) find the English genitive alternation to be sensitive to rhythm, though the former identify it as "a minor player" compared to weight, which was "a very crucial factor" (p. 298). As further discussed in §5.6, prosodic end-weight cannot be reduced to eurythmy, but rather instantiates an independent phenomenon.

5.5 Subsyllabic factors in end-weight

Certain properties of syllables are well established as contributing to end-weight, at least in the context of binomials, compounds, and echo reduplication. Specifically, seven subsyllabic properties correlate with greater end-weight: vowel length, vowel

---

[7] NONFINALITY is used in varying senses in the literature as referring to final stress avoidance, final foot avoidance, or both (e.g. Prince and Smolensky 1993/2004). In this chapter, for simplicity, it can be taken to refer only to phrase-final stress, as footing is not considered here. See §2.3.3 on NONFINALITY in the analysis of stress placement. NONFINALITY may be related both to extrametricality (Liberman and Prince 1977, Hayes 1979a, 1982) and to the neutralization of weight contrasts in final position that owes in part to final lengthening (Lunden 2010, 2013, Gordon et al. 2010).

lowness (likely also connected to duration), onset complexity, onset obstruency, coda complexity, coda sonority, and stress. These properties (except coda complexity and stress) are posited as an ensemble first by Cooper and Ross (1975:71), and have continued to receive support from subsequent corpus-based and experimental research. This section comprises four subsections, treating the nucleus (§5.5.1), onset (§5.5.2), coda (§5.5.3), and stress (§5.5.4), respectively. The effect of syllable count is then treated in §5.6, after which a summary of prosodic factors in end-weight is provided in §5.7. Furthermore, as this and the following sections (§§5.8–5.9) argue, all of these syllabic properties are associated with syllable weight more generally. This view, which is given the slogan END-WEIGHT IS WEIGHT, has been implied by previous studies, but is taken to an even greater extreme here, so as to bring onset size, onset sonority, and coda sonority effects explicitly into its purview.

5.5.1 Vowel length and quality

First, long(er) vowels are heavier than short(er) vowels, where "heavier" in the context of end-weight refers to favoring final position. This tendency is first noted by the ancient grammarian Kātyāyana, accounting for Sanskrit dvandvas such as *kuśa -kāśa-m* (two kinds of grass). It is also one of the core generalizations of Cooper and Ross (1975)—their second rule of seven, after syllable count—and likewise of Ross (1982) in their studies of (mainly) English binomials: Long/tense vowels consistently favor second position over short/lax vowels, as in *trick or treat* and *slip and slide*. Müller (1997) demonstrates the same length effect for German. Pinker and Birdsong (1979) wug-test English and French binomials, analyzing vowel length separately from quality (e.g. *motching and moatching* for length, *fim and fum* for quality). They find both length and quality to be significant predictors of end-weight in both languages. Minkova (2002) concludes the same for English. Oakeshott-Taylor (1984) conducts a detailed study of the correlation between several phonetic factors and end-weight propensity in largely nonsensical binomials (e.g. *peat and poot*) in South African English, Dutch, and Afrikaans, finding phonetic duration (beyond just phonemic tenseness/length) to be a significant predictor of end-weight in all three languages. Consider, for instance, the English front vowels in Figure 5.1, where end-weight propensity refers to the percentage of the time that the vowel is chosen to be in the second item in a balanced binomial ordering task. As the Figure illustrates, end-weight propensities reflect gradient duration, not just binary length.

Benor and Levy (2006) and Mollin (2012), in their respective corpus studies of English binomials, test for effects of vowel length, with largely, though not entirely, null results.[8] Nevertheless, these studies are not designed to probe specifically phonetic/phonological factors, as those in the previous paragraph were. Benor and Levy (2006), for instance, evaluate 411 binomial types against nineteen predictors, meaning that phonological tendencies might easily be swamped by semantic factors or might otherwise be poorly instantiated by the selection of data. A null result, after all, is not

---

[8] Mollin (2012) does find a significant contribution of length to end-weight, but only in the subset of data in which semantics, rhythm, and syllable count are held constant.

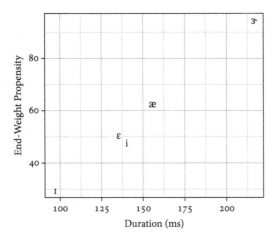

FIGURE 5.1 End-weight propensity vs. duration for five South African English front vowels under nuclear stress, based on data from Oakeshott-Taylor (1984:228, 233). Propensity is the percentage of the time that the vowel was chosen for final position in a balanced ordering task.

the same as a negative result. It can arise from a test that is not sufficiently powerful, or a paucity of relevant forms. Finally, Lohmann and Takada (2014) find a significant effect of mora count in Japanese binomials, which is related to length, though they do not include syllable and mora count in the same model, meaning that it is not possible to interpret the mora count result as a nucleus length effect.

Vowel quality is also widely documented to correlate with end-weight, in ways that likely also ultimately reflect duration, in which case the length and quality effects can be collapsed. English, for one, exhibits a well-known tendency for a high(er), front(er) vowel to precede a low(er), back(er) vowel, as in *tit for tat, brain and brawn, wend and wander*, and numerous similar cases (Wheatley 1866, Biese 1939, Thun 1963, Gustafsson 1975, etc.). Wescott (1970) and Minkova (2002) provide tables of combinatory rates, supporting a general tendency for items to increase in F1 (i.e. lowness). Jespersen (1961), Marchand (1969), Minkova (2002), and Stephanie S. Shih (2016) also single out vowel height. Cooper and Ross (1975) initially suggest that F2 (i.e. backness) is the relevant dimension, but Ross (1982) revises this to height, in line with the other literature, further suggesting that backness is decisive only when height is held constant. Pinker and Birdsong (1979) and Oden and Lopes (1981) both demonstrate that the height effect is productive in binomial wug-tests. Beyond English, a high-before-low tendency has been described for German (Müller 1997), Hungarian (Pordany 1986), and Jingpho (Mortensen 2006). Jespersen (1961:176) mentions also Greek, Lithuanian, and Bantu (sic). Pāṇini's rule 2.2.32 for Sanskrit, which states that a stem in *-i* or *-u* precedes one in *-a* (Wackernagel 1905, 1938), may reflect the generalization as well, though the rule specifies only the stem-final vowel, which points rather to morphological conditioning.

Increasing F1 jibes with the more general short-before-long tendency, given that F1 is positively correlated with duration, both in English and cross-linguistically (Lehiste

1970). In other words, lower vowels are usually longer than higher vowels, all else being equal. This correlation likely arises from the greater jaw displacement required for low vowels (Westbury and Keating 1980).

Nevertheless, certain languages, such as Turkish and Tungus, are claimed to invert the height generalization, such that the lowness favors initial position (Marchand 1952, 1969, Swadesh 1962, Wescott 1970, Pinker and Birdsong 1979).[9] Being head-final, with the basic word order SOV (subject–object–verb), these languages might be expected to exhibit beginning-weight rather than end-weight. If this is the case, it arguably follows that the phonological generalizations should be inverted, so as to favor greater weight in initial position. See §5.12 for further discussion of beginning-weight, its evidence, and its motivation.

5.5.2 Onset size and sonority

The structure and features of onsets are also fairly widely reported to affect prosodic end-weight, with two generalizations approaching consensus in the literature. First, onsets containing more segments pattern as heavier, again in the sense of favoring final position in compounds, binomials, etc. Second, lower sonority onsets pattern as heavier. These two generalizations are considered in turn.

Cooper and Ross (1975) are perhaps first to articulate the onset complexity effect, which they state as their third phonological principle or ordering, drawing on English examples such as *meet and greet, helter-skelter,* and *fair and square.* This view has generally since been corroborated. It is demonstrated by wug-testing in Oden and Lopes (1981) (e.g. *sash-sprash, atten-dratten*), where it is significant, albeit not as strong an effect as vowel identity or onset sonority. Ross (1982) notes that the contrast between a null and simple onset (Ø vs. C) is greater than that between a simple and complex onset (C vs. C_2), though both hold. The corpus studies of Benor and Levy (2006) and Mollin (2012) also support the onset size effect, though it is not highly significant in either, perhaps owing to the small number of relevant data and the large number of factors in their data samples, which are not designed to probe specifically phonology. Indeed, this factor, though borderline, is the strongest subsyllabic effect in Benor and Levy (2006): "When the confounding effects of semantic and metrical constraints are controlled for, the only phonological constraint for which we found compelling evidence was a preference for larger initial consonant clusters on [item] B." Wright and Hay (2002), by contrast, find no significant effect of onset size in their study of binomials of personal names. As mentioned in §5.4, they hypothesize that complexity would favor initial rather than final position due to phonotactics, but this hypothesis is not borne out.

A simple experiment on Amazon's Mechanical Turk (Daland et al. 2011, Gibson et al. 2011, Sprouse 2011, Yu and Lee 2014, Ryan 2018) further supports the productivity of the onset effect in English. Each critical item is a nonce binomial consisting of two monosyllables that differ only in onset complexity, as shown

[9] Pinker and Birdsong (1979) also mention Hindi and Yiddish as inverters, apparently based on some examples in Cooper and Ross (1975), but the examples involve semantic reversals vis-à-vis English.

in (9). Participants are asked to select the ordering of the binomial that sounds better to them. They are presented with a total of nineteen forced-choice prompts, of which fourteen are fillers and five are critical items. For critical items, the spelling varies slightly between the two monosyllables so that they have the same number of letters, ruling out the alternative possible explanation that participants are ignoring phonology and placing the visually larger element second. Fillers consisted of real binomial "freezes" for which one order is clearly more natural than the other (e.g. *black* ∼ *white* and *near* ∼ *far*). For each prompt, filler and critical alike, both orders are presented in random order as radio-button options. Critical items and fillers are randomly interleaved, except that the initial and final prompts are always fillers. Participants were paid $0.34 for this approximately two-minute task and retained for analysis only if they complete all of the prompts, err on no more than one of the fillers, provide informed consent, are located in the United States, are identified by the service as "Masters," and have a 97 per cent or higher approval rating based on a record of a hundred or more tasks. These criteria were met by twenty-seven subjects. Among them, the (phonologically) longer onset was preferred in second position 2.6 times as frequently as in the first position, a significant departure from the 50 per cent chance baseline (goodness-of-fit $\chi^2(1) = 25.8$, $p < .0001$). This test therefore corroborates the findings reported in the previous paragraph.

(9)

Binomial (in preferred order)	N Agree	N Disagree	% Agree
1. beck and brek	23	4	85
2. keph and klef	20	7	74
3. phum and frum	16	11	59
4. spimm and sprim	19	8	70
5. temm and trem	19	8	70

Among other languages, Pordany (1986) supports the onset complexity effect for Hungarian. Müller (1997) supports it for German. Shih and Zuraw (2016) find it in Tagalog, in the sense that null onsets are avoided in second position, though they speculate that this avoidance might be due to a penalty on resyllabification. Note, however, that this explanation would not carry over to languages like English and German, where the same tendency is also attested. To wit, in (9), phonotactics favors the complex-first order, since that order minimizes the cluster after the conjunction (Wright et al. 2005:541). But the observed preference is the opposite. In Sanskrit, Pāṇini's second rule for dvandva order, 2.2.33, states that a vowel-initial element (of the regular inflectional class in -*a*) occupies first position. Like Tagalog, this rule admits two (not mutually exclusive) possible explanations. First, it may reflect the intrinsic weights of null vs. filled onsets. Second, it may reflect phonotactics, in the sense that placing the vowel-initial element second would induce vowel fusion sandhi. For example, *uṣṭra-kharam* is a dvandva meaning "camel and donkey." If it were reversed, the -*a* of *khara* would have to fuse with the *u*- of *uṣṭra*, yielding the -*o*- in **kharoṣṭram*. Wackernagel (1905) conjectures that the rule might therefore be driven by sandhi avoidance.

Beyond segment count, it has long been noted that English "freezes" (i.e. relatively fixed binomials and compounds) favor certain featural configurations of onsets. In particular, given a sonority difference, the more sonorous onset is preferred in initial position. This effect is perhaps clearest when other factors are held constant, as in *wear and tear*, *wheel and deal*, *surf and turf*, and *huff and puff* (or comparable compounds, e.g. *namby-pamby*). Cooper and Ross (1975), Ross (1982), and independently Campbell and Anderson (1976) state the sonority generalization clearly as such, though indications of it can also be found in earlier work such as Wheatley (1866), Biese (1939), Abraham (1950), and Marchand (1969). It is the fourth phonological principle of Cooper and Ross (1975). Frequency tables in Campbell and Anderson (1976:75) underscore the strength of the effect. Müller (1997) suggests that the same onset sonority effect is active in German.

The onset sonority generalization has been further upheld by several experiments. Pinker and Birdsong (1979) find it to be significant in English, though not in French. Moreover, onset sonority is one of the stronger effects in Oden and Lopes (1981), ahead of, for instance, onset size. Parker (2002) confirms the effect in doublets of the type *roly-poly*, generally supporting falling sonority, as in the example just cited (with isolated exceptions such as *k* before *g*). Finally, in their study of name pairs, Wright et al. (2005) observe a trend for the placement of the more sonorous onset first, though it is nonsignificant.

Potentially related to sonority, *h* shows a strong tendency to occupy the first position in English (Wheatley 1866, Biese 1939, Abraham 1950, Marchand 1969, Campbell and Anderson 1976, Parker 2002). In other words, *h* patterns with sonorant onsets and null onsets, as if it were light. If *h* is regarded as highly sonorous, its behavior can be subsumed by the sonority principle. Laryngeals such as *h* and *ʔ*, after all, are well-known to be ambivalent in sonority both typologically and within English (e.g. Parker 2002:224; recall also Huehuetla Tepehua, in which laryngeals count as sonorants for weight; §2.7.2). Alternatively, *h* may pattern as light due to its proximity to nullity. In some phonological systems, *h* composes a natural class with null onsets. In Ancient Greek, for instance, a coda resyllabifies with the following word iff the latter begins with *h* or a vowel. Thus, *h* might pattern as light either by virtue of its sonority (which in onsets correlates with lightness; §5.9) and/or by virtue of its inchoateness as a segment, lacking supralaryngeal place. The latter would be consistent with the fact that ostensibly vowel-initial words in English are often pronounced with an initial glottal stop, but this glottal stop, if present, does not count towards weight in the same way that other consonants do (Ryan 2014).

Next, labials are sometimes claimed to be favored in second position (Jespersen 1961, Cooper and Ross 1975, Campbell and Anderson 1976, Dienhart 1999). This tendency has not, however, been tested systematically for binomials, so as to deconfound it from sonority and other factors. Since it is tentative, I make no attempt here to explain it. Furthermore, Campbell and Anderson (1976), in their extensive survey of English doublets, find at least one subtype, usually associated with cuteness or baby talk, that reverses the sonority generalization, placing a *w*-initial copy in second position (e.g. *boogie-woogie, fuzzy-wuzzy, Betsy-Wetsy*).[10] As they admit, this subtype appears to operate by a more idiosyncratic principle (cf. the "islands of reliability" of Albright 2002). In conclusion, the only two arguably consensus principles regarding onsets in end-weight are that (a) longer onsets pattern as heavier and (b) more obstruent onsets pattern as heavier.

5.5.3 *Coda size and sonority*

In the coda, unlike in the onset, greater sonority correlates with greater weight, as in *thick and thin, push and pull*, and *pots and pans*. This generalization is one of the core phonological principles of Cooper and Ross (1975) and Ross (1982). It is also supported by experimental data, with strong results in the aforementioned direction in Bolinger (1962) and Wright et al. (2005) (Pinker and Birdsong 1979, for their part, do not test it). Additionally, Mollin (2012) finds a highly significant effect of coda sonority in English corpus data, though Benor and Levy (2006) obtain a null result for it in their study (as they do for some other well-known phonological factors, given their design, as discussed in §5.5.1).

Although it has not been investigated systematically, post-hoc analysis of wug-test data from Bolinger (1962) suggests that this sonority effect is gradient. As the sonority difference between the items' codas increases, the more sonorant-ending item is increasingly skewed towards second position, as illustrated in Figure 5.2 for three sonority classes (obstruent, nasal, and liquid). Wug binomials were identical

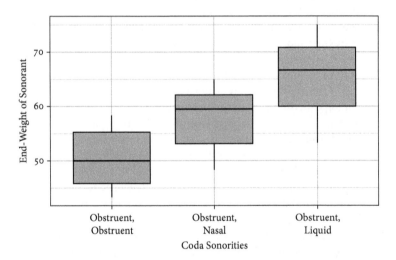

FIGURE 5.2 The greater the sonority difference between codas, the more the higher sonority coda is preferred in final position, based on wug-test data from Bolinger (1962). Once again, the y-axis is the percentage of time that the more sonorant coda was chosen for final position in a balanced ordering task.

---

[10] Andrew Nevins (p.c.) notes that labials are prevalent in echo reduplication cross-linguistically.

except for their codas (e.g. *skrit* and *skrill*). In the obstruent-obstruent category, one of the obstruents is classified as being more sonorant than the other by virtue of its voicing and/or continuancy. The y-axis is the percentage of the time that Bolinger's subjects (in Test 4) preferred the more sonorant-final order of each relevant pair. If the sonority generalization were categorical, sensitive only to, say, [±*son*], the fact that nasals are approximately halfway between obstruents and liquids in their inferred end-weight would be missed.

A few studies (Cooper and Ross 1975, Bolinger 1962, Mollin 2012) further claim that open syllables pattern as heavier than closed syllables, as in *hem and haw* and *lock and key*. This generalization likely folds in with the coda sonority generalization, as the open syllables in question, usually monosyllables, are typically long vowels or diphthongs, as in both examples just provided. In other words, if the comparison is between VC and VV, the second timing slot of the rime is more sonorous in the latter. More generally, greater sonority anywhere in the rime, including a lower vowel, contributes to greater end-weight.

The coda sonority effect cannot be explained away by phonotactics or vowel duration. Consider first phonotactics. For example, type *thick and thin* could conceivably be preferred to *thin and thick* because the latter alone places a highly sonorous nasal coda next to a highly sonorous nasal(ized) nucleus, as penalized by Syllable Contact or OCP constraints (see §5.8.3). However, the coda sonority effect persists when phonotactics is neutralized, a situation that arises when the codas are conjunct-internal. For example, nonce *zick me and zill me* has the same phonotactic violations as *zill me and zick me*, but speakers still prefer the former.

This preference is confirmed by a forced-choice experiment conducted via Amazon's Mechanical Turk, set up similarly to the experiment just described in §5.5.2. In this case, seventy-two participants met the screening criteria. Each evaluated twenty-five binomials, including ten critical items and fifteen fillers. As always, both orders of each binomial are presented in random order, and the order of the prompts is also randomized. Critical items are nonce binomials generated by a formula to pair coda {p, k} in one conjunct with coda {b, g, l, m, n} in the other.[11] Critical items were distributed stochastically across three conditions, namely, "Simple," "Suffix," and "Clitic," which are exemplified in (10) (the conditions are weighted so that the "Suffix" condition is approximately three times as populous as the others, for reasons presently irrelevant). In every condition, the sonorant coda (or ambisyllabic consonant) was significantly favored finally, as shown in (10) by χ^2 goodness-of-fit tests (based on the counts excluding obstruent–obstruent pairings). In conclusion, the productivity of the coda sonority effect is confirmed here not only for the simple case (e.g. *zick and zill*), but also for forms in which the critical coda is insulated by a suffix (e.g. *zicker*

[11] Wugs are generated by randomly pairing orthographic stems (*shi, zi, floo, je, gro, gri, bla, tre, fe, vi, bi, pli, fli*) with orthographic codas (*p, ck, b, g, l, m, n*). In the suffix condition, the word is further appended with *-er*, *-a*, *-y*, or *-o*, adjusting spelling as appropriate. In the clitic condition, *me, one, it,* or *you* is appended. Wugs containing *lVl* or *ag* are excluded, as are accidental real English words, as determined by checking a lexicon.

and ziller) or clitic (e.g. *zick me and zill me*). In these latter two cases, phonotactics cannot motivate the preference, but weight remains viable.[12]

(10)

	Simple	Suffix	Clitic
1.	zick and zill	zicker and ziller	zick me and zill me
2.	grop and grom	groppy and grommy	grop one and grom one
3.	trep and tren	treppo and trenno	trep it and tren it
...	(etc.)	(etc.)	(etc.)

[+*son*]-final:

62.5% of 112 selections	57.2% of 299 selections	63.4% of 93 selections
$\chi^2(1) = 7.0, p = .008$	$\chi^2(1) = 6.2, p = .013$	$\chi^2(1) = 6.7, p = .010$

A second logically possible—but ultimately not viable—explanation for the coda sonority effect is that vowels tend to be longer before sonorant than obstruent codas. If so, perhaps vowel duration drives the effect. After all, vowel duration is known independently to contribute to end-weight (§5.5.1). But it cannot be the sole cause of the coda sonority effect. In particular, lateral codas pattern as heavier than nasal codas. In the data in (10), laterals are final in 66 per cent of their binomials, while nasals are final 56 per cent of the time (Fisher's exact test $p = .02$). This distinction is also evident from Bolinger (1962), as shown in Figure 5.2. However, vowels are shorter before laterals than before nasals in English. To confirm this, all 3,583 monosyllabic nouns of the form $C_0V\{l, n, m\}$ were retrieved from the Buckeye corpus (Pitt et al. 2007). In a mixed-effects regression with random intercepts for onset and vowel identity, vowels are significantly shorter before laterals ($\beta = -19$ ms, $t = -4.9$). Figure 5.3 shows that this generalization is consistent across vowels in English (cf. also Katz 2012 for a production study).[13] Thus, the coda sonority effect cannot be written off to properties of the vowel; it is at least partly intrinsic to the coda. Laterals are longer and more sonorous than nasals, which presumably drives their greater weight.

Sonority aside, greater coda complexity in terms of segment count correlates with greater weight. This means that unlike sonority, the complexity factor works in the same direction for both onsets and codas. Ross (1982) documents this generalization for English binomials.[14] Ross also mentions Arabic as complying (cf. Pinker and Birdsong 1979:506). In their wug-test of French binomials, Pinker and Birdsong (1979) find a significant finality-favoring effect of coda complexity, though in their English test, it is only a nonsignificant trend. The English corpus study of Benor

---

[12] Pairs like *zicker and ziller* suggest that so-called ambisyllabic consonants pattern as codas rather than onsets for the determination of weight: If they were (exclusively) onsets, a preference for the reverse order might be expected, given that obstruent onsets behave as (if anything) heavier than sonorant onsets (§5.2; see also §5.9.4).

[13] The following vowels are excluded from the figure due to a paucity of data in the corpus. First, [æ] and [ɔɪ] both occur only once before [l] in the relevant frame, and [aʊ] and [ʌ] never occur in this context in the corpus. [ʊ] does not occur in the frame before [n].

[14] Ross (1982) corrects Cooper and Ross (1975) on this point. The latter had tentatively suggested that greater coda complexity is favored in initial position (as in *betwixt and between*), though they also cite counterexamples. Most of their positive examples involve vowel length confounds.

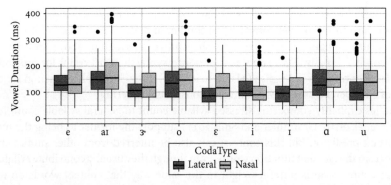

FIGURE 5.3 Vowels are aggregately longer before nasal codas than before lateral codas in English, based on monosyllabic nouns in the Buckeye corpus. Despite this, syllables with lateral codas pattern as heavier.

and Levy (2006) reveals a nonsignificant trend favoring complex codas in final position, and that of Mollin (2012) obtains null results. On the whole, then, coda complexity appears to be relatively weak as a predictor, possibly subordinate even to onset complexity. One possible explanation for its weakness is that longer codas tend to cooccur with shorter vowels, both phonemically (e.g. *betwixt and between*) and durationally, even when the vowel is held constant (e.g. *beet* has a shorter vowel than *bee*). The previous paragraph also alluded to this trade-off: There is a partial compensatory timing relationship between the durations of the nucleus and coda (Abercrombie 1967, Maddieson 1985, Browman and Goldstein 1988, Katz 2010, 2012). Therefore, increasing coda size might not contribute to the overall duration of the syllable to the same extent that increasing the nucleus or onset size does. But regardless of relative effect sizes and their explanations, the overall picture is that coda complexity can contribute to weight, just as coda sonority can.

5.5.4 Stress level

Finally, stress level affects weight, in the sense that stressed syllables contribute more to weight than unstressed syllables. This factor is sometimes operationalized as the number of PWds, given that each PWd has a single primary stress. Whether syllables with secondary stress pattern in this context as stressed, unstressed, or intermediate remains an outstanding question (cf. Anttila et al. 2010:974 for a preliminary result favoring their intermediate status).

English heavy NP shift and Serbo-Croatian topicalization are claimed by Zec and Inkelas (1990) to target branching phonological phrases, that is, phrases comprising two or more PWds (cf. also Zubizarreta 1998:150 for a similar branchingness constraint in Italian). Unstressed words do not count towards this minimum, since they do not head their own PWds. Thus, in these cases, it is not syntactic word count that matters, but rather the number of primary stressed elements. Anttila et al. (2010:975) study this requirement more systematically for the dative alternation in Switchboard, a corpus of spoken English. They find that primary stress count strongly affects end-weight, but syntactic word count has no significant effect when primary stress count is also in the model. Similarly, Grafmiller and Shih (2011) find that primary stress count is significant in the English genitive alternation, above and beyond word count.[15] Finally, PWd count is superior to syntactic word count for predicting auxiliary contraction in English (MacKenzie 2012), though this phenomenon is not a case of end-weight, as it does not involve constituent ordering.

Studies explicitly comparing stressed syllable count to general syllable count (e.g. Anttila et al. 2010, Grafmiller and Shih 2011) support the former as being the more important predictor. But this contrast can also be inferred from other studies cited above from the fact that function words, even though they usually contribute syllables, do not count towards phrasal weight in the same way that content words do (e.g. this treatment is implicit in Zec and Inkelas 1990). Stressed syllable count is also expected to affect binomial ordering (as in cases like *I'll huff, and I'll puff, and I'll blow your house in*), but existing phonological studies on binomial ordering analyze single-word conjuncts, shedding no light on this prediction. To be sure, foundational work on end-weight by Behaghel (1909) offers many examples of conjunctions in which a one-word conjunct precedes a multiword conjunct, but without a quantitative study, it is unclear to what extent prosodic vs. syntactic complexity motivates such cases. Thus, experimental and corpus-based studies of multiword conjuncts remain a desideratum.

5.6 The syllable-count effect in end-weight

In addition to the subsyllabic factors in prosodic end-weight described in the preceding sections, the total number of syllables in a constituent affects its prosodic weight, termed here the SYLLABLE-COUNT EFFECT. While rhythmic optimization of phrases is an established phenomenon (e.g. Hayes 1984, Selkirk 1984, Schlüter 2005, Shih 2014) and likely has some effect on word order preferences in end-weight constructions (cf. e.g. Bolinger 1962, Campbell and Anderson 1976, Kelly and Bock 1988, McDonald et al. 1993, Müller 1997, Wright et al. 2005, Benor and Levy 2006, Anttila 2008, Ehret et al. 2014, Shih 2014, Shih et al. 2015), it cannot explain away the syllable-count effect in end-weight in the general case. This section surveys the evidence for a syllable-count effect as independent from other factors, especially eurythmy and frequency. It is divided into four subsections, treating English (§5.6.1), Latin (§5.6.2), French (§5.6.3), and other languages (§5.6.4), respectively.

The syllable-count effect is the best-known phonological principle of ordering, being cited by the vast majority of studies that consider the prosodic aspect of end-weight (e.g. Pāṇini 2.2.34, Jespersen 1905 et seq., Behaghel 1909, Abraham 1950, Malkiel 1959, Jakobson 1960, Bolinger 1962, Friedman 1971, Hetzron 1972, Gustafsson 1975, Cooper and Ross 1975, Pinker and Birdsong 1979, Ross 1982, Kelly 1986, Pordany 1986, Fenk-Oczlon 1989, McDonald et al. 1993, Müller 1997, Wasow

---

[15] Grafmiller and Shih (2011) include a factor for syntactic complexity ("node count"), which is the most important predictor tested. Independent of node count, however, primary stress count is also significant, and a stronger effect than word count.

2002, Wright and Hay 2002, Wright et al. 2005, Benor and Levy 2006, Mollin 2012, 2013, Wolf 2008, Ingason and MacKenzie 2011, MacKenzie 2012, Thuilier 2012, Lohmann and Takada 2014, Shih and Zuraw 2016). Focus in this section is on the subset of these studies that address syllable account while controlling for rhythm and frequency.

To illustrate these two confounds, consider the binomial *salt and pepper*. At least three motivations for this ordering are conceivable. First, it might reflect syllable count (monosyllable before disyllable). Second, it might reflect frequency (§5.3), since *salt* is more frequent than *pepper*. Third, it might reflect rhythm, as just mentioned in §5.4, since *pepper and salt* violates LAPSE and NONFINALITY, while *salt and pepper* violates neither. Thus, to demonstrate that syllable count asserts itself as an independent weight effect, one needs to control for these sorts of confounds. Note that many binomial types permit syllable count to be disentangled from rhythm and other confounds. For example, whether a monosyllable is favored before or after an iamb depends on whether syllable count or rhythm is dominant. Frequency and syllable count can be similarly deconfounded.

5.6.1 *The syllable-count effect in English*

Prosodic end-weight cannot be reanalyzed as being purely an artifact of rhythm, frequency, or phonotactics, the sorts of phonological effects discussed above in §§5.3–5.4. Rather, it must (at least in many cases) reflect bona fide weight. First, several subsyllabic factors, such as long vowels patterning as heavier than short vowels, are robust components of end-weight (§5.5). These cannot be motivated by rhythmic principles such as clash and lapse. For example, consider two monosyllables in conjunction: "X́ and Ý." The clash and lapse violations are the same in either order. The same holds for the effect of primary stress count, whereby phrases with a greater number of PWds, regardless of syntactic word count, are more likely to be final (§5.5.4).[16] Moreover, the syllable-count effect is observed in English and other languages even in contexts in which putting the heavier word second is neutral or anharmonic with respect to rhythm, as discussed presently.

As mentioned in §5.4, rhythm could motivate (which is not to say that it necessarily does motivate) the localization of a monosyllable before a trochee (or longer initially stressed word), since these pairs exhibit lapse in the non-end-weight order (όσ *and* ό), but no lapse in the end-weight order (ό *and* όσ). For a monosyllable plus iamb (or longer finally stressed word), however, the generalization is reversed: The end-weight order exhibits lapse (ό *and* σό), while the non-end-weight order does not (σό *and* ό). In this context, then, the syllable-count factor and eurythmy make opposite predictions, permitting the two effects to be disentangled. Moreover, for other pairs, such as a monosyllable plus amphibrach (σόσ), the two orders are equivalent on lapse (ό *and* σόσ compared to σόσ *and* ό). If the syllable-count effect still obtains in such cases, it cannot be explained by eurythmy. Finally, even among cases in which

---

[16] Anttila et al. (2010) analyze this effect in terms of a principle that may sound rhythmic, namely, STRESS-TO-STRESS, but has nothing to do with favoring evenly spaced stresses, the usual definition of rhythm in phonology. See §5.9 for a more clearly weight-based extension of this constraint.

lapse favors the end-weight order, a syllable-count effect might still be in evidence, as the lapse and syllable-count factors are not perfectly correlated. For example, compare two binomials, (a) *ó and óσ* and (b) *σó and óσσ*. Lapse favors the given order for both (a) and (b), as does syllable count. But the lapse discrepancy between (a) and (b) is more extreme than the syllable-count discrepancy, assuming that both constraints are gradient. A regression model might therefore assign different weights to the two effects based on such comparisons, potentially uncovering a syllable-count effect even among lapse-obeying data. In short, the syllable-count and lapse factors are far from fully confounded in English, permitting their independent contributions to be gauged by several types of binomial data.

Several previous studies, both experimental and corpus-based, include both rhythmic factors and syllable count as predictors, permitting the two factors to be separated. Benor and Levy (2006), for one, analyze binomials (692 tokens and 411 types) in a combined corpus of written and spoken English. In their analyses (namely, logistic regression based on types, logistic regression based on tokens, and stochastic Optimality Theory), the syllable-count factor is highly significant and relatively highly weighted in the hierarchy of predictors—the strongest non-semantic predictor—despite the models' inclusion of the rhythmic factors of Lapse and NonFinality. (Clash, for its part, is irrelevant, given that an unstressed conjunction serves as a buffer.) This finding suggests that a syllable-count effect exists independent of eurythmy. Indeed, because Benor and Levy (2006) include their annotated data set at the end of the article, further analysis is possible, underscoring this conclusion.

Benor and Levy (2006) code their binomials for several phonological and semantic factors. Of 411 types, 234 are coded as neutral on semantic factors (namely, iconicity, power, perceptual markedness, and relative and absolute formal markedness), meaning that there is no obvious determinism of ordering from syntax or semantics (e.g. *calm and relaxed*). Of these 234 semantically neutral binomials, only six are attested in both orders. These six are put aside here, leaving 228 one-order types for a type-based logistic regression, as in Benor and Levy (2006). The regression is set up as in Lohmann and Takada (2014), such that the dependent variable is uniformly one and no intercept is employed (see also Levy forthcoming:§6.8.4 on this use of a dummy dependent variable). Each factor is coded according to whether the given binomial agrees (positive) or disagrees (negative) with it. Factors are defined so that they correspond to positive values in their hypothesized directions, and negative values otherwise. If the factor is equal between orders or otherwise irrelevant, it is coded as zero. For example, more frequent items are predicted to be favored initially (§5.3). Thus, the frequency factor is defined to be higher as the first item more greatly exceeds the second in frequency. If the hypothesized polarity is supported by the model, the factor is assigned a positive coefficient.

The present model comprises the four factors in (11), which cover syllable count, frequency, and the two potentially relevant rhythmic factors, Lapse and NonFinality. Where possible, factors are interpreted gradiently, as defined. For lapse, for instance, a single unstressed syllable between two stresses does not count as a violation, but every subsequent intervening syllable adds one violation. For example, *slowly and thoughtfully* has a lapse of one in the given order (corresponding to two unstressed syllables) and a lapse of two in the reverse order. Its score on the lapse factor in (11) is therefore one: The given order improves on lapse by one violation relative to its transposition. This score is positive, meaning that it accords with the hypothesized direction of lapse: If speakers are sensitive to lapse, they are expected to avoid it, not favor it.

(11)   a. Syllables: # of syllables in item B minus the # in item A.
       b. Frequency: Log frequency of item A minus log frequency of item B.
       c. Lapse: Lapse size in reverse order minus lapse size in given order.
       d. Nonfinality: 1 if the given order is finally unstressed but the reversal
                          would not be; −1 if vice versa; 0 if neutral.

The resulting regression table is given in (12) (for more details on such tables, see §4.4). Syllable count is the only significant ($p < .05$) factor. Neither rhythmic factor is significant in these data (though Benor and Levy 2006 find that they are significant in their fuller data set that includes semantically influenced binomials). This result therefore suggests that syllable count is more important than rhythm among binomials whose order is not syntactically or semantically determined, a data set one would expect to be particularly amenable to phonological factors.

(12)

Factor	β	SE	z	p
a. Syllables	0.3413	0.1457	2.343	= .019
b. Frequency	0.0805	0.0695	1.158	= .247
c. Lapse	−0.0604	0.1503	−0.402	= .688
d. Nonfinality	0.5890	0.3848	1.531	= .126

Because the model is fairly collinear ($\kappa = 7.10$) and "Nonfinality" comes out significant if "Syllables" is removed, it is worth further probing the relative independent contributions of the factors. Two methods of assessing relative predictor importance are employed here, namely, drop-one AIC_c and random forests, the former following Shih and Zuraw (2016) and the latter Shih (2013) (cf. Strobl et al. 2009, Tagliamonte and Baayen 2012, etc.). AIC_c is a measure of goodness-of-fit that corrects for sample size and number of parameters. A drop-one AIC_c test gauges the contribution of a predictor by comparing the AIC_c of the full model to the AIC_c of the subset model in which the predictor is excluded. The greater this difference, the more important the predictor. A random forest is an ensemble of (in this case 5,000) classification trees in which each tree randomly samples a subset of data and (in this case 2) predictors. The importance of a predictor can then be gauged by comparing the overall classification accuracy of the ensemble when the predictor has its true values to the overall accuracy when the predictor's values are randomly permuted, with the assumption that shuffling the values of unimportant predictors will have less of an impact on overall accuracy. Refer to the aforementioned sources for more details concerning implementation and motivation; the emphasis here is on the results.

As Figure 5.4 suggests, both methods agree that syllable count contributes the greatest explanatory power, followed by a weak effect of nonfinality and little to no effect of frequency and lapse. Once again, these null results should not be interpreted

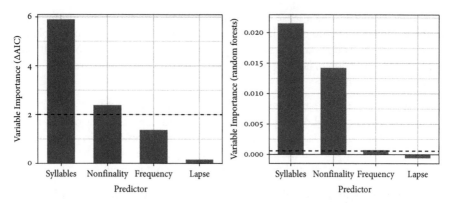

FIGURE 5.4 Two measures of relative variable importance: ΔAIC_c (left) and random forests ("ntree = 5000, mtry = 2"; right). Dashed lines are cutoffs for significance, as operationalized by Burnham and Anderson (2004) and Strobl et al. (2009), respectively.

as negative results: Frequency and lapse are, after all, significant in Benor and Levy's (2006) full model. But they reinforce that the syllable-count effect cannot be reduced to rhythm, even when semantics and frequency are controlled. Indeed, these results imply that even when rhythm *could* be invoked, as with Jespersenian binomials of the type ό *and* όσ, syllable count may still be doing more work than rhythm to motivate the end-weight preference. Just because rhythm could motivate such cases does not imply that it does.

As a second case study, consider binomials of personal names, such as *Joan and Margery*. These binomials are useful for investigating factors like phonology and frequency because many of the semantic factors analyzed by Benor and Levy (2006) and others, such as iconicity, are irrelevant.[17] Wright and Hay (2002) and Wright et al. (2005) examine such pairs in corpora and experiments and find syllable count to be a strong predictor of ordering. But they do not analyze syllable count separately from rhythm, leaving open the possibility that the syllable-count effect is an artifact of rhythm. Therefore, a new corpus of personal name binomials is analyzed here in order to shed more light on the syllable count vs. rhythm question. See also later in this section for a new experimental study of personal name ordering supporting the same conclusion.

The binomials were derived from the Google Books Ngram corpus of English Fiction (Michel et al. 2011), specifically, the "2012 5-gram punctuation" file. From the portion of this corpus tagged for part of speech, all "(NOUN *and* NOUN)," "#NOUN *and* NOUN VERB" ("#" indicates the beginning of a sentence), and "#NOUN *and*

---

[17] In real situations, pragmatic factors may well apply. For example, in a particular conversation, one of the two persons might be discourse-given while the other is not, or the two might differ in importance. However, in a large data set, one expects these sorts of discourse-local confounds to "wash out" in the aggregate, since they are not usually intrinsically tied to names. In other words, they are noise, not systematic confounds.

NOUN ADVERB" strings were retrieved in which both nouns consist of a capital letter trailed by lower-case letters. Unlike a normal internet search, Google Books permits punctuation- and capitalization-sensitive queries, allowing orthographic parentheses and sentence boundaries to be exploited as a proxy for phrase structure without a treebank. Many of the binomials extracted were not personal names (e.g. *Sense and Sensibility, France and England*); these are excluded. Furthermore, because the regression analysis is type-based, as before, only orders attested in one order (or at least twice as frequently in one order as in the other) are retained (in their dominant order), each serving as a single data point. The final corpus comprises 539 binomial types.

The factors labeled Syllables, Frequency, Lapse, and Nonfinality are defined as in (11). Furthermore, because Wright and Hay (2002) (among others) establish that male names tend to precede female names, a factor for Gender is added and coded as 1 if a male name precedes a female name, −1 if vice versa, and 0 if the names are of the same gender or indeterminate. Moreover, given that writers sometimes also consciously alphabetize names, "Alphabetical" is now also included, coded as 1 if the pair is in alphabetical order and −1 if not.

The resulting regression table is presented in (13). Among the six predictors, only "Gender" and "Syllables" are significant. The two rhythmic factors, lapse and nonfinality, are nonsignificant, with the former trending in the unexpected (i.e. lapse-favoring) direction, just as in (12). If this model were subjected to a routine process of stepwise backwards elimination, as in Wright et al. (2005) and Shih and Zuraw (2016), only "Gender" and "Syllables" would survive, both highly significant ($p < .0001$). But since the model in (13) is relatively collinear ($\kappa = 9.5$), it is once again informative to subject the predictors to metrics of relative importance.

(13)

	Factor	β	SE	z	p
a.	Gender	1.0861	0.2806	3.870	< .001
b.	Syllables	0.3217	0.1444	2.228	= .026
c.	Lapse	−0.2288	0.1225	−1.868	= .062
d.	Nonfinality	0.3713	0.2692	1.379	= .168
e.	Frequency	0.0156	0.0340	0.459	= .646
f.	Alphabetical	0.0047	0.0905	0.052	= .958

Explanatory contributions are assessed by ΔAIC_c and random forests, as in Figure 5.5. The former largely replicates the regression table. The latter finds syllables to be the most robust predictor, somewhat ahead of gender (as confirmed under multiple random seeds; see Shih 2013). Note that gender and syllable count are highly correlated, in that male names tend to be shorter than female names. Thus, the tendency for male names to precede female names may reflect a conspiracy between cultural norms and purely phonological factors (Wright et al. 2005). This sort of collinearity can skew coefficient estimates in regression, which might explain why random forests arrive at a different ranking from the regression table. But under every approach, the same subset of factors is significant; their precise ranking is not important here.

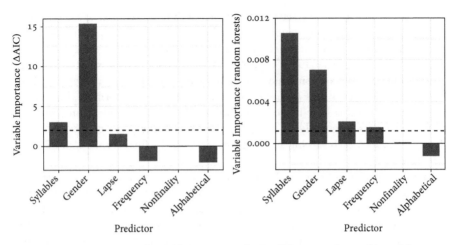

FIGURE 5.5 Two measures of variable importance for English personal name binomials, set up as in Figure 5.4.

The overall picture is therefore confirmed by several methods. From every modeling perspective tested, the syllable-count factor is significant, in contrast to the rhythmic factors of lapse and nonfinality. Lapse, for its part, consistently trends in the *negative* (lapse-favoring) direction, being near-significantly so in the second study. The results for personal name binomials therefore corroborate the findings earlier in this section based on the Benor and Levy (2006) corpus, underlining that the syllable-count effect, not lapse or nonfinality, is the primary driver of prosodic end-weight in binomials with syllable-count differentials.

Three additional corpus studies of English binomials that address syllable count include the following. First, Mollin (2012) also finds syllable count to be highly significant, separately from rhythm and frequency, though she does not employ regression. Second, Kelly (1986), in his corpus studies of binomials in written and spoken English, finds significant effects of syllable count independently in both genres. In particular, he demonstrates that this effect arises not only from monosyllable–disyllable pairings, but also from disyllable–trisyllable pairings, among which it is independently significant. Trisyllable–quadrisyllable pairings are also tested and trend heavy-final, albeit nonsignificantly, given the small sample size. While Kelly (1986) interprets these effects as reflecting syllable count and treats rhythm separately, he does not control for rhythm in testing syllable count. Finally, Lohmann and Takada (2014), in their study of English binomials, find syllable count to be a powerful predictor ($z = 7.0$), while frequency, also in the model, is not significant ($z = 1.0$). However, Lohmann and Takada (2014) do not include rhythmic predictors.

Aside from corpus studies, experiments also largely support a syllable-count effect (with one exception discussed below), and provide further evidence that it exists independently of rhythm. Pinker and Birdsong (1979) find consistent effects of syllable count ("Panini's Law," as they call it) among both English and French speakers, which they argue cannot be explained by rhythm: "[A]lthough it seems clear that

English speakers do not shelve their appreciation of the rhythms of the language when creating or judging freezes, our data indicate that Panini's Law is not simply an artifact of stress patterns" (p. 507). For example, their subjects generally favored monosyllable-before-iamb orders such as *bóof and kabóof,* for which rhythm predicts the anti-end-weight order. Moreover, because the words are wugs, frequency is moot. Of five phonological factors that they test, syllable count is the strongest effect in both English and French. In French, it is trivially the case that the syllable-count effect cannot be motivated by rhythm, as explained in §5.6.3.

The ratings experiments of Bolinger (1962) further support the coexistence of the syllable-count effect and rhythm, though they probe only monosyllable-plus-trochee combinations. In his first two experiments, Bolinger elicits preferred orderings of pairs of real adjectives, one being a monosyllable and one a trochee (e.g. *frank* and *candid*), as in (14). In Experiment 1, the adjectives modify initially stressed nouns, such as *statement* in (a–b). Experiment 2 employs the same adjectives, but replaces the nouns with noninitially stressed counterparts, as in (c–d). No pause or high-level intonational boundary intervenes between the adjective and noun; therefore, final placement of the monosyllable creates clash in (a–b) but not in (c–d). The end-weight preference is attenuated somewhat (from 91% to 84%) from the first set (a–b) to the second (c–d), suggesting that the sentential context of the binomial matters and eurythmy plays some role in ordering (see also Kelly and Bock 1988).

(14)   a. Type *frank and candid statement*   [no lapse or clash]   91%
       b. Type *candid and frank statement*   [one lapse and one clash]   9%

       c. Type *frank and candid appraisal*   [one lapse but no clash]   84%
       d. Type *candid and frank appraisal*   [one lapse but no clash]   16%

But the fact that the end-weight order is still strongly preferred (at 84%) in the second set (c–d) cannot be explained by rhythm alone, since (c) and (d) have equally (an)harmonic rhythmic profiles: Each has a two-syllable lapse, and neither violates clash or nonfinality. It seems necessary in such cases to invoke weight per se (via syllable count) to justify end-weight, even now in the context of the Jespersenian monosyllable–trochee combination. Frequency, for its part, cannot motivate the end-weight tendency in Bolinger's Experiment 2: The end-weight order is still strongly preferred when the longer adjective is more frequent (e.g. *frank and candid, bleak and lonely*).[18]

---

[18] One could not salvage rhythm by maintaining that end-weight in (c–d) is computed for the coordinated adjective phrase (AP) before the AP is merged with the noun, for at least two reasons. First, Bolinger's experiments (including the third, not discussed here, and corroborated by Kelly and Bock 1988) demonstrate that the rhythm of the sentential context into which the binomial is inserted affects its ordering, undermining an architecture in which order is determined without consideration of the noun (see §5.11 below for further discussion). Second, altering the construction slightly so that the first adjective is syntactically external (as in [*frank,* [*candid opinions*]NP]NP) does not eliminate the preference for end-weight between the adjectives. If end-weight were computed solely based on rhythm, even if such a computation were cyclical, [*frank opinions*]NP is rhythmically optimal, and then so is [*candid,* [*frank opinions*]NP]NP, leaving no explanation for end-weight among stacked APs in this type of case. The proposal here (§5.9) will be that rising phrasal stress can explain such cases.

McDonald et al. (1993) conduct seven closely related experiments on binomial ordering. Unlike the studies discussed thus far, their results are mixed, but largely null (not to be confused with negative), for syllable count, so it is appropriate to engage with these results at some length here, as methodological points likely motivate the discrepancy. The first five experiments involve a recall-and-production task, in which participants are asked to recount sentences or conjunctions involving lexemes varying in length and in other properties. The authors compare the participants' volunteered orders to the (balanced) orders in which they were originally presented. None of these five experiments finds a significant effect of length, but with three caveats raised by the authors. First, in every word pair, the conjuncts differ not only in length, but also animacy (e.g. *child* and *music*). Animacy is always a strong effect, and may eclipse attention to length. Second, the prompts and responses often involve whole sentences, which participants are asked to recreate in free-form writing (e.g. *The music soothed the child* ~ *The child was soothed by the music*). It is not clear that one would expect syllable count to affect the choice to passivize; at least, nobody has proposed that it should. Further, attempting to reconstruct whole sentences in a written format could conceivably also help to distract the participants from euphonic principles in favor of conceptual ones. Finally, as discussed in the following paragraphs, the recall methodology may independently compete with any length effect.

The sixth experiment of McDonald et al. (1993) is more relevant here, as it removes interference from animacy and sentence structure, examining only con-joined inanimate nouns. This experiment also fails to support a length effect. When iambs are analyzed separately from trochees, no monosyllable-before-trochee prefer-ence is evident, and iambs are weakly preferred before monosyllables, contradicting the length hypothesis (this result is significant, though small in magnitude, being only a 4% deviation from the chance baseline of 50%). These findings are surprising given the foregoing discussion: Monosyllable–trochee combinations in particular are expected to be a Paradebeispiel of end-weight in English (Jespersen 1905, et seq.), and the vast majority of experiments and corpus studies support a monosyllable-before-trochee preference. As McDonald et al. (1993) intimate in their discussion, differences in methodology might explain this discrepancy. In particular, theirs was a recall-and-production task, while most others are acceptability or corpus studies. Ratings experiments such as those of Bolinger (1962), Pinker and Birdsong (1979), and Wright et al. (2005) may heighten participants' sensitivity to euphony by explicitly tasking them with comparing alternatives.

Moreover, the recall component of the recall-and-production task possibly inter-feres with end-weight. After all, word length interacts with recall. For example, in a free recall task using lists of words in which words vary in length within each list, Katkov et al. (2014) find that length in syllables significantly *positively* correlates with recall. While shorter words are generally more accessible (Kelly 1986) and lists of uniformly short words are easier to recall than lists of uniformly long words (Baddeley et al. 1975), in the context of a mixed-length recall task, the opposite can sometimes hold: Longer words can stand out more and perhaps "be accorded a special place in working memory or short-term storage" (McDonald et al. 1993:223), evincing priority in retrieval, as noted by Levelt and Maassen (1981) and Katkov et al. (2014)

(cf. also Cowan et al. 2003 on a recall advantage for long words when long words are in the minority). Given that the paired presentation of words differing in length in McDonald et al. (1993) does not align perfectly with these other recall studies, it is unclear whether longer items would be expected to exhibit improved or faster recall, but it is possible.

Indeed, consistent with a possible damping effect of recall on end-weight, the seventh and final experiment of McDonald et al. (1993), which features ratings rather than recall, offers some relief to the syllable-count hypothesis. This experiment recycles all of the materials from the previous experiments, but presents the alternatives for rating without any recall component. The ratings data for each experiment are analyzed separately, so no omnibus result can be reported. But a short-before-long preference emerges significantly for two of the sets, near-significantly for a third, and is null but not significantly reversed in the remaining three (all of which have the animacy confound). Furthermore, in sets designed to probe metrical differences (e.g. iamb vs. trochee), metrical structure is never significant, while length sometimes is, indirectly lending some support to a syllable-count effect independent from rhythmic considerations. In sum, with the exception of one condition in one of seven experiments, the findings of McDonald et al. (1993) are a mix of null (not to be confused with negative) and positive for the syllable-count effect.

As a final consideration favoring the syllable-count effect, take multinomials, in which three or more items are conjoined, as in *friends, Romans, countrymen* in (1). The alternative order *Romans, friends, countrymen* is equivalently harmonic on the three rhythmic factors of clash, lapse, and final stress avoidance.[19] Thus, insofar as monosyllables tend to precede trochees in such triplets and other factors are equal, it must reflect a syllable-count effect. That said, however, I am not aware of any systematic studies of trinomials that would bear on the syllable-count question while controlling for other factors such as frequency (Oden and Lopes 1981, for one, analyze trinomials, but only for vowel modulations). Therefore, this last point concerning trinomials, though supported by intuition (e.g. Cooper and Ross 1975:104), must remain tentative for English. Pordany (1986) provides a somewhat more systematic account of trinomials in Hungarian, reporting that "[t]he ones I have found—and they are quite numerous in Hungarian—invariably show either a partial or a gradual linear increase in the number of syllables" (p. 119). At least some of his examples would be better rhythmically in the reverse, long-to-short order, for example, *bort, búzát, békességet* 'wine, wheat, peace,' which would avoid clash in the reverse order.

In general, then, insofar as syllable count can be disentangled from frequency, rhythm, and other factors based on existing corpus-based, typological, and experimental studies, it is broadly supported. This section on English now concludes with a short follow-up experiment on monosyllable–iamb binomials, serving as an addi-

---

[19] This conclusion is true regardless of whether or not the two prosodic breaks corresponding to the commas count as beats (essentially the same as unstressed syllables) for the purposes of evaluating clash and lapse. If the commas are not beats, both orders violate clash once, but not lapse. If the commas are beats, both orders violate lapse once, but not clash. Finally, if the commas mitigate both clash and lapse, rhythm remains indecisive.

tional check on a key case mentioned above. Monosyllable and iamb combinations are particularly informative for rhythm vs. syllable count, since the two factors make opposite predictions. End-weight favors the monosyllable–iamb order, while rhythm if anything favors the iamb–monosyllable order (clash is moot; lapse favors σσ́ *and* σ́ over σ́ *and* σσ́). To this end, a short Mechanical Turk experiment (as in §§5.5.2–5.5.3) investigates such pairs in female name binomials (e.g. *Deb and Denise*; cf. Wright et al. 2005, described earlier in this section). Participants are presented with twenty-one forced-choice prompts, of which fourteen are fillers and seven are critical items. In each critical item, a monosyllabic name is paired with an iambic name using *and*. Fillers consist of real binomial freezes, as before, in part to screen participants. Critical items randomly combine one monosyllable from {*Bree, Deb, Fay, Jade, Kai, Pam, Trish*} with one iamb from {*Annette, Denise, Diane, Elaine, Louise, Michelle, Nicole*}. Fillers and critical items are randomized as before, both in terms of which ordering of the binomial is presented first and in the sequence of the prompts themselves. Thirty-five subjects met the inclusion criteria, as described in §5.5.2.

Of 245 critical-item prompts completed by these participants, iamb-final orders were chosen almost twice as frequently as iamb-initial orders (157 vs. 88), a significant departure from the chance rate of 50 per cent (goodness-of-fit $\chi^2(1) = 19.4$, $p < .0001$). Frequency is not a confound: The eight monosyllables were chosen to be uniformly less frequent than the eight iambs. This selection entails that frequency would if anything favor the iamb–monosyllable order. In other words, the syllable-count effect defeated both frequency and rhythm, which conspire to favor the monosyllable-final order. These results therefore converge with the other results in this section in support of an irreducible syllable-count effect.

5.6.2 *The syllable-count effect in Latin*

Beyond English, the syllable-count effect is widely attested cross-linguistically. This section demonstrates it for Latin using Book I of Julius Caesar's *Commentaries on the Gallic War* (58 BC). From this corpus, all binary conjunctions in which both conjuncts are single words (or, in a few cases, single words with identical proclitics) were extracted, regardless of part of speech and conjunction strategy, whether enclitic *que* or medial *et, ac*, etc. Binomials whose order is clearly fixed by semantic constraints (e.g. the temporal sequencing of verbs) were excluded, leaving the ninety-seven binomials in (15). Macrons follow Francese (2011), but are irrelevant here, as only syllable count is analyzed.

(15)	Mātrona et Sēquana	cultū atque hūmānitāte	Sēquanīs et Helvētiīs
	Messālā et Pisōne	lātissimō atque altissimō	Sēquanōs et Helvētiōs
	iūmentōrum et carrōrum	pācem et amīcitiam	fidem et iūs
	potentissimōs ac firmissimōs	clientēs obaerātōsque	angustum et difficile
	facilius atque expeditius	Helvētiōrum et Āllobrogum	Nammēius et Verucloetius
	iniūriā et maleficiō	gratia et largitione	maleficiō et iniūriā
	Sēquanōrum et Haeduōrum	Grāiocelī et Caturigēs	angustias et fines
	vīcōs possessiōnēsque	Haeduōrum et Sēquanōrum	ratibus et lintribus
	patribus māiōribusque	dolō aut īnsidiīs	Āmbarrōs quod Āllobrogās
	vītae necisque	nōbilissimō ac potentissimō	grātiae atque honōris

fidem iūstitiam
opibus ac nervīs
Boī et Tulingī
matarās ac trāgulās
oppida vīcōsque
ferī ac barbarī
diciōne atque imperiō
ad nūtum aut ad voluntātem
ferōs ac barbarōs
rēx atque amīcus
Nasuam et Cimberium
mentēs animōsque
quaerendum aut cōgitandum
ūsus ac disciplīna
barbarōs atque imperitōs
dubitāsse neque timuisse
pulsās ac superātās
nōbilibus prīncipibusque
ārvernōs et Rutēnōs
virtūte et hūmānitāte
vēlocissimī ac fortissimī
rēdīs et carrīs
tam barbarum neque tam imperītum

alacritās et cupiditās
voluntātī ac precibus
impedīmenta et carrōs
impedīmentīs castrīsque
Galliae Āllobrogibusque
proeliīs calamitātibusque
locus ac sēdēs
frātrēs cōnsanguineōsque
Cimbrī Teutonīque
grātiam atque amīcitiam
frūmentāriae commeātūsque
vōcibus ac timōre
furōre atque āmentiā
armātōs ac victōrēs
pudor atque officium
beneficiō ac līberālitāte
ōrnāmentō et praesidiō
grātiam atque amīcitiam
lapidēs tēlaque
frūmentō commeātūque
inlātīs et acceptīs
repentē celeriterque

petit atque hortātur
trānsfīxīs et conligātīs
carrōs rotāsque
litterās nūntiōsque
iūris lībertātisque
hospitiō atque amīcitiā
superbē et crūdēliter
inservitūte atque indiciōne
commeātū atque mōlīmentō
ab Haeduīs et ā Treveris
Gallōrum ac mercatōrum
mīlitēs centuriōnēsque
Cimbrīs et Teutonīs
ratiōne et cōnsiliō
iūstitiam temperantiam
sociōs atque amīcōs
voluptāte et grātulātiōne
labōre et perīculō
alacritās studiumque
Sēquanīs et Haeduīs
sortibus et vāticinātiōnibus
familiārem et hospitem

These conjunctions were coded for the factors "Syllables," "Lapse," and "Frequency," as defined in §5.6.1. "Frequency" is based on the total frequency of the inflected word in the Perseus Digital Library (Crane 2017). "Nonfinality" is not considered here as monosyllables are the only words in Latin with final stress, and only two conjuncts in (15) are monosyllables. "Lapse" takes into account the different conjunction types (medial or enclitic) and computes stress accordingly (using the rule for enclitic stress in Newcomer 1908); it also corrects for elision (e.g. *atque* is read as *atqu'* before a vowel).

(16)

Factor	β	SE	z	p
a. Syllables	0.8530	0.2509	3.400	= .0007
b. Frequency	0.1478	0.1462	1.011	= .312
c. Lapse	0.2450	0.2074	1.181	= .237
d. Nonfinality	N/A			

As the regression table in (16) and the corresponding variable importance measures in Figure 5.6 make clear, "Syllables" is significant, while neither "Frequency" nor "Lapse" is significant in any test. In the aggregate, 71 per cent of binomials with syllable count differentials are heavy-final. Moreover, the end-weight tendency becomes stronger as the discrepancy in syllable count increases. For pairs differing in one syllable ($n = 41$), 29.3 per cent are heavy-initial. For pairs differing in more than one syllable ($n = 26$), the heavy-initial rate is approximately halved, to 15.4 per cent (nevertheless, given the sample size, this difference is not significant; Fisher's exact test odds ratio = 2.25, $p = .25$).

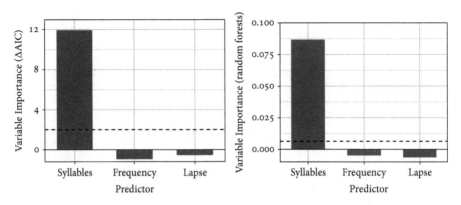

Figure 5.6 Two measures of variable importance for Latin binomials, as in Figure 5.4.

5.6.3 *The syllable-count effect in French*

As a final case study of the syllable-count effect, French is examined in this section. French exhibits stress that is if anything final in the accentual phrase (putting aside final schwa and special rules for focus; Walker 1975). Given this system, a monosyllable–disyllable order (e.g. *beurre et fromage*) fares no better than the reverse (*fromage et beurre*) with respect to rhythm. If anything, the heavy-final order is worse rhythmically, as it contains a lapse, while the reverse does not. More generally, any short-before-long order in French exhibits a greater lapse than its reversal, assuming that both conjuncts receive some degree of stress. (If they do not, of course, then rhythm is trivially nonexplanatory.)

In spite of this, heavy-final orders are favored in French, just as in English, Latin, and many other languages. As mentioned in §5.6.1, Pinker and Birdsong (1979) demonstrate this preference experimentally for French using wugs (e.g. *veli et velinochet*). Furthermore, Forsgren (1978), Abeillé and Godard (1999), and Thuilier (2012) find that adjective–noun order is affected by syllable count. In (17), for instance, the adjective (*avide*) becomes more felicitous prenominally as the noun becomes longer. For example, it is more likely to be prenominal with *hippopotame* than it is with *air*. Thuilier (2012) also reports that typically prenominal adjectives in French (such as *grand*) tend to be short; the longer they are, the more likely they are to be typically postnominal. Finally, French exhibits heavy NP shift, just as English does, though Thuilier (2012) finds that it is better predicted by word count than by syllable count.

(17)   a. un air avide   'an avid air'
        b. un avide hippopotame   'an avid hippopotamus'

Syllabic end-weight in French is further corroborated here through a new corpus study of binomials, once again derived from the Google Books Ngram corpus, this time the files labeled "French 2012 5-grams." All binomials were extracted from the frames "(X CONJ Y)" and "#X CONJ Y PUNC," where X and Y are both nouns or both adjectives, CONJ is *et* or *ou*, # is sentence-initial position, and PUNC is any punctuation. In both frames, X CONJ Y is almost always a coordinated noun or adjective phrase.

Lacking a treebank, this constituency is not guaranteed, but any exceptions (of which spot-checking revealed none) would be at most a small source of noise. As in §5.6.1, only binomials attested at least twice as frequently in one order as in the other are retained (in their dominant order) for a type-based analysis; 4,757 binomial types fit this description.

The regression table in (18) includes four factors. Syllable count and frequency are both significant in the expected directions, such that more syllables favor final position and higher frequency favors initial position. Alphabetical order is also weakly significant in the predicted direction.[20] "Characters" is coded as the number of characters in the second item minus the number of characters in the first. The fact that this predictor is not significant, while syllable count is highly significant, underscores that the observed end-weight propensity does not reflect a (conscious) tendency on the part of writers to put the orthographically longer item second. Rather, here as elsewhere, phonological structure is decisive. Moreover, the variable importance measures in Figure 5.7 confirm the robustness of syllable count independent from frequency. Though frequency has greater weight in Figure 5.7, syllable count is roundly significant by every measure.

(18)

Factor	β	SE	z	p
a. Syllables	0.3323	0.0453	7.634	< .0001
b. Frequency	0.1313	0.0161	8.161	< .0001
c. Alphabetical	0.0778	0.0305	2.551	= .011
d. Characters	0.0283	0.0176	1.612	= .107

The French results just reported do not control for semantic and pragmatic factors that might interfere with noun or adjective order. While one approach to controlling for such factors is to code as many as possible, as in Benor and Levy (2006), it is

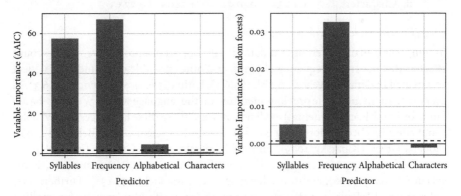

FIGURE 5.7 Two measures of variable importance for French binomials, as in Figure 5.4.

[20] That alphabetical order is significant does not necessarily mean that orthography per se sometimes determines order. It could also reflect phonology. For instance, if vowel-initial words tend to precede consonant-initial words, it could favor alphabetical order in the aggregate.

also possible to augment the logistic model with random effects structure in order to factor out any idiosyncratic "firstness" tendencies of individual items, regardless of their causes. This latter approach follows more closely the logistic analysis of Shih and Zuraw (2016).

To employ word-based random effects, it is necessary to change the basic design of the model in (18). In particular, each word is now taken as a data point, with the dependent variable being 1 if the word is in final position in its binomial and 0 if it is initial. In other words, the model is now PARADIGMATIC, evaluating typical properties of initial as opposed to final position, rather than SYNTAGMATIC, as before, comparing pairs of words on various criteria, with each pair serving as an individual data point. Predictors can accordingly now be interpreted in simpler fashion, since they refer only to single words. "Syllables" is the number of syllables in the word; "Frequency" is its log frequency; "Characters" is its character count; and "Alphabetical" is the place of its (lowercased) first letter in the alphabet. Moreover, each word is now assigned its own intercept, which is the maximal viable random effects structure in this case (cf. Barr et al. 2013).[21]

As the resulting table in (19) reveals (not showing intercepts), the mixed-effects paradigmatic model is qualitatively the same as the fixed-effects-only syntagmatic model earlier in this section. In particular, "Syllables" and "Frequency" are both highly significant in the expected directions (for the latter, the sign has switched to negative because the dependent variable is uniformly operationalized as final position), and their ΔAIC_c ratio (not shown) is approximately the same as before.

(19)

Factor	β	SE	z	p
a. Syllables	0.2423	0.0485	5.000	< .0001
b. Frequency	−0.0765	0.0120	−6.402	< .0001
c. Alphabetical	0.0039	0.0020	2.008	= .045
d. Characters	0.0233	0.0191	1.220	= .223

5.6.4 The syllable-count effect: conclusion

In sum, nearly all of numerous tests converge in support of a productive syllable-count effect as distinct from frequency, rhythm, and other possible confounds. This effect was treated in detail above for English (§5.6.1), Latin (§5.6.2), and French (§5.6.3), in every case augmenting the previous literature on the language with new corpus-based (and, for English, experimental) evidence. Beyond these three languages, the syllable-count effect has been reported for Sanskrit (Pāṇini), Ancient Greek (Behaghel 1909), Modern Greek (Kiparsky 2009), Finnish (Kiparsky 1968), German (Malkiel 1959, Fenk-Oczlon 1989, Müller 1997), Hebrew (Friedman 1971, Hetzron 1972), Hungarian (Pordany 1986), and other languages (e.g. Malkiel 1959:151). Furthermore, Lohmann and Takada (2014) document a mora-count effect for Japanese (controlling for frequency and semantics), though they do not find evidence for a syllable-count effect, consistent with the marginal role of the syllable in Japanese phonology. Finally,

---

[21] Random slopes cannot be employed here, as the other predictors are fixed for each word.

Choi (2007) finds a syllable-count effect in Korean beginning-weight (see §5.12.1 below), but does not deconfound it from word count. See also §5.12.2 regarding evidence for syllable-count beginning-weight in Turkish.

5.7 Summary of prosodic factors in end-weight

Eight near-consensus principles of prosodic end-weight are summarized in (20). For each, the specified property is associated with greater end-weight. Although (a) denotes a subset of (b), it is stated as a separate principle because stressed syllables count more towards weight than unstressed syllables do (§5.5.4). In other words, (a) and (b) are in a stringency relationship (§1.5).

(20) a. More stressed syllables
      b. More syllables
      c. Longer vowel
      d. Lower vowel
      e. Longer onset
      f. Less sonorant onset
      g. More sonorant coda
      h. Longer coda

The factors are cumulative, in the sense that they add up if combined within a syllable, but their relative weights are not as important here as their directionalities (on gauging their relative weights, cf. e.g. Cooper and Ross 1975, Pinker and Birdsong 1979, Oden and Lopes 1981, Benor and Levy 2006, and Mollin 2012).[22] Properties (c–h) are presumably also cumulative in the sense that they would be expected to combine across syllables of the word(s). In a polysyllable, after all, there are multiple nuclei, (possibly) onsets, and (possibly) codas to consider. Once again, however, existing studies reveal little about how the subsyllabic factors combine across syllables, especially when multiple levels of stress are involved. The theory proposed in §5.9 makes certain predictions about both types of cumulativity—within syllables and across them—but assessing its full range of predictions on these questions is beyond the scope of this chapter, which sets out mainly to cover the established generalizations.

Finally, most of the principles in (20) are correlated with greater duration, as recognized by many scholars over the last century. However, the sonority generalization is reversed between the onset, where less sonority favors weight, and the rime, where more sonority favors weight. This reversal is consistent with phonological weight in other domains (see §5.8), but is not explicable in terms of total duration. Moreover, the effect of stress level may not reduce to raw duration. On the one hand, stressed syllables are longer than their unstressed counterparts, given accentual lengthening (Turk and Sawusch 1997, Turk and White 1999, Turk and

---

[22] The order of the list in (20) roughly corresponds to the importance of the factors based on §§5.5.1–5.5.4, but only impressionistically. In particular, based on existing studies, it is difficult to compare the effect size of (stressed) syllable count to that of the subsyllabic factors.

Shattuck-Hufnagel 2000). In that sense, stressed syllables are expected to be heavier. On the other hand, the stress effect likely exceeds what accentual lengthening alone predicts, in that promoting a syllable from unstressed to stressed (e.g. from [ɪ] to [ˈɪ]) usually adds less to the total duration of an item than adding one or more whole unstressed syllables would. Yet studies such as Zec and Inkelas (1990) suggest that only primary stress count matters, with no number of unstressed syllables able to compensate for a subminimal (i.e. < 2) number of stresses. For Zec and Inkelas (1990), this is because the branchingness of the prosodic constituent, not its duration, is argued to be decisive for the phenomena that they analyze. The theory presented in §5.9 provides a further mechanism by which stressed elements count more towards prosodic weight than unstressed elements, extending a constraint to similar effect in Anttila et al. (2010).

5.8 Explanations for prosodic end-weight

Five explanations have been suggested for prosodic end-weight, or at least certain aspects of it. These include final lengthening, rhythm, phonotactics, phonological complexity, and nuclear stress. This section reviews these proposals in turn and ultimately argues (continuing in §5.9) that nuclear stress is the primary force behind prosodic end-weight, while the other considerations, while perhaps not irrelevant, are more parochial, unable to motivate most of the core properties of prosodic end-weight. Meanwhile, phrasal stress provides a unified explanation of all of its core properties, as explicated further in §5.9.

5.8.1 Final lengthening

First, phrase-final lengthening (PFL) is sometimes invoked as an explanation for the phonological aspect of end-weight (Pinker and Birdsong 1979, Ross 1982, Oakeshott-Taylor 1984, Minkova 2002, Wright et al. 2005, Wolf 2008). PFL refers to the phenomenon whereby prosodic constituents of a certain level are prolonged at their right edges (Delattre 1966, Lindblom 1968, Wightman et al. 1992, Turk and Shattuck-Hufnagel 2000, 2007, Lunden 2006). This process applies clearly at the level of the phonological phrase and above; it is less clear whether it applies to PWds that are not phrase-final (Turk and Shattuck-Hufnagel 2000). The domain of lengthening is to a first approximation the ultima, though this description oversimplifies in two respects: First, different parts of the ultima are stretched to different degrees. For example, the final onset, though perhaps not wholly unaffected, is not affected to nearly the same extent that the rime is, and within the rime, the coda is lengthened substantially more than the vowel (*op. cit.*). Second, a small amount of lengthening affects material preceding the ultima, though it is quite minor by comparison—perhaps an order of magnitude less in English—and may be confined to the stressed syllable, assuming that stress is nonfinal (Turk and Shattuck-Hufnagel 2007:455–7).

In the context of end-weight, the insight is generally that placing the longer item second better aligns inherent length with the locus of PFL, though this rationale has not been formalized, and faces several problems. As is argued here, PFL plays no role in end-weight. First, end-weight applies just as strongly to binomials in which the second item is not in prosodic phrase-final position (e.g. *check and discipline himself*), a point raised and supported by corpus data by Benor and Levy (2006:244). It is also demonstrated experimentally by Bolinger (1962) (see (14) above). Bolinger finds that end-weight is strongly preferred for adjectival binomials before a noun, a context in which no prosodic phrase boundary normally intervenes (e.g. *frank and candid appraisal*). In fact, end-weight is significantly stronger when the adjectival binomial is prenominal than when it is sentence-final (Bolinger 1962:40), the opposite of what PFL would predict. Furthermore, trinomials exhibit end-weight, despite pause after every conjunct (§5.6.1). One might counter that the final pause is greatest in magnitude, but as with binomials, this is not necessarily true. Pause often follows every conjunct *except* the final one, apparently without affecting end-weight, much less reversing it (e.g. *the lock, stock, and barrel of a gun*). In sum, end-weight is not determined by the boundary structures of binomials and multinomials.

A second point against PFL as an explanation for end-weight is that PFL is almost entirely confined to the phrase-final syllable (Lindblom 1968, et seq.), but end-weight remains highly (if not more) sensitive to nonfinal syllables. For instance, in experiments on binomials, the deterministic modulation is sometimes two or more syllables from the ends of the words, as in the trisyllabic pairs such as *neeminy-nominy* tested by Oden and Lopes (1981). Additionally, I ran a small experiment on Amazon's Mechanical Turk, set up as in §5.6.1, to check whether binomial ordering is more sensitive to a medial, stressed vowel or to a final, unstressed vowel when the two make crossed predictions for end-weight. For example, consider the wug pair *climmo ~ clamma*. If end-weight is more sensitive to the weight of the final vowel, as predicted by PFL, *climmo* should be preferred in final position, since [oʊ] is heavier than [ə]. If, however, it is more sensitive to the stressed vowel, as predicted by a nuclear stress, *clamma* should be preferred finally, since [æ] is heavier than [ɪ]. Five such pairs were tested on thirty-seven qualifying participants meeting all of the same criteria as described for the Turk experiment in §5.6.1. As before, presentation of the two orders of each binomial is randomized and wug prompts are interleaved with real English freezes serving both as fillers and as criteria to ensure that participants understand the task and are paying attention.

The results are summarized (21), showing each binomial only in its most frequently selected order, which was always the stress-sensitive order. In the aggregate, speakers chose orders agreeing with stress-sensitive weight 1.45 times as frequently as they did orders agreeing with ultima-sensitive weight (goodness-of-fit $\chi^2(1) = 6.6$, $p = .01$). Thus, speakers are significantly more sensitive to stressed syllables than ultimas in assessing end-weight, contradicting the PFL account. Indeed, this same conclusion is implicit in Benor and Levy (2006) and Mollin (2012), who code the vowel features of their binomials for stressed vowels, not final vowels, when the two differ, as well as in experimental studies of binomials (e.g. Pinker and Birdsong 1979, Oden and Lopes 1981), which modulate stressed as opposed to final vowels. To be sure, the finding here is not that speakers ignore properties of unstressed ultimas in assessing end-weight; it is that they attribute greater importance to stressed syllables.

(21)	Binomial (in stress-sensitive order)	N Agree	N Disagree	% Agree
	1. bitnaw and batnee	19	18	51
	2. brimminaw and bromminee	22	15	59
	3. climmo and clamma	21	16	57
	4. minto and monta	28	9	76
	5. pihvo and pahva	20	17	54

A third point against PFL is that it offers no explanation for the syllable-count effect, one of the best-established principles of prosodic end-weight (§5.6). Given that PFL is almost entirely confined to the ultima, it is not clear why adding more syllables to the word would assist PFL. In fact, PFL predicts the opposite: Another well-established timing principle is that of polysyllabic shortening (Lehiste 1972, et seq.; §1.2), which entails that ultimas are progressively shorter in words with progressively more syllables, all else being equal (Turk and Shattuck-Hufnagel 2000:403 and references therein). It follows that the locus of PFL is more compressed in longer words, and PFL therefore predicts a reverse syllable-count effect in end-weight, by which polysyllables are avoided in final position. This argument is not undermined by the fact that PFL can also slightly affect certain nonfinal syllables in English. As mentioned, Turk and Shattuck-Hufnagel (2007) find a pre-ultima effect of PFL only for the stressed syllable in English, and even then the magnitude of PFL is roughly a tenth of what it is for the ultima. But as demonstrated in §§5.6.1–5.6.3, adding unstressed nonfinal syllables significantly affects end-weight in English, Latin, and French, as seen, for instance, with monosyllable-plus-iamb pairs in English and French. Not only can PFL not motivate this effect, if anything it predicts the opposite directionality.

Beyond the syllable count effect, a fourth point against PFL-driven end-weight is that PFL and end-weight diverge with respect to the treatment of subsyllabic factors. In PFL, the coda of the word-final syllable is lengthened to a much greater extent than the nucleus, on the order of 1.5 to four times as much (based on Dutch, English, and Hebrew; Turk and Shattuck-Hufnagel 2007:462). Meanwhile, the final onset is unaffected by PFL, or at most only slightly affected. Turk and Shattuck-Hufnagel (2007), for one, find no consistent effect of onset lengthening in English PFL. Thus, if end-weight reflected PFL, one might expect coda structure to have the strongest effect on end-weight, followed (substantially) by the nucleus, followed by little to no effect of the onset; in short, coda $\gtrsim$ nucleus $\gtrsim$ (onset). This is almost the mirror image of the hierarchy actually observed for end-weight. In end-weight, the nucleus is the most decisive factor (as made explicit by Pinker and Birdsong 1979:502 and Oden and Lopes 1981:677, among others; see §5.5). Meanwhile, among syllable margins, both the onset and coda contribute significantly to end-weight (§§5.5.2–5.5.3).[23] These facts are more consistent with weight than with PFL. In gradient weight systems,

---

[23] If anything, the onset is more important than the coda in end-weight (as made explicit, for example, by Ross 1982:280), though the coda size effect has possibly been underestimated due to a compensatory relationship between the nucleus and coda (§5.5.3). Therefore, it is more cautious to conclude merely that both the onset and coda contribute significantly.

nuclei take priority over onsets and codas, but both of the latter also contribute significantly (e.g. Ryan 2014:333ff, 2016:726–8).

Fifth, PFL also misses the mark for onsets in another respect. While onsets are not lengthened in prosodic phrase-final position, they *are* lengthened in prosodic phrase-initial position (Turk and Shattuck-Hufnagel 2000:402 and references therein). Thus, insofar as the left edges of binomials coincide with prosodic breaks, one would expect longer onsets to be preferred in initial, not final, position, given the timing-based approach to end-weight. This is the opposite of what is found for end-weight, where longer onsets are favored in final position, including when the binomial follows a prosodic break (§5.5.2). Once again, weight makes the correct prediction: Longer onsets are associated with (if anything) greater weight (Ryan 2014), and are thus predicted to be (if anything) favored in final position, the locus of nuclear stress.

Sixth, the PFL account predicts that only prosodic end-weight, not beginning-weight, should be attested typologically, given that there is no phrase-initial analog of PFL in any language.[24] Preliminary indications, however, support the existence of languages exhibiting prosodic beginning-weight (see §5.12). If these cases hold up to further scrutiny, it is an additional point against PFL-driven weight effects. If they do not, the previous points are unaffected.

In summary, six empirical problems are raised here for the PFL explanation of end-weight. First, end-weight is not affected by boundary structure. Second, end-weight is more sensitive to stressed syllables than to ultimas. Third, PFL cannot motivate the syllable-count effect. Fourth, PFL predicts the primacy of the coda and the irrelevance of the onset, both erroneously. Fifth, if phrase-initial consonant lengthening is also considered, longer onsets would be predicted to be favored initially by a timing-based account, also contradicting the end-weight facts. Finally, if prosodic beginning-weight exists, as seems likely given currently available evidence, the PFL-based explanation does not go through, while the weight-based explanation remains viable.

In addition to these empirical points, it is worth noting that the logic of the PFL explanation has never been explicated in a formal model, which may conceal further issues of implementation and typology. For example, if PFL serves a communicative function (White 2014), that function could conceivably favor *more expandable* as opposed to *longer* elements in PFL position. Turk and Shattuck-Hufnagel (2007), for instance, find that in English "a final reduced-vowel syllable appears to be more (rather than less) lengthenable than a final full-vowel syllable," while the opposite may hold of Dutch (Cambier-Langeveld et al. 1997). Without a formal model of PFL-driven end-weight, one cannot gauge how such considerations might be predicted to affect end-weight. At any rate, given the empirical issues, a formalized interface between PFL and end-weight is not worth pursuing.

---

[24] To be sure, domain-initial lengthening occurs, perhaps universally, but it is not the mirror image of PFL, as it only affects the domain-initial onset (Fougeron and Keating 1997, Fougeron 1998, Byrd 2000, Turk and Shattuck-Hufnagel 2000).

5.8.2 Rhythm

Outside of PFL, eurythmy has been put forth as an explanation for end-weight, particularly in the context of the syllable-count effect. As treated extensively in §§5.6.1–5.6.4, however, the potential explanatory scope of eurythmy is limited compared to the full range of the syllable-count effect. In English, for example, favored long-final orders are often not metrically optimizing; indeed, they are often worse rhythmically, as with monosyllable–iamb combinations, which evidently still abide by end-weight. In nearly all studies permitting syllable count and rhythm to be disentangled, syllable count remains significant. Moreover, eurythmy cannot explain any aspect of the syllable-count effect in certain other languages, such as French, where it is equally robust. Thus, rhythm cannot motivate the syllable-count effect in general. What's more, beyond syllable count, rhythm cannot explain any of the seven remaining core principles of prosodic end-weight enumerated in §5.7. These other principles include the primary stress-count effect (§5.5.4), as well as six subsyllabic factors, such as the fact that longer vowels contribute more to end-weight than shorter vowels do. As argued below in §5.9, all eight principles, including the two count effects, are amenable to a unified explanation in terms of weight. This is not to deny that rhythm plays a role in word order. But it is not at the core of prosodic end-weight.

5.8.3 Phonotactics

The situation is similar for phonotactics, which can sometimes affect word order (e.g. through OCP effects such as sibilant–sibilant avoidance; §5.4), though mostly in ways that are orthogonal to end-weight. While particular instances of longer onsets patterning as heavier in certain languages could in principle be due to the avoidance of hiatus or resyllabification (e.g. putting a vowel-initial conjunct out first to avoid hiatus with a vowel-final conjunction; §5.4), phonotactics is far from a general solution to end-weight. For one thing, it does not cover the same effect in languages like English and German. In fact, phonotactics predicts that increasingly complex onsets should be increasingly avoided after a consonant-final conjunction, the opposite of the observed complex-final preference.

As a second case attributed to phonotactics, the onset sonority effect, whereby less sonorous onsets are favored finally (§5.5.2), is claimed by Parker (2002) to be driven by a GENERALIZED SYLLABLE CONTACT LAW that promotes deep sonority troughs between nuclei by favoring low-sonority onsets intersyllabically (cf. also Murray and Vennemann 1983:520). Parker (2002) bases this analysis on reduplicative compounds such as *roshy-toshy* > *toshy-roshy*. In this case, *roshy-toshy*, with its deep trough, is preferred to *toshy-roshy*, with its shallower trough. That said, another possible explanation for this asymmetry is the nuclear stress account developed below in §5.9. In brief, weight systems generally treat obstruent onsets as (if anything) heavier than sonorant onsets. Because greater stress usually falls on the second item in English echo reduplication (i.e. *ròshy-tóshy*), the more obstruent onset is favored in that position.

The same onset sonority effect is found in binomials (§5.5.2). Thus, *ròshy and tóshy* is also expected to be favored over *tòshy and róshy* (using the grave accent to indicate a lesser degree of word stress). So far, this observation remains compatible with both the syllable contact and nuclear stress analyses. However, the two analyses can be teased apart using other data. For example, if each conjunct is buffered by an article, as in *a ròshy (and) a tóshy*, syllable contact no longer asserts a preference; both orders have identical violation profiles. Meanwhile, nuclear stress remains unaltered in its prediction of an onset sonority effect in this context. Similarly, if the relevant onsets are word-medial, as in *maròshy (and) matóshy*, syllable contact predicts the sonority effect to vanish, while nuclear stress predicts it to remain.

Five such binomials are tested on Amazon's Mechanical Turk, with the same design as before (§5.8.1). The wugs are designed to be most naturally stressed on their peninitial syllables (e.g. *ayárma* as opposed to *áyarma*), such that the critical consonants occupy the onsets of stressed syllables, though it is not crucial that participants assign stress in this manner (an effect is merely expected to be stronger when the modulation is in a more salient position; §5.5.4). Eighteen participants met the inclusion criteria. As summarized in (22), they aggregately favored the obstruent in second position for every binomial tested. Overall, obstruent-final orders were preferred 1.8 times as frequently as sonorant-final orders ($\chi^2(1) = 7.5, p = .006$). This result cannot be motivated by syllable contact, but is expected under the weight-based account, given that greater stress falls on the second conjunct and onset obstruency generally correlates with stress (§5.9).

(22) | Binomial (in obstruent-second order) | N Agree | N Disagree | % Agree |
|---|---|---|---|
| 1. ayarma and akarma | 10 | 8 | 56 |
| 2. aloompt and atoompt | 12 | 6 | 67 |
| 3. lemonte and leponte | 12 | 6 | 67 |
| 4. mameert and mapeert | 14 | 4 | 78 |
| 5. siroof and sicoof | 10 | 8 | 56 |

Moreover, Parker's (2002) syllable-contact analysis makes the wrong prediction for the coda sonority effect. Parker (2002) defines the syllable-contact constraint as in (23).

(23)   "Generalized Syllable Contact Law: A heterosyllabic sequence of two segments A.B is more harmonic the higher the sonority of A and the lower the sonority of B."

This constraint therefore predicts that higher-sonority codas should be favored finally in binomials, since, for instance, *thin and thick* locates higher sonority in A (of A.B) than *thick and thin* does. This contradicts the well-documented preference reported in §5.5.3, which was further argued in §5.5.3 not to be phonotactically driven based on independent considerations. In conclusion, phonotactics cannot explain away end-weight with respect to the onset sonority effect, one of the only aspects of prosodic end-weight for which a phonotactic explanation has been suggested.

5.8.4 Complexity

As a final logically possible non-weight-based explanation for prosodic end-weight, consider raw phonological complexity, for example the number of segments, features, or prosodic nodes. Under this approach, the more phonologically complex item would be favored in final position (or, equivalently, the simpler item in initial position). One could imagine various processing motivations for such a tendency, borrowing from the literature on the role of syntactic complexity in (non-prosodic) end-weight (e.g. Hawkins 1994, Gibson 1998, Wasow 2002, Temperley 2007, Tily 2010; for more discussion of the relation between prosodic and syntactic end-weight, see §5.13). First, speakers might tend to defer complexity, postponing elements anticipated to have a high processing cost (cf. Wasow 2002:56 on syntactic weight). Second, speakers might seek to minimize dependency distances between a head and its arguments (cf. Hawkins 1990, 1994, 2004, Gibson 1998, and Chang 2009 on syntactic weight). For example, for a ditransitive verb such as *give*, placing the shorter argument first means that the left edge of the second argument is closer to the verb than it would be in the alternative order.[25] Finally, placing the more complex item adjacent to pause (e.g. sentence-finally) might facilitate comprehension, favoring a more uniform processing load over time, given that medial items are in a more taxing context for processing (e.g. Pinker and Birdsong 1979:507).[26]

While complexity deferral, whatever its motivations, may play some role in prosodic end-weight, it is not a viable explanation for most of the core phonological principles of end-weight identified in §5.7. Several of the principles have weight-like properties that cannot be derived from complexity. First, sonority is positively correlated with weight in the coda, whereas it is not the case that more sonorous segments are generally more complex than less sonorous ones. Second, in the onset, this generalization is reversed, which again eludes complexity, but is explicable in terms of weight (see §5.9). Third, as discussed above in §5.5.1, weight correlates gradiently with the durations of vowels, which again is not a function of their phonological complexity. Fourth, vowel effects are generally stronger than consonant effects, as mentioned earlier in this section, a well-established principle of weight, but orthogonal to complexity. Fifth, a rime comprising a long or tense vowel typically patterns as (if anything) heavier than one comprising a short vowel followed by a consonant (i.e. VV $\gtrsim$ V̌C; see the discussion of open syllables in §5.5.3), just as in weight systems more generally, where VV is virtually always heavier than V̌C if the two are distinguished. In this case, the greater number of segments corresponds with less, not more, weight.

Additional problems for complexity-driven end-weight apply more specifically to the individual processing explanations just enumerated. For instance, dependency distance minimization predicts that if a binomial exhibits end-weight, it should do so only as a right-side complement, for example as the object of a verb or preposition. Meanwhile, a binomial in preverbal position is expected to exhibit beginning-weight on this account, and binomials standing alone are expected to exhibit neither beginning- nor end-weight. These predictions are erroneous; binomials exhibit

---

[25] To be clear, neither of these processing accounts has been proposed to apply to prosodic complexity. This section merely considers some problems that they would face if they were applied to it.

[26] Additionally, Cutler and Cooper (1978) argue that stereotyped orders of binomials facilitate processing, though this question does not bear on the causes of the stereotypes.

end-weight across the board in end-weight languages. Pause-facilitated processing, for its part, does not account for the fact that end-weight occurs even in non-pause-adjacent positions, as discussed in §5.8.1 as the first argument against the PFL analysis. Moreover, like dependency distance minimization, it incorrectly predicts beginning-weight sentence-initially and ambivalence for stand-alone binomials. An account in terms of postponing difficult constituents would need to address PERSISTENT EUPHONY, that is, the fact that binomials are heavy-final not only in spontaneous production, but also when one bears both orders in mind for a ratings task. It would also have to contend with beginning-weight languages, in which heavier items are preferred initially (§5.12).

In conclusion, complexity is not a viable motivation for prosodic end-weight, mainly because it cannot explain its weight-like properties, in addition to issues of implementation. It therefore joins phrase-final lengthening, eurythmy, and eutaxy as being a possible mechanism by which phonology can influence word order, but one that is largely orthogonal to prosodic end-weight per se. The phrasal stress analysis developed in the next section, by contrast, provides a unified account of the weight-like properties of end-weight without any of the shortcomings of the four approaches outlined in this section.

5.9 Phrasal stress as an explanation for end-weight

5.9.1 Constraints

Above the level of the PWd, stress is normally right-oriented in English.[27] Following Chomsky and Halle (1968:15–24), Liberman (1975), Liberman and Prince (1977), among many others, this generalization is sometimes termed the NUCLEAR STRESS RULE, as in Selkirk (1995:562): "The most prominent syllable of the rightmost constituent in a phrase P is the most prominent syllable of P." Nothing here hinges on the question of whether this "rule" is in fact language-specific or the reflex of a universal (cf. e.g. Cinque 1993, Zubizarreta 1998, Arregi 2002). Only the fact that phrasal stress tends to be right-oriented in end-weight constructions is relevant here. While some authors employ the term NUCLEAR STRESS to refer only to the stress maximum of the sentence or intonational phrase, here it refers more generally to the maximum stress of any supraword constituent. This usage follows, for example, Anttila (2016:145), among many others: "Nuclear Stress Rule: In a phrase (NP, VP, AP, S), assign stress to the rightmost word bearing lexical stress."

Because prosodic constituents are nested, phrasal stress tends to be cumulative, exhibiting progressively higher phrasal maxima.[28] Consider the example in (24),

---

[27] There are exceptions to this generalization involving contrastive focus and lexical factors (Zubizarreta 1998, Zubizarreta and Vergnaud 2000, Katz and Selkirk 2011, Ahn 2016). See §5.11 on the Rhythm Rule. Additionally, compounds, which can comprise multiple PWds, vary in their prosodic headedness (e.g. prosodically left-headed *kétchup factory* vs. right-headed *hoity-tóity*). The next section treats end-weight in compounds.

[28] As acknowledged since at least Chomsky and Halle (1968), nuclear stress is perceived to be a stress maximum, but may not translate straightforwardly to acoustic extrema; see Büring (2013:862, 891) for

adapted from Anttila et al. (2010:955). Phrasal stress might be represented, for example, as a bracketed grid (a), where column height indicates phrasal stress level (only relative, not absolute, column heights are relevant here), or as a tree (b), where constituency is depicted along with the S(trong) vs. W(eak) status of each constituent (see, e.g., overviews and references in Burzio 1994, Hayes 1995, and Samek-Lodovici 2005). The lowest level shown in (24) is the PWd. As both representations make explicit, prosodic constituents are right-headed above the PWd.

(24) (a)

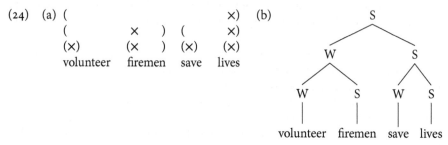

The nuclear stress explanation of end-weight proposes that greater weight is preferred in final position because that is normally also the locus of greater stress. In short, prosodic end-weight reflects end-stress. As such, prosodic end-weight folds in with the more general interface between weight and stress, which has been documented extensively at the level of the syllable (Chapter 2). For example, consider the grids in (25). The freeze *trick or treat* is taken as an example of vowel length correlating with weight in binomials. In (a), the attested order, the long vowel is associated with greater stress than the short vowel. In (b), the opposite holds. Thus, (a) better aligns weight with stress than (b).

(25) (a) (×)   (b) (×)
          (×) (×)   (×) (×)
          trick or treat   treat or trick

This explanation of prosodic end-weight, though not new here, remains overlooked by the vast majority of prosodic end-weight studies. Surveys by Wright et al. (2005) and Wolf (2008), for instance, mention final lengthening, rhythm, and phonotactics as possible causes of end-weight, but say nothing about rising phrasal stress (as distinct from rhythm, which concerns clash, lapse, and nonfinality). Some earlier studies suggest that sentential prosody is relevant for end-weight, but do not clearly distinguish among independent aspects of prosody such as nuclear stress, final lengthening, and nonfinality (Bolinger 1962, Oakeshott-Taylor 1984). Additionally, several studies have linked focus to nuclear stress, some arguing for movement (or "p-movement") of a narrowly focused constituent from its (nonfinal) base position to final position, driven by the requirement that focus and stress coincide (cf. Zubizarreta 1998, Zubizarreta and Vergnaud 2000, Büring and Gutiérrez-Bravo 2001, Samek-Lodovici 2005,

references concerning this issue. The Rhythm Rule can sometimes also interfere with rising stress, as treated below in §5.11.

Vogel 2006). In some cases, this stress–focus interface could motivate what might be recognized as end-weight, since, for example, a heavy, focused constituent might come to follow a lighter constituent, such as English *it*. Nevertheless, this stress–focus interface is orthogonal to the prosodic end-weight generalizations being examined here. For instance, the fact that long vowels are preferred in final position in all-new, broad-focus binomials, such as the *trick or treat* example just mentioned, must reflect a narrowly phonological rather than information-theoretic principle. The same argument applies to all of the generalizations in §5.7 under similar conditions.[29]

To my knowledge, only two previous studies explicitly propose a link between nuclear stress and prosodic end-weight, as distinct from focus.[30] First, Benor and Levy (2006) argue for nuclear stress over final lengthening as an explanation for end-weight on the grounds that binomials exhibit end-weight regardless of their prosodic boundary context. This was one of several arguments raised against final lengthening above in §5.8. Benor and Levy (2006) mention it as a functional principle, though it plays no formal role in their analysis. Second, Anttila et al. (2010) formalize the role of nuclear stress in end-weight via the constraint STRESS-TO-STRESS: "Each lexical stress occurs within the prosodic phrase that receives sentence stress." They employ this constraint to account for the primary stress count effect in the English dative alternation (§5.5.4), offering examples such as (26) (p. 955, their grids). Phrasing (a) receives three violations of STRESS-TO-STRESS, since three lexical stresses (bottom layer) occur in the nonfinal prosodic phrase (middle layer). Meanwhile, (b) incurs only two violations, and is therefore predicted to be favored. In a weighted-constraints framework, STRESS-TO-STRESS predicts a stronger end-weight tendency as the primary stress count discrepancy between the direct and indirect objects increases.

(26) (a) (×)
           (×)   (×)
           (×   ×   ×)   (×)
           gave critical backing   to   Bush

      (b) (×)
           (×)   (×)
           (×   ×)   (×   ×)
           gave   Bush   critical backing

Anttila et al. (2010) highlight three novel predictions of STRESS-TO-STRESS. First, function words, lacking lexical stresses, are predicted to be ignored for end-weight, an asymmetry for which they present evidence from the dative alternation (as described above in §5.5.4; but cf. the syllable-count effect for binomials in §5.6, which extends to unstressed syllables). Second, if nuclear stress is lured away, non-end-weight orders

[29] Zubizarreta (1998), for one, admits that English has weight-driven p-movement that does not serve to align focus with nuclear stress, as for example in heavy NP shift, but does not formalize an analysis (pp. 148–9).
[30] This statement puts aside studies such as MacDonald (2015) that cite one of these articles for the nuclear stress point without adding to the argument. Additionally, Müller (1997) invokes nuclear stress, but uses it only in the context of rhythmic constraints.

should be ameliorated, as in, to give an attested example, *never send someone them in the mail éither*, which has nuclear stress on *either*, and other real tokens collected by Bresnan and Nikitina (2003:20); cf. **never send someone thém*. Finally, if a language has left- instead of right-oriented nuclear stress, it is predicted to exhibit beginning-weight. As Anttila et al. (2010) admit, it is unclear whether this last prediction is borne out. On the one hand, as discussed in §5.12 below, beginning-weight is well established; on the other, its prosodic aspect is not well studied. While STRESS-TO-STRESS capitalizes on the insight that end-weight reflects nuclear stress, it does not address weight per se, and therefore fails to motivate the seven remaining principles of prosodic end-weight enumerated in §5.7. For one, insofar as a more general syllable count effect exists, as argued in §5.6, STRESS-TO-STRESS cannot motivate it. Moreover, all of the six subsyllabic principles of end-weight are lost on STRESS-TO-STRESS. That said, however, the same rationale for end-weight can be extended to weight, as in the remainder of this section.

The proposed constraints require heavy elements to be set in phrasally strong positions, consistent with the constraint family in §1.5. Phrasally strong positions are operationalized as φ_s, where φ denotes a prosodic node at or above the level of PWd and s denotes that it is strong, that is, a head. A preliminary segmental weight hierarchy is defined as in (27) (cf. Zec 1988, 1995, 2003). VV indicates any long vowel or diphthong, V any vowel or syllabic consonant, N_μ any moraic sonorant, X_μ any moraic segment, and X any segment. These categories are formulated stringently (Prince 1999, de Lacy 2004; §1.5), such that each is a subset of the category listed below it in (27), as visualized by Figure 5.8. On the use of segment types rather than rime or syllable types as weight predicates, see §5.9.4 below.

(27) a. VV→φ_s
      b. V→φ_s
      c. N_μ→φ_s
      d. X_μ→φ_s
      e. X→φ_s

Definition: For each heavy element η_i, assign a violation for each node φ_{wj} such that φ_{wj} dominates η_i.

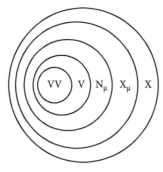

FIGURE 5.8 A stringent weight hierarchy, in which the most embedded set is the heaviest.

Each constraint in (27) penalizes a heavy element of the specified type for each φ_w that dominates it. The nuance "for each" was not relevant in the previous chapters, as mapping constraints did not invoke recursive layers (e.g. σ is not recursive). But in the present context, φs are nested. This is not just a consequence of my defining φ as generalizing over higher levels of the prosodic hierarchy, but follows also from the assumption that PWds are recursive (§3.2.2). Therefore, it is now necessary to clarify that conditionals are interpreted universally rather than existentially. As explained in §1.5, a constraint such as $VV \rightarrow \varphi_s$ could equivalently be stated $^*VV/\varphi_w$, as indeed I have elsewhere (Ryan 2018). I opt for the former here for consistency with the rest of the book. The constraints in (27) are akin to WEIGHT-TO-STRESS (i.e. $\sigma_{\mu\mu} \rightarrow$ STRESS; §2.3), except that stress is now interpreted phrasally and weight is atomized. Anttila et al.'s (2010) constraint STRESS-TO-STRESS could be folded into this scheme as STRESS $\rightarrow \varphi_s$, though it is omitted from the tableaux below, which exemplify only single-word conjuncts, a context in which such a constraint is never decisive. The hierarchy in (27) is incomplete; additional sonority effects are addressed later in this section.

This use of generic φ permits prosodic end-weight to emerge in contexts not involving the stress maximum of the sentence. After all, end-weight is still observed in binomials in which neither conjunct contains the matrix nuclear stress. Because φ_ws can be embedded, a single segment can incur multiple violations from a single constraint. No harm comes from this eventuality, since these extra violations are constant across reorderings of the binomial. For example, if the binomial as a whole is set in a weak intonation group φ_w, both orders of the binomial will receive identical violations from that head, rendering it irrelevant. Finally, because the constraints in (27) are stringent, the factorial typology excludes grammars that negate weight universals. For example, a consonant is putatively never heavier than a vowel (Gordon 2006, Ryan 2016; §1.3). If the constraints had been stated as $V \rightarrow \varphi_s$ and $C \rightarrow \varphi_s$, the latter could be ranked above the former to implement the counter-universal. But with $V \rightarrow \varphi_s$ and $X \rightarrow \varphi_s$, a consonant always receives a subset of the violations of a vowel, and therefore can never be more penalized in φ_w.

As an illustration, consider once again *trick or treat*, presented alongside its transposition in the tableau in (28). For additional cases of constraint-based grammar adjudicating between word orders and for further discussion of the architectural issues that such an approach raises, see recently Elfner (2012, 2015), Shih (2014), Bennett et al. (2016), Clemens and Coon (2016), Shih and Zuraw (2016), among others (cf. also the TRY-AND-FILTER approach; Büring 2013:872). In (28), $VV \rightarrow \varphi_s$ is decisive, which (b) alone violates due to the tense vowel in the weak branch of the binomial. The constraints are not crucially ranked at this point, hence the dashed dividers. The issues of ranking and variation are treated presently. In (28), $X_\mu \rightarrow \varphi_s$ incurs two violations from (a) because two segments under a φ_w are moraic, namely, $[\text{ɪ}_\mu]$ and $[\text{k}_\mu]$. Meanwhile, $X \rightarrow \varphi_s$ incurs four violations from (a), as φ_w dominates four segments, $[\text{t}]$, $[\text{ɹ}]$, $[\text{ɪ}_\mu]$, and $[\text{k}_\mu]$. That the coda of *trick* is moraic is reinforced by prosodic minimality in English (Morén 1997), though it would not affect anything here if final codas were nonmoraic.

(28)

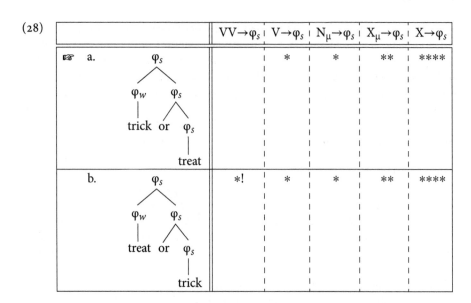

		VV→φ_s	V→φ_s	N_μ→φ_s	X_μ→φ_s	X→φ_s
☞ a.	φ_s [φ_w | trick] [φ_s or [φ_s treat]]		*	*	**	****
b.	φ_s [φ_w | treat] [φ_s or [φ_s trick]]	*!	*	*	**	****

In general, at least for the simple binomials under consideration, the prosodic structures of binomials can be assumed to align with their right-branching syntactic structures, consistent with highly-ranked MATCH constraints (Selkirk 2011). Thus, the prosodic structure on the left in (29) matches its syntactic structure on the right (cf. Munn 1993, Wagner 2005). The conjunction, lacking stress, is taken to adjoin to a recursive PWd, but this analysis of clitics is not critical here. The only critical assumption about prosodic phonology here is that the right branch of a binomial is prosodically strong, which is a matter of consensus.

(29)   Prosody: Syntax:

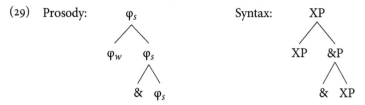

Couched in OT, this analysis predicts that candidate (a) in (28) wins categorically. In the case of *trick or treat*, this might be acceptable. In general, however, the vowel length effect is only a tendency in binomials (§5.5.1). To encode a tendency, the constraints could be numerically weighted in a probabilistic version of HG (e.g. Goldwater and Johnson 2003, Wilson 2006, Hayes and Wilson 2008, Pater 2009, Boersma and Pater 2016). To generate variation in the presence of subsetted violation vectors, as in (28), where (a) would harmonically bound (b) in OT, maxent HG can be employed (e.g. Goldwater and Johnson 2003, Wilson 2006, Hayes and Wilson 2008), since harmonic bounding is not a property of that framework (Jesney 2007). At the same time, lexicalized binomials (FREEZES or IDIOMS) can be exempted from variation via faithfulness (which itself might be weighted in order to implement the variable strengths of idioms). For example, *trick or treat* is more frozen than a comparable but non-idiomatic binomial such as *clip or pleat*. This situation, in which a grammar must encode statistical regularities but at the same time defer to listed items, is a common one in phonology; see, for example, Zuraw (2010) and Morgan and Levy (2016) for discussion and references, the latter treating specifically binomials. At any rate, the implementation of lexicalized phrases is not pursued here, as the emphasis is on the productive aspect of end-weight.

The present analysis also captures the syllable-count effect (§5.6) without further stipulation. Though there is no dedicated constraint for syllable count, its aggregate effect emerges from the fact that additional syllables incur additional violations of the other constraints (e.g. *baba* has double the violations of *ba*, at least if stress is put aside).[31] Consider a binomial such as *bread and butter*, as in (30). The long-initial order (b) is in this case redundantly excluded by $V \to \varphi_s$ and $N_\mu \to \varphi_s$, though this redundancy does not hold in general, as the next example will illustrate. Although (a) wins categorically (30), in reality, both candidates are grammatical. As just discussed, this variation can be achieved through weighting. All that is critical here is that (a) is favored as long as at least one of the decisive constraints has any weight. Additionally, given that these are real binomials, other constraints also come into play, including frequency, rhythm, prototypicality, idiomaticity, and so forth. As the focus here is on the contribution of phonology, only phonological constraints are shown. This presentation is not meant to imply that other types of constraints are not active as well.

(30)

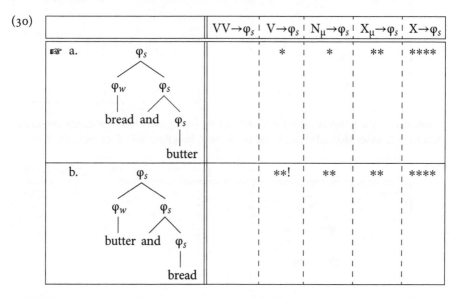

Tableau (31) exemplifies an outcome that depends on ranking/weighting: *beer and butter* ~ *butter and beer*. In this case, syllable count conflicts with vowel length, and the empirical preference is unclear. With the arbitrary ranking shown in (31)—a solid vertical line now isolates the top constraint—(a) wins, since it is more important to avoid a long vowel under weak phrasal stress than any number of short vowels, given strict domination. With other rankings, however, (b) would win. Moreover, with

---

[31] This analysis leaves open the possibility that syllable count might not be decisive if other constraints such as vowel length interfere. See (31).

weighting, counting cumulativity is possible, meaning that even if a constraint has a lower weight, it might overcome a dominant constraint if the former receives enough violations (Jäger and Rosenbach 2006, Pater 2009:1008). At any rate, no attempt is made here to determine precise weights of these constraints in English. With any nonzero weights, the generalizations in §5.7 emerge, which is the main concern here. Previous work addressing ranking or weighting in some form includes Cooper and Ross (1975), Pinker and Birdsong (1979), Oden and Lopes (1981), Benor and Levy (2006), and Mollin (2012), among others.

(31)

	VV→φ$_s$	V→φ$_s$	N$_\mu$→φ$_s$	X$_\mu$→φ$_s$	X→φ$_s$
☞ a. butter and beer		**	**	**	****
b. beer and butter	*!	*	**	**	***

Another core generalization concerning end-weight is that sonorant codas are treated as heavier than obstruent codas. N$_\mu$→φ$_s$ handles this effect, as in (32).

(32)

	VV→φ$_s$	V→φ$_s$	N$_\mu$→φ$_s$	X$_\mu$→φ$_s$	X→φ$_s$
☞ a. thick and thin		*	*	**	***
b. thin and thick		*	**!	**	***

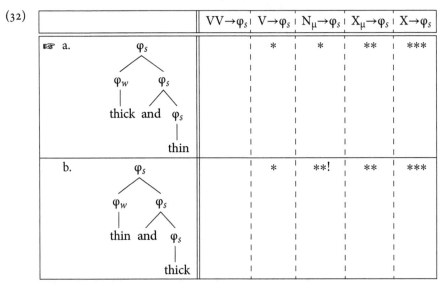

The analysis also captures onset size effects via X→φ_s, as in (34). Coda consonants, for their part, incur violations from X→φ_s, X_μ→φ_s, and potentially also N_μ→φ_s. This analysis therefore predicts that coda size matters at least as much as onset size, as coda consonants incur a superset of the violations of onset consonants. Nevertheless, as discussed in §5.5.3, coda length usually trades off (gradiently if not categorically) with nucleus length, potentially damping some of the apparent effect of coda size in real data.

(33)

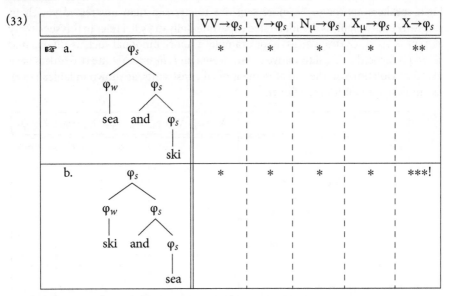

	VV→φ_s	V→φ_s	N_μ→φ_s	X_μ→φ_s	X→φ_s
☞ a.	*	*	*	*	**
b.	*	*	*	*	***!

The constraint set is more fine-grained than the five constraints illustrated so far. For example, coda sonority appears to be gradient (§5.5.3), in which case N_μ→φ_s could be broken down further, for example, into [+*approx*]→φ_s, [+*son*]→φ_s, and so forth. Vowel sonority effects (§5.5.1) can be treated similarly. For instance, [+*low*]→φ_s penalizes low vowels in weak positions. On the onset sonority effect, which has not yet been analyzed, see §5.9.4.

All of these generalizations are consistent with the phonology of weight more generally across languages and systems, hence the slogan: PROSODIC END-WEIGHT IS WEIGHT. First, nucleus and coda size are well known as canonical determinants of weight (Hyman 1985, Hayes 1995, Gordon 2006). Second, greater coda sonority and vowel lowness are also widely reported to correlate with weight, as they increase the duration or total energy of the rime (e.g. Zec 1988, 1995, 2003, Prince 1999, Gordon 2002b, 2006, de Lacy 2004, Crowhurst and Michael 2005). Third, the treatment of onsets in end-weight, including both the complexity and obstruency effects, is convergent with the onset weight typology across systems (Gordon 2005, Topintzi 2010, Ryan 2011b, 2014, 2016). For example, the stress system of Pirahã famously exhibits both effects (Everett and Everett 1984, Daniel Everett 1988, Keren Everett 1998); but they are more widely attested (§5.9.4). On the implementation of the sonority reversal between the onset and rime and the phonetic rationale for this reversal, see §5.9.4. In short, the phrasal stress explanation for prosodic end-weight, unlike the other explanations in §5.8, correctly predicts that prosodic end-weight should exhibit the same features as syllable weight in other systems, given that they all instantiate the constraint family in §1.5.

5.9.2 *Stress-modulated weight*

I now turn to three outstanding issues for the phrasal stress analysis of prosodic end-weight, namely, stress-modulated weight, multinomials (§5.9.3), and the onset sonority effect (§5.9.4). (The behavior of compounds will be addressed in §5.10.) First, speakers appear to be more sensitive to stressed than unstressed vowels in assessing end-weight, as demonstrated experimentally in §5.8. I refer to this sensitivity as STRESS-MODULATED WEIGHT. For example, a nonce binomial such as *climmo and cleema* is favored to the alternative order, *cleema and climmo*. Yet the two orders have identical violations on the five aforementioned constraints, as shown in tableau (34). "🌢" indicates an undesired winner.

(34)

		$VV{\to}\varphi_s$	$V{\to}\varphi_s$	$N_\mu{\to}\varphi_s$	$X_\mu{\to}\varphi_s$	$X{\to}\varphi_s$
☞ a.	φ_s / φ_w φ_s / climmo and φ_s / cleema	*	**	**	**	*****
🌢 b.	φ_s / φ_w φ_s / cleema and φ_s / climmo	*	**	**	**	*****

The problem is that the unstressed vowel *o* [oʊ] and the stressed vowel *ee* [ˈiː] are treated identically by $VV{\to}\varphi_s$, when the latter should be heavier. A stressed element is heavier than its unstressed counterpart (as least for vowel length; other distinctions are expected to behave similarly, but have not been tested). STRESS$\to\varphi_s$ (cf. Anttila et al. 2010) alone does not capture this stress modulation, since both orders in (34) have a single stressed vowel under φ_w. But further dissolving STRESS$\to\varphi_s$ into its own stringency hierarchy by adding $\acute{V}V{\to}\varphi_s$, which targets only stressed long vowels and diphthongs, achieves this effect, as in (35). Stringency ensures that under all rankings, $\acute{V}V$ is at least as heavy as VV, since a stressed long vowel violates both constraints, but an unstressed long vowel violates only the latter.[32]

---

[32] In an HG setting, an alternative to expanding the constraint set would be to posit a multiplier for stress level (on multipliers, cf. Kimper 2011, Zymet 2015, McPherson and Hayes 2016).

(35)

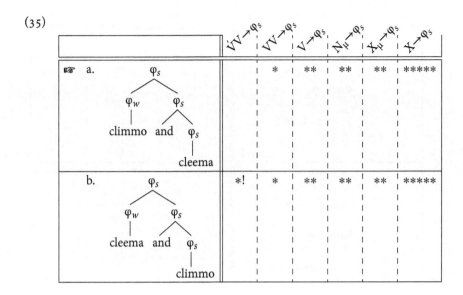

5.9.3 Multinomials

End-weight is generally thought to apply not only to binomials, but also to series of any length (e.g. *tic-tac-toe*; *lock, stock, and barrel*; see §5.2, §5.6.1). Given the constraints and prosodic assumptions laid out in this section, trinomials and longer lists are predicted to exhibit prosodic end-weight only in the sense that the final member will tend to be the heaviest. Nonfinal members are not predicted to be susceptible to end-weight among themselves, as illustrated by (36). Because each of the first two conjuncts is under a single φ_w, (a) and (b) have identical violation vectors. Due to space constraints, the tableau shows only four of six possible orders of three elements.

(36)

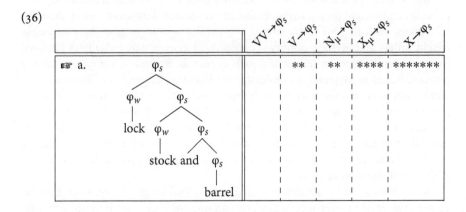

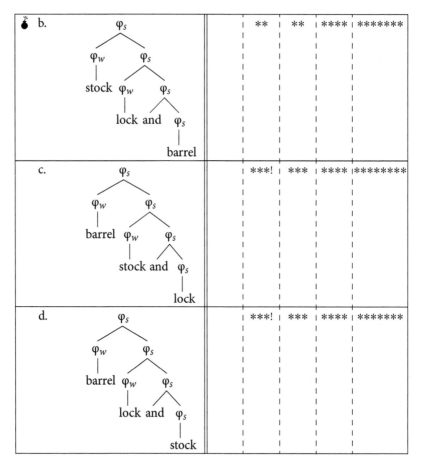

First, as an empirical matter, it is worth investigating more systematically whether prosodic end-weight productively obtains among nonfinal conjuncts. After all, many trinomials, such as *Tom, Dick, and Harry*, exhibit seemingly gratuitous non-end-weight orders among their nonfinal conjuncts. Moreover, many examples cited for increasing end-weight in trinomials, such as *friends, Romans, countrymen*, involve confounds such as frequency. In this case, *friends* is more frequent than *Romans*. Thus, some caution is warranted in assuming that trinomials in fact exhibit incremental prosodic end-weight across positions. An unrelated complication is that trinomials are sometimes susceptible to the Rhythm Rule (see §5.11), which can result in the promotion of stress on the first element and the demotion of it on the second. For example, *tic-tac-toe*, ostensibly a case of incremental end-weight, can be pronounced with greater stress on *tic* than *tac*.

These caveats aside, assuming that prosodic end-weight is confirmed to be cumulative among nonfinal conjuncts, certain assumptions about prosodic phrasing in (36) should be revisited. For instance, if nonfinal conjuncts formed a prosodic constituent, as in (37), rising end-weight would follow on the present analysis. Indeed, prosodic structure is known sometimes to depart from syntactic structure in order to promote evenly balanced constituents (cf. Nespor and Vogel 1986, Taglicht

1998, Steedman 2000). This adjustment was not relevant for binomials above, but may be relevant for multinomials. I leave the prosodic phrasing of more complex coordinated structures and their implications for this proposal to future research (cf. Wagner 2005, 2010).

(37)

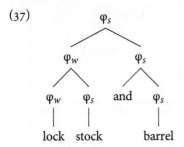

One fairly well circumscribed class of exceptions to end-weight in multinomials concerns series of the type *hickory-dickory-dock, eeny-meeny-miny-mo*, and so forth, which end sharply with a monosyllable (Campbell and Anderson 1976). In such cases, a principle of euphony seems to compete with both NonFinality and end-weight, since the monosyllable is preferred rather than avoided in final position.[33] Note also that this pattern is confined to multinomials; it does not work as well for hypothetical binomials such as *hickory-dock* or *minie-mo*. Hayes and MacEachern (1998) and Kiparsky (2006b) motivate this construction in terms of saliency; see also Blumenfeld (2016a). Saliency, as a constraint, penalizes a fully parallel list, favoring instead a distinctive cadence. This analysis explains the confinement of saliency to multinomials, since no parallelism can be established if only one item precedes the final item. Therefore, this special case can be put aside as motivated by an independent consideration. Indeed, aside from the salient cadence, end-weight appears to obtain as normal in such lists: *hickory-dickory* follows the onset sonority rule, *eenie-meenie-minie* follows the onset complexity and vowel duration rules, and so forth.

5.9.4 *Onset sonority*

The only phonological generalization regarding prosodic end-weight in §5.7 that is yet to be implemented at this point is the onset sonority effect, whereby obstruent onsets pattern as heavier than sonorant onsets (§5.5.2). $N_\mu \rightarrow \varphi_s$, for its part, covers the coda sonority effect, but ignores onsets, which lack moras in English. At any rate, even if onsets were moraic in English, $N_\mu \rightarrow \varphi_s$ is the opposite of what is needed. $T_{ons} \rightarrow \varphi_s$, where T_{ons} is an onset obstruent, achieves the needed effect, as in (38). I first address the justification for this constraint and then turn to problems that it faces.

---

[33] Donca Steriade (p.c.) notes that these phrases are extracted from verse: *Hickory dickory dóck / The mouse ran up the clóck; Eeny, meeny, miny, mó / Catch a tiger by the tóe.* In each case, the cadence is iambic, and the rhyme must occupy the final strong position. That said, these formulas may be productive outside of verse, as in law firm names (Adam Albright, p.c.). For example, a poster for the 2012 film *The Three Stooges* features the gag business names *Dewey, Burnham, and Howe; Proba, Keister, and Wince;* and *Ditcher, Quick, and Hyde.* The verse confound also cannot motivate the confinement of the pattern to multinomials as opposed to binomials.

(38)

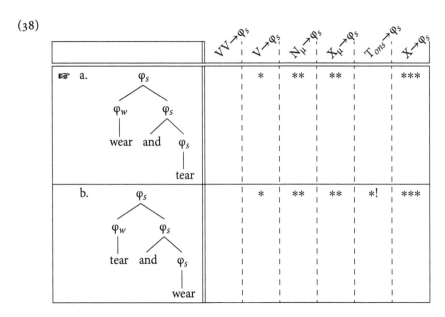

	$VV \to \varphi_s$	$V \to \varphi_s$	$N_\mu \to \varphi_s$	$X_\mu \to \varphi_s$	$T_{ons} \to \varphi_s$	$X \to \varphi_s$
☞ a. φ_s [φ_w wear, φ_s [and, φ_s tear]]	*	**	**			***
b. φ_s [φ_w tear, φ_s [and, φ_s wear]]	*	**	**		*!	***

$T_{ons} \to \varphi_s$ reflects the universal phonology of weight, in that cross-modally and cross-linguistically, obstruent onsets behave as (if anything) heavier than sonorant onsets, the opposite directionality of what is observed in the rime. Stress systems treating obstruent or voiceless onsets as heavier than sonorant or voiced onsets include genealogically diverse Pirahã (Everett and Everett 1984, Daniel Everett 1988, Keren Everett (1998)), Arabela (Payne and Rich 1988), Tümpisa Shoshone (Dayley 1989), and perhaps Karo (Gabas Jr. 1999, Topintzi 2010:39; cf. Blumenfeld 2006). See Gordon (2005), Topintzi (2010), and Ryan (2014) for overviews. Similarly, Ryan (2014) finds that simplex voiceless onsets pattern as significantly more stress-attracting than simplex voiced onsets in English, and also demonstrates the same voicing effect for Sanskrit meter, in which syllables pattern as gradiently heavier if they contain a voiceless as opposed to voiced onset. Finally, the onset sonority effect is well established for end-weight, the present concern (§5.5.2).

The phonetic rationale for the onset sonority effect is treated by Gordon (2005) and Ryan (2014). Gordon (2005) invokes auditory recovery and adaptation, observing that a vowel immediately following a voiceless consonant is perceived as louder, and hence heavier, than one immediately following a voiced consonant, owing to the more distinct transition characterizing the former. Ryan (2014) adds to this consideration the fact that the perceptual beat (p-CENTER) of a syllable (Morton et al. 1976; see more recently Port 2007, Wright 2008, Villing 2010, and references therein) is typically perceived as occurring slightly earlier in the presence of a longer onset, a phenomenon that extends to the phonetic durations of singletons, which are typically longer as (especially aspirated) voiceless obstruents than as voiced obstruents or sonorants. Some tasks that elicit p-center data include chanting over a metronome and isochronizing a series (e.g. turning a knob until successive syllables sound evenly timed).

These two explanations are not mutually exclusive. On the contrary, they complement each other in motivating aspects of onset weight that the other cannot explain. First, as Ryan (2014) and Mai (2018) observe, the total energy of the rime (incorporating adjustments such as auditory adaptation and recovery) cannot account for more complex onsets attracting stress in languages like English because rimes are progressively shorter, not longer, after progressively more complex onsets (Figure 1.1). Second, auditory recovery and adaptation cannot explain onset complexity effects outside of an approximately 40 ms window from the beginning of the vowel, given a physiological ceiling effect (Delgutte 1982:135, Gordon 2005). For example, they predict no perceived weight difference between *ba* [ˈbɑ] and *spa* [ˈspɑ̥], given that the stop is typically longer than 40 ms, effectively rendering the [s] invisible (Ryan 2014:332). Third, recovery and adaptation make the wrong prediction for empty (or glottal stop) onsets, which pattern as phonologically light despite the salient attack that they furnish for the rime (but cf. Gordon 2005 for discussion). P-center theory is compatible with all of these effects, since onset complexity favors earlier p-center placement. At the same time, p-center theory struggles in certain respects that recovery and adaptation do not. For instance, it fails to motivate certain weight contrasts, such as [d] vs. [n]. It follows that recovery, adaptation, and p-centers may well simultaneously affect the weight percept, such that one might refer to the total energy of the p-center interval to incorporate the benefits of both proposals (Ryan 2014, Hirsch 2014, Mai 2018).

Returning to the formalization, a problem with $T_{ons} \rightarrow \varphi_s$ is that it breaks the stringency hierarchy, as depicted by Figure 5.9: It is not a superset of heavier elements. As such, it can be ranked anywhere with respect to the other constraints, generating markedness reversals. For example, one language might be sensitive to vowel length but ignore onset sonority, while another ignores vowel length but heeds onset sonority. The latter is likely an impossibility. With a fully stringent hierarchy, such reversals are precluded.

I now outline a few logically possible recourses. The first is to relax stringency and let the theory overgenerate. After all, overgeneration is a common and commonly ignored defect of constraint systems (for discussion of overgeneration pathologies, see Steriade 2009, Blumenfeld 2006), so the situation might not be viewed as grave. Moreover, it is empirically unclear how to integrate T_{ons} into the stringency hierarchy, with some evidence suggesting that markedness reversals do in fact occur. As discussed in §1.5, languages have been described that both (1) heed coda absence/presence while

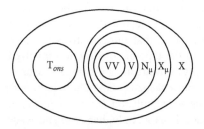

FIGURE 5.9 T_{ons} breaks the stringency hierarchy.

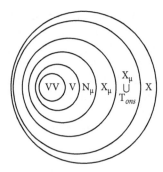

FIGURE 5.10 A disjunctive solution to the onset sonority problem for stringency.

ignoring onset sonority and (2) ignore coda absence/presence while heeding onset sonority. If the cases of (2) (Karo and Tümpisa Shoshone; Topintzi 2010, §1.5) hold up to scrutiny, then at least a limited breach of stringency is justified.

The second possible recourse is to preserve stringency through disjunction. For instance, perhaps between the rings X_μ and X in Figure 5.9 resides the ring $X_\mu \cup T_{ons}$, as in Figure 5.10, yielding the constraint $X_\mu \cup T_{ons} \rightarrow \varphi_s$. (If one were so inclined, one could give $X_\mu \cup T_{ons}$ a name and a label, such as the "submora," say, v.) The stipulativeness of such a disjunction is tempered by its being phonetically grounded in the weight percept. De Lacy (2004) makes a similar analytical move with his stringent mapping constraints. For example, he posits $^*\text{HD}_{Ft}/i,\partial,i{\cdot}u$ and other constraints whose predicates are not natural classes according to standard feature theories (§1.5). They would have to be expressed as disjunctions. But de Lacy (2004) argues that sonority can be regarded as a (richly) multivalued feature, obviating the need for disjunction. The present case can be treated similarly, if sonority is understood to mean total energy: The labels of elements are not important; what matters is that they refer to contiguous, heavy-aligned subsections of a scale, namely, the normalized weight percept. In this sense, $X_\mu \cup T_{ons} \rightarrow \varphi_s$ is natural.

A third possible solution is what might be termed the DIRECT INTERFACE approach, that is, to abandon reference to discrete heavy elements altogether and employ instead a real-valued constraint such as $t \rightarrow \varphi_s$, where t is normalized total energy. Stringency would then be irrelevant, lacking a constraint family. I discuss my rationale for not adopting such an approach in the conclusion, especially §6.4.

At this point, then, all eight phonological principles of end-weight in §5.7 have been addressed, assuming that STRESS-TO-STRESS (Anttila et al. 2010) or its φ_s equivalent, STRESS$\rightarrow\varphi_s$, is retained to handle the primary stress effect. Moreover, while only binomials have been illustrated, the same analysis applies to all prosodic end-weight phenomena, given that phrasal stress is generally right-oriented, and φ_s is indiscriminate as to the type of construction involved. The question of when constructional optionality is available is a complex issue at the interfaces and not considered here, as the present focus is the phonological aspect of end-weight (see e.g. Embick 2007, Büring 2013, Shih and Zuraw 2016). See also §5.14 concerning the attenuation of phonological factors in higher-level end-weight constructions such as heavy NP shift.

5.10 End-weight in compounds

Compounds are another context in which stress above the PWd is not necessarily right-oriented. The phrasal stress account of end-weight predicts that insofar as compounds comprise multiple PWds, they should exhibit weight polarity mirroring their prosodic headedness. As discussed in §5.2, the earliest claim for end-weight comes from Pāṇini's rules for dvandva compounds in Sanskrit. It is therefore natural to ask whether these compounds are prosodically head-final. This is plausible, on the grounds that if a Sanskrit dvandva is single-accented, that accent normally falls on the final member (with lexical exceptions; Pāṇini 6.1.223, 6.2.34–7; Kiparsky 2010).[34]

Binary compounds in English are usually prosodically left-headed (e.g. *kétchup factory, bláckboard*),[35] though in more complex compounds, prosodic headedness can be affected by syntax (Chomsky and Halle 1968, Liberman and Prince 1977, Arregi 2002). Nevertheless, the order of most compounds is syntactically determined, rendering end-weight moot. For example, because *ketchup factory* means something different from *factory ketchup*, prosodic weight has no opportunity to assert itself. That said, there is one major type of compound in English for which end-weight is potentially applicable, namely, echo reduplication. Syntax has nothing to do with, say, *hoity-toity* being preferred to *toity-hoity*. Following Dienhart (1999), echo compounds include ONSET REDUPLICATIVES, in which onsets vary (e.g. *hoity-toity*), and ABLAUT REDUPLICATIVES, in which vowels vary (e.g. *dilly-dally*). Because their stress patterns differ, these types are treated separately here.

For onset reduplicatives, stress is normally on the initial element if the elements are monosyllables (e.g. *hóbnob*), and otherwise on the final element (e.g. *artsy-fártsy*). Consistent with the phrasal stress theory of prosodic end-weight, end-weight is observed in onset reduplicatives when they are disyllable pairs, but not when they are monosyllable pairs. Specifically, judging by Dienhart's (1999) data, when monosyllable pairs differ in onset complexity (e.g. *crúmbum*), the longer onset is second 55 per cent of the time, essentially chance (6 of 11; goodness-of-fit $\chi^2(1) = .1, p = .76$). For disyllable pairs, the longer onset is second 89 per cent of the time, significantly greater than chance (17 of 19; $\chi^2(1) = 11.8, p < .001$). When monosyllable pairs comprise members beginning with simplex onsets differing in sonority, the second element begins with the less sonorous onset 45 per cent of the time, again, essentially chance (14 of 31; $\chi^2(1) = .29, p = .59$). For disyllable pairs, the less sonorous onset is second 90 per cent of the time (28 of 31; $\chi^2(1) = 20.2, p < .0001$). In sum, monosyllable pairs, which have left-oriented stress, lack end-weight, while disyllable pairs, which have right-oriented stress, observe end-weight. This asymmetry, visualized in Figure 5.11, is precisely what the phrasal stress theory of prosodic end-weight predicts.[36]

---

[34] Dvandvas can also be accented on all or none of their members, particularly in Vedic Sanskrit (Wackernagel 1905, Oliphant 1912, Kiparsky 2010). These cases are not informative about the prosodic headedness of the compound as a whole.

[35] Accents here indicate the stress maxima of compounds, not word stress in general.

[36] Monosyllable pairs exhibit neither beginning- nor end-weight. Phrasal stress predicts that they should exhibit beginning-weight only if they are parsed into multiple PWds. However, monosyllable pairs are plausibly parsed into feet (f) of a single PWd, for example, $((hob)f_s(nob)f_w)\varphi$, in which case phrasal stress

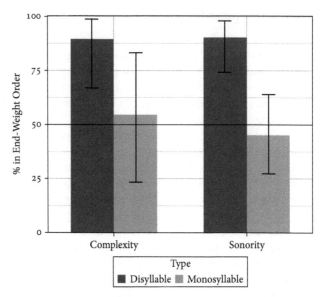

FIGURE 5.11 End-weight among onset reduplicatives consisting of disyllables vs. monosyllables, based on data from Dienhart (1999). Disyllable pairs exhibit end-weight in terms of both complexity and sonority, while monosyllable pairs exhibit neither.

For ablaut reduplicatives, stress is usually initial for both monosyllable and disyllable pairs (e.g. *chítchat, dílly-dally*) (Dienhart 1999), though it is final for polysyllables and more complex disyllables (e.g. *twinkum-twánkum, Jiminy Jáminy, clickety-cláck*) (Minkova 2002). These compounds are at first glance problematic for the phrasal stress analysis, in that they exhibit a high-before-low tendency even when peak stress is initial (*ibid.*). However, initially stressed ablaut reduplicatives do not comprise multiple PWds, rendering phrasal stress moot. For example, φ_w constraints do not affect the internal organization of $((dilly)f_s(dally)f_w)\varphi$. This foot parse is supported by the fact that stress shifts to the final member in forms in which the members exceed minimal foot size, as in $((twinkum)\varphi_w(twankum)\varphi_s)\varphi$, as depicted in (39). These longer cases are prosodified as separate PWds, and end-weight applies as expected.

(39) (a)

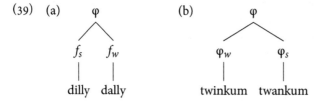

correctly predicts that weight is ignored. Meanwhile, a longer form such as *artsy-fartsy* is prosodified as separate PWds—it has the same prosody as *artsy and fartsy*—and φ_s constraints apply, favoring end-weight.

Nevertheless, the question remains: If short ablaut reduplicatives such as *dilly-dally* are not subject to φ_w constraints, why do they exhibit a high-before-low vocalism consistent with end-weight? The proposal here is that this vocalism does not synchronically reflect weight, but is rather a case of FIXED SEGMENTISM (Alderete et al. 1999, Keane 2001). For comparison, consider another type of English echo reduplication, of the type *fancy-shmáncy* (Nevins and Vaux 2003, Southern 2005). Overwriting the onset with *shm* usually results in a longer onset in second position, consistent with end-weight. However, this may be a coincidence; there could be other motivations for placing the faithful copy first. Moreover, while the Yiddish etymology of the construction is obvious, the use of [ʃm] in particular (as opposed to [ʃl], etc.) is fairly arbitrary from a synchronic perspective. In some other cases of fixed segmentism, the origin of the fixed material is completely obscure. Thus, while a pattern of fixed segmentism might originate with the help of functional or sociolinguistic principles, once it is sufficiently entrenched in the language, its use might spread to contexts where those initial conditions do not apply. As discussed in the following paragraphs, this is possibly the situation with fixed segmentism in English ablaut reduplicatives.

One way to distinguish between end-weight and fixed segmentism is to assess the range of vowels involved. If the range is highly limited (at the extreme, one vowel per position), it is more symptomatic of fixed segmentism than of the free operation of end-weight. Coordinate binomials, for their part, must exhibit end-weight as opposed to fixed segmentism, since the vowels entering into the binomial are unrestricted. Similarly, onset reduplicatives must exhibit end-weight, since the onsets involved vary widely. For ablaut reduplicatives, by contrast, the situation is more akin to fixed segmentism. Statistics here are based on a table in Thun (1963:220; repeated in Minkova 2002:157). In the overwhelming majority (92.2%) of ablaut reduplicatives, the first element has the vowel /ɪ/. /i/ is the next most frequent at 5 per cent, but as Minkova (2002) points out, it is often motivated by length agreement (cf. Tamil, where echo reduplication always copies length but not quality; Keane 2001). The remainder is fewer than 3 per cent of ablaut reduplicatives, and almost all of this remainder is the vowels /ʌ/ (1.6%) and /ɛ/ (1.2%), both close to /ɪ/. Meanwhile, in the second element of the reduplicative, the vowel is almost always (95.4%) either /æ/ or /ɑ~ɔ/.

In short, ablaut reduplicatives normally exhibit the limited vocalism /ɪ - æ~ɑ~ɔ/, a situation resembling fixed segmentism. If it were end-weight alone, one would expect vowels to combine more freely (in orders favored by end-weight), as with hypothetical compounds such as *booty-boaty* (/u-o/), *babble-bobble* (/æ-ɑ/), and *matey-Matty* (/e-æ/), all of which have the longer vowel in second position, though they flout the stereotyped vocalism. To claim that /ɪ - æ~ɑ~ɔ/ is synchronically fixed is not to deny that the specific vowels in that formula might ultimately be influenced by end-weight. After all, /ɪ/ is the shortest full vowel in English, and /æ~ɑ~ɔ/ are located opposite from it in the vowel space; these facts hardly seem arbitrary. However, the vocalism might have been more transparently related to stress in earlier stages of its entrenchment. For example, it was always reinforced by binomials (e.g. *tit-for-tát, riff for ráff*), which remain stressed on their final elements. Moreover, some pairs were borrowed from French, where they were finally stressed, before being reanalyzed as initially stressed at some point in English (e.g. *rif et ráf* > *ríffraff; bric à brác* > *bríc-a-brac*). Even among Germanic compounds, Dienhart (1999) and Minkova (2002) mention that stress can vary for some ablaut reduplicatives, such as *tip-top*, depending on part of speech and other factors. Thus, changing stress patterns may have partially opacified the conditions under which the fixed segmentism originated. At any rate, as long as there are not multiple PWds involved, these cases are outside of the purview of the phrasal stress theory proposed in §5.9.

5.11 The Rhythm Rule

As mentioned in §5.9.3, in a phrase with three stressed elements, the Rhythm Rule sometimes promotes stress on the first and demotes it on the second (Liberman and Prince 1977, Kiparsky 1979, Hayes 1984, Selkirk 1984, Hayes and Puppel 1985, Gussenhoven 1991). For example, *Mississippi* is pronounced in isolation as [ˌmɪsɪˈsɪpi]. But followed by, say, *mud*, the primary stress on *Mississippi* usually retracts to its initial syllable, as shown in (40-b), though (a) is also grammatical (Hayes and Puppel 1985).

(40) (a)   ×   (b)   ×
                          ×   ×   ×   ×
              ×   ×   ×   ×   ×   ×
              ×   ×   ×   ×   ×   ×   ×   ×   ×   ×
              Mis   sis   sip   pi   mud   Mis   sis   sip   pi   mud

The same rule potentially applies to certain binomials, such as in *rough-and-tumble play* in (41), where both (a–b) are felicitous.[37] Note, however, that freezes such as *rough and tumble* usually acquire a compound reading when used as modifiers, as implied by their hyphenation (*rough and tumble* vs. *rough-and-tumble play*). Idiomaticity and sense modulate the likelihood of a compound reading and hence the likelihood of initial stress; compare *black-and-white issues* to *black and white crayons*.

(41) (a)   ×   (b)   ×
                          ×   ×   ×   ×
              ×   ×   ×   ×   ×   ×
              ×   ×   ×   ×   ×   ×   ×   ×   ×   ×
              rough and tum ble play   rough and tum ble play

Turning to "ADJ *and* ADJ NOUN" more broadly, my intuition, supported by examination of the few tokens of this frame in the Buckeye corpus (Pitt et al. 2007), is that the Rhythm Rule does not usually apply to this configuration. In practice, it is difficult to discern for most naturally occurring tokens whether it has applied. Buckeye contains only four instances of this configuration without numerals, compound stress (e.g. *elementary or middle school*), or a noticeable hesitation between adjectives. These tokens are given in (42) along with the mean f_0 and intensity of the first adjective,

---

[37] Adam Albright (p.c.) first brought this issue to my attention. See Ryan (2018) for further discussion.

second adjective, and noun, respectively, as measured from the middle 50 per cent of the stressed vowel. Most of the changes are decreasing, but that does not mean that the phonological stress level is decreasing, given declination (Ladd 1984, 2008; footnote 28). Indeed, the noun, ostensibly the stress maximum of the phrase, usually has the lowest f_0 and intensity of all three words, revealing the strength of declination. Experimental data with a control condition or a model of declination would be better to gauge how much and often the Rhythm Rule applies in this configuration.

(42)

Phrase	Pitch (f_0 in Hz)	Intensity (dB µE)
calm and reasonable way	73, 75, creaky	58, 59, 54
physical and mental traits	99, 92, 83	72, 69, 66
interesting and wrong things	117, 107, 109	61, 65, 62
equal and fair society	89, 81, 85	64, 65, 69

The relevance of the Rhythm Rule to the phrasal stress theory of prosodic end-weight is that it has the potential to create a beginning-weight context. If greater stress falls on the first conjunct, I predict greater weight to be attracted to that position (modulo certain complications discussed below). For "ADJ *and* ADJ NOUN," prosodic end-weight clearly applies as normal to the binomial, as supported presently. This means that either (1) prosodic end-weight is not affected by the Rhythm Rule or (2) the Rhythm Rule does not often apply in this context. Bolinger (1962) tests adjectival binomials both sentence-finally and prenominally before initially and noninitially stressed nouns (e.g. *bleak and lonely*, *bleak and lonely countryside*, *bleak and lonely ravine*). There is no Rhythm Rule possibility sentence-finally, but there is one prenominally. Nevertheless, Bolinger (1962) finds that end-weight applies just as strongly (at a higher rate, in fact) prenominally. Therefore, if the participants were applying the Rhythm Rule frequently in this context, it had no attenuating effect on end-weight. Of course, it is also possible that they were not applying the Rhythm Rule frequently, in which case these figures reveal nothing about whether it affects end-weight. Moreover, Bolinger (1962) finds a higher rate of adjectival end-weight before initially stressed than noninitially stressed nouns (92% vs. 84%, Fisher's exact test OR = 1.93, $p = .02$), even though one would expect the Rhythm Rule to apply if anything more frequently before an initially stressed noun, as the clash is then more local.

Thus, the empirical situation is unclear on a few fronts. First, it is unclear how often English speakers apply the Rhythm Rule in cases like *bleak and lonely ravine*. My own intuition is that the Rhythm Rule is unlikely for such an item (assuming that it is all-new), but becomes more felicitous for more frequent or familiar binomials such as *rough and tumble*. Second, it is unclear whether applications of the Rhythm Rule correlate with a greater likelihood of beginning-weight. For example, in (42), all heavy-initial orders have higher f_0 on the initial item, and the one heavy-final order has higher f_0 on the final item. It is possible that such a correlation obtains more generally, such that greater weight does tend to accompany greater stress or f_0, though a proper study is needed. Third, lexicalization might interfere with stress–weight alignment. That is, speakers might be unwilling to reverse familiar binomials such as *rough and tumble* due to their listedness, regardless of the stress pattern. Indeed, beyond listedness and phrasal stress, numerous other factors influence ordering (§§5.3–5.4). Finally, the order of the conjoined adjective phrase might be decided at least partly independently of the noun, "before" the Rhythm Rule has an opportunity to apply. The noun cannot be ignored altogether, as Bolinger (1962) and Kelly and Bock (1988) demonstrate an effect of phrasal context. But given the recent resurgence in derivational constraint-based grammar (e.g. McCarthy 2009, 2010), on the one hand, and phase-based spellout (e.g. Kratzer and Selkirk 2007), on the other, a derivational model of binomial ordering may be feasible. More research is needed on contextual stress patterns such as the Rhythm Rule and their correlations, if any, with weight polarity preferences.

5.12 Beginning-weight

5.12.1 Overview of prosodic and syntactic beginning-weight

While phrasal stress is generally right-oriented in English (§5.9), this is not universally the case across languages. In many verb-final languages, for instance, stress is left-oriented in phonological phrases, such that the leftmost PWd heads the prosodic phrase. For example, the phrasal prosodies of Bengali, Persian, and Turkish are comparatively well documented in the phonological literature, and all three fit this generalization (Hayes and Lahiri 1991, Kahnemuyipour 2003, and Kabak and Vogel 2001, respectively). Note that left-headedness does not necessarily continue above the prosodic phrase: Hayes and Lahiri (1991:55) claim that while phrasal stress is leftmost in prosodic phrases in Bengali, it is rightmost in the intonation group under neutral focus. Similarly, Kahnemuyipour (2003:337) claims that in Persian, stress is leftmost in the prosodic phrase, rightmost in the intonation group, and then leftmost again in the utterance.

Following the phrasal stress account of end-weight, insofar as such languages exhibit left-oriented phrasal stress and weight-polarity effects of some kind, they are expected to exhibit BEGINNING-WEIGHT rather than end-weight. A few caveats are in order. First, given the possible inconsistency of prosodic headedness, prosodic beginning- vs. end-weight is not necessarily a language-wide parameter. For example, assuming the analysis of Hayes and Lahiri (1991) for Bengali, one would expect to find prosodic beginning-weight in (if anything) phrases but not intonation groups. Second, syntactic weight and prosodic weight might not behave identically. In English, they happen to coincide: Syntactic complexity (while holding phonology constant) contributes to end-weight, and phonological weight (while holding syntax constant) does the same. But depending on the explanation for syntactic weight effects, it is not logically required that the two types of weight converge. The end of this section considers a possible syntactic vs. prosodic weight discrepancy from Japanese. The final caveat is that the nuclear stress account of end-weight depends on stress per se, that is, differences in stress prominence between prosodic phrases. It is not clear that all languages realize phrasal prosodic headedness in terms of stress (as opposed to, say, pitch phenomena such as register and range). Again, this nuance may be relevant for Japanese.

The evidence for prosodic (as opposed to syntactic) weight at the phrasal level in prosodically head-initial contexts is limited at this point, but what evidence exists tentatively favors the phrasal stress account of weight. In the context of binomials, Tungus (Swadesh 1962, Wescott 1970) and Turkish (Marchand 1952, 1969:431, Pinker and Birdsong 1979) exhibit the reverse vocalism as English, that is, low-before-high, ostensibly a case of heavy-before-light. A few Turkish ablaut reduplicatives and binomials that illustrate this trend are given in (43) (from Marchand 1952). As Marchand (1952) emphasizes, the /ɑ/ – /u/ vocalism in particular has a status comparable to the stereotypical /ɪ/ – /æ∼ɑ∼ɔ/ vocalism in English.

(43) a. takur tukur   'harsh'
      b. cak cuk   'noisy'
      c. yamuk yumuk   'swollen'
      d. çalı çırpı   'wood chip'
      e. para pul   'money'

These compounds are prosodically head-initial, like phrases and compounds more generally in Turkish (Kabak and Vogel 2001). Kabak and Vogel (2001) analyze binary compounds as comprising two PWds, even though little to no stress is perceived on the second member. Consultation with a native speaker suggests that the same prosody applies to the reduplicative compounds in (43). For example, *takúr tukur* (stressed as accented) has the structure in (44). Under either ordering, the stress peak is *kur*. But placing *takur* before *tukur* avoids a violation of $[+low] \rightarrow \varphi_s$ (§5.9). Thus, stress and weight align as predicted by the nuclear stress account, though further investigation of phrasal constructions, beyond stereotyped compound vocalism, is needed to secure the case.

(44)

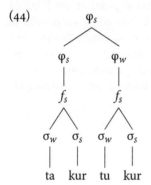

Other cases of low-before-high vocalism, though perhaps not previously discussed as such, come from South Asian languages such as Tamil, which, like Bengali, is verb-final and prosodically left-headed in the word and phrase (Keane 2003, 2006). This vocalism is clear as a stereotype from at least two contexts in Tamil, including deictic oppositions and echo reduplication. First, in deictic pairs, the distal is favored before the proximal, as in (45). This is the opposite of the order found in English, where the proximal usually goes first (e.g. *this and that, here and there, now and then*; Cooper and Ross 1975). In Tamil, the distal form differs from its proximal counterpart in substituting [ɑ] for [i] (Asher and Annamalai 2002:18). It is possible that the proximity reversal vis-à-vis English is motivated by stress–weight alignment in phrases, that is, once again, $[+low] \rightarrow \varphi_s$, as it applies to structures such as (46).[38]

(45) a. atu itu   'that [and] this'
      b. avan̠ ivan̠   'he (distal) [and] he (proximal)'
      c. aṅkē iṅkē   'there [and] here'
      d. appōtu ippōtu   'then [and] now'
      e. appaṭi ippaṭi   'in that way [and] in this way'

(46)

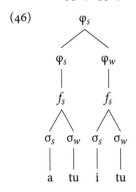

A low-first vocalism is also encountered in ablaut reduplication in Tamil. This construction involves copying a word, but replacing the initial CV of the second copy with *ki* [gi] or *kī* [giː], matching the vowel length of the base, as in (47) (Keane 2001). Because [i] is the shortest stressed vowel in Tamil (and [iː] the shortest stressed long vowel), this vocalism guarantees that the vowel in initial position, the locus of greatest stress, is at least as phonetically long as the vowel in second position. In sum, Tamil, like Turkish, exhibits stereotyped vocalism that approximately reverses the /ɪ/ – /æ~ɑ~ɔ/ pattern found in languages such as English and German. This mirror-image vocalism must be stipulated if the mirror-image stress patterns are ignored. In general, however, research on the prosodic properties of binomials and other weight-sensitive constructions in verb-final languages is lacking.

(47) a. taṇṇīr-kiṇṇīr   'water and such'
      b. pāmpu-kīmpu   'snakes and such'
      c. puli-kili   'tigers and such'
      d. pai-kī   'bag and such'

Moving beyond vocalism, I am aware of four languages for which the case for syntactic beginning-weight has been made, always in head-final contexts. These are Japanese (Dryer 1980, Hawkins 1994, 2004, Yamashita and Chang 2001, 2006, Chang 2009, Jaeger and Norcliffe 2009), Korean (Choi 2007), Cantonese (Matthews and

---

[38] Beyond Tamil, Cooper and Ross (1975:101) offer a few examples of Hindi binomials suggesting that "Hindi contradicts the English ordering fairly systematically." Judging by their data, it is not clear whether this discrepancy arises from phonology or semantics.

Yeung 2000), and Persian (Faghiri and Samvelian 2014) (cf. also Hawkins 2004:131 on Hungarian). Japanese and Korean, like Bengali and Tamil, are rigidly head-final. Insofar as ordering alternatives are available in these languages (e.g. for coarguments of the verb), longer elements are favored earlier, the mirror image of English. For example, Choi (2007) demonstrates beginning-weight for dative–accusative constructions in Korean, in which the dative and accusative arguments can be realized in either order. Persian, though not rigidly head-final, evidently behaves similarly in its preverbal field (Faghiri and Samvelian 2014; cf. Rasekh-Mahand et al. 2016). Finally, while Cantonese has a basic word order of SVO (subject–verb–object), Matthews and Yeung (2000) show that prenominal relative clauses, a head-final context, exhibit beginning-weight.

Thus, beginning-weight appears to be associated with head-finality. Hawkins (1994, 2004) capitalizes on this correlation to explain beginning-weight in terms of minimizing dependency distances (§5.8.4; cf. Yamashita and Chang 2001 for a different approach). For example, in a VO (verb–object) language like English, placing the shorter of two post-verbal arguments first entails that the left edges of both arguments are closer to their head than they would be in the reverse order. In an OV language, by contrast, locating the shorter argument second maximally aligns the arguments' (now right) edges with their head. In short, beginning-weight is predicted before the head, end-weight after it.

Existing studies of beginning-weight in East Asian languages and Persian (*op. cit.*) all conceive of weight in terms of syntactic complexity (or at least word count),[39] and their functional explanations follow suit by invoking processing or conceptual factors that relate to syntactic or lexical complexity. It is not presently clear whether specifically *prosodic* beginning-weight also exists in these languages. That is, it is uncertain whether increasing syllable count while holding syntactic complexity constant would affect beginning-weight, or whether any of the subsyllabic factors in §5.5 matter.

One study that addresses aspects of this question for Japanese is Lohmann and Takada (2014). The article analyzes Japanese binomial ordering using logistic models that include predictors for syllable count, mora count, frequency, and four pragmatic factors. Syllable count is nonsignificant in their data, while mora count weakly favors end-weight, not beginning-weight. However, caution is warranted on this point, as mora count is fairly borderline (*p* between 0.01 and 0.05, judging by their annotations) and its effect size is small compared to that of syllable count in English, which they also test using the same model. Given the clear evidence for syntactic beginning-weight in Japanese, it is perhaps surprising at first glance that no tendency for prosodic beginning-weight is observed. If anything, Lohmann and Takada (2014) point towards prosodic end-weight, though if it exists, it is considerably weaker than its counterpart in English.

Upon further reflection, however, this discrepancy between syntactic beginning-weight and a null or weakly reverse effect in the prosody may not be surprising.

---

[39] Choi (2007), for one, measures phrasal length in syllables, but interprets it as a proxy for word count, and therefore does not disentangle syntactic and phonological weight.

After all, the explanations for beginning-weight put forth by Hawkins (1994, 2004) and Yamashita and Chang (2001) apply to syntactic or lexical complexity, and are thus moot for single-word binomials. Meanwhile, Japanese is a pitch accent language, perhaps lacking in nuclear stress qua stress, although prominence can be signaled through pitch phenomena. As Venditti et al. (2008) emphasize, "standard Japanese has no analog to the notion 'accent' when it is used as a synonym for 'nuclear stress' in these Germanic languages." If this holds, the nuclear stress theory of end-weight is mute concerning beginning- vs. end-weight in Japanese, and the near-null result for prosodic weight in Japanese in Lohmann and Takada (2014) becomes a point in favor of the nuclear stress account rather than a liability for it. To the extent that a weak long-last tendency in terms of moras exists (*ibid.*), it may be symptomatic of complexity deferral rather than weight, given that longer words tend to be less accessible (Kelly 1986). At any rate, stress languages with head-initial prosodic phrases, such as Persian and Turkish, are better test cases for prosodic beginning-weight.

5.12.2 *A pilot study of prosodic beginning-weight in Turkish*

This section presents a pilot study of binomial ordering in Turkish, a language just mentioned in §5.12.1 as being a candidate for possible prosodic beginning-weight within the phonological phrase. Specifically, binary conjunctions of simple color terms are investigated in a written corpus of Turkish, the 3.4-billion-word "TenTen" corpus available on SketchEngine.[40] The corpus is web-based, but curated to avoid most of the pitfalls of an internet search, which include language mixing (e.g. words like *gri* and *mor* appear in many languages, and are also often typos or acronyms), duplicate pages, boilerplate and other garbage, and estimated rather than exact hit counts. It also permits more advanced searches, such as regular expressions in multiword phrases and control over capitalization and punctuation. Finally, results are presented in a fixed window of context that facilitates hand-checking.

The eleven color terms in (48) were tested in every binary combination (11 choose 2 = 55) in both orders with *ve* 'and' or *veya* 'or' as a conjunction (e.g. *gri ve beyaz*, *beyaz ve gri*, etc.).[41] Because this corpus lacks a treebank, initial results included "ADJ CONJ ADJ" strings that were not self-contained constituents. For example, the adjectives might occur at the end of a longer list, or might be modified, and so forth. Results were therefore counted by hand in order to exclude nonconstituents. For "ADJ CONJ ADJ" strings with more than twenty hits, the first twenty hits were examined by hand, and the mean constituency rate (usually around 75%) was then extrapolated to the remaining hit count. In practice, there is no reason to suspect that nonconstituency, even if it were left uncontrolled, would be a pernicious confound. The rate of nonconstituency was similar across pairs, meaning that hit counts ended up being reduced by a near-constant factor, leaving the relative frequencies of pairs close to what they would have been if constituency had not been addressed.

---

[40] This corpus was created in 2012 and accessed from www.sketchengine.co.uk in April 2017.

[41] *Kahverengi* 'coffee-colored, i.e. brown' is not included because it is transparently compound-like, and this test seeks to avoid interference from morphosyntactic complexity.

(48)

	Word	IPA	Gloss	Syllables	Log$_{10}$ Frequency
a.	*gri*	[ˈgriː]	'gray'	1	4.66
b.	*mor*	[ˈmoɾ]	'purple'	1	4.52
c.	*beyaz*	[beˈjaz]	'white'	2	5.59
d.	*siyah*	[siˈjah]	'black'	2	5.39
e.	*mavi*	[ˈmaːvi]	'blue'	2	5.12
f.	*yeşil*	[jeˈʃil]	'green'	2	5.44
g.	*sarı*	[saˈɾɯ]	'yellow'	2	5.24
h.	*pembe*	[pemˈbe]	'pink'	2	4.78
i.	*kırmızı*	[kɯɾmɯˈzɯ]	'red'	3	5.49
j.	*lacivert*	[ˈlad͡ʒivert]	'navy'	3	4.11
k.	*turuncu*	[tuˈrund͡ʒu]	'orange'	3	4.36

As Figure 5.12 shows, in the aggregate, the longer the color term in syllables, the more likely it is to be first in its binomial. For one vs. two syllables, frequency is a possible confound, since the disyllables are aggregately more frequent than the monosyllables. Therefore, the long-first tendency in that subset might reflect a frequent-first effect. However, frequency makes the wrong prediction for two vs. three syllables. Trisyllables are aggregately less frequent than disyllables, and yet trisyllables are still significantly more likely to be initial.

More to the point, regressing on syllable count and frequency, as in (49), reveals both to be significant. The model is paradigmatic in the sense defined in §5.6.3: Each word is coded as an individual datum, with the dependent variable being its initiality in the binomial, one if first and zero if second. Given the paucity of types relative to tokens, the model is token- rather than type-based. Factors are scaled (i.e. expressed in standard deviations from the mean) so that their magnitudes can be

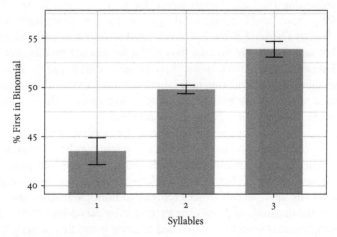

FIGURE 5.12 As the number of syllables in the color term increases, it is more likely to be initial in its binomial.

meaningfully compared. "Syllables" is positive, meaning that a higher syllable count favors first position. "Frequency," perhaps surprisingly, is negative (albeit slightly), such that more frequent terms tend to be final. Both of these factors are reversed vis-à-vis their expected polarities from languages like English and French.

(49) | Factor | β | SE | z | p |
| --- | --- | --- | --- | --- |
| a. scale(Syllables) | 0.1096 | 0.0076 | 14.247 | < .00001 |
| b. scale(Frequency) | −0.0494 | 0.0077 | −6.411 | < .00001 |

This study therefore suggests that prosodic beginning-weight might well exist in Turkish not just in terms of vocalism (§5.12.1) but also in terms of syllable count. It is limited, however, in that it addresses only color term binomials in a corpus, and thus should not be considered to be strong evidence for this conclusion.

5.13 Prosodic vs. syntactic end-weight

The foregoing discussion has consistently distinguished between prosodic and syntactic end-weight. The phrasal stress theory advocated here motivates only the former, while at the same time, theories of end-weight in terms of syntactic complexity (e.g. Hawkins 1994, 2004, Wasow 2002) motivate only the latter (see §5.8.4 on why the latter fail to cover prosodic end-weight). But given that syntactic end-weight and prosodic end-weight are both end-weight, is this not a case of duplication? Is it possible that a better theory would generalize to both aspects of end-weight? This section briefly makes the case that analyzing syntactic and prosodic end-weight with separate mechanisms does not constitute a case of duplication.

As Hawkins (1994, et seq.) observes, syntactic end-weight is found in syntactically head-initial languages (or contexts), while syntactic beginning-weight is found in syntactically head-final languages (or contexts), an asymmetry that he motivates in terms of processing (§5.8.4). Phrasal stress, for its part, tends to be left-oriented in syntactically head-final languages and right-oriented in syntactically head-initial languages, perhaps because prominence is related to degree of embedding (Cinque 1993) or because objects are favored over verbs for phrasal prominence for other reasons (Kahnemuyipour 2004, 2008, Kratzer and Selkirk 2007). Thus, it is no coincidence that syntactic end-weight is found in languages that also happen to have right-oriented nuclear stress: Both share a single, deep cause in the basic word order of the language. They are not independent parameters.

As discussed in §5.12, Japanese is a test case for a possible divergence between syntactic and prosodic weight, in that beginning-weight may be confined to syntactic weight. Evidence from Lohmann and Takada (2014) suggests that prosodic polarization in Japanese is weak, but if anything errs on the side of end-weight. If this discrepancy holds up, it lends further credence to multiple mechanisms of weight, as tailored to the demands of processing vs. phonological optimization. At any rate, if a processing account were to be expanded to cover prosodic end-weight, it would have to cover the eight generalizations in §5.7 and address the additional problems in §5.8.4.

5.14 Prosodic end-weight beyond binomials

Numerous constructions exhibit end-weight, but the specifically phonological aspect of end-weight has been studied most intensively for single-word coordination and echo reduplication, which have therefore also been the foci here. For higher-level end-weight phenomena such as heavy NP shift and the dative alternation, the contribution of phonology is evidently more modest. For example, Anttila et al. (2010), in their corpus study of the English dative alternation, find a strong effect of PWd count as distinct from syntactic word count, but little to no effect of syllable count. Similarly, Shih and Grafmiller (2013) compare syntactic vs. phonological measures of weight for the English dative and genitive alternations, concluding that syntactic factors are dominant in "higher-level constituent ordering," as they put it. Insofar as prosodic weight affects such constructions, they find, it is mostly in terms of PWd count; the syllable-count effect is marginal (see also Ingason and MacKenzie 2011, MacKenzie 2012). Thus, a kind of DEPTH-OF-FIELD effect appears to be in evidence, such that the available grain of detail scales with the complexity of the constituents involved. For simple constituents, such as monosyllables, segmental properties are clearly available (§5.7). For complex constituents, such as multiword phrases, these features are more likely to be ignored.

Some form of depth of field is predicted by the constraint-based theory advocated in §5.9, assuming that it is implemented in a weighted-constraints setting such as maxent HG. In such a framework, the more material a constituent contains, the more negligibly individual segments will affect its total weight. As relative effect size decreases, likelihood of detection in experiments and corpus studies decreases with it. Moreover, depth of field might also arise from processing. Specifically, for increasingly complex phrases, it becomes increasingly infeasible for the speaker to plan every phonological detail in advance. Indeed, at a certain level of complexity, the speaker might not even completely plan both phrases at the point at which their order is determined (Wasow 2002:45–6). A more detailed treatment of depth of field must be left for future work, in part because its empirical properties are not well established for prosody. For one thing, processing complexity predicts that depth of field should be complexity-dependent, not construction-dependent. For example, segmental detail may become available for dative alternants consisting of monosyllables, and it may become unavailable for multiword binomials. The task may also be relevant, in that, for instance, ratings might diverge from production.

5.15 Conclusion

This chapter first made the case for the existence of PROSODIC END-WEIGHT as independent of syntactic complexity and other non-phonological factors (frequency, semantics, etc.). When these other factors are controlled, either through wug-testing or multifactorial models, the following phonological properties consistently correlate with greater end-weight: (1) more syllables, with stressed syllables counting for more than unstressed syllables, (2) longer and/or lower vowels, such that both phonemic length and phonetic duration matter, (3) more sonorous codas, (4) less sonorous onsets, (5) longer onsets, and (6) longer codas. As discussed in §§5.5–5.9, all of these properties contribute to heaviness more generally in weight-sensitive systems typo-logically. For example, across languages and phenomena, greater sonority correlates with greater weight when it occurs in the rime, but the opposite holds of onsets, where greater sonority is (if anything) lighter. Moreover, the syllable-count effect cannot be explained away by metrical optimization (§5.6). Even when the heavy-final order is metrically degrading, as with binomials in French or monosyllable-plus-iamb binomials in English, end-weight still obtains. More generally, Lapse, Clash, and NonFinality, while not inert, were found to be weaker effects than syllable count in a number of corpus studies and experiments in §5.6. Thus, end-weight does not reduce to rhythm, and when weight and rhythm compete, weight usually takes precedence.

The core motivation for prosodic end-weight was argued here to be nuclear (i.e. phrasal) stress. As such, prosodic end-weight is a manifestation of the more general weight–stress interface in phonology. In English and many other languages, phrasal prominence is generally right-oriented. Therefore, realizing phonologically heavier elements later better aligns phrasal weight with phrasal stress. This explanation of end-weight was demonstrated in §5.8 to be superior to several other explanations that have been put forth in the literature, including final lengthening, eurythmy, phonotactics, and complexity deferral.

The phrasal stress theory of end-weight was formalized in §5.9 in terms of con-straints of the form $X \rightarrow \varphi_s$, where X is a segment type (including its linkage to a mora) and φ_s refers to any strong prosodic constituent at the level of the PWd or higher. For example, $V \rightarrow \varphi_s$ penalizes every nucleus under a weak phrasal node, effectively pres-suring constituents with more syllables to occupy the strong branch. The constraint family is expressed stringently, instantiating the more general prominence mapping family posited in §1.5.

The remainder of the chapter treated contexts in which phrasal stress is sometimes left- rather than right-oriented, namely, compounds (§5.10), Rhythm Rule contexts (§5.11), and the phrasal prosodies of certain other languages (§5.12). The outlook is generally promising for the phrasal stress proposal. In English compounds, end-weight is only relevant for echo reduplicatives, since ordering is syntactically deter-mined in other types. In general, when reduplicatives are parsed as separate PWds, end-weight is observed, and when they are not, it is not (except for the stereotyped vocalism /ɪ/ + low vowel, which was argued to synchronically reflect fixed segmentism rather than weight). Beyond English, some head-final languages exhibit left-oriented phrasal stress, in which case the phrasal stress theory predicts prosodic beginning-weight in prosodic phrases. Potential cases of beginning-weight from Turkish and Tamil were discussed, including a corpus study of Turkish binomials. While prelim-inary indications suggest that prosodic beginning-weight is not found in Japanese, this may be because Japanese realizes prominence primarily through pitch rather than stress, and therefore falls outside of the purview of the phrasal stress account. At any rate, because most studies of beginning-weight focus on syntactic complexity rather than phonology, the treatment of prosodic weight in head-final languages remains understudied.

In conclusion, this chapter maintains that prosodic weight is not confined to syllables: Higher-level prosodic constituents such as words and phrases also bear weight. While almost all previous treatments of phonological weight treat exclusively the syllable (or components thereof, or the interval; §4.6), the present proposal is perhaps less surprising in light of the literature on timing, which finds various respects in which speakers compute local prosodic adjustments by taking properties of a larger domain into account. For example, as mentioned in §5.8, one robust finding of word-level prosody is the phenomenon of polysyllabic shortening, whereby speakers compress syllables as a function of the total number of syllables in the word (Lehiste 1972, et seq.; §1.2). This behavior entails that even at the point of starting to produce a word, the speaker anticipates the overall weight of the word in some sense. Similarly, the domains for final lengthening and even accentual lengthening are sometimes larger than the syllable (e.g. Turk and Sawusch 1997, Turk and White 1999). Compensatory effects within the foot—as one syllable increases in the duration, the other decreases—are also well established (e.g. Borise 2017 on Slavic and Türk et al. 2018 on Sami and Finnic). Thus, speakers are sensitive to prosodic weight above the syllable for purposes of both timing and, as proposed here, for purposes of stress–weight alignment.

6

Conclusion and further issues

This book treats the phonological analysis of weight, especially complex scales, in four metrical systems, namely, stress, prosodic minimality, poetic meter, and prosodic end-weight. Several universals of weight hold across these systems, finding a common explanation in the nature of the weight percept. For example, increasing length or complexity contributes to weight in every part of the syllable (albeit to varying degrees for the onset vs. coda), but greater sonority contributes to weight only in the rime; in the onset, it detracts from weight. Onset-driven weight is established in every system, including cases that I am first to report (e.g. onset weight effects in quantitative meters) or first to bring within the purview of phonological weight (e.g. onset weight effects in prosodic end-weight). Even onset sonority-driven weight is instantiated across systems (except, to my knowledge, prosodic minimality), always treating greater sonority as lighter.

Weight effects are implemented here by mapping constraints that relate strong elements to each other via implication. Dimensions of strength include stress prominence (e.g. STRESS, MAIN), metrical prominence or ictus (e.g. STRONG), and weight prominence, that is, phonologized perceptual energy (§6.1) (e.g. $\sigma_{\mu\mu}$, $V_\mu[+son]_\mu$). As motivated in §1.5 and Ryan (2017b), mapping constraints invoke only strong predicates and are formulated stringently, such that any set of elements serving as a strong predicate is contiguous on that scale and includes the strongest element. Constraints are then expressed as conditionals linking strong predicates from different dimensions of prominence, which can be invoked in any order. Some examples of licit constraints are STRESS $\rightarrow \sigma_{\mu\mu}$, $\sigma_{\mu\mu} \rightarrow$ STRESS, STRONG $\rightarrow \sigma_{\mu\mu}$, and STRONG $\rightarrow$ STRESS.

Analyses of weight-driven stress in Chapter 2 focus on ternary and higher n-ary systems, which I argue cannot generally be analyzed in terms of moraic Coercion, by which codas are contextually moraic. Rather, they must at least sometimes invoke Vowel Prominence, by which syllables containing long vowels or diphthongs attract stress (e.g. VV $\rightarrow$ STRESS). I further maintain that given the availability of Vowel Prominence, it is unnecessary to analyze geminates as being nonmoraic in "VG light" systems. In other words, I tentatively uphold the Moraic Theory of Geminates. Chapter 2 also surveys cases of gradient weight for stress, in which scalar relations are fine-grained and quantifiable. Naturally occurring weight gradience for stress has been reported for several languages; it is additionally brought out by experiments.

Prosodic Weight. First edition. Kevin M. Ryan.
© Kevin M. Ryan 2019. First published 2019 by Oxford University Press.

Prosodic minimality typically evinces binary weight, though see §6.4 below on a context in which it appears to reveal gradient weight. Chapter 3 has two major contributions. First, it analyzes PWd minimality for PWds that are embedded in larger prosodic phrases. Minimality-in-context is complicated by resyllabification: In the languages studied, a word-final coda is forced to resyllabify as an onset when the following word begins with a vowel. Resyllabification therefore threatens the minimality of an otherwise minimal C_0VC word. Languages respond to this threat in three ways. They either suppress resyllabification iff it threatens minimality, repair C_0VC words undergoing resyllabification to bring them back up to size, or let the resulting degenerate word stand as such. Second, with Tamil, I describe and analyze perhaps the first reported case of a language in which only a subset of possible word-final consonants contributes to prosodic minimality.

The world's quantitative meters are characterized by both categorical and gradient weight, sometimes coexisting within the same meter. Their categorical aspect is obvious. For example, a particular position of the line might accept only a heavy or only a light. More subtly, positions sometimes exhibit varying tolerances for heavier heavies or lighter lights, revealing gradient weight. Chapter 4 presents case studies of gradient weight in meters of Sanskrit, Finnish, Ancient Greek, and Latin; for others, see Ryan (2011a, 2011b).

Finally, prosodic end-weight is nearly always gradient (on which, see §6.4 below). Chapter 5 supports the view that prosodic end-weight reflects phonological weight, not complexity or duration. For one thing, it folds in with the weight typology in every respect, including the onset-rime sonority reversal. I propose that stress–weight mapping is the cause of prosodic end-weight. In particular, heavier constituents are attracted to loci of greater phrasal stress, thanks to a phrasal generalization of WEIGHT-TO-STRESS, namely, the constraint family WEIGHT $\rightarrow \varphi_s$.

In what remains, I turn to residual general issues and prospects for a theory of weight. Much of this discussion concerns the degree of phonetic detail available to phonological weight-mapping, including the viability of DIRECT-INTERFACE approaches. I begin with questions concerning phonetically driven phonology in §6.1. Next, §6.2 treats opacity in weight criteria. §6.3 addresses the domain of the weight percept in light of onset effects. §6.4 concludes by returning to the definition of gradient weight and the issue of explaining its relative frequency vis-à-vis low n-ary categorical weight across phenomena.

6.1 The phonetics–phonology interface

The present work focuses on the phonological analysis of weight systems. As such, it complements research treating the phonetic underpinnings of weight distinctions. In particular, Gordon (1999, 2002b, 2005, 2006) maintains that languages select weight criteria that maximize the perceptual distance between categories. This distance is operationalized as follows. For each syllable token, Gordon (2002b) computes the total energy (that is, energy integrated over duration) of its rime. For a candidate criterion, say, V < VX, he then subtracts the mean total energy of V syllables from the mean total energy of VX syllables, yielding the PHONETIC EFFECTIVENESS of the criterion. He does the same for other criteria, including, for instance, VC < VV. The simple criterion[1] with the greatest phonetic effectiveness is predicted to be the criterion employed by the language. More succinctly, in languages in which VC is light, VC is expected to be perceptually closer to V than to VV, and vice versa for languages in which VC is heavy (see also Broselow et al. 1997).

This phonetic approach to weight differs from the factorial typology approach implied by OT (and by HG, mutatis mutandis). The weight-mapping constraints developed in this book, or indeed any such constraints, can in principle be ranked (or weighted) any way in any language, regardless of the phonetic properties of the language. For example, nothing prevents VV → STRESS from being the dominant weight-mapping constraint in a language in which VC < VV is a relatively ineffective criterion phonetically. In this sense, the purely phonological approach overgenerates.[2]

At the same time, phonetic effectiveness is not an analysis of a weight-based system; it is only a metric for criteria. Establishing that, say, V < VX is the optimal binary criterion for some system in some language says nothing about how that criterion is implemented as part of the system, including how it is incorporated into mapping or foot-form constraints, how those constraints are ranked with respect to each other and other constraints, and so forth—the issues that have been at the center of this book.

Thus, both approaches are needed, which raises the question of how they are related and whether they can be unified. I now sketch some general strategies for unification along with some problems that they face. One strategy would be to implant Gordonian effectiveness directly into the weight predicates of mapping constraints. Take PEH to refer to "phonetically effective heavies," that is, the set of syllables that are heavy according to the most phonetically effective criterion for the language and system in question.[3] PEH would then serve as the strong predicate in weight-mapping constraints, replacing options such as VV and $\sigma_{\mu\mu}$ in the present system. For example, PEH → STRESS would require phonetically effective heavies to be stressed. This tack partially addresses overgeneration, as mapping is forced to utilize the phonetically optimal criterion. (On a different, acategorical phonetic approach to weight-mapping, t → STRESS, see §6.4 below.)

Nevertheless, PEH-mapping faces several challenges. The first is that it is viable as a replacement of the present approach only if there are no exceptions to phonetic effectiveness in the typology. A system with a less-than-optimal criterion would be unlearnable under such an approach, as the suboptimal mapping constraint would

---

[1] I specify "simple criterion" here because Gordon (2002b) further argues that languages avoid complex criteria even when they outperform simple criteria in phonetic effectiveness. Complex criteria are defined as criteria involving disjunctions or multiple place predicates (*id.*:57).

[2] This problem is not specific to the constraints employed here. For example, if one were to implement the difference between V < VX and VC < VV for stress by using WEIGHT-TO-STRESS along with different rankings of WbyP, the same objection would apply.

[3] Because different systems within a language can employ different criteria (Gordon 2006), PEH would have to be relativized to the system in question, for example, PEH$_{stress}$.

not be available.[4] PEH is successful for the six case studies presented by Gordon (2002b) (with one exception to be addressed presently), but it is uncertain that it would succeed uniformly for the many hundreds of weight-sensitive systems cross-linguistically. Indeed, there are indications in Gordon (2002b) that it likely would not. First, one of the case studies is Telugu, which Gordon (2002b) characterizes as ternary $V < VC < VV$ based on collapsing the distinct binary criteria from metrics ($V < VX$) and stress ($VC < VV$). Gordon (2002b) proposes that the most phonetically effective ternary scale is the scale that combines the two most effective binary criteria, and proceeds to demonstrate that $V < VX$ and $VC < VV$ are the two most effective binary criteria in Telugu, in that order. However, this reveals that Telugu stress employs a suboptimal criterion, as $VC < VV$ is second-best.[5] Second, Gordon (2002b) shows that the obstruent-to-sonorant ratio of a language's coda inventory correlates with the choice of criterion, such that a preponderance of coda obstruents favors $VC < VV$ over $V < VX$. However, there were five exceptions in his sample.

Moreover, in experimental settings, subjects can learn a stress system with a phonetically suboptimal criterion. For example, Carpenter (2010) demonstrates that English and French speakers can learn through passive exposure an artificial grammar in which stress is conditioned by vowel height (§2.8.3). This is not the most phoneti-cally effective criterion in the subjects' native language,[6] nor is it the most phonetically effective criterion in the artificial language: The mean total energy of syllables in the high vowel condition was greater than that of syllables in the low vowel condition (Carpenter 2010:379), and yet subjects still favored the phonetically less effective $I < A$ criterion. Additionally, de Lacy (2007) finds that height-driven stress criteria do not always correspond to differences in vowel duration. Thus, available evidence suggests that speakers are capable of learning non-PEH criteria in both natural and experimental settings, though further study is needed, as relevant experimental evidence is not extensive. One might reply that speakers are only learning non-PEH criteria *in addition* to PEH criteria; on the unsatisfactoriness of this response, see the next paragraph.

Complex weight scales pose a further problem for the PEH approach. Gordon (2002b) hypothesizes that if a system has a complex scale with n levels, the scale will combine the most effective $n - 1$ binary criteria. For example, for ternary $x < y < z$, the top two binary criteria should be $x < \{y, z\}$ and $\{x, y\} < z$, in any order. Under the

---

[4] One might respond that non-PEH constraints could be constructed if needed, but this concession vitiates the appeal of the direct interface approach, as it permits languages to freely adopt ad hoc criteria, reintroducing the need for a traditional, non-PEH-based theory of weight-mapping, and, in doing so, resurrecting the factorial typology problem. On the possibility of biased constraints, see below.

[5] Gordon (2002b) would be vindicated in this case if his assumption about the criterion for Telugu stress were incorrect; as I discussed in §2.6.1, it is not secure empirically. Furthermore, the phonetic effectiveness scores for $V < VX$ and $VC < VV$ in Gordon (2002b) are close to being tied, being possibly within the margin of error. The existence of such "close calls" might be taken to provide some wiggle room for criteria, but this move would also weaken the predictions of the theory.

[6] This is unnecessary to test for English. Even if $I < A$ were the most phonetically effective criterion in English, it would still mean that English speakers have learned a stress system based on a suboptimal criterion, only it would be their native stress system rather than the experimental one.

PEH-mapping approach just outlined, one would have to further articulate PEH to account for such systems: PEH_1 could refer to heavies according to the best criterion, PEH_2 to heavies according to the second-best, and so forth. These PEHs could then be encoded in mapping constraints such as $PEH_1 \to$ STRESS, $PEH_2 \to$ STRESS, and so forth. However, once $PEH_2 \to$ STRESS is part of the constraint system, there is nothing to prevent it from being highly ranked while $PEH_1 \to$ STRESS is buried, thus generating a language with a suboptimal binary criterion. One would have to impose a metacondition on ranking to the effect that if PEH_n is active, then $PEH_{k<n}$ is also active. But it is unclear how exactly such a metacondition could be formulated so as to constrain learning, aside from which such metaconditions are anathema to a core tenet of OT (and HG), namely, the notion of factorial (or weighting) typology.

It is also worth noting that the PEH approach in Gordon (2002b) makes predictions only about what the optimal cutoff points are for a given arity; it does not predict the arity itself. For example, given that Chickasaw employs a ternary scale for stress (V < VC < VV), Gordon (2002b) demonstrates that the two constituent binary criteria (V < VX and VC < VV) are the two most effective in that language. But Gordon (2002b) does not suggest that phonetic effectiveness determines arity. If Chickasaw were identical phonetically but happened to exhibit only binary VC < VV for stress, it would still be compatible with Gordon's (2002b) theory, VC < VV being the optimal binary criterion. Similarly, if Chickasaw exhibited no weight sensitivity at all (i.e. an arity of one), it would be equally compatible with the theory. It might be possible to extend phonetic effectiveness to make predictions about arity (which includes whether a system is weight-sensitive in the first place, as unarity is an arity), but such a pursuit remains for the future.

Finally, as Mai (2018) observes, predicting a language's favored criterion on the basis of the phonetics of that language risks circularity. After all, diachronically, stressed elements tend to lengthen or otherwise fortify, while unstressed elements tend to reduce. Gordon (2002b) implies a unidirectional relationship, the title of the article being "A phonetically-driven account of syllable weight." But phonology can also drive phonetics, as is clear from the progressive dispersion of stressed and unstressed elements over time even while the criterion remains constant. A theory to the effect that a language selects the most phonetically effective criterion does not explain such enhancement, assuming that the criterion was optimal all along (if it were not, the theory would be refuted). Gordon (2002b) controls for the influence of phonology by computing total energies based only on syllables of a uniform stress level. This does not, however, eliminate the confound altogether, as a segment's target duration/place under stress might be affected by its target duration/place across the board, given allophony avoidance. In other words, if there is historical dispersion between light and heavy syllables, it could conceivably influence their respective realizations even under stress. To be clear, this paragraph does not describe an objection to the phonetic approach to weight, but an area for continuing research.

In conclusion, constraint-based weight-mapping, as conceived of here and else-where, misses a generalization: Languages tend to promote weight-mapping con-straints with weight predicates that are both simple and phonetically effective vis-à-vis the language and system in question. At the same time, phonetic assessments of criteria are no substitute for phonological analyses of weight-based systems. More-over, given the foregoing discussion, weight-based systems appear unlikely to be slav-ishly natural in every instance; suboptimal and opaque (§6.2) criteria are learnable. Finally, discriminant analysis, at least as developed to date, says nothing about where complex scales—the focus of this book—are expected to be found or how they can be instantiated in constraint systems without reintroducing the overgeneration problem (see §6.4 for further discussion). A challenge going forward is thus to unify insights from these two fields. In particular, phonetics appears to serve as a bias on constraint systems. Biases can be implemented via learning, where certain analyses are favored a priori, but can be overridden given sufficient evidence.[7] In maxent HG, biases have been implemented by μ, which serves as a center of gravity of each constraint (White 2017), and by σ^2, which modulates the plasticity of each constraint (Wilson 2006); see recently Beguš (2018) for extensive references and discussion in the context of segmental phonology. In the present context, one could imagine that categorical mapping constraints such as MAIN $\rightarrow$ VV are biased by their phonetic effectiveness. This could explain trends in typology without incurring the problems just outlined with a hardline PEH approach. I expect that in my future work on weight, bias will play a greater role.

6.2 Opacity

Stress systems can be opaque, meaning that a weight criterion might not be surface-true. Diachronically, stress might remain fixed on a particular syllable while sound changes undo the conditions that originally motivated its placement on that syllable. Synchronically, this situation can result in a generalization holding only when the effects of certain independent processes are factored out. For example, consider Levantine Arabic, in which stress is generally predictable, landing on a heavy penult. The two forms in (1), however, have distinct stress patterns despite being realized with identical segmental structure (Brame 1974, Kager 1999, Kiparsky 2000). The explanation for this discrepancy resides in their differing underlying forms: [i] is not stressed when it is epenthetic. As Kiparsky (2000) argues, it is not sufficient merely to ban stress on epenthetic vowels, as they are not just unstressable, but metrically invisible in all respects.

(1)   a. /fihim-na/   →   [fiˈhimna]   'he understood us'
      b. /fihm-na/   →   [ˈfihimna]   'our understanding'

A similar case of opacity can be found in Tiberian Hebrew. Stress normally falls on final VC. But a word such as [ˈmelex] 'king' receives penultimate stress because the final vowel is epenthetic, the underlying form being /malk/ (Prince 1975:373). The analysis of Tiberian Hebrew stress in §2.7.2 put forth yet another kind of opacity, in

---

[7] Some of the phonetic bias in the typology could conceivably also arise from historical transmission rather than synchronic pressures (on this opposition, see Moreton 2008). Experiments on the learnability of suboptimal criteria would help to disentangle these explanations.

that vowels that are long due to final lengthening do not count as VV for purposes of stress assignment.

In Huehuetla Tepehua, which was also treated in §2.7.2, I have noted from Kung (2007) no fewer than seven independent ways in which weight-sensitive stress is opaque. Recall that stress is claimed to fall on the ultima if it ends with a sonorant consonant (including laryngeals and glides), and otherwise on the penult. Some surface exceptions are explained in (2). Throughout, I assume Kung's (2007) analysis of underlying forms.

(2) a. Stress falls on final [ɬ] from /l/ (e.g. [ˌʔamakˈʃtaɬ] ← /ʔamakʃtal/ 'trash') but not from /ɬ/ (e.g. [ˈʔiːsmiɬ] ← /iːsmiɬ/ 'watercress').

   b. Stress is conditioned by the plural suffix -*ni* which then sometimes deletes on the surface, as in [ˌlapaˈnak] ← /lapanakni/ 'persons'; cf. [laˈpanak] ← /lapanak/ 'person.'

   c. /q/ and /ʔ/ optionally neutralize to [ʔ], but only the latter attracts stress. Compare [tʃaˈqaʔ] ← /ʃ-tʃaqaʔ/ 'his/her house' to [ˈɬʔapaʔ] ← /ɬqapaq/ 'walking stick bug.'

   d. As in Levantine Arabic and Tiberian Hebrew, epenthetic vowels are not stressed, which in the present case can yield antepenultimate stress, as in [ˈʔaqatsuɬ] ← /aqtsuɬ/ 'head.'

   e. Stem-final /ʔ/ is deleted before a suffix, and yet still conditions stress, as in [tʼaˈkuːtʃ] ← /tʼakuʔ-tʃ/ 'woman.' (The deletion also triggers compensatory lengthening of the vowel, but VVT does not otherwise attract stress.)

   f. /h/-deletion and subsequent syllable fusion can leave stress on an obstruent-closed ultima, as in [makˈtaiɬtʃ] ← /maktahi-li-tʃ/ 'it flamed'; compare 'watercress' in (a).

   g. /uw/ and /ij/ merge with /uː/ and /iː/, respectively, on the surface. The former attract stress (e.g. [ʔaˈβiː] ← /awij/ 'mouse'); the latter do not (e.g. [laˈqasiː] ← /laqasiː/ 'first'). (Under the reanalysis suggested in §2.7.2, however, this case would be rendered transparent, as final /iː/ is reinterpreted as /i/.)

Cross-linguistically, opacity is not limited to weight-based phenomena, but widespread among phonological processes. In that sense, it is orthogonal to the present work. Numerous proposals for its analysis are debated in the literature (e.g. McCarthy 2007, Nazarov and Pater 2017, and references therein).

6.3 Onset effects and the domain of the weight percept

As I have argued elsewhere (Ryan 2014), the domain over which the weight percept is computed can be neither the rime nor the syllable. This is generally accepted in the case of the syllable, given onset-rime asymmetries. For one thing, criteria are often sensitive to the presence vs. absence of a coda while ignoring the structure of the onset. Rime-based weight easily captures such asymmetries, but can explain onset weight effects only insofar as heavier onsets increase the total energy of the rime, either directly (e.g. via auditory adaptation and recovery) or indirectly (if heavier onsets cooccur with longer vowels) (Gordon 2005).

Ryan (2014) documents aspects of onset-driven weight that rime-based perceptual energy cannot explain. For example, in English, onset complexity correlates with stress propensity (*ibid.*, Kelly 2004). At the same time, increasing onset complexity correlates with shorter, not longer, vowels in English (Figure 1.1 above). Rime-based weight therefore predicts the opposite effect: Longer onsets should repel stress. Auditory adaptation and recovery likewise provide incomplete coverage of onset effects. Due to a ceiling effect, for instance, rime attacks have the same adaptation and recovery profiles after onsets such as *sp* and lenis *b*, despite the former being heavier phonologically. Furthermore, recovery and adaptation make the unwanted prediction that the empty or glottal stop onset should be the heaviest, since the transition from silence is the most salient attack (Ryan 2014; cf. Gordon 2005).

I therefore propose in Ryan (2014) that the domain for the weight percept is the p-center interval, as explained above in §4.6 and §5.9.4. In this book, it has been mostly unnecessary to delve into the p-center proposal, as most of the studies do not involve onset weight, and for those that do, the emphasis is on their phonological analysis, not their phonetic profile. Nevertheless, as discussed in §1.5 and §5.9.4, an outstanding problem for stringent weight-mapping involves the question of whether and how onset and rime effects can be integrated. For the reasons given there, this book tentatively treats onset effects as being outside of the stringency hierarchy for moras/rimes, albeit still stringent among themselves. This picture may change as more cases of onset weight are unveiled typologically (building on e.g. Gordon 2005, Topintzi 2010) and as more studies probe phonetics–phonology correlations of onset effects in gradient weight systems (building on e.g. Ryan 2014, Mai 2018).

6.4 Categorical vs. gradient weight

For syllables to compose a category of weight, they must behave indistinguishably with respect to the diagnostic phenomenon. A categorical scale can in principle comprise any number of categories, though in practice the typological frequency of an arity is inversely proportional to its complexity. Unary weight, that is, no distinctions, is the most prevalent scale (§2.1). For binary or higher-order scales, one can get a rough idea of their relative frequencies for stress by examining the sixty-seven languages in Figure 2.6: 64 per cent are binary,[8] 18 per cent ternary, 6 per cent quaternary, and 12 per cent higher arities (though some of this 12% might instead be gradient; see below). For phenomena other than stress, these rates vary, but they universally taper off monotonically with increasing complexity.

Independent of arity is the possibility of variation. Imagine that a language stresses the rightmost heavy, if one is present, 70 per cent of the time, and otherwise the ultima. Let us assume that the rightmost heavy is equally likely to attract stress regardless of its

---

[8] In Gordon (2006), 87 per cent of criteria are binary. See §2.1 on why such figures are likely to be overestimates.

structure. Despite the presence of free variation, weight in this hypothetical language is categorical: Syllables are either heavy or light. Only one mapping constraint is needed, say, STRESS $\rightarrow \sigma_{\mu\mu}$, which can be weighted appropriately against ALIGN-R to achieve the variation.[9]

In the present text, gradient weight refers not to the type of situation just described, but rather to situations in which weight itself is gradient, there being no evidence for the stratification of syllable types into discrete, well-defined categories. Note that a system can combine categorical and gradient weight. In the Homeric hexameter, for example, the longum tolerates only a heavy syllable, diagnosing a binary criterion (on ostensible exceptions, see West 2018). At the same time, however, positional discrepancies diagnose a continuum of weight within the heavies (§4.4.2). Similarly, compare the treatment of weight in Tamil vs. Finnish meters in Figure 6.1, from Ryan (2011b). Although both Tamil meter (qua Kamban's epic; see §3.4.1) and Finnish meter (qua the Kalevala; see §4.4.1) exhibit gradient weight, weight is significantly more dichotomized in Finnish. The x-axis is mean estimated rime duration and the y-axis is metrical weight as estimated from skews between strong and weak positions, as in §4.4. Both corpora exhibit V $\lesssim$ VC $\lesssim$ VV $\lesssim$ VVC, if one aggregates over those four groups. But in Tamil, the correlation between rime duration and meter is tighter than it is in Finnish, where there is a large gap between V and VC corresponding to the light–heavy cutoff. Thus, Finnish meter exhibits binary categorization alongside intraheavy gradience, while Tamil meter appears to treat weight as wholly gradient by this diagnostic (see Ryan 2017b for more details on the meter).

In the gradient weight studies in this book, I often aggregate over syllable types for purposes of illustration or testing. For example, Figure 6.1 superimposes category means for V, VC, VV and VVC onto continuous distributions. This labeling is expository; it is not meant to imply that weight is quaternary. Similarly, the regressions in Chapter 4 isolate classes of syllables for testing purposes. For example, I show that VN is aggregately heavier than VT in Finnish and Greek. The purpose of such aggregations is to test the significance of relevant factors, in this case coda sonority, on weight. It does not suggest that the groups being tested constitute categories in the above sense.

Insofar as weight instantiates categories, it can be implemented by categorical mapping constraints of the type posited in §1.5. Gradient weight, for its part, can be implemented in one of two ways, which I term true gradience and apparent gradience. TRUE GRADIENCE can be achieved by a mapping constraint in which the weight predicate is a real-valued perceptual measure such as total energy (t). For example, $t \rightarrow$ STRESS is violated by the sum of the total energies of all unstressed syllables, a real-valued number (cf. Flemming 2001, Ryan 2014). If such a constraint is employed in maxent HG, it modulates the probabilities of candidates in proportion to their real-valued violations. As a simple illustration, consider /baːba/. Assume that the normalized total energies of its two syllables are 100 and 50, respectively,

---

[9] It would not work to say that stress placement is fixed for a given weight profile but would-be heavies (say, VC and VV) have a 70 per cent chance of being parsed as bimoraic. Such an analysis predicts that stress should sometimes land on non-rightmost heavies.

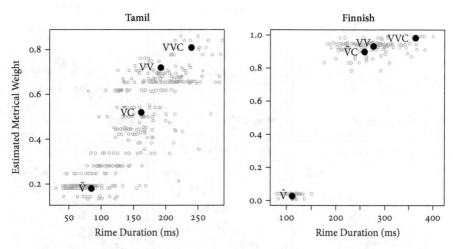

FIGURE 6.1 Mean estimated rime duration (x-axis) vs. inferred metrical weight (y-axis) in the meters of Kamban's Tamil (left) and the Finnish Kalevala (right). Both exhibit gradient weight, but weight is significantly more dichotomized in Finnish.

in arbitrary units.[10] In (3), the violations of each candidate on $t \rightarrow$ STRESS, expressed as nonpositive integers, are multiplied by the constraint's weight, which is stipulated to be 0.03, yielding the candidate's total penalty in the middle column. Candidate i's probability is then $\exp(\text{penalty}_i)/\sum_k \exp(\text{penalty}_k)$, where k ranges over all candidates (Hayes and Wilson 2008; see also §2.8.1). In this example, /baːba/ receives initial stress 82 per cent of the time.

(3)

/baːba/		p	penalty	$t \rightarrow$ STRESS weight = 0.03
a.	ˈbaːba	0.82	−1.5	−50
b.	baːˈba	0.18	−3.0	−100

With the same grammar but a different input, say, /baːban/ in (4), initial stress is generated less frequently. Let us say that *ban* has an energy of 80. Initial stress is still favored, but now at a rate of 65 per cent.

(4)

/baːban/		p	penalty	$t \rightarrow$ STRESS weight = 0.03
a.	ˈbaːban	0.65	−2.4	−80
b.	baːˈban	0.35	−3.0	−100

[10] A theory of normalization must accompany such models in order to preclude stress shifts driven by low-level factors such as speech rate (Flemming 2001, Steriade 2009, Ryan 2014). The assumption of such a theory is a major promissory note of any such approach.

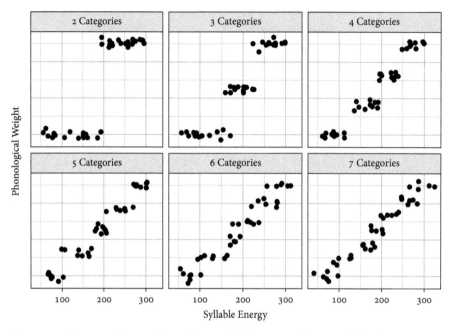

FIGURE 6.2 Increasingly complex scales quickly become indistinguishable from gradient weight in the presence of noise. Each dot is a syllable type. The x-axis is normalized syllable energy (or more properly, energy of the weight percept; §6.3) and the y-axis is syllable weight as inferred from phonological behavior, all hypothetical.

Gradient weight can also be analyzed in terms of APPARENT GRADIENCE, which invokes only categorical constraints, the approach adopted in this book.[11] In particular, if a sufficient number of categorical mapping constraints are active, the resulting system will be indistinguishable from a continuum. Figure 6.2 illustrates this effect using hypothetical distributions. The upper left panel, for two categories, resembles Finnish in Figure 6.1. Despite manifesting categories, the systems in Figure 6.2 exhibit some variation: On the y-axis, inferred weight is noisy, perhaps reflecting exceptions, and on the x-axis, categories overlap somewhat, perhaps due to criterial simplicity outweighing phonetic precision (Hayes 1999, Gordon 2002b). Crucially, even with only a small amount of noise, an n-ary categorical scale and a gradient scale become empirically indistinguishable at relatively low ns.

Most if not all real situations involving gradient weight also involve noise (free variation), making apparent gradience a viable approach to gradient weight. Indeed, it is often empirically unclear in the first place whether a noisy system is gradient or high n-ary categorical. Nevertheless, a fault of apparent gradience is that it uses several constraints to accomplish what could perhaps be achieved by a single t-mapping

---

[11] Gradient weight approximated by PEH-mapping constraints, as in §6.1, would also involve apparent gradience.

constraint. This objection is tempered by the fact that the categorical constraints that are necessary to achieve apparent gradience are independently motivated by categorical systems. Indeed, given this point, the objection could be turned on its head: A fault of the *t*-mapping approach is that it analyzes categorical and gradient systems using completely different devices. With apparent gradience, gradience reduces to a special case of categoricity. With *t*-mapping, the subtle shift from high *n*-ary to gradient involves a switch in theories.

To be sure, *t*-mapping can analyze certain types of categorical weight. Consider tableaux (5) and (6), which are based on (3) and (4), except that the weight of *t*→ STRESS is adjusted and ALIGN-R is added. The outcomes are now categorical: Stress is initial in *baːba* and final in *baːban*.

(5)

/baːba/		*p*	penalty	ALIGN-R weight = 17.93	*t*→ STRESS weight = 0.53
☞ a.	'baːba	1	−44.4	−1	−50
b.	baː'ba	0	−53.0		−100

(6)

/baːban/		*p*	penalty	ALIGN-R weight = 17.93	*t*→ STRESS weight = 0.53
a.	'baːban	0	−60.3	−1	−80
☞ b.	baː'ban	1	−53.0		−100

However, this example also illustrates a pathology of *t*-mapping. The cost of shifting to the penult is 17.93, the weight of ALIGN-R.[12] This means that for shifting to be preferred, the initial syllable's *t* must exceed that of the ultima by at least 33.8 (17.93 ÷ 0.53), as depicted in Figure 6.3. If ALIGN-R were weighted higher, this threshold would increase. Thus, *t*-mapping generates systems that are acategorical and relative: Stress shifts from syllable *x* to *y* only when *y* exceeds *x* by at least *z* units. Where *x* and *y* stand with respect to some fixed cutoff for heavy vs. light, say, *q*, is irrelevant. This last point is illustrated by Figure 6.3: There is no cutoff on either axis that can be said to represent a heavy–light boundary; all that matters is the energy differential between the syllables.

Weight is evidently not treated as relative in this sense in real systems. For example, imagine a grammar in which penultimate VVC attracts stress away from final V and VC (but not VV), while penultimate VV attracts stress away from final V (but not VC). In other words, stress shifts only if the two syllables are at least two rungs apart on the scale V < VC < VV < VVC. To my knowledge, no system works like this, though it would be worth exploring further experimentally.

---

[12] The fact that this example involves alignment is irrelevant. The pathology is not an alignment pathology (McCarthy 2003, Pater 2009). The argument would not be altered by the substitution of any comparable categorical constraint (e.g. EDGEMOST).

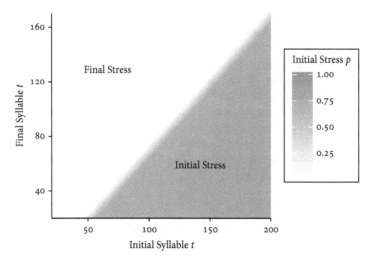

FIGURE 6.3 A pathology of *t*-mapping. Given the grammar in (5) and (6), the penult lures stress away from the ultima iff the penult's *t* exceeds that of the ultima by a constant.

Thus, *t*-mapping overgenerates. It also undergenerates. For example, it cannot implement an unbounded binary system. Consider a language in which the rightmost heavy (with the Latin criterion) is stressed, else rightmost. Let *t* be fifty for *ba*, a hundred for *baː*, and seventy for *bat*; any reasonable estimates would do. Unweighted tableaux are provided in (7) and (8) to illustrate desired winners and violation profiles. No weighting scheme can account for both tableaux simultaneously. For (7) to succeed, one violation of ALIGN-R must outweigh thirty violations of $t \rightarrow$ STRESS. If w_1 and w_2 are the weights of these two constraints, respectively, then $w_1 > 30 \cdot w_2$. For (8), two violations of ALIGN-R must be outweighed by twenty violations of $t \rightarrow$ STRESS, that is, $2 \cdot w_1 < 20 \cdot w_2$, or $w_1 < 10 \cdot w_2$. The two conditions contradict each other; w_1 cannot be both greater than $30 \cdot w_2$ and less than $10 \cdot w_2$. I tested this example with additional potentially relevant constraints in the tableaux, including NONFINALITY and ALIGN-L, and it still did not converge. For a direct interface theory to be maintained in the face of unboundedness, one would need PEH-style constraints such as $(\sigma > 60) \rightarrow$ STRESS. PEH-mapping was addressed in §6.1.[13]

(7)

/baːbat/	ALIGN-R	$t \rightarrow$ STRESS
☞ a. baːˈbat		−100
b. ˈbaːbat	−1	−70

---

[13] One might further consider how this grammar would play out without an alignment constraint. For instance, perhaps all heavies are footed, and a categorical constraint penalizes a head (primary stress) foot that is followed by another foot. This reintroduces the problem of defining "heavy" under *t*-mapping, as feet must now be associated with heavy (or appropriately binary) syllables. Once again, PEH-mapping may provide a solution, with the caveats in §6.1.

(8)

/batbaba/		ALIGN-R	$t \rightarrow$ STRESS
☞ a.	'batbaba	−2	−100
b.	batba'ba		−120

Finally, none of the discussed theories captures the fact that some phenomena are more likely to be gradient than others. Specifically, stress and prosodic minimality tend to exhibit low *n*-ary weight (though gradience is probably underestimated; §2.8), while prosodic end-weight is nearly always gradient. Poetic meter is intermediate, sometimes combining categorical and gradient aspects. Nothing in the constraint system predicts these differences. Categoricity could be modeled just as easily for end-weight as it is for stress. For example, with $VV \rightarrow \varphi_s$ sufficiently highly weighted, VV-containing conjuncts could be mandated to occupy final position rather than merely preferred there.

That said, no phenomenon appears to completely ban either categorical or gradient weight. Prosodic end-weight, for one, tends strongly to be gradient, but has categorical aspects. For example, clitics are sometimes fixed in end-weight order. Compare (9), in which the sentences progressively improve as weight is added to the direct object. At least (a) is ungrammatical: *It* needs to occupy the first position.[14] Aside from clitic ordering, categorical effects have also been addressed for prosodic end-weight in the context of idioms (Morgan and Levy 2016) and prosodic branchingness conditions (Zec and Inkelas 1990).

(9) a. Give her it.
　　 b. Give her them.
　　 c. Give her those.
　　 d. Give her something.
　　 e. Give her everything.

At the other extreme, prosodic minimality is typically binary, but may exhibit gradient aspects, as observed in §3.1. In particular, in languages with exceptionful minima, exceptions may become increasingly marked as they deviate from the minimum. English, for instance, has a bimoraic minimum, with tense vowels counting as long. Words in (b–d) of (10) are subminimal. Nevertheless, such words occur as slang or ideophones, revealing a sonority scale: The lower the vowel, the more acceptable and prevalent as slang the subminimal word becomes. Words like *yeah* are borderline regular, non-slang words of English; words like *duh* are less frequent and more ideophonic in tone; and words like [mʊ] are fully unacceptable qua words—it is no coincidence that they cannot even be spelled.[15]

---

[14] I do not mark sentences with asterisks in (9) because it is debatable how far to go with them. Moreover, these judgments may vary by dialect; I refer here to General American.

[15] *The* and *a* end with [ʌ] when stressed, but they are normally clitics, rarely stressed. The lax vowels in (b–d) are illicit word-finally in polysyllables as well. Indeed, they may be banned altogether at the ends of polysyllables (the CMU Pronouncing Dictionary suggests some cases, such as *Yahweh*, but they are generally loanwords with alternants). At any rate, the sonority scale among monosyllables remains to be explained.

(10)   a. *spa* [spɑ], *flaw* [flɔ], *spur* [spɝ]
      b. *yeah* [jæ], *nah* [næ], *waah* [wæ]
      c. *duh* [dʌ], *meh* [mɛ]
      d. [mʊ], [mɪ]

Across phenomena, the incidence of gradience correlates with domain size, such that larger domains favor gradience. Stress and prosodic minimality are canonically intraword phenomena (the latter concerned expressly with the smallest of words), while meter and end-weight are predominately phrasal.[16] As noted in §5.14, even within a phenomenon—prosodic end-weight—one finds a depth-of-field effect, whereby sensitivity to elements declines with their depth of embedding. For example, subsyllabic effects are clearer for monosyllables than for complex phrases. Moreover, learning a categorical prosodic rule for end-weight, say, that a VV-containing conjunct must be final, is a nonstarter, as conjunct order is often forced to violate phonological constraints for extraneous reasons. For instance, conjuncts' order might be temporally fixed ("break and enter"); speakers might not plan both conjuncts in advance ("green and…red"); VV-heavy might conflict with other desiderata such as syllable count ("tried and tested"); and so forth. The learning data for phrasal phenomena will always be noisier due to such considerations. Finally, word-sized chunks are more likely to be listed (memorized) than phrase-sized chunks, rendering the former more susceptible to invariable prosody by virtue of listing.

---

[16] Donca Steriade (p.c.) raised this point.

Appendix: Key constraints

This list is not exhaustive, especially as concerns variants. Definitions here are stubs; see the text for details. Note that I argue against some of these constraints in the text.

*3μ	Penalize a syllable with three or more moras.
*(__ __)	Penalize a foot comprising two heavy syllables.
*('◡__)	Penalize a light–heavy trochee.
ALIGN-L (or R)	All stresses are leftmost (or rightmost) (pp. 34, 106).
ALIGN-L-MAIN (or R)	Primary stress is leftmost (or rightmost) (*ibid.*).
ALIGN-L(x, y) (or R)	Penalize each left (or right) edge of x that does not coincide with the left (or right) edge of y (*ibid.*).
*APPEND	Penalize a segment that attaches directly to the syllable node.
BINMIN(φ, ω)	Penalize a non-binary prosodic phrase.
BRANCH	Penalize each non-branching mora under primary stress.
CLASH	Penalize each pair of adjacent stressed syllables.
CODACOND(-ŏ̆)	Penalize a coda with its own place node (in an unstressed syllable).
DEP	Penalize the insertion of a segment.
DEP-μ	Penalize the insertion of a mora (e.g. lengthening).
DEP-μ-OO	Penalize the insertion of a mora vis-à-vis the base.
(Faith)	Stub for irrelevant faithfulness constraints.
FTBIN	Penalize a non-binary foot.
GRAMWD=PWD	Penalize a grammatical word that is not prosodified (p. 104).
IAMB	Penalize a finally unstressed foot.
IDENT(*feat*)	Penalize a change to the value of the specified feature.
LAPSE	Penalize each span of two or more adjacent unstressed syllables.
*μ	Penalize a mora.
*μ/X	Penalize each X that heads a mora.
MAIN→CODA	Penalize an open syllable with primary stress.
MAIN→FULL	Penalize a reduced-voweled syllable with primary stress.
MAIN→VV	Penalize a short-voweled syllable with primary stress.
MAX	Penalize the deletion of a segment.
MAX-μ	Penalize the deletion of a mora (e.g. shortening).
MAX-μ-V	Penalize the deletion of a vocalic mora.
MAX(place)	Penalize the deletion of a place node.
NONFINALITY	Penalize word-final stress (or sometimes, as noted, a final foot).
ONSET	Penalize a syllable with an empty onset.
PARSE	Penalize an unfooted syllable.
PK-PROM	Penalize primary stress on a syllable that is not the heaviest (p. 32).

RH-CONTOUR	Penalize uneven (HL) trochees and even (LL) iambs.
$\sigma_{\mu\mu} \rightarrow S(\text{TRESS})$	Penalize an unstressed heavy (a.k.a. WSP).
$\sigma_{\mu\mu\mu} \rightarrow S(\text{TRESS})$	Penalize an unstressed superheavy.
$S(\text{TRESS}) \rightarrow \sigma_{\mu\mu}$	Penalize a stressed light (a.k.a. SWP).
STRESS-TO-STRESS	Penalize each stress that is not in a strong p-phrase (p. 203).
$t \rightarrow \text{STRESS}$	Penalize an unstressed syllable by its total energy (p. 240).
TROCHEE	Penalize an initially unstressed foot.
*V.V	Penalize a sequence of two adjacent vowels.
WbyP	Penalize each coda consonant that does not head a mora.
$X \rightarrow \varphi_s$	Penalize each X under a weak prosodic node of type φ.

References

Abbott, Stan. 1985. A tentative multilevel multiunit phonological analysis of the Murik language. *Papers in New Guinea Linguistics* 22.339–373.

Abeillé, Anne, and Danielle Godard. 1999. La position de l'adjectif épithète en français: le poids des mots. *Recherches Linguistiques de Vincennes* 28.9–32.

Abercrombie, David. 1967. *Elements of general phonetics*. Edinburgh: Edinburgh University Press.

Abraham, Richard D. 1950. Fixed order of coordinates: A study in comparative lexicography. *The Modern Language Journal* 34.276–287.

Abrahamson, Arthur. 2003. Acoustic cues to word-initial stop length in Pattani Malay. *Proceedings of the 15th International Congress of Phonetic Sciences, Barcelona*. 387–390.

Ahn, Byron. 2016. There's nothing exceptional about the phrasal stress rule. MS, Princeton University, submitted.

Ahn, Mee-Jin. 2000. Phonetic and functional bases of syllable weight for stress assignment. Doctoral Dissertation, University of Illinois at Urbana-Champaign.

Albright, Adam. 2002. Islands of reliability for regular morphology: Evidence from Italian. *Language* 78.684–709.

Alderete, John, Jill Beckman, Laura Benua, Amalia Gnanadesikan, John McCarthy, and Suzanne Urbanczyk. 1999. Reduplication with fixed segmentism. *Linguistic Inquiry* 30.327–364.

Allan, Keith. 1987. Hierarchies and the choice of left conjuncts (with particular attention to English). *Journal of Linguistics* 23.51–77.

Allen, W. Sidney. 1953. *Phonetics in ancient India*. Oxford University Press.

Allen, W. Sidney. 1973. *Accent and rhythm*. London: Cambridge University Press.

Allen, W. Sidney. 1978. *Vox Latina: A guide to the pronunciation of Classical Latin*. London: Cambridge University Press.

Anttila, Arto. 1997a. Deriving variation from grammar. *Variation, change and phonological theory*, ed. by Frans Hinskens, Roeland van Hout, and Leo Wetzels, 35–68. Amsterdam: John Benjamins.

Anttila, Arto. 1997b. Variation in Finnish phonology and morphology. Doctoral Dissertation, Stanford University.

Anttila, Arto. 2006. Prosodic constraints on /-ntV/ in Finnish. *A man of measure: Festschrift in honour of Fred Karlsson on his 60th birthday*, ed. by Mickael Suominen et al., volume 19 of *Special Supplement to SKY Journal of Linguistics*, 119–127. Turku: The Linguistic Association of Finland.

Anttila, Arto. 2008. Gradient phonotactics and the Complexity Hypothesis. *Natural Language and Linguistic Theory* 26.695–729.

Anttila, Arto. 2010. Word stress in Finnish. Colloquium talk, Yale University, February 1.

Anttila, Arto. 2016. Stress, phrasing, and auxiliary contraction in English. *The morphosyntax-phonology connection: Locality and directionality at the interfaces*, ed. by Vera Gribanova and Stephanie S. Shih, 143–170. Oxford: Oxford University Press.

Anttila, Arto, Matthew Adams, and Michael Speriosu. 2010. The role of prosody in the English dative alternation. *Language and Cognitive Processes* 25.946–981.

Arnold, E. Vernon. 1905. *Vedic metre in its historical development*. Cambridge, UK: Cambridge University Press.

Arnold, Jennifer, Thomas Wasow, Anthony Losongco, and Ryan Ginstrom. 2000. Heaviness vs. newness: The effects of complexity and information structure on constituent ordering. *Language* 76.28–55.

Arregi, Karlos. 2002. Focus on Basque movements. Doctoral Dissertation, MIT.

Asher, R. E., and T. C. Kumari. 1997. *Malayalam*. London: Routledge.

Asher, Ronald E., and Elayaperumal Annamalai. 2002. *Colloquial Tamil: The complete course for beginners*. London: Routledge.

Baayen, Rolf Harald, Richard Piepenbrock, and Léon Gulikers. 1993. The CELEX lexical database [CD-ROM]. Philadelphia, PA: Linguistics Data Consortium, University of Pennsylvania.

Baddeley, Alan D., Neil Thomson, and Mary Buchanan. 1975. Word length and the structure of short-term memory. *Journal of Verbal Learning and Verbal Behavior* 14.575–589.

Baker, Brett J. 1997. Edge crispness: Segment to mora isomorphism. WCCFL 16.33–47.

Baker, Brett J. 1999. Word structure in Ngalakgan. Doctoral Dissertation, University of Sydney.

Baker, Brett J. 2008. *Word structure in Ngalakgan*. Stanford: CSLI Publications.

Baković, Eric. 2008. Unbounded stress and factorial typology. *Optimality Theory in phonology: A reader*, ed. by John J. McCarthy, 202–214. Malden, MA: Blackwell.

Baković, Eric J. 1996. Foot harmony and quantitative adjustments. MS, Rutgers University.

Balcaen, M. Jean. 1995. The prosody of Tiberian Hebrew. Master's thesis, University of Saskatchewan, Saskatoon.

Bandhu, Chudamani, Balabh Mani Dahal, Andreas Holzhausen, and Austin Hale. 1971. *Nepali segmental phonology*. Kirtipur, Nepal: Summer Institute of Linguistics.

Barker, Muhammad Abd-al-Rahman. 1963. *Klamath dictionary*. Berkeley, CA: University of California Press.

Barker, Muhammad Abd-al-Rahman. 1964. *Klamath grammar*. Berkeley, CA: University of California Press.

Barr, Dale J., Roger Levy, Christoph Scheepers, and Harry J. Tily. 2013. Random effects structure for confirmatory hypothesis testing: Keep it maximal. *Journal of Memory and Language* 68.255–278.

Beckman, Jill N. 1998. Positional faithfulness. Doctoral Dissertation, University of Massachusetts, Amherst.

Beckman, Jill N. 2013. *Positional faithfulness: An Optimality Theoretic treatment of phonological asymmetries*. Routledge.

Beguš, Gašper. 2018. Unnatural phonology: A synchrony-diachrony interface approach. Doctoral Dissertation, Harvard University.

Behaghel, Otto. 1909. Beziehungen zwischen Umfang und Reihenfolge von Satzgliedern. *Indogermanische Forschungen* 25.110–142.

Beltzung, Jean-Marc. 2008. Compensatory lengthening in phonological representations: Nature, constraints and typology. Doctoral Dissertation, University of Paris-3 (Sorbonne-Nouvelle). Available on Rutgers Optimality Archive, record 1056.

Bennett, Charles E. 1918. *New Latin grammar*. Ithaca, NY: Allyn and Bacon.

Bennett, Ryan. 2012. Foot-conditioned phonotactics and prosodic constituency. Doctoral Dissertation, University of California, Santa Cruz.

Bennett, Ryan, Emily Elfner, and James McCloskey. 2016. Lightest to the right: An anomolous displacement in Irish. *Linguistic Inquiry* 47.169–234.

Benor, Sarah, and Roger Levy. 2006. The chicken or the egg? A probabilistic analysis of English binomials. *Language* 82.233–278.

Benua, Laura. 1995. Identity effects in morphological truncation. *Papers in Optimality Theory [Occasional Papers 18]*, ed. by Jill Beckman, Laura Walsh Dickey, and Suzanne Urbanczyk, volume 18, 77–136. Amherst, MA: University of Massachusetts.

Benua, Laura. 1997. Transderivational identity: Phonological relations between words. Doctoral Dissertation, University of Massachusetts, Amherst.

Berko, Jean. 1958. The child's learning of English morphology. *Word* 14.150–177.

Bever, Thomas G. 1970. The cognitive basis of linguistic structures. *Cognition and the development of language*, ed. by John R. Hayes, 279–362. New York: John Wiley & Sons.

Bhatt, Rakesh. 1989. Syllable weight and metrical structure of Kashmiri. MS, Department of Linguistics, University of Illinois.

Biese, Yrjo Mooses. 1939. Neuenglisch tick-tack und Verwandtes. *Neuphilologische Mitteilungen* 40.146–205.

Biggs, Henry. 1996. A statistical analysis of the metrics of the classic French decasyllable and classic alexandrine. Doctoral Dissertation, University of California, Los Angeles.

Blevins, Juliette. 1994. The bimoraic foot in Rotuman phonology and morphology. *Oceanic Linguistics* 33.491–516.

Blevins, Juliette. 1995. The syllable in phonological theory. *The handbook of phonological theory*, ed. by John A. Goldsmith, 206–244. Malden, MA: Blackwell.

Blevins, Juliette. 1996. Mokilese reduplication. *Linguistic Inquiry* 27.523–530.

Blumenfeld, Lev. 2006. Constraints on phonological interactions. Doctoral Dissertation, Stanford University.

Blumenfeld, Lev. 2011. Coercion and minimality. *The Linguistic Review* 28.207–240.

Blumenfeld, Lev. 2015. Meter as faithfulness. *Natural Language and Linguistic Theory* 33.79–125.

Blumenfeld, Lev. 2016a. End-weight effects in verse and language. *Studia Metrica et Poetica* 3.7–32.

Blumenfeld, Lev. 2016b. Generative metrics: An overview. *Language and Linguistics Compass* 10.413–430.

Boas, Franz. 1947. Kwakiutl grammar with a glossary of the suffixes. *Transactions of the American Philosophical Society*, ed. by Helene Boas Yampolsky and Zelig Harris, volume 37.3. 201–377.

Bock, J. Kathryn. 1977. The effect of a pragmatic presupposition on syntactic structure in question answering. *Journal of Verbal Learning and Verbal Behavior* 16.723–734.

Bock, J. Kathryn. 1982. Toward a cognitive psychology of syntax: Information processing contributions to sentence formation. *Psychological Review* 89.1–47.

Bock, Kathryn, and Richard Warren. 1985. Conceptual accessibility and syntactic structure in sentence formulation. *Cognition* 21.47–67.

Boersma, Paul, and Joe Pater. 2016. Convergence properties of a gradual learning algorithm for Harmonic Grammar. *Harmonic grammar and harmonic serialism*, ed. by John McCarthy and Joe Pater. London: Equinox Press.

Boersma, Paul, and David Weenink. 2017. Praat: Doing phonetics by computer [computer program]. Version 6.0.28, retrieved 23 March 2017 from www.praat.org.

Böhtlingk, Otto. 1887. *Pâṇiniʾs Grammatik*. Leipzig: H. Haessel.

Boldrini, Sandro. 1999. *Prosodie und Metrik der Römer*. Stuttgart and Leipzig: Teubner. Trans. by Bruno W. Häuptli.

Bolinger, Dwight L. 1962. Binomials and pitch accent. *Lingua* 11.34–44.

Booij, Geert. 1983. Principles and parameters in Prosodic Phonology. *Linguistics* 21.249–280.

Borise, Lena. 2017. Prominence redistribution in the Aŭciuki dialect of Belarusian. *Proceedings of Formal Approaches to Slavic Linguistics (FASL)* 24.94–109.

Borise, Lena. 2018. Pretonic prominence in the Aŭciuki dialect of Belarusian. Paper presented at WCCFL, Los Angeles.

Bosch, Anna R. K. 1991. Phonotactics at the level of the phonological word. Doctoral Dissertation, University of Chicago.

Bradley, Travis G. 2001. The phonetics and phonology of rhotic duration contrast and neutralization. Doctoral Dissertation, The Pennsylvania State University.

Brame, Michael. 1974. The cycle in phonology: Stress in Palestinian, Maltese and Spanish. *Linguistic Inquiry* 5.39–60.

Braver, Aaron, and Shigeto Kawahara. 2012. Complete and incomplete neutralization in Japanese monomoraic lengthening. MS, Rutgers University.

Braver, Aaron, and Shigeto Kawahara. 2014. Incomplete vowel lengthening in Japanese: A first study. *Proceedings of the 31st West Coast Conference on Formal Linguistics*, ed. by Robert E. Santana-LaBarge, 86–95. Somerville, MA: Cascadilla Proceedings Project.

Bresnan, Joan. 2007. Is syntactic knowledge probabilistic? Experiments with the English dative alternation. *Roots: Linguistics in search of its evidential base*, ed. by Sam Featherston and Wolfgang Sternefeld, Studies in Generative Grammar, 77–96. Berlin: Mouton de Gruyter.

Bresnan, Joan, Anna Cueni, Tatiana Nikitina, and Harald Baayen. 2007. Predicting the dative alternation. *Cognitive foundations of interpretation*, ed. by G. Boume, I. Kraemer, and J. Zwarts, 69–94. Amsterdam: Royal Netherlands Academy of Science.

Bresnan, Joan, and Marilyn Ford. 2010. Predicting syntax: Processing dative constructions in American and Australian varieties of English. *Language* 86.186–213.

Bresnan, Joan, and Jennifer Hay. 2008. Gradient grammar: An effect of animacy on the syntax of *give* in New Zealand and American English. *Lingua* 118.245–259.

Bresnan, Joan, and Tatiana Nikitina. 2003. On the gradience of the dative alternation. MS, Stanford University.

Bresnan, Joan, and Tatiana Nikitina. 2009. The gradience of the dative alternation. *Reality exploration and discovery: Pattern interaction in language and life*, ed. by Linda Uyechi and Lian Hee Wee. Stanford, CA: CSLI Publications.

Broselow, Ellen. 1982. On predicting the interaction of stress and epenthesis. *Glossa* 16.115–132.

Broselow, Ellen, Su-I Chen, and Marie Huffman. 1997. Syllable weight: convergence of phonology and phonetics. *Phonology* 14.47–82.

Bross, Christoph, Dieter Gunkel, Olav Hackstein, and Kevin M. Ryan. 2013. Tocharian B versification. Paper presented at Tocharian Texts in Context, University of Vienna, June 2013.

Bross, Christoph, Dieter Gunkel, and Kevin M. Ryan. 2014. Caesurae, bridges, and the colometry of four Tocharian B meters. *Indo-European Linguistics* 2.1–23.

Browman, Catherine P., and Louis Goldstein. 1988. Some notes on syllable structure in articulatory phonology. *Phonetica* 45.140–155.

Büring, Daniel. 2013. Syntax, information structure, and prosody. *The Cambridge handbook of generative syntax*, ed. by Marcel den Dikken, 860–896. Cambridge, UK: Cambridge University Press.

Büring, Daniel, and Rodrigo Gutiérrez-Bravo. 2001. Focus-related constituent order variation without the NSR: A prosody-based crosslinguistic analysis. *Syntax at Santa Cruz* 3.41–58.

Burnham, Kenneth P., and David R. Anderson. 2004. Multimodal inference: Understanding AIC and BIC in model selection. *Sociological Methods & Research* 33.261–304.

Burzio, Luigi. 1994. *Principles of English stress*. Cambridge, UK: Cambridge University Press.

Bye, Patrik, and Paul de Lacy. 2008. Metrical influences on fortition and lenition. *Lenition and fortition*, ed. by Joaquim de Carvalho, Tobias Scheer, and Philippe Ségéral, 173–206. Berlin: Mouton de Gruyter.

Bye, Patrik, Elin Sagulin, and Ida Toivonen. 2009. Phonetic duration, phonological quantity and prosodic structure in Inari Saami. *Phonetica* 66.199–221.

Byrd, Dani. 2000. Articulatory vowel lengthening and coordination at phrasal junctures. *Phonetica* 57.3–16.

Byrne, Brian, and Elizabeth Davidson. 1985. On putting the horse before the cart: Exploring conceptual bases of word order via acquisition of a miniature artificial language. *Journal of Memory and Language* 24.377–389.

Cambier-Langeveld, Tina, Marina Nespor, and Vincent J. van Heuven. 1997. The domain of final lengthening in production and perception in Dutch. *Linguistics in the Netherlands*, ed. by Helen de Hoop and Jane Coerts, 13–24. Amsterdam: John Benjamins.

Campbell, Mary Ann, and Lloyd Anderson. 1976. Hocus pocus nursery rhymes. *Papers from the 12th Regional Meeting of the Chicago Linguistic Society*, ed. by Salikoko S. Mufwene, Carol A. Walker, and Sanford B. Steever, 72–95. Chicago: Chicago Linguistic Society.

Campbell, Nick. 1999. A study of Japanese speech timing from the syllable perspective. *Journal of Phonetic Society of Japan* 3.29–39.

Cardona, George. 1988. *Pāṇini, his work and traditions, vol. 1: Background and introduction.* Delhi: Motilal Banarsidass.

Carpenter, Angela C. 2010. A naturalness bias in learning stress. *Phonology* 27.345–392.

Cei, Erica, and Bruce Hayes. 2012. Multiple factors affecting Italian word stress. Phonology Seminar, UCLA, March 7.

Chang, Franklin. 2009. Learning to order words: A connectionist model of heavy NP shift and accessibility effects in Japanese and English. *Journal of Memory and Language* 61.374–397.

Chen, Matthew Y. 2000. *Tone sandhi: Patterns across Chinese dialects*, volume 92 of *Cambridge Studies in Linguistics*. Cambridge, UK: Cambridge University Press.

Choi, Hye-Won. 2007. Length and order: A corpus study of Korean dative-accusative construction. *Discourse and Cognition* 14.207–227.

Chomsky, Noam. 1958/1962. A transformational approach to syntax. *Proceedings of the Third Texas Conference on Problems of Linguistics Analysis in English*, ed. by Archibald A. Hill, volume 3, 124–158. Austin: University of Texas Press.

Chomsky, Noam. 1961. On the notion 'rule of grammar'. *Structure of language and its mathematical aspects, proceedings of the twelfth symposium in applied mathematics*, ed. by Roman Jakobson, volume 12, 6–24. Providence, RI: American Mathematical Society.

Chomsky, Noam. 1975. *The logical structure of linguistic theory*. Chicago: University of Chicago Press.

Chomsky, Noam, and Morris Halle. 1968. *The sound pattern of English*. Cambridge, MA: Massachusetts Institute of Technology Press.

Christdas, Prathima. 1988. The phonology and morphology of Tamil. Doctoral Dissertation, Cornell University.

Christdas, Prathima. 1996. Syllable prominence and stress in Tamil. MS, Cornell University.

Cinque, Guglielmo. 1993. A null theory of phrase and compound stress. *Linguistic Inquiry* 24.239–297.

Clemens, Lauren, and Jessica Coon. 2016. Deriving verb-initial word order in Mayan. MS, University at Albany, SUNY and McGill University, submitted.

Colantoni, Laura, and Jeffrey Steele. 2005. Phonetically-driven epenthesis asymmetries in French and Spanish obstruent-liquid clusters. *Experimental and theoretical approaches to Romance linguistics*, ed. by Randall Gess and Edward Rubin, 77–96. Amsterdam: John Benjamins.

Connell, Bruce A., Richard J. Hayward, and John Abraha Ashkaba. 2000. Observations on Kunama tone. *Studies in African Linguistics* 29.1–41.

Cooper, William E., and John R. Ross. 1975. World order. *Papers from the Parasession on Functionalism*, ed. by R. Grossman, L.J. San, and T. Vance, 63–111. Chicago: Chicago Linguistic Society.

Copestake, Ann, and Aurélie Herbelot. 2011. Exciting and interesting: Issues in the generation of binomials. *Proceedings of the UCNLG+ Eval: Language Generation and Evaluation Workshop*, 45–53. Association for Computational Linguistics.

Cowan, Nelson, Alan D. Baddeley, Emily M. Elliott, and Jennifer Norris. 2003. List composition and the word length effect in immediate recall: A comparison of localist and globalist assumptions. *Psychonomic Bulletin & Review* 10.74–79.

Crane, Gregory R. 2017. Perseus digital library. Tufts University. www.perseus.tufts.edu (accessed May 5, 2017).

Crosswhite, Katherine. 1999. Vowel reduction in Optimality Theory. Doctoral Dissertation, University of California, Los Angeles.

Crosswhite, Katherine. 2001. *Vowel reduction in Optimality Theory*. New York: Routledge.

Crowhurst, Megan J., and Lev D. Michael. 2005. Iterative footing and prominence-driven stress in Nanti (Kampa). *Language* 81.47–95.

Crowley, Terry. 1981. The Mpakwithi dialect of Anguthimri. *Handbook of Australian languages, volume II*, ed. by Robert M. W. Dixon and Barry Blake, 147–194. Amsterdam: John Benjamins.

Curtis, Emily. 2003. Geminate weight: Case studies and formal models. Doctoral Dissertation, University of Washington.

Cutler, Anne, and William E. Cooper. 1978. Phoneme-monitoring in the context of different phonetic sequences. *Journal of Phonetics* 6.221–225.

Daland, Robert, Bruce Hayes, James White, Marc Garellek, Andrea Davis, and Ingrid Norrmann. 2011. Explaining sonority projection effects. *Phonology* 28.197–234.

Davidson, Lisa. 2006. Phonology, phonetics, or frequency: Influences on the production of non-native sequences. *Journal of Phonetics* 34.104–137.

Davis, Stuart. 1999. On the representation of initial geminates. *Phonology* 16.93–104.

Davis, Stuart. 2003. The controversy over geminates and syllable weight. *The syllable in Optimality Theory*, ed. by Caroline Féry and Ruben van de Vijver, 77–98. Cambridge, UK: Cambridge University Press.

Davis, Stuart. 2011. Geminates. *Companion to phonology*, ed. by Marc van Oostendorp, Colin J. Ewen, Elizabeth Hume, and Keren Rice, chapter 37. Malden, MA: Wiley-Blackwell Publishers.

Dayley, Jon Philip. 1989. *Tümpisa (Panamint) Shoshone grammar*, volume 115 of *University of California Publications in Linguistics*. Berkeley, CA: University of California Press.

Delattre, P. 1966. A comparison of syllable length conditioning among languages. *International Review of Applied Linguistics* 4.183–198.

Delgutte, Bertrand. 1982. Some correlates of phonetic distinctions at the level of the auditory nerve. *The representation of speech in the peripheral auditory system*, ed. by R. Carlson and B. Granström, 131–150. Amsterdam: Elsevier.

Dell, François. 2011. Singing in Tashlhiyt Berber, a language that allows vowel-less syllables. *Handbook of the syllable*, ed. by Charles Cairns and Eric Raimy, 173–193. Leiden: Brill.

Dell, François, and Mohamed Elmedlaoui. 2017. Syllabic weight in Tashlhiyt Berber. *Syllable weight in African languages*, ed. by Paul Newman, 83–96. Amsterdam: John Benjamins.

Deo, Ashwini. 2007. The metrical organization of Classical Sanskrit verse. *Journal of Linguistics* 43.

Deo, Ashwini, and Paul Kiparsky. 2011. Poetries in contact: Arabic, Persian, and Urdu. *Frontiers of comparative metrics*, ed. by M. Lotman. Bern and New York: Peter Lang.

Devine, Andrew M., and Laurence Stephens. 1994. *The prosody of Greek speech*. Oxford University Press.

Dienhart, John M. 1999. Stress in reduplicative compounds: Mish-mash or hocus-pocus? *American Speech* 74.13–38.

Dixon, Robert M. W. 1977. Some phonological rules in Yidinʸ. *Linguistic Inquiry* 8.1–34.

Doherty, Cathal. 1991. Munster Irish stress. *Phonology at Santa Cruz* 2.19–32.

Downing, Laura J. 2005. Morphological complexity and prosodic minimality. *Catalan Journal of Linguistics* 4.83–106.

Dresher, B. Elan. 2009. Stress assignment in Tiberian Hebrew. *Contemporary views on architecture and representations in phonology*, ed. by Eric Raimy and Charles E. Cairns, 213–224. Cambridge, MA: MIT Press.

Dresher, B. Elan, and Harry van der Hulst. 1998. Head-dependent asymmetries in phonology: Complexity and visibility. *Phonology* 15.317–352.

Dryer, Matthew S. 1980. The positional tendencies of sentential noun phrases in universal grammar. *Canadian Journal of Linguistics* 25.123–195.

Duckworth, George Eckel. 1969. *Vergil and classical hexameter poetry: A study in metrical variety*. Ann Arbor, MI: University of Michigan Press.

Dupoux, E., Y. Hirose, K. Kakehi, C. Pallier, and J. Mehler. 1998. Epenthetic vowels in Japanese: A perceptual illusion? *Journal of Experimental Psychology: Human Perception and Performance* 25.1568–1578.

Ehret, Katharina, Christoph Wolk, and Benedikt Szmrecsányi. 2014. Quirky quadratures: On rhythm and weight as constraints on genitive variation in an unconventional data set. *English Language and Linguistics* 18.263–303.

Eichinger, Ludwig M. 1992. Ganz natürlich—aber im Rahmen bleiben. Zur Reihenfolge gestufter Adjektivattribute. *Deutsche Sprache* 4.312–329.

El Zarka, Dina. 2005. On the borderline of reduplication: Gemination and other consonant doubling in Arabic morphology. *Studies on reduplication*, ed. by Bernhard Hurch, 369–394. Berlin: Mouton de Gruyter.

Elfner, Emily. 2012. Syntax-prosody interactions in Irish. Doctoral Dissertation, University of Massachusetts, Amherst.

Elfner, Emily. 2015. Recursion in prosodic phrasing: Evidence from Connemara Irish. *Natural Language and Linguistic Theory* 33.1169–1208.

Elias-Ulloa, José. 2004a. Quantity (in)sensitivity and underlying glottal-stop deletion in Capanahua. *Coyote Papers* 13.15–30.

Elias-Ulloa, José. 2004b. Variable syllable weight and quantity-insensitive allomorphy in Shipibo. *North Eastern Linguistic Society (NELS)* 35.171–186.

Embick, David. 2007. Linearization and local dislocation: Derivational mechanics and interactions. *Linguistic Analysis* 33.303–336.

Emeneau, Murray B. 1939. The vowels of the Badaga language. *Language* 15.43–47.

van Engelenhoven, Aone. 1994. A description of the Leti language. Doctoral Dissertation, University of Leiden.

Erdmann, Peter. 1988. On the principle of 'weight' in English. *On language, rhetorica phonologica syntactica: A Festschrift for Robert P. Stockwell from his friends and colleagues*, ed. by Caroline Duncan-Rose and Theo Vennemann, 325–339. London: Routledge.

Evans, Nicholas. 1995. *A grammar of Kayardild: With historical-comparative notes on Tangkic*. New York: Mouton.

Everett, Daniel. 1988. On metrical constituent structure in Pirahã. *Natural Language and Linguistic Theory* 6.207–246.

Everett, Daniel, and Keren Everett. 1984. On the relevance of syllable onsets to stress placement. *Linguistic Inquiry* 15.705–711.

Everett, Keren. 1998. The acoustic correlates of stress in Pirahã. *Journal of Amazonian Linguistics* 1.105–162.

Fabb, Nigel, and Morris Halle. 2008. *Meter in poetry. With a chapter on Southern Romance meters by Carlos Piera*. Cambridge, UK: Cambridge University Press.

Faghiri, Pegah, and Pollet Samvelian. 2014. Constituent ordering in Persian and the weight factor. *Empirical issues in syntax and semantics*, ed. by Christopher Piñón, volume 10, 215–232. Paris: CNRS.

Fenk-Oczlon, Gertraud. 1989. Word frequency and word order in freezes. *Linguistics* 27.517–556.

Ferreira, V. S., and H. Yoshita. 2003. Given-new ordering effects on the production of scrambled sentences in Japanese. *Journal of Psycholinguistic Research* 32.669–692.

Fitzgerald, Colleen. 1997. O'odham rhythms. Doctoral Dissertation, University of Arizona.

Flemming, Edward. 2001. Scalar and categorical phenomena in a unified model of phonetics and phonology. *Phonology* 18.7–44.

Forsgren, Mats. 1978. *La place de l'adjectif épithète en français contemporain, étude quantitative et sémantique*. Stockholm: Almqvsit & Wilksell.

Fougeron, Cécile. 1998. *Variations articulaires en début de constituants prosodiques de différents niveaux en français*. Paris: Université Paris III-Sorbonne Nouvelle.

Fougeron, Cécile, and Patricia Keating. 1997. Articulatory strengthening at edges of prosodic domains. *Journal of the Acoustical Society of America* 101.3728–3740.

Fox, Barbara, and Sandra Thompson. 2007. Relative clauses in English conversation: Relativizers, frequency, and the notion of construction. *Studies in Language* 31.293–326.

Francese, Christopher. 2011. *Caesar: Selection from the Gallic War*. Carlisle, PA: Dickinson College Commentaries.

Francis, Elaine J. 2010. Grammatical weight and relative clause extraposition in English. *Cognitive Linguistics* 21.35–74.

Francis, Elaine J., and Laura A. Michaelis. 2014. Why move? How weight and discourse factors combine to predict relative clause extraposition in English. *Competing motivations in grammar and usage*, ed. by B. Macwhinney, A. Malchukov, and E. Moravcsik, 71–87. Oxford: Oxford University Press.

Friedman, Sh. Y. 1971. Kol hakatsar kodem ['the shorter precedes,' in Hebrew]. *Leš* 35.117–129.

Gabas Jr., Nilson. 1998. *Estudo fonológica da língua karo*. Munich and Newcastle: LINCOM Europa.

Gabas Jr., Nilson. 1999. A grammar of Karo (Tupi). Doctoral Dissertation, University of California, Santa Barbara.

Gandour, Jack. 1979. Tonal rules for English loanwords in Thai. *Studies in Tai and Mon-Khmer phonetics and phonology in honour of Eugenie J.A. Henderson*, ed. by T.L. Thongkum, V. Panupong, P. Kullavanijaya, and M.R.K. Tingsabadh. Bangkok: Chulalongkorn University Press.

Garcia, Guilherme D. 2016. The computation of weight in Portuguese: Syllables and intervals. *Proceedings of the 33rd West Coast Conference on Formal Linguistics*, ed. by Kyeong-min Kim et al., 137–145. Somerville, MA: Cascadilla Proceedings Project.

Garcia, Guilherme D. 2017a. Weight effects on stress: Lexicon and grammar. Doctoral Dissertation, McGill University.

Garcia, Guilherme D. 2017b. Weight gradience and stress in Portuguese. *Phonology* 34.41–79.

Garcia, Guilherme D. 2017c. When lexical statistics and the grammar conflict: Learning and repairing weight effects on stress. MS, McGill University, submitted.

Garrett, Edward. 1999. Minimal words aren't minimal feet. *Papers in Phonology 2: UCLA Working Papers in Linguistics, Vol. 1*, ed. by Matthew Gordon, 68–105. University of California, Los Angeles.

Gibson, Edward. 1998. Linguistic complexity: Locality and syntactic dependencies. *Cognition* 68.1–76.

Gibson, Edward. 2000. The dependency locality theory: A distance-based theory of linguistic complexity. *Image, language, brain*, ed. by Y. Miyashita, A. Marantz, and W. O'Neil, 95–126. Cambridge, MA: Massachusetts Institute of Technology Press.

Gibson, Edward, Steve Piantadosi, and Kristina Fedorenko. 2011. Using Mechanical Turk to obtain and analyze English acceptability judgments. *Language and Linguistics Compass* 5.509–524.

Goedemans, Rob, and Harry van der Hulst. 2013. Weight-sensitive stress. *The world atlas of language structures online*, ed. by Matthew S. Dryer and Martin Haspelmath. Max Planck Institute for Evolutionary Anthropology.

Goedemans, Rob, Jeffrey Heinz, and Harry van der Hulst. 2017. StressTyp2. Web Download Archive, st2.ullet.net, April 2017.

Goldwater, Sharon, and Mark Johnson. 2003. Learning OT constraint rankings using a Maximum Entropy model. *Proceedings of the Stockholm Workshop on Variation within Optimality Theory*, ed. by Jennifer Spenader, Anders Eriksson, and Osten Dahl, 111–120.

Golenbock, Janice. 2000. Binomial expressions—does frequency matter? MS, Carnegie Mellon University.

Golston, Chris. 1998. Constraint-based metrics. *Natural Language and Linguistic Theory* 16.719–770.

Golston, Chris, and Tomas Riad. 2000. The phonology of Classical Greek meter. *Linguistics* 38.99–167.

Golston, Chris, and Tomas Riad. 2005. The phonology of Greek lyric meter. *Journal of Linguistics* 41.77–115.

Gordon, Matthew. 1999. *Syllable weight: phonetics, phonology, and typology*. Doctoral Dissertation, University of California, Los Angeles.

Gordon, Matthew. 2001. The tonal basis of final weight criteria. *Proceedings of the Chicago Linguistic Society* 36.141–156.

Gordon, Matthew. 2002a. A factorial typology of quantity insensitive stress. *Natural Language and Linguistic Theory* 20.491–552.

Gordon, Matthew. 2002b. A phonetically-driven account of syllable weight. *Language* 78.51–80.

Gordon, Matthew. 2004a. A phonological and phonetic study of word-level stress in Chickasaw. *International Journal of American Linguistics* 70.1–32.

Gordon, Matthew. 2004b. Positional weight constraints in Optimality Theory. *Linguistic Inquiry* 35.692–703.

Gordon, Matthew. 2005. A perceptually-driven account of onset-sensitive stress. *Natural Language and Linguistic Theory* 23.595–653.

Gordon, Matthew. 2006. *Syllable weight: phonetics, phonology, typology*. New York, NY: Routledge Press.

Gordon, Matthew. 2011. Stress systems. *The handbook of phonological theory, 2nd edition*, ed. by John Goldsmith, Jason Riggle, and Alan C. L. Yu, 141–163. Oxford: Blackwell Publishing.

Gordon, Matthew. 2017. Syllable weight: A typological and theoretical overview. *Syllable weight in African languages*, ed. by Paul Newman, 27–48. Amsterdam: John Benjamins.

Gordon, Matthew, and Ayla Applebaum. 2010. Prosodic fusion and minimality in Kabardian. *Phonology* 27.45–76.

Gordon, Matthew, Carmen Jany, Carlos Nash, and Nobutaka Takara. 2008. Vowel and consonant sonority and coda weight: A cross-linguistic study. *Proceedings of the 26th West Coast Conference on Formal Linguistics (WCCFL)*, ed. by Charles B. Chang and Hannah J. Haynie, 208–216. Somerville, MA: Cascadilla Proceedings Project.

Gordon, Matthew, Carmen Jany, Carlos Nash, and Nobutaka Takara. 2010. Syllable structure and extrametricality: a typological and phonetic study. *Studies in Language* 34.131–166.

Gordon, Matthew, and Edmundo Luna. 2004. An intergenerational study of Hupa stress. *Annual Meeting of the Berkeley Linguistics Society* 30.105–117.

Gorgadze, Sergi. 1912. *Gruzinskoe stixosloženie*. Tbilisi.

Gouskova, Maria. 2003. Deriving economy: Syncope in Optimality Theory. Doctoral Dissertation, University of Massachusetts-Amherst. Distributed as Rutgers Optimality Archive 610. Available at http://roa.rutgers.edu.

Grafmiller, Jason, and Stephanie Shih. 2011. New approaches to end weight. Paper presented at Variation and Typology: New Trends in Syntactic Research, 25–7 August 2011, Helsinki.

Green, Anthony Dubach. 1996. Stress placement in Munster Irish. *Proceedings of the Chicago Linguistic Society* 32.77–92.

Griffin, Zenzi M., and J. Kathryn Bock. 1998. Constraint, word frequency, and the relationship between lexical processing levels in spoken word production. *Journal of Memory and Language* 38.313–338.

Guion, Susan G., J. J. Clark, Tetsuo Harada, and Ratree P. Wayland. 2003. Factors affecting stress placement for English nonwords include syllabic structure, lexical class, and stress patterns of phonologically similar words. *Language and Speech* 46.403–427.

Gunkel, Dieter, and Olav Hackstein. 2018. *Language and meter*. Leiden: Brill.

Gunkel, Dieter, and Kevin M. Ryan. 2011. Hiatus avoidance and metrification in the Rigveda. *Proceedings of the 22nd Annual UCLA Indo-European Conference*, ed. by Stephanie W. Jamison, H. Craig Melchert, and Brent Vine, 53–68. Bremen: Hempen.

Gupta, Abha. 1987. Hindi word stress and the obligatory branching parameter. *Papers from the Annual Regional Meeting, Chicago Linguistic Society* 23.134–148.

Gussenhoven, Carlos. 1986. English plosive allophones and ambisyllabicity. *Gramma* 10.119–141.

Gussenhoven, Carlos. 1991. The English Rhythm Rule as an accent deletion rule. *Phonology* 8.1–35.

Gussenhoven, Carlos. 1993. The Dutch foot and the chanted call. *Journal of Linguistics* 29.37–63.

Gussenhoven, Carlos. 2008. Vowel duration, syllable quantity and stress in Dutch. *The nature of the word: Essays in honor of Paul Kiparsky*, ed. by Kristin Hanson and Sharon Inkelas, 181–198. Cambridge, MA: MIT Press.

Gustafsson, Marita. 1974. The phonetic length of the members in present-day English binomials. *Neuphilologische Mitteilungen* 75.663–677.

Gustafsson, Marita. 1975. *Binomial expressions in present-day English*. Turku: Annales Universitatis Turkunsis.

Hajek, John. 2000. How many moras? Overlength and maximal moraicity in Italy. *Phonological theory and the dialects of Italy*, ed. by Lori Repetti, 111–136. Amsterdam: John Benjamins Publishing Company.

Hajek, John, and Rob Goedemans. 2003. Word-initial geminates and stress in Pattani Malay. *The Linguistic Review* 20.79–94.

Hall, Tracy Alan. 1999. The phonological word: A review. *Studies on the phonnological word*, ed. by Tracy Alan Hall and Ursula Kleinhenz. Amsterdam: John Benjamins.

Hall, Tracy Alan. 2002. The distribution of superheavy syllables in Standard German. *The Linguistic Review* 19.377–420.

Halle, Morris. 1970. On meter and prosody. *Progress in linguistics*, ed. by Manfred Bierwisch and Karl Erich Heidolph, 64–80. The Hague: Mouton & Co.

Halle, Morris, and G. N. Clements. 1983. *Problem book in phonology*. Cambridge, MA: MIT Press.

Halle, Morris, and Samuel Jay Keyser. 1966. Chaucer and the study of prosody. *College English* 28.187–219.

Halle, Morris, and Jean-Roger Vergnaud. 1987. *An essay on stress*. Cambridge, MA: MIT Press.

Halporn, James W., Martin Ostwald, and Thomas G. Rosenmeyer. 1980. *The meters of Greek and Latin poetry: Revised edition*. Norman, OK: University of Oklahoma Press.

Hammond, Michael. 1986. The obligatory-branching parameter in metrical theory. *Natural Language and Linguistic Theory* 4.185–228.

Hanson, Kristin, and Paul Kiparsky. 1996. A parametric theory of poetic meter. *Language* 72.287–335.

Harris, James. 1983. *Syllable structure and stress in Spanish: A nonlinear analysis*. Cambridge, MA: Massachusetts Institute of Technology Press.

Hart, George, and Hank Heifetz. 1988. *The Forest Book of the Rāmāyaṇa of Kampaṉ*. Berkeley, CA: University of California Press.

Hart, Kausalya. 1999. *Tamil for beginners*. University of California, Berkeley: International and Areal Studies.

Hart, Michele. 1991. The moraic status of initial geminates in Trukese. *Proceedings of the 7th Annual Meeting of the Berkeley Linguistics Society*. 107–120.

Hawkins, John A. 1990. A parsing theory of word order universals. *Linguistic Inquiry* 21.223–261.

Hawkins, John A. 1994. *A performance theory of order and constituency*. Cambridge, UK: Cambridge University Press.

Hawkins, John A. 2000. The relative order of prepositional phrases in English: Going beyond manner-place-time. *Language Variation and Change* 11.231–266.

Hawkins, John A. 2004. *Efficiency and complexity in grammars*. Oxford: Oxford University Press.

Hawkins, W. Neil. 1950. Patterns of vowel loss in Macushi (Carib). *International Journal of American Linguistics* 16.87–90.

Hayes, Bruce. 1979a. Extrametricality. *MIT Working Papers in Linguistics* 1.77–86.

Hayes, Bruce. 1979b. The rhythmic structure of Persian verse. *Edebiyāt* 4.193–242.

Hayes, Bruce. 1980. A metrical theory of stress rules. Doctoral Dissertation, Massachusetts Institute of Technology.

Hayes, Bruce. 1982. Extrametricality and English stress. *Linguistic Inquiry* 13.227–276.

Hayes, Bruce. 1983. A grid-based theory of English meter. *Linguistic Inquiry* 14.357–393.

Hayes, Bruce. 1984. The phonology of rhythm in English. *Linguistic Inquiry* 15.33–74.

Hayes, Bruce. 1988. Metrics and phonological theory. *Linguistics: The Cambridge survey, vol. ii, Lingustic theory: Extensions and implications*, ed. by Frederick J. Newmeyer, 220–249. Cambridge University Press.

Hayes, Bruce. 1989. Compensatory lengthening in moraic phonology. *Linguistic Inquiry* 20.253–306.

Hayes, Bruce. 1995. *Metrical stress theory: Principles and case studies*. Chicago, IL: University of Chicago Press.

Hayes, Bruce. 1997. Phonetically-driven phonology: the role of Optimality Theory and inductive grounding. *Proceedings of the 1996 Milwaukee Conference on Formalism and Functionalism in Linguistics*.

Hayes, Bruce. 1999. Phonetically-driven phonology: the role of Optimality Theory and inductive grounding. *Functionalism and formalism in linguistics*, ed. by Michael Darnell, Edith Moravscik, Michael Noonan, Frederick Newmeyer, and Kathleen Wheatly, volume 1, 243–285. John Benjamins.

Hayes, Bruce. 2009. *Introductory phonology*. West Sussex: Wiley-Blackwell.

Hayes, Bruce. 2012. How predictable is Italian word stress? Paper presented at National Chiao Tung University, May 11.

Hayes, Bruce, and Aditi Lahiri. 1991. Bengali intonational phonology. *Natural Language and Linguistic Theory* 9.47–96.

Hayes, Bruce, and Margaret MacEachern. 1998. Quatrain form in English folk verse. *Language* 74.473–507.

Hayes, Bruce, and Claire Moore-Cantwell. 2011. Gerard Manley Hopkins's Sprung Rhythm: Corpus study and stochastic grammar. *Phonology* 28.235–282.

Hayes, Bruce, and Stanislaw Puppel. 1985. On the rhythm rule in Polish. *Advances in nonlinear phonology*, ed. by Harry van der Hulst and Norval Smith, 59–81. Dordrecht: Foris.

Hayes, Bruce, and Colin Wilson. 2008. A Maximum Entropy model of phonotactics and phonotactic learning. *Linguistic Inquiry* 39.379–440.

Hayes, Bruce, Colin Wilson, and Anne Shisko. 2012. Maxent grammars for the metrics of Shakespeare and Milton. *Language* 88.691–731.

Heeschen, Volker. 1983. *Wörterbuch der Eipo-Sprache: eipo, deutsch, englisch*. Berlin: D. Reimer.

Heinz, Jeffrey. 2014. Culminativity times harmony equals unbounded stress. *Word stress: Theoretical and typological issues*, ed. by Harry van der Hulst, chapter 8. Cambridge: Cambridge University Press.

Heinz, Jeffrey, Rob Goedemans, and Harry van der Hulst, ed. by. 2016. *Dimensions of phonological stress*. Cambridge: Cambridge University Press.

Hetzron, Robert. 1972. Phonology in syntax. *Journal of Linguistics* 8.251–262.

Hinrichs, Lars, and Benedikt M. Szmrecsányi. 2007. Recent changes in the function and frequency of Standard English genitive constructions: a multivariate analysis of tagged corpora. *English Language and Linguistics* 11.437–474.

Hinton, Leanne, and Herb Luthin. 2002. Stress & syllable weight in Yahi. Paper presented at the Society for the Study of the Indigenous Languages of the Americas.

Hirsch, Aron. 2014. What is the domain for weight computation: The syllable or the interval? *Proceedings of the 2013 Meeting on Phonology*, ed. by John Kingston, Claire Moore-Cantwell, Joe Pater, and Robert Staubs. Washington, DC: Linguistic Society of America.

Hoenigswald, Henry M. 1989. Overlong syllables in Ṛgvedic cadences. *Journal of the American Oriental Society* 109.559–563.

Hoenigswald, Henry M. 1991. The prosody of the epic adonius and its prehistory. *Illinois Classical Studies* XVI.1–15.

Hubbard, Kathleen. 1994. Duration in moraic theory. Doctoral Dissertation, University of California, Berkeley.

Hume, Elizabeth. 1997. Vowel preservation in Leti. *Oceanic Linguistics* 36.65–101.

Hume, Elizabeth, Jennifer Muller, and Aone van Engelenhoven. 1997. Nonmoraic geminates in Leti. *Phonology* 14.371–402.

Hyde, Brett. 2006. Towards a uniform account of prominence-sensitive stress. *Wondering at the natural fecundity of things: Essays in honor of Alan Prince*, ed. by Eric Baković, John J. McCarthy, and Junko Itô, 139–183. Santa Cruz, CA: Linguistics Research Center.

Hyman, Larry. 1977. On the nature of linguistic stress. *Studies in stress and accent*, ed. by Larry Hyman, volume 4 of *Southern California Occasional Papers in Linguistics*, 37–82. Los Angeles: University of Southern California.

Hyman, Larry. 1985. *A theory of phonological weight*. Dordrecht: Foris.

Hyman, Larry M. 1992. Moraic mismatches in Bantu. *Phonology* 9.255–266.

Ibragimov, Garun X. 1990. *Tsaxurskij jazyk*. Moscow: Nauka.

Idemaru, Kaori, and Susan G. Guion. 2008. Acoustic covariants of length contrast in Japanese stops. *Journal of the International Phonetic Association* 38.167–186.

Ingason, Anton Karl, and Laurel MacKenzie. 2011. 'Heaviness' as evidence for a derive-and-compare grammar. Poster presented at the 19th Manchester Phonology Meeting.

Inkelas, Sharon, and Draga Zec. 1995. The phonology/syntax interface. *Handbook of phonological theory*, ed. by John A. Goldsmith, 535–549. Oxford: Blackwell Publishing.

Itô, Junko. 1986. Syllable theory in prosodic phonology. Doctoral Dissertation, University of Massachusetts, Amherst.

Itô, Junko. 1989. A prosodic theory of epenthesis. *Natural Language and Linguistic Theory* 7.217–259.

Itô, Junko, and Armin Mester. 1999. Realignment. *The prosody-morphology interface*, ed. by René Kager, Harry van der Hulst, and Wim Zonneveld, 188–217. Cambridge, UK: Cambridge University Press.

Itô, Junko, and Armin Mester. 2009. Recursive prosodic phrasing in Japanese. *Prosody matters: Essays in honor of Lisa O. Selkirk*, ed. by Toni Borowsky, Shigeto Kawahara, Takahito Shinya, and Mariko Sugahara. London: Equinox Publishing.

Jacobs, Haike. 1997. Latin enclitic stress revisited. *Linguistic Inquiry* 28.648–661.

Jacobs, Haike. 2003. Why preantepenultimate stress in Latin requires an OT-account. *Development in prosodic systems*, ed. by Paula Fikkert and Haike Jacobs, 395–418. Berlin: Mouton de Gruyter.

Jaeger, T. Florian, and Elisabeth J. Norcliffe. 2009. The cross-linguistic study of sentence production. *Language and Linguistics Compass* 3.866–887.

Jäger, Gerhard, and Anette Rosenbach. 2006. The winner takes it all—almost: Cumulativity in grammatical variation. *Linguistics* 44.937–971.

Jakobson, Roman. 1960. *Linguistics and poetics*. Cambridge, MA: Massachusetts Institute of Technology Press.

Jakobson, Roman. 1971/1931. Die Betonung und ihre Rolle in der Wort- and Syntagmaphonologie. *Selected writings I*. The Hague: Mouton.

Jensen, John T. 1977. *Yapese reference grammar*. Honolulu: University Press of Hawaii.

Jensen, John T. 2000. Against ambisyllabicity. *Phonology* 17.187–235.

Jesney, Karen. 2007. The locus of variation in weighted constraint grammars. Poster presented at the Workshop on Variation, Gradience, and Frequency in Phonology, Stanford, CA.

Jespersen, Otto. 1905. *Growth and structure of the English language*. Stuttgart: Teubner Verlag.

Jespersen, Otto. 1938. *Growth and structure of the English language*. Stuttgart: Teubner Verlag.

Jespersen, Otto. 1961. *A Modern English grammar on historical principles. Part VI, Morphology*. London: George Allen and Unwin Ltd.

Jha, Subhadra. 1940–44. Maithili phonetics. *Indian Linguistics* 8.435–459.

Jha, Subhadra. 1958. *The formation of the Maithili language*. London: Luzac.

Kabak, Baris, and Irene Vogel. 2001. The phonological word and stress assignment in Turkish. *Phonology* 18.315–360.

Kachru, Braj B. 1969. *A reference grammar of Kashmiri*. Urbana, IL: University of Illinois Press.

Kachru, Braj B. 1973. An introduction to Spoken Kashmiri. MS, Department of Linguistics, University of Illinois.

Kager, René. 1990. Dutch schwa in moraic phonology. *Proceedings of Chicago Linguistics Society* 26.241–256.

Kager, René. 1996. On affix allomorphy and syllable counting. *Interfaces in phonology*, ed. by Ursula Kleinhenz, 155–171. Berlin: Akademie Verlag.

Kager, René. 1999. *Optimality Theory*. Cambridge, UK: Cambridge University Press.

Kager, René. 2007. Feet and metrical stress. *The Cambridge handbook of phonology*, ed. by Paul de Lacy, 195–227. Cambridge, UK: Cambridge University Press.

Kager, René. 2012. Stress in windows: Language typology and factorial typology. *Lingua* 122.1454–1493.

Kahn, Daniel. 1976. Syllable-based generalizations in English phonology. Doctoral Dissertation, Massachusetts Institute of Technology.

Kahnemuyipour, Arsalan. 2003. Syntactic categories and Persian stress. *Natural Language and Linguistic Theory* 21.333–379.

Kahnemuyipour, Arsalan. 2004. The syntax of sentential stress. Doctoral Dissertation, University of Toronto.

Kahnemuyipour, Arsalan. 2008. Phases as domains of linguistic computation. Second Prosody-Syntax Interface Workshop (PSI 2). ZAS, Berlin, 13–14 June 2008.

Kamban. 1956. *Kampar Iyaṟṟiya Irāmāyaṇam*. Annamalai, India: Annamalai University Press. Critical edition of the *Kamparāmāyaṇam* (c. 1200 CE).

Karimi, Simin. 2003. On object positions, specificity, and scrambling in Persian. *Word order and scrambling*, ed. by Simin Karimi, 91–124. Oxford: Blackwell Publishing.

Karvonen, Daniel. 2005. Word prosody in Finnish. Doctoral Dissertation, University of California, Santa Cruz.

Karvonen, Daniel. 2008. A three-way distinction in syllable weight: Evidence from Finnish. Paper presented at the 16th Manchester Phonology Meeting.

Katkov, Mikhail, Sandro Romani, and Misha Tsodyks. 2014. Word length effect in free recall of randomly assembled word lists. *Frontiers in Computational Neuroscience* 8.129.

Katz, Jonah. 2010. Compression effects, perceptual asymmetries, and the grammar of timing. Doctoral Dissertation, Massachusetts Institute of Technology.

Katz, Jonah. 2012. Compression effects in English. *Journal of Phonetics* 40.390–402.

Katz, Jonah, and Elisabeth Selkirk. 2011. Contrastive focus vs. discourse-new: Evidence from prosodic prominence in English. *Language* 87.771–816.

Kavitskaya, Darya. 2002. *Compensatory lengthening: Phonetics, phonology, diachrony*. London and New York: Routledge.

Keane, Elinor. 2001. *Echo words in Tamil*. Doctoral Dissertation, University of Oxford.

Keane, Elinor. 2003. Word-level prominence in Tamil. *Proceedings of the 15th International Congress of the Phonetic Sciences*, volume 2, 1257–1260.

Keane, Elinor. 2004. Illustrations of the IPA: Tamil. *Journal of the International Phonetic Association* 34.111–116.

Keane, Elinor. 2006. Prominence in Tamil. *Journal of the International Phonetic Association* 36.1–20.

Kelkar, Ashok R. 1968. *Studies in Hindi-Urdu I: Introduction to word phonology*. Deccan College.

Kelly, Michael. 2004. Word onset patterns and lexical stress in English. *Journal of Memory and Language* 50.231–244.

Kelly, Michael H. 1986. On the selection of linguistic options. Doctoral Dissertation, Cornell University.

Kelly, Michael H., and J. Kathryn Bock. 1988. Stress in time. *Journal of Experimental Psychology: Human Perception and Performance* 14.389–403.

Kelly, Michael H., J. Kathryn Bock, and Frank C. Keil. 1986. Prototypicality in a linguistic context: Effects on sentence structure. *Journal of Memory and Language* 25.59–74.

Kendall, Tyler, Joan Bresnan, and Gerard Van Herk. 2011. The dative alternation in African American English: Researching syntactic variation and change across sociolinguistic datasets. *Corpus Linguistics and Linguistic Theory* 7.229–244.

Kenstowicz, Michael. 1993. Peak prominence stress systems and Optimality Theory. *Proceedings of the 1st International Conference on Linguistics at Chosun University*. Kwangju, Korea: Choseun University Foreign Culture Research Institute.

Kenstowicz, Michael. 1994a. *Phonology in generative grammar*. Oxford: Blackwell Publishing.

Kenstowicz, Michael. 1994b. Sonority-driven stress. Rutgers Optimality Archive ROA-33.

Kenstowicz, Michael. 1996a. Base-identity and uniform exponence: Alternatives to cyclicity. *Current trends in phonology: Models and methods*, ed. by J. Durand and B Laks, 363–393. CNRS, Paris X, and the University of Salford: University of Salford Publications.

Kenstowicz, Michael. 1996b. Quality-sensitive stress. *Rivista di Linguistica* 9.157–187.

Kessler, Brett. 1998. Ambisyllabicity in the language of the Rigveda. MS, Stanford University.

Ketner, Katherine Heidel. 2006. Size restrictions in Prosodic Morphology. Doctoral Dissertation, University of Cambridge.

Khan, Geoffrey. 1987. Vowel length and syllable structure in the Tiberian tradition of Biblical Hebrew. *Journal of Semitic Studies* 32.23–82.

Kimball, Geoffrey. 1991. *Koasati grammar*. Lincoln: University of Nebraska Press.

Kimball, Geoffrey. 1994. *Koasati dictionary*. Lincoln: University of Nebraska Press.

Kimball, John P. 1973. Seven principles of surface structure parsing in natural language. *Cognition* 2.15–47.

Kimper, Wendell A. 2011. Competing triggers: Transparency and opacity in vowel harmony. Doctoral Dissertation, University of Massachusetts-Amherst.

Kiparsky, Paul. 1968. Metrics and morphophonemics in the Kalevala. *Studies presented to Roman Jakobson by his students*, ed. by Charles Gribble. Cambridge, MA: Slavica.

Kiparsky, Paul. 1977. The rhythmic structure of English verse. *Linguistic Inquiry* 8.189–248.

Kiparsky, Paul. 1979. Metrical structure assignment is cyclic. *Linguistic Inquiry* 10.421–441.

Kiparsky, Paul. 2000. Opacity and cyclicity. *The Linguistic Review* 17.351–367.

Kiparsky, Paul. 2006a. Amphichronic linguistics vs. evolutionary phonology. *Theoretical Linguistics* 32.217–236.

Kiparsky, Paul. 2006b. A modular metrics for folk verse. *Formal approaches to poetry*, ed. by B. Elan Dresher and Nila Friedberg, 7–49. Mouton.

Kiparsky, Paul. 2008. Universals constrain change, change results in typological generalizations. *Linguistic universals and language change*, ed. by Jeff Good, 23–53. Oxford: Oxford University Press.

Kiparsky, Paul. 2009. Verbal co-compounds and subcompounds in Greek. *MIT Working Papers in Linguistics* 57.

Kiparsky, Paul. 2010. Dvandvas, blocking, and the associative: The bumpy ride from phrase to word. *Language* 86.302–331.

Kiparsky, Paul. 2011. Compensatory lengthening. *Handbook of the syllable*, ed. by Charles Cairns and Eric Raimy, 33–70. Leiden: Brill.

Kiparsky, Paul. 2018. Indo-European origins of the Greek hexameter. *Language and meter*, ed. by Dieter Gunkel and Olav Hackstein, 77–128. Leiden: Brill.

Knight, W. F. Jackson. 1931. Homodyne in the fourth foot of the Vergilian hexameter. *The Classical Quarterly* 25.184–194.

Knight, W. F. Jackson. 1950. *Accentual symmetry in Vergil*. Oxford: Blackwell, 2nd edition.

Kolachina, Sudheer. 2016. Stress and vowel harmony in Telugu. Master's thesis, Massachusetts Institute of Technology.

Kotowski, Sven. 2016. *Adjectival modification and order restrictions: The influence of temporariness on prenominal word order*. Berlin and Boston: Walter de Gruyter.

Kotowski, Sven, and Holden Härtl. 2016. How real are adjective order constraints? Multiple prenominal adjectives at the grammatical interfaces. MS, Universität Kassel.

Koul, Omkar N. 2003. Kashmiri. *The Indo-Aryan languages*, ed. by Danesh Jain and George Cardona, 895–952. New York, NY: Routledge.

Kraehenmann, Astrid. 2001. Swiss German stops: Geminates all over the word. *Phonology* 18.109–145.

Kraehenmann, Astrid. 2003. *Quantity and prosodic asymmetries in Alemannic: Synchronic and diachronic perspectives*. Berlin: Mouton de Gruyter.

Kratzer, Angelika, and Elisabeth Selkirk. 2007. Phase theory and prosodic spellout: The case of verbs. *The Linguistic Review* 24.93–135.

Krisch, Thomas. 2009. On vowel quantity in the Rigvedic Auslaut. *Protolanguage and prehistory. Akten der XII. Fachtagung der Indogermanischen Gesellschaft, vom 11.–15. Oktober 2004 in Krakau*, ed. by Rosemarie Lühr and Sabine Ziegler, 255–270. Wiesbaden: Reichert-Verlag.

Krishnamurti, Bhadriraju. 2003. *The Dravidian languages*. Cambridge, UK: Cambridge University Press.

Kubozono, Haruo. 1999. Mora and syllable. *The handbook of Japanese linguistics*, ed. by Natsuko Tsujimura, 31–61. Oxford: Blackwell.

Kuiper, Franciscus Bernardus Jacobus. 1955. Shortening of final vowels in the Rigveda. *Mededelingen der Koninklijke Nederlandse Akademie van Wetenschappen, Nieuwe Reeks* 18. 253–289.

Kümmel, Martin. 2018. Silbenstruktur und Metrik: Neues zum Altavestischen. *Language and meter*, ed. by Dieter Gunkel and Olav Hackstein, 129–157. Leiden: Brill.

Kung, Susan Smythe. 2007. A descriptive grammar of Huehuetla Tepehua. Doctoral Dissertation, University of Texas, Austin.

Kurisu, Kazutaka. 2001. The phonology of morpheme realization. Doctoral Dissertation, University of California, Santa Cruz.

Kuznecova, A. N., E. A. Xelimskij, and E. V. Gruškina. 1980. *Očerki po sel'kupskomu jazyku.* Moscow: Izdatel'stvo Moskovskogo Universiteta.

de Lacy, Paul. 1997. Prosodic categorization. Available on Rutgers Optimality Archive, ROA-236, http://ruccs.rutgers.edu/roa.html.

de Lacy, Paul. 2002a. The formal expression of markedness. Doctoral Dissertation, University of Massachusetts-Amherst.

de Lacy, Paul. 2002b. The interaction of tone and stress in Optimality Theory. *Phonology* 19.1–32.

de Lacy, Paul. 2004. Markedness conflation in Optimality Theory. *Phonology* 21.145–199.

de Lacy, Paul. 2007. The interaction of tone, sonority, and prosodic structure. *The Cambridge handbook of phonology*, ed. by Paul de Lacy, 281–307. Cambridge University Press.

de Lacy, Paul. 2014. Evaluating evidence for stress systems. *Word stress: Theoretical and typological issues*, ed. by Harry van der Hulst, 149–193. Cambridge, UK: Cambridge University Press.

Ladd, D. Robert. 1984. Declination: A review and some hypotheses. *Phonology* 1.53–74.

Ladd, D. Robert. 1986. Intonational phrasing: The case for recursive prosodic structure. *Phonology* 3.311–340.

Ladd, D. Robert. 2008. *Intonational phonology.* Cambridge, UK: Cambridge University Press.

Ladefoged, Peter, and Ian Maddieson. 1996. *The sounds of the world's languages.* Blackwell Publishing.

Larson, Richard K. 1988. On the double object construction. *Linguistic Inquiry* 19.335–391.

Lehiste, Ilse. 1970. *Suprasegmentals.* Cambridge, MA: MIT Press.

Lehiste, Ilse. 1972. The timing of utterances and linguistic boundaries. *The Journal of the Acoustical Society of America* 51.2018–2024.

Lehmann, Thomas. 1994. *Grammatik des Alttamil unter besonderer Berücksichtigung der Cankam-Texte des Dichters Kapilar.* Stuttgart: Franz Steiner Verlag. Revision of 1992 Doctoral Dissertation, University of Heidelberg.

Leino, Pentti. 1994. The Kalevala Metre and its development. *Songs beyond the Kalevala: Transformations of oral poetry*, ed. by Anna-Leena Siikala and Sinikka Vakimo, 56–74. Helsinki: Suomalaisen Kirjallisuuden Seura (SKS).

Levelt, Willem, and Ben Maassen. 1981. Lexical search and order of mention in sentence production. *Crossing the boundaries in linguistics*, ed. by W. Klein and W. Levelt, 221–252. Dordrecht: Reidel.

Levin, Juliette. 1985. A metrical theory of syllabicity. Doctoral Dissertation, Massachusetts Institute of Technology.

Levy, Roger. Forthcoming. *Probabilistic models in the study of language.* Cambridge, MA: MIT Press.

Liberman, Mark. 1975. The intonational system of English. Doctoral Dissertation, Massachusetts Institute of Technology.

Liberman, Mark, and Alan Prince. 1977. On stress and linguistic rhythm. *Linguistic Inquiry* 8.249–336.

Lindblom, Björn. 1968. Temporal organization of syllable production. *Speech transmission laboratory quarterly progress*, volume 2–3, 1–6. Stockholm, Sweden: Royal Institute of Technology.

Lindblom, Björn, and Karin Rapp. 1973. *Some temporal regularities of spoken Swedish.* Stockholm: Institute of Linguistics.

Lohmann, Arne. 2012. A processing view on order in reversible and irreversible binomials. *Views: Vienna English Working Papers.* 25–50.

Lohmann, Arne, and Tayo Takada. 2014. Order in NP conjuncts in spoken English and Japanese. *Lingua* 152.48–64.

Lohse, Barbara, John Hawkins, and Thomas Wasow. 2004. Processing domains in English verb-particle constructions. *Language* 80.238–261.

Lönnrot, Elias. 1849. *Kalevala taikka vanhoja Karjalan runoja Suomen kansan muinoisista ajoista.* Helsinki: Suomalaisen Kirjallisuuden Seura.

Loos, Eugene Emil. 1967. *The phonology of Capanahua and its grammatical basis.* Norman: Summer Institute of Linguistics of the University of Oklahoma.

Loporcaro, Michele. 1991. Compensatory lengthening in Romanesco. *Certamen phonologicum II: Papers from the 1990 Cortona Phonology Meeting,* ed. by Pier Marco Bertinetto, Michael Kenstowicz, and Michele Loporcaro, 279–307. Turin: Rosenberg and Sellier.

Lunden, Anya. 2006. Weight, final lengthening and stress: A phonetic and phonological case study of Norwegian. Doctoral Dissertation, University of California, Santa Cruz.

Lunden, Anya. 2010. *A phonetically-motivated phonological analysis of syllable weight and stress in the Norwegian language.* New York, NY: Edwin Mellen Press.

Lunden, Anya. 2013. Reanalyzing final consonant extrametricality: A proportional theory of weight. *Journal of Comparative Germanic Linguistics* 16.1–31.

Maas, Paul. 1962. *Greek metre.* Oxford University Press.

MacDonald, Jonathan E. 2015. A movement analysis of some double object constructions. *Proceedings of the 32nd West Coast Conference on Formal Linguistics,* ed. by Ulrike Steindl, Thomas Borer, Huilin Fang, Alfredo García Pardo, Peter Guekguezian, Brian Hsu, Charlie O'Hara, and Iris Chuoying Ouyang, 276–285. Somerville, MA: Cascadilla Proceedings Project.

Macdonell, Arthur Anthony. 1910. *Vedic grammar.* Strassburg: Trübner.

MacKenzie, Laurel. 2012. Location variation above the phonology. Doctoral Dissertation, University of Pennsylvania.

Maddieson, Ian. 1985. Phonetic cues to syllabification. *Phonetic linguistic essay in honor of Peter Ladefoged,* ed. by Victoria Fromkin, 203–221. New York: Academic Press.

Mai, Anna. 2018. Phonetic effects of onset complexity on the English syllable. MS, UC San Diego, submitted.

Malkiel, Yakov. 1959. Studies in irreversible binomials. *Lingua* 8.113–160.

Marchand, Hans. 1952. Alliteration, Ablaut und Reim in den Türkischen Zwillingsformen. *Oriens* 5.60–69.

Marchand, Hans. 1969. *The categories and types of present-day English word-formation.* Wiesbaden, Germany: Harrossowitz.

de Marneffe, Marie-Catherine, Scott Grimm, Inbal Arnon, Susannah Kirby, and Joan Bresnan. 2012. A statistical model of the grammatical choices in child production of dative sentences. *Language and Cognitive Processes* 27.25–61.

Matthews, Stephen J., and L. Y. Y. Yeung. 2000. Processing motivations for topicalization in Cantonese. *Cognitive-functional linguistics in an East Asian context,* ed. by Kaoru Horie and Shigeru Sato, 81–102. Tokyo: Kurosio Publishers.

McCarthy, John J. 1979a. Formal problems in Semitic phonology and morphology. Doctoral Dissertation, MIT.

McCarthy, John J. 1979b. On stress and syllabification. *Linguistic Inquiry* 10.443–465.

McCarthy, John J. 1981. Stress, pretonic lengthening, and syllabification in Tiberian Hebrew. *MIT Working Papers in Linguistics* 3.73–100.

McCarthy, John J. 2002. *A thematic guide to Optimality Theory.* Cambridge. UK: Cambridge University Press.

McCarthy, John J. 2003. OT constraints are categorical. *Phonology* 20.75–138.

McCarthy, John J. 2005. Optimal paradigms. *Paradigms in phonological theory*, ed. by Laura Downing, T. A. Hall, and Renate Raffelsiefen, 170–210. Oxford University Press.

McCarthy, John J. 2007. *Hidden generalizations: Phonological opacity in Optimality Theory.* London: Equinox Press.

McCarthy, John J. 2008. The gradual path to cluster simplification. *Phonology* 25. 271–319.

McCarthy, John J. 2009. Harmony in Harmonic Serialism. *Linguistics Department Faculty Publication Series* 41.1–52.

McCarthy, John J. 2010. An introduction to harmonic serialism. *Language and Linguistics Compass* 4.1001–1018.

McCarthy, John J. 2011. *Doing Optimality Theory: Applying theory to data.* Malden, MA: John Wiley & Sons.

McCarthy, John J., and Alan Prince. 1986. Prosodic morphology I. MS, University of Massachusetts at Amherst and Brandeis University.

McCarthy, John J., and Alan Prince. 1993. Generalized alignment. *Yearbook of morphology*, ed. by Geert Booij and Jaap van Marle, volume 1993, 79–153. Dordrecht: Kluwer.

McCarthy, John J., and Alan Prince. 1995. Faithfulness and reduplicative identity. *Papers in Optimality Theory*, ed. by Jill Beckman, Laura Walsh Dickey, and Suzanne Urbanczyk, volume 18 of *University of Massachusetts Occasional Papers in Linguistics*, 249–384. University of Massachusetts, Amherst: Graduate Linguistics Student Association.

McCawley, James D. 1965. The accentual system of Standard Japanese. Doctoral Dissertation, Massachusetts Institute of Technology.

McCawley, James D. 1968. *The phonological component of a grammar of Japanese.* The Hague and Paris: Mouton.

McDonald, Janet L., Kathryn Bock, and Michael H. Kelly. 1993. Word and world order: Semantic, phonological, and metrical determinants of serial position. *Cognitive Psychology* 25.188–230.

McDonough, Joyce, and Keith Johnson. 1997. Tamil liquids: An investigation into the basis of the contrast among five liquids in a dialect of Tamil. *Journal of the International Phonetic Association* 27.1–26.

McGarrity, Laura W. 2003. Constraints on patterns of primary and secondary stress. Doctoral Dissertation, Indiana University.

McIntosh, Mary. 1984. *Fulfulde syntax and verbal morphology.* London: Routledge & Kegan Paul.

McLaughlin, Fiona, and Caroline R. Wiltshire. 2017. Syllable weight in the phonology of Pulaar. *Syllable weight in African languages*, ed. by Paul Newman, 161–176. Amsterdam: John Benjamins Publishing Company.

McPherson, Laura, and Bruce Hayes. 2016. Relating application frequency to morphological structure: The case of Tommo So vowel harmony. *Phonology* 33.125–167.

Meira, Sergio. 1998. Rhythmic stress in Tiriyó (Cariban). *International Journal of American Linguistics* 64.352–378.

Mester, Armin. 1994. The quantitative trochee in Latin. *Natural Language and Linguistic Theory* 12.1–61.

Michael, Lev. 2004. Between grammar and poetry: The structure of Nanti Karintaa chants. *Texas Linguistic Forum* 47.251–262.

Michel, Jean-Baptiste, Yuan Kui Shen, Aviva Presser Aiden, Adrian Veres, Matthew K. Gray, William Brockman, The Google Books Team, Joseph P. Pickett, Dale Hoiberg, Dan Clancy, Peter Norvig, Jon Orwant, Steven Pinker, Martin A. Nowak, and Erez Lierberman Aiden. 2011. Quantitative analysis of culture using millions of digitized books. *Science* 331.176–182.

Minkova, Donka. 2002. Ablaut reduplication in English: The criss-crossing of prosody and verbal art. *English Language and Linguistics* 6.133–169.

Mohanan, K. P. 1986. *The theory of Lexical Phonology*. Dordrecht: Reidel.

Mohanan, Tara. 1989. Syllable structure in Malayalam. *Linguistic Inquiry* 20.589–625.

Mollin, Sandra. 2012. Revisiting binomial order in English: Ordering constraints and reversibility. *English Language and Linguistics* 16.81–103.

Mollin, Sandra. 2013. Pathways of change in the diachronic development of binomial reversibility in Late Modern American English. *Journal of English Linguistics* 41.168–203.

Moore-Cantwell, Claire. 2016. *The representation of probabilistic phonological patterns: Neurological, behavioral, and computational evidence from the English stress system*. Doctoral Dissertation, University of Massachusetts-Amherst.

Morén, Bruce T. 1997. Markedness and faithfulness constraints on the association of moras: The dependency between vowel length and consonant weight. Master's thesis, University of Maryland, College Park.

Morén, Bruce T. 1999. Distinctiveness, coercion, and sonority. Doctoral Dissertation, University of Maryland, College Park.

Morén, Bruce T. 2000. The puzzle of Kashmiri stress: Implications for weight theory. *Phonology* 17.365–396.

Morén, Bruce T. 2001. *Distinctiveness, coercion and sonority: A unified theory of weight*. London: Routledge.

Morgan, Emily, and Roger Levy. 2016. Abstract knowledge versus direct experience in processing of binomial expressions. *Cognition* 157.384–402.

Mori, Yoko. 2002. Lengthening of Japanese monomoraic nouns. *Journal of Phonetics* 30.689–708.

Mortensen, David. 2006. Logical and substantive scales in phonology. Doctoral Dissertation, University of California, Berkeley.

Morton, John, Steve Marcus, and Clive Frankish. 1976. Perceptual centers (P-centers). *Psychological Review* 83.405–408.

Mudzingwa, Calisto. 2010. Shona morphophonemics: Repair strategies in Karanga and Zezuru. Doctoral Dissertation, University of British Columbia.

Müller, Gereon. 1997. Beschrankungen für Binomialbildungen im Deutschen. *Zeitschrift für Sprachwissenschaft* 16.5–51.

Muller, Jennifer. 1999. A unified mora account of Chuukese. *WCCFL* 18.393–405.

Muller, Jennifer. 2001. The phonology and phonetics of word-initial geminates. Doctoral Dissertation, The Ohio State University.

Munn, Alan. 1993. Topics in the syntax and semantics of coordinate structures. Doctoral Dissertation, University of Maryland.

Munro, Pamela. 1996. The Chickasaw sound system. MS, University of California, Los Angeles.

Munro, Pamela, and Charles Ulrich. 1984. Structure-preservation and Western Muskogean rhythmic lengthening. *West Coast Conference on Formal Linguistics* 3.191–202.

Munshi, Sadaf. 2012. The metrical structure of Kashmiri Vanivun. *Ars Metrica* 5.1–36.

Munshi, Sadaf, and Megan J. Crowhurst. 2012. Weight sensitivity and syllable codas in Srinagar Koshur. *Journal of Linguistics* 48.427–472.

Mürk, Harry W. 1991. The structure and development of Estonian morphology. Doctoral Dissertation, Indiana University.

Murray, Robert W., and Theo Vennemann. 1983. Sound change and syllable structure in Germanic phonology. *Language* 59.514–528.

Murugan, V. 2000. *Tolkappiyam in English*. Chennai, India: Institute of Asian Studies.

Myers, Scott. 1987. Vowel shortening in English. *Natural Language and Linguistic Theory* 5.485–518.

Nagarajan, H. 1995. Gemination of stops in Tamil: Implications for the phonology-syntax interface. *UCL Working Papers in Linguistics* 7.495–509.

Nanni, Debbie. 1977. Stressing words in -ative. *Linguistic Inquiry* 8.752–763.

Narayanan, Shrikanth, Dani Byrd, and Abigail Kaun. 1999. Geometry, kinematics, and acoustics of Tamil liquid consonants. *Journal of the Acoustical Society of America* 106.1993–2007.

Nazarov, Aleksei, and Joe Pater. 2017. Learning opacity in Stratal Maximum Entropy Grammar. *Phonology* 34.299–324.

Neilsen, Konrad. 1926. *Lærebok i Lappisk. 3 vols.* Oslo: Brøggers.

Nespor, Marina, and Irene Vogel. 1986. *Prosodic phonology*. Dordrecht: Foris.

Nespor, Marina, and Irene Vogel. 2007. *Prosodic phonology: With a new foreword*. Berlin: Mouton de Gruyter.

Nevins, Andrew, and Keith Plaster. 2008. Review of Paul de Lacy, Markedness: reduction and preservation in phonology. *Journal of Linguistics* 44.770–781.

Nevins, Andrew, and Bert Vaux. 2003. Metalinguistic, shmetalinguistic: The phonology of shm-reduplication. *Proceedings of the Chicago Linguistic Society* 39.702–721.

Newcomer, Charles B. 1908. The effect of enclitics on the accent of words in Latin. *The Classical Journal* 3.150–153.

Niang, Mamadou Ousmane. 1995. Syllable 'sonority' hierarchy and Pulaar stress: A metrical approach. *Kansas Working Papers in Linguistics* 20.53–68.

Niang, Mamadou Ousmane. 1997. *Constraints on Pulaar phonology*. Lanham, Maryland: University Press of America.

Niklas, Ulrike. 1988. *Introduction to Tamil prosody*. Bulletin de l'Ecole française d'Extrême-Orient 77.

Oakeshott-Taylor, John. 1984. Phonetic factors in word order. *Phonetica* 41.226–237.

O'Connor, Ellen. 2010. A stringent analysis of Peak Prominence in quantity sensitive stress systems. MS, University of Southern California.

Oden, Gregg C., and Lola L. Lopes. 1981. Preference for order in freezes. *Linguistic Inquiry* 12.673–679.

Ohala, Manjari. 1983. *Aspects of Hindi phonology*. Delhi: Motilal Banarsidass.

Oldenberg, Hermann. 1888. *Die Hymnen des Ṛgveda I: Metrische und textgeschichtliche Prolegomena*. Berlin: Hertz.

Oldenberg, Hermann. 1906. Vedische Untersuchungen. 15. Der vedische Quantitätswechsel auslautender Vokale und Verwandtes. *Zeitschrift der Deutschen Morgenländischen Gesellschaft* 60.115–164.

Olejarczuk, Paul, and Vsevolod Kapatsinski. 2016. The metrical parse is coarse-grained: Phonotactic generalizations in stress assignment. MS, University of Oregon, submitted.

Oliphant, Samuel Grant. 1912. The Vedic dual: Part VI, the elliptic dual; part VII, the dual dvandva. *Journal of the American Oriental Society* 32.33–57.

Ollett, Andrew. 2012. Moraic feet in Prakrit metrics: A constraint-based approach. *Transactions of the Philological Society* 110.241–282.

van Oostendorp, Marc. 2000. *Phonological projection: A theory of feature content and prosodic structure*. Berlin: Mouton de Gruyter.

Ọla Orie, Ọlanikẹ, and Douglas Pulleyblank. 2002. Yoruba vowel elision: Minimality effects. *Natural Language and Linguistic Theory* 20.101–156.

Parker, Steve. 1998. Disjoint metrical tiers and positional markedness in Huariapano. MS, University of Massachusetts, Amherst.

Parker, Steve. 2002. Quantifying the sonority hierarchy. Doctoral Dissertation, University of Massachusetts, Amherst.

Parker, Steve, ed. by. 2012. *The sonority controversy*, volume 18 of *Phonology and Phonetics*. Berlin and Boston: De Gruyter Mouton.

Parthasarathy, R. 1992. *The tale of an anklet: An epic of South India*. New York: Columbia University Press.

Pater, Joe. 2009. Weighted constraints in generative linguistics. *Cognitive Science* 33.999–1035.

Payne, David, and Furne Rich. 1988. Sensitivity to onset in Arabela stress. MS, Información de Campo 743. Yarinacocha, Pucallpa, Perú: Instituto Lingüístico de Verano.

Peperkamp, Sharon. 1997. Prosodic words. Doctoral Dissertation, University of Amsterdam. Published as HIL Dissertations 34, The Hague, Academic Graphics.

Pharr, Clyde. 1964. *Vergil's Aeneid books I-VI: Revised edition*. Lexington, Massachusetts: D. C. Heath and Company.

Pingali, Sailaja. 1985. Some aspects of the vowel phonology of Telugu and Telugu-English. Doctoral Dissertation, Central Institute of English and Foreign Languages, Hyderabad.

Pinker, Steven, and David Birdsong. 1979. Speakers' sensitivity to rules of frozen word order. *Journal of Verbal Learning and Verbal Behavior* 18.497–508.

Pipping, Hugo. 1903. *Bidrag till eddametriken*, volume 50 of *Skrifter utgifna af svenska litteratursällskapet i Finnland*. Helsingfors: Tidnings- & Tryckeri-Aktiebolagets Tryckeri.

Pitt, Mark, Laura Dilley, Keith Johnson, Scott Kiesling, William Raymond, Elizabeth Hume, and Eric Fosler-Lussier. 2007. Buckeye Corpus of Conversational Speech (2nd release). [www.buckeyecorpus.osu.edu]. Columbus, OH: Department of Psychology, Ohio State University.

Pittayaporn, Pittayawat, and Jakrabhop Iamdanush. 2014. Metrical stress in Pattani Malay. Paper presented at the 24th Annual Meeting of the Southeast Asian Linguistics Society, Yangon, Myanmar.

Plank, Frans. 2005. The prosodic contribution of clitics: Focus on Latin. *Lingue e Linguaggio* 4.281–292.

Podesva, Robert J. 2002. Segmental constraints on geminates and their implications for typology. Paper presented at the Annual Meeting of the Linguistic Society of America.

Pordany, Laszlo. 1986. A comparison of some English and Hungarian freezes. *Papers and Studies in Contrastive Linguistics* 21.117–125.

Port, Robert. 1981. Linguistics timing factors in combination. *Journal of the Acoustical Society of America* 69.262–274.

Port, Robert. 2007. The problem of speech patterns in time. *The Oxford handbook of psycholinguistics*, ed. by M. Gareth Gaskell, 503–514. Oxford: Oxford University Press.

Prince, Alan. 1975. The phonology and morphology of Tiberian Hebrew. Doctoral Dissertation, Massachusetts Institute of Technology.

Prince, Alan. 1980. A metrical theory of Estonian quantity. *Linguistic Inquiry* 11.

Prince, Alan. 1983. Relating to the grid. *Linguistic Inquiry* 14.19–100.

Prince, Alan. 1989. Metrical forms. *Rhythm and meter*, ed. by Paul Kiparsky and Gilbert Youmans, volume 1 of *Phonetics and Phonology*, 45–81. San Diego, CA: Academic Press.

Prince, Alan. 1990. Quantitative consequences of rhythmic organization. *CLS: Papers from the parasession on the syllable in phonetics and phonology*, ed. by Karen Deaton, Manuela Noske, and Michael Ziolkowski, volume 26, 355–398. Chicago: Chicago Linguistic Society.

Prince, Alan. 1999. Paninian relations. Handout, University of Marburg.

Prince, Alan, and Paul Smolensky. 1993/2004. *Optimality Theory: Constraint interaction in Generative Grammar*. Malden, MA: Blackwell. Technical Report, Rutgers University and University of Colorado at Boulder, 1993. Revised version Blackwell, 2004.

Probert, Philomen. 2002. On the prosody of Latin enclitics. *Oxford University Working Papers in Linguistics, Philology and Phonetics*, ed. by A. Hartmann, I. J. an Willi, volume vii, 181–206. Oxford: Oxford University, Centre for Linguistics, Philology and Phonetics.

Prokosch, Eduard. 1939. *A comparative Germanic grammar*. Baltimore: Linguistic Society of America.

Prunet, Jean-François, and Christine Tellier. 1984. Interaction des niveaux en phonologie: L'abrègement vocalique en pulaar. *McGill Working Papers in Linguistics* 2.65–90.

Quirk, Randolph, Sidney Greenbaum, Geoffrey Leech, and Jan Svartvik. 1972. *A grammar of Contemporary English*. London: Longman.

Quirk, Randolph, Sidney Greenbaum, Geoffrey Leech, Jan Svartvik, and David Crystal. 1985. *A comprehensive grammar of the English language*. London: Longman.

Radford, Robert S. 1903. The Latin monosyllables in their relation to accent and quantity. A study in the verse of Terence. *Transactions and Proceedings of the American Philological Association* 34.60–103.

Rajam, V. S. 1992. *A reference grammar of classical Tamil poetry*. Philadelphia, PA: American Philosophical Society.

Rasekh-Mahand, Mohammad, Mojtaba Alizadeh-Sahraie, and Raheleh Izadifar. 2016. A corpus-based analysis of relative clause extraposition in Persian. *Ampersand* 3.21–31.

Raven, D. S. 1962. *Greek metre*. London: Faber and Faber.

Raven, D.Š. 1965. *Latin metre: An introduction*. London: Faber and Faber.

Riad, Tomas. 1992. Structures in Germanic prosody: A diachronic study with special reference to Nordic languages. Doctoral Dissertation, Stockholm University.

Rice, Curt. 1992. Binarity and ternarity in metrical theory: Parametric extensions. Doctoral Dissertation, University of Texas, Austin.

Rice, Curt. 2006. Norwegian stress and quantity: Implications of loanwords. *Lingua* 116.1171–1194.

Rickford, John, Thomas Wasow, Norma Mendoza-Denton, and Juli Espinoza. 1995. Syntactic variation and change in progress: Loss of the verbal coda in topic-restricting as far as constructions. *Language* 71.102–131.

Ridouane, Rachid. 2010. Geminates at the junction of phonetics and phonology. *Laboratory Phonology* 10.61–90.

Rijkhoff, Jan. 2002. *The noun phrase.* Oxford: Oxford University Press.

Ringen, Catherine, and Robert M. Vago. 2011. Geminates: Heavy or long? *Handbook of the syllable*, ed. by Charles Cairns and Eric Raimy, 155–170. Leiden: Brill.

Roberts, John R. 1987. *Amele.* New York: Croom Helm.

Rosenbach, Anette. 2002. *Genitive variation in English: Conceptual factors in synchronic and diachronic studies.* Berlin and New York: Mouton de Gruyter.

Rosenbach, Anette. 2005. Animacy versus weight as determinants of grammatical variation in English. *Language* 81.613–644.

Rosenthall, Sam, and Harry van der Hulst. 1999. Weight-by-position by position. *Natural Language and Linguistic Theory* 17.499–540.

Ross, David. 2007. *Virgil's Aeneid: A reader's guide.* Malden, MA: Blackwell Publishing.

Ross, John Robert. 1967. Constraints on variables in syntax. Doctoral Dissertation, Massachusetts Institute of Technology.

Ross, John Robert. 1982. The sound of meaning. *Linguistics in the morning calm*, ed. by The Linguistic Society of Korea, 275–290. Seoul: Hanshin Publishing Co.

Ross, John Robert. 1986. *Infinite syntax.* Norwood, NJ: Ablex.

Rothstein-Dowden, Zachary. 2018. Syntax, phonology and verbal raising in the R̥gveda. MS, Harvard University.

Rubach, Jerzy. 1996. Shortening and ambisyllabicity in English. *Phonology* 13.197–237.

Ryan, Kevin M. 2007. Two dimensions of correspondence in half-rhyme. Paper presented at Poetics Fest II, University of California, Santa Cruz.

Ryan, Kevin M. 2010. Variable affix order: Grammar and learning. *Language* 86.758–791.

Ryan, Kevin M. 2011a. Gradient syllable weight and weight universals in quantitative metrics. *Phonology* 28.413–454.

Ryan, Kevin M. 2011b. *Gradient weight in phonology.* Doctoral Dissertation, University of California, Los Angeles.

Ryan, Kevin M. 2013a. Against final indifference. Slides, M@90: Metrical Structure: Meter, Text-Setting, and Stress, MIT.

Ryan, Kevin M. 2013b. Contextual and non-contextual prosodic minimality. *NELS 41: Proceedings of the 41st Meeting of the North Eastern Linguistics Society*, ed. by Lena Fainleib, Nicholas LaCara, and Yangsook Park, 165–178. University of Massachusetts, Amherst: GLSA Publications.

Ryan, Kevin M. 2014. Onsets contribute to syllable weight: Statistical evidence from stress and meter. *Language* 90.309–341.

Ryan, Kevin M. 2016. Phonological weight. *Language and Linguistics Compass* 10.720–733.

Ryan, Kevin M. 2017a. Attenuated spreading in Sanskrit retroflex harmony. *Linguistic Inquiry* 48.299–340.

Ryan, Kevin M. 2017b. The stress–weight interface in meter. *Phonology* 34.581–613.

Ryan, Kevin M. 2018. Prosodic end-weight reflects phrasal stress. To appear in *Natural Language & Linguistic Theory*.

Sadeniemi, Matti. 1951. *Die Metrik des Kalevala-Verses*. Helsinki: Folklore Fellows Communications.

Samek-Lodovici, Vieri. 2005. Prosody-syntax interaction in the expression of focus. *Natural Language and Linguistic Theory* 23.687–755.

Sande, Hannah. 2014. Amharic infixing reduplication targets heavy syllables. *UC Berkeley Phonology Lab Annual Report*. 182–208.

Sande, Hannah, and Andrew Hedding. 2017. Syllable weight in Amharic. *Syllable weight in African languages*, ed. by Paul Newman, 69–82. Amsterdam: John Benjamins.

Sankoff, Gillian. 1980. *The social life of language*. Philadelphia: University of Pennsylvania Press.

Sapir, Edward, and Victor Golla. 2001. Hupa texts, with notes and lexicon. *Northwest California linguistics [The collected works of Edward Sapir XIV]*, ed. by Victor Golla and Sean O'Neill, 19–1011. New York: Mouton.

Sapir, Edward, and Morris Swadesh. 1960. *Yana dictionary*. Berkeley, CA: University of California Publications in Linguistics 22.

Schiffman, Harold F. 1999. *A reference grammar of spoken Tamil*. Cambridge, UK: Cambridge University Press.

Schlie, Perry, and Ginny Schlie. 1993. A Kara phonology. *Phonologies of Austronesian languages* 2, ed. by John M. Clifton, 99–130. Ukarumpa, Papua New Guinea: Summer Institute of Linguistics.

Schlüter, Julia. 2005. *Rhythmic grammar: The influence of rhythm on grammatical variation and change in English*. Berlin and New York: Mouton de Gruyter.

Schneider, Cynthia. 2010. *A grammar of Abma: A language of the Pentecost Island, Vanuatu*. Canberra: Pacific Linguistics.

Seiler, Hansjakob. 1965. Accent and morphophonemics in Cahuilla and Uto-Aztecan. *International Journal of American Linguistics* 31.50–59.

Seiler, Hansjakob. 1977. *Cahuilla grammar*. Banning, CA: Malki Museum Press.

Selkirk, Elisabeth O. 1982. The syllable. *The structure of phonological representations, part II*, ed. by Harry van der Hulst and Norval Smith, 337–384. Dordrecht: Foris.

Selkirk, Elisabeth O. 1984. *Phonology and syntax: The relationship between sound and structure*. Massachusetts Institute of Technology Press.

Selkirk, Elisabeth O. 1990. A two-root theory of length. *University of Massachusetts Occasional Papers in Linguistics*.

Selkirk, Elisabeth O. 1995. Sentence prosody: Intonation, stress, and phrasing. *The handbook of phonological theory*, ed. by John A. Goldsmith, 550–569. Oxford: Blackwell Publishing.

Selkirk, Elisabeth O. 2011. The syntax-phonology interface. *The handbook of phonological theory, 2nd edition*, ed. by John Goldsmith, Jason Riggle, and Alan C. L, Yu, 435–484. Oxford: Blackwell Publishing.

Shaw, Patricia A. 1985. Coexistent and competing stress rules in Stoney (Dakota). *International Journal of American Linguistics* 51.1–18.

Shelton, Michael. 2007. An experimental approach to syllable weight and stress in Spanish. Doctoral Dissertation, The Pennsylvania State University.

Sherer, Tim. 1994. Prosodic phonotactics. Doctoral Dissertation, University of Massachusetts-Amherst.

Shih, Shu-Hao. 2016. Sonority-driven stress does not exist. *Proceedings of the Annual Meeting on Phonology (2015)* 1–11.

Shih, Shu-Hao. 2017. On the existence of sonority-driven stress: Gujarati. *Phonology* 35.327–364.

Shih, Stephanie. 2013. Random forests, for model (and predictor) selection. Handout, Stanford University and UCLA.

Shih, Stephanie. 2014. Towards optimal rhythm. Doctoral Dissertation, Stanford University.

Shih, Stephanie, and Jason Grafmiller. 2013. Weighing in on end weight. Paper presented at the LSA 85th Annual Meeting, 6–9 January 2011, Pittsburgh, PA.

Shih, Stephanie, Jason Grafmiller, Richard Futrell, and Joan Bresnan. 2015. Rhythm's role in genitive construction choice in spoken English. *Rhythm in cognition and grammar*, ed. by Ralf Vogel and Ruben van de Vijver, 207–34. Berlin: De Gruyter Mouton.

Shih, Stephanie, and Kie Zuraw. 2016. Phonological conditions on variable adjective-noun word order in Tagalog. MS, submitted, UC Merced and UCLA, available at ling.auf.net/lingbuzz/002796.

Shih, Stephanie S. 2016. Phonological influences in syntactic alternations. *The morphosyntax-phonology connection: Locality and directionality at the interfaces*, ed. by Vera Gribanova and Stephanie S. Shih, 223–254. Oxford: Oxford University Press.

Shinohara, Shigeko, and Masako Fujimoto. 2011. Moraicity of initial geminates in the Tedumuni dialect of Okinawan. *Proceedings of ICPhS* 17.1826–1829.

Silagadze, Apollon. 2009. Problem of the qualification of Georgian verse. *Bulletin of the Georgian National Academy of Sciences* 3.190–197.

Sitapati, G. V. 1936. Accent in Telugu speech and verse. *Journal of Indian Linguistics* 6.201–245.

Southern, Mark R. V. 2005. *Contagious couplings: Transmission of expressives in Yiddish echo phrases*. Westport, CT: Greenwood Publishing Group.

Spahr, Christopher. 2011. Dialectal gemination in Finnish: Phonetics/phonology interplay in moraic theory. Master's thesis, University of Toronto.

Sprouse, Jon. 2011. A validation of Amazon Mechanical Turk for the collection of acceptability judgments in linguistic theory. *Behavior Research Methods* 43.155–167.

Stallings, Lynne M., and Maryellen C. MacDonald. 2011. It's not just the "heavy NP": Relative phrase length modulates the production of heavy-NP shift. *Journal of Psycholinguistic Research* 40.177–187.

Steedman, Mark. 2000. Information structure and the syntax-phonology interface. *Linguistic Inquiry* 31.649–689.

Steriade, Donca. 1982. Greek prosodies and the nature of syllabification. Doctoral Dissertation, Massachusetts Institute of Technology.

Steriade, Donca. 1991. Moras and other slots. *Proceedings of the Formal Linguistics Society of Midamerica*, volume 1, 254–280.

Steriade, Donca. 1999. Alternatives to the syllabic interpretation of consonantal phonotactics. *Proceedings of the 1998 Linguistics and Phonetics Conference*, ed. by O. Fujimura, B. Joseph, and B. Palek, 205–242. Prague: The Karolinum Press.

Steriade, Donca. 2000. Paradigm uniformity and the phonetics-phonology boundary. *Papers in laboratory phonology V: Acquisition and the lexicon*, ed. by M. B. Broe and J. B. Pierrehumbert, 313–334. Cambridge, UK: Cambridge University Press.

Steriade, Donca. 2008. Resyllabification in the quantitative meters of Ancient Greek: Evidence for an Interval Theory of Weight. MS, MIT.

Steriade, Donca. 2009. The phonology of perceptibility effects: The P-map and its consequences for constraint organization. *The nature of the word: essays in honor of Paul Kiparsky*, ed. by Kristin Hanson and Sharon Inkelas. Cambridge, MA: MIT Press.

Steriade, Donca. 2011. Rhyming evidence for intervals. Colloquium presentation at the UCLA Department of Linguistics, March 4.

Steriade, Donca. 2012. Invervals vs. syllables as units of linguistic rhythm. Handouts, EALING, Paris.

Strobl, Carolin, James Malley, and Gerhard Tutz. 2009. An introduction to recursive partitioning: Rationale, application, and characteristics of classification and regression trees, bagging, and random forests. *Psychological Methods* 14.323–348.

Sturtevant, Edgar H. 1919. The coincidence of accent and ictus in the Roman dactylic poets. *Classical Philology* 14.373–385.

Sturtevant, Edgar H. 1923a. Harmony and clash of accent and ictus in the Latin hexameter. *Transactions of the American Philological Association* 54.51–73.

Sturtevant, Edgar H. 1923b. The ictus of classical verse. *The American Journal of Philology* 44.319–338.

Swadesh, Morris. 1962. Archaic doublets in Altaic. *American studies in Altaic linguistics*, ed. by Nicholas Poppe, volume 13 of *Uralic and Altaic Series*, 293–330. Bloomington, IN: Indiana University Publications.

Szendroi, Kriszta. 2001. Focus and the syntax-phonology interface. Doctoral Dissertation, University College London.

Szmrecsányi, Benedikt M. 2004. On operationalizing syntactic complexity. *Journées internationales d'Analyse statistique des Données Textuelles (JADT-04)* 2.1032–1039.

Tagliamonte, Sali A., and R. Harald Baayen. 2012. Models, forests, and trees of York English: Was/were variation as a case study for statistical practice. *Language Variation and Change* 24.135–178.

Taglicht, Josef. 1998. Constraints on intonational phrasing in English. *Linguistics* 34.181–211.

Takagi, N., and V. Mann. 1994. A perceptual basis for the systematic phonological correspondences between Japanese loan words and their English source words. *Journal of Phonetics* 22.343–356.

Taylor, Frank William. 1953. *A grammar of the Adamawa dialect of the Fulani language (Fulfulde) (2nd edition)*. Oxford: Clarendon Press.

Temperley, David. 2007. Minimization of dependency length in written English. *Cognition* 105.300–333.

Thinnappan, S. P. 1976. Alapetai in Tamil. *Dravidian linguistics*, ed. by S. Agesthialingom and P. S. Subrahmanyam, volume 5, 539–560. Annamalai, India: Annamalai University Press.

Thornton, Anna M. 1996. On some phenomena of prosodic morphology in Italian: Accorciamenti, hypocoristics, and prosodic delimitation. *Probus* 8.81–112.

Thuilier, Juliette. 2012. *Contraintes préférentielles et ordre des mots en français*. Doctoral Dissertation, Université Paris Diderot.

Thun, Nils. 1963. *Reduplicative words in English*. Lund, Sweden: Carl Bloms Boktryckeri.

Tily, Harry Joel. 2010. The role of processing complexity in word order variation and change. Doctoral Dissertation, Stanford University.

Topintzi, Nina. 2005. Onset weight in Arabela and Bella Coola. Paper presented at the 13th Manchester Phonology Meeting, Manchester, UK, 26–28 May 2005.

Topintzi, Nina. 2008. On the existence of moraic onset geminates. *Natural Language and Linguistic Theory* 26.147–184.

Topintzi, Nina. 2010. *Onsets: suprasegmental and prosodic behaviour*. Cambridge, UK: Cambridge University Press.

Topintzi, Nina, and Stuart Davis. 2017. On the weight of edge geminates. *The phonetics and phonology of geminate consonants*, ed. by Haruo Kubozono, 260–282. Oxford: Oxford University Press.

Topintzi, Nina, and Eva Zimmermann. 2014. As alive as ever: The geminate debate under Containment. *Topics at InfL*, ed. by A. Assmann, S. Bank, D. Georgi, T. Klein, P. Weisser, and E. Zimmermann, volume 92, 65–90. Leipzig: Linguistische Arbeits Berichte, Universität Leipzig.

Tranel, Bernard. 1991. CVC light syllables, geminates and Moraic Theory. *Phonology* 8.291–302.

Tranel, Bernard, and Francesca Del Gobbo. 2002. Local conjunction in Italian and French phonology. *Romance phonology and variation: Selected papers from the 30th Linguistic Symposium on Romance Languages, Gainesville, Florida, February 2000*, Current Issues in Linguistic Theory, 191–218. Amsterdam: Benjamins.

Trubetzkoy, Nikolai S. 1958. *Grundzüge der Phonologie*. Göttingen: Vandenhoeck & Ruprecht.

Turk, Alice E., and James R. Sawusch. 1997. The domain of accentual lengthening in American English. *Journal of Phonetics* 25.25–41.

Turk, Alice E., and Stefanie Shattuck-Hufnagel. 2000. Word-boundary-related duration patterns in English. *Journal of Phonetics* 28.397–440.

Turk, Alice E., and Stefanie Shattuck-Hufnagel. 2007. Multiple targets of phrase-final lengthening in American English words. *Journal of Phonetics* 35.445–472.

Turk, Alice E., and Laurence White. 1999. Structural influences on accentual lengthening in English. *Journal of Phonetics* 27.171–206.

Türk, Helen, Pärtel Lippus, Karl Pajusalu, and Pire Teras. 2018. The acoustic correlates of quantity in Inari Saami. MS, University of Tartu, submitted.

Tyler, Stephen. 1969. *Koya: An outline grammar*. Berkeley, CA: University of California Press.

University of Madras. 1924–1936. *Tamil lexicon*. Madras: University of Madras.

University of Madras. 1992. *Kariyāviṉ taṟkālat Tamiḻ akarāti*. Cre-A, Madras: University of Madras.

Ussishkin, Adam. 1999. The inadequacy of the consonantal root: Modern Hebrew denominal verbs and output-output correspondence. *Phonology* 16.401–442.

Ussishkin, Adam. 2000. The emergence of fixed prosody. Doctoral Dissertation, University of California, Santa Cruz.

Vasu, Srisa Chandra. 1898. *The Ashtádhyáyí of Pánini, translated into English by Śríśa Chandra Vasu*. Allahabad: Indian Press.

Venditti, Jennifer J., Kikuo Maekawa, and Mary E. Beckman. 2008. Prominence marking in the Japanese intonation system. *Handbook of Japanese linguistics*, ed. by Shigeru Miyagawa and Mamoru Saito, 456–512. Oxford: Oxford University Press.

Vendler, Zeno. 1968. *Adjectives and nominalizations*. The Hague: Mouton & Co.

Vennemann, Theo. 1972. On the theory of syllabic phonology. *Linguistische Berichte* 18.1–18.

van de Vijver, Ruben. 1998. *The iambic issue: Iambs as a result of constraint interaction*. The Hague: Holland Academic Graphics.

Villing, Rudi C. 2010. Hearing the moment: Measures and models of the perceptual centre. Doctoral Dissertation, National University of Ireland Maynooth.

Vogel, Ralf. 2006. Weak function word shift. *Linguistics* 44.1059–1093.

Volkmann, Richard Emil. 1885. *Die Rhetorik der Griechen und Römer*. Leipzig: B. G. Teubner.

Wackernagel, Jakob. 1896. *Altindische Grammatik*, volume I. Göttingen: Vandenhoeck & Ruprecht.

Wackernagel, Jakob. 1905. *Altindische Grammatik*, volume II. Göttingen: Vandenhoeck & Ruprecht.

Wackernagel, Jakob. 1938. Eine Wortstellungsregel des Pāṇini und Winklers Aleph-Beth-Regel. *Indogermanische Forschungen* 56.161–170.

Wackernagel, Jakob. 1955. *Kleine Schriften*. Göttingen: Vandenhoeck & Ruprecht.

Wagner, Michael. 2005. Prosody and recursion. Doctoral Dissertation, Massachusetts Institute of Technology.

Wagner, Michael. 2010. Prosody and recursion in coordinate structures and beyond. *Natural Language and Linguistic Theory* 28.183–237.

Walker, Douglas C. 1975. Word stress in French. *Language* 51.887–900.

Walker, James A., and Marjory Meechan. 1999. The decreolization of Canadian English: Copula contraction and prosody. *Actes du Congrès annuel de l'Association canadienne de linguistique 1998*, ed. by John T. Jensen and Gerard Van Herk, 431–441.

Walker, Rachel. 1996. Prominence-driven stress. MS, University of California, Santa Cruz. Rutgers Optimality Archive ROA-172.

Walker, Rachel. 1997. Mongolian stress, licensing, and factorial typology. MS, University of California, Santa Cruz, Rutgers Optimality Archive 172.

Wasow, Thomas. 1997. Remarks on grammatical weight. *Language Variation and Change* 9. 81–105.

Wasow, Thomas. 2002. *Postverbal behavior*. Stanford, CA: CSLI Publications.

Wasow, Thomas, and Jennifer Arnold. 2003. Post-verbal constituent ordering in English. *Determinants of grammatical variation in English*, ed. by G. Rohdenburg and B. Mondorf, 119–154. Mouton.

Watson, Janet C. E. 2002. *The phonology and morphology of Arabic*. Oxford: Oxford University Press.

Weiss, Michael. 2011. *Outline of the historical and comparative grammar of Latin (2nd corr. printing)*. Ann Arbor: Beech Stave Press.

Wescott, Roger W. 1970. Types of vowel alternations in English. *Word* 26.309–343.

West, M. L. 1970. A new approach to Greek prosody. *Glotta* 48.185–194.

West, M. L. 1982. *Greek metre*. Oxford: Clarendon Press.

West, Martin. 2018. Unmetrical verses in Homer. *Language and meter*, ed. by Dieter Gunkel and Olav Hackstein, 362–379. Leiden: Brill.

Westbury, John, and Patricia Keating. 1980. Central representation of vowel duration. *Journal of the Acoustical Society of America* 67.S37(A).

Wheatley, Henry B. 1866. *A dictionary of reduplicated words in the English language*, volume 17. Transactions of the Philological Society.

White, James. 2017. Accounting for the learnability of saltation in phonological theory: A maximum entropy model with a P-map bias. *Language* 93.1–36.

White, Laurence. 2002. English speech timing: A domain and locus approach. Doctoral Dissertation, University of Edinburgh.

White, Laurence. 2014. Communicative function and prosodic form in speech timing. *Speech Communication* 63–64.38–54.

White, Laurence, and Alice E. Turk. 2010. English words on the Procustean bed: Polysyllabic shortening reconsidered. *Journal of Phonetics* 38.459–471.

Whitney, William Dwight. 1889. *Sanskrit grammar, including both the Classical language and the older dialects, of Veda and Brahmana.* Cambridge, MA: Harvard University Press, 2nd edition.

Wiese, Richard. 2001. The phonology of /r/. *Distinctive feature theory*, ed. by T. Allan Hall, 335–368. Berlin: Mouton de Gruyter.

Wightman, C. W., Stefanie Shattuck-Hufnagel, M. Ostendorf, and P. J. Price. 1992. Segmental durations in the vicinity of prosodic phrase boundaries. *Journal of the Acoustical Society of America* 92.1707–1717.

Willis, Erik W., and Travis G. Bradley. 2008. Contrast maintenance of taps and trills in Dominican Spanish: Data and analysis. *Selected Proceedings of the 3rd Conference on Laboratory Approaches to Spanish Phonology*, ed. by Laura Colantoni and Jeffrey Steele, 87–100. Somerville, MA: Cascadilla Proceedings Project.

Wilson, Colin. 2006. Learning phonology with substantive bias: An experimental and computational study of velar palatalization. *Cognitive Science* 30.945–982.

Wilson, Colin, and Benjamin George. 2008. Maxent grammar tool. Software package. University of California, Los Angeles.

Wiltshire, Caroline R. 2006. Pulaar's stress system: A challenge for theories of weight typology. *Selected Proceedings of the 35th Annual Conference on African Linguistics*, ed. by John Mugane, John P. Hutchison, and Dee A. Worman, 181–192. Somerville, MA: Cascadilla Proceedings Project.

Windsor, Joey. 2016. Contrast, phonological features, and phonetic implementation: Aspiration in Blackfoot. *Calgary Working Papers in Linguistics* 29.61–80.

Wolf, Matthew. 2008. Optimal interleaving: Serial phonology-morphology interaction in a constraint-based model. Doctoral Dissertation, University of Massachusetts-Amherst.

Wolk, Christoph, Joan Bresnan, Anette Rosenbach, and Benedikt Szmrecsányi. 2013. Dative and genitive variability in Late Modern English: Exploring cross-constructional variation and change. *Diachronica* 30.382–419.

Woodbury, Anthony C. 1985. Graded syllable weight in Central Alaskan Yupik Eskimo (Hooper Bay-Chevak). *International Journal of American Linguistics* 51.620–623.

Wright, Matthew James. 2008. The shape of an instant: Measuring and modeling perceptual attack time with probability density functions. Doctoral Dissertation, Stanford University.

Wright, Saundra, and Jennifer Hay. 2002. Fred and Wilma: A phonological conspiracy. *Gendered practices in language*, ed. by Sarah Benor, Mary Rose, Devyani Sharma, Julie Sweetland, and Qing Zhang, 175–191. Stanford, CA: CSLI Publications.

Wright, Saundra, Jennifer Hay, and Tessa Bent. 2005. Ladies first? Phonology, frequency, and the naming conspiracy. *Linguistics* 44.531–561.

Yamashita, Hiroko, and Franklin Chang. 2001. "Long before short" preference in the production of a head-final language. *Cognition* 81.B45–55.

Yamashita, Hiroko, and Franklin Chang. 2006. Sentence production in Japanese. *Handbook of East Asian psycholinguistics*, ed. by Mineharu Nakayama, Reiko Mazuka, and Yasuhiro Shirai, volume 2, 291–297. Cambridge, UK: Cambridge University Press.

Yu, Alan C. L. 2004. Explaining final obstruent voicing in Lezgian: Phonetics and history. *Language* 80.73–97.

Yu, Alan C. L., and Hyunjung Lee. 2014. The stability of perceptual compensation for coarticulation within and across individuals: A cross-validation study. *The Journal of the Acoustical Society of America* 136.382–388.

Yupho, Nawanit. 1989. Consonant clusters and stress rules in Pattani Malay. *Mon-Khmer Studies* 15.125–137.

Zec, Draga. 1988. Sonority constraints on prosodic structure. Doctoral Dissertation, Stanford University.

Zec, Draga. 1995. Sonority constraints on syllable structure. *Phonology* 12.85–129.

Zec, Draga. 1999. Footed tones and tonal feet: Rhythmic constituency in a pitch-accent language. *Phonology* 16.225–264.

Zec, Draga. 2003. Prosodic weight. *The syllable in Optimality Theory*, ed. by Caroline Féry and R. van de Vijer. Cambridge, UK: Cambridge University Press.

Zec, Draga. 2007. The syllable. *The Cambridge handbook of phonology*, ed. by Paul de Lacy, 161–194. Cambridge, UK: Cambridge University Press.

Zec, Draga, and Sharon Inkelas. 1990. Prosodically constrained syntax. *The phonology-syntax connection*, ed. by Sharon Inkelas and Draga Zec, 365–378. CLSI.

Zewen, François-Xavier Nicolas. 1977. *The Marshallese language: A study of its phonology, morphology, and syntax*. Berlin: Verlag von Dietrich Reimer.

Zhang, Jie. 2002. *The effects of duration and sonority on contour tone distribution: A typological survey and formal analysis*. London and New York: Routledge.

Zhang, Jie. 2004. Contour tone licensing and contour tone representation. *Language and Linguistics* 5.925–968.

Zimmermann, Eva. 2017. *Morphological length and prosodically defective morphemes*. Oxford: Oxford University Press.

Zipf, George Kingsley. 1936. *The psycho-biology of language: An introduction to dynamic philology*. Cambridge, MA: MIT Press.

Zubizarreta, Maria-Luisa. 1998. *Prosody, focus and word order*. Cambridge, MA: MIT Press.

Zubizarreta, Maria-Luisa, and Jean-Roger Vergnaud. 2000. Phrasal stress and syntax. MS, University of Southern California.

Zuraw, Kie. 2010. A model of lexical variation and the grammar with application to Tagalog nasal substitution. *Natural Language and Linguistic Theory* 28.417–472.

Zuraw, Kie. 2013. *MAP constraints. MS, UCLA.

Zuraw, Kie. 2018. Beyond trochaic shortening. To appear in *Phonological Data and Analysis*.

Zuraw, Kie, and Bruce Hayes. 2017. Intersecting constraint families: An argument for Harmonic Grammar. *Language* 93.497–548.

Zvelebil, Kamil. 1970. *Comparative Dravidian phonology*. The Hague: Mouton.

Zvelebil, Kamil. 1989. *Classical Tamil prosody: an introduction*. Madras, India: Hoe & Co.

Zwicky, Arnold M. 1987. Suppressing the zs. *Journal of Linguistics* 23.133–148.

Zymet, Jesse. 2015. Distance-based decay in long-distance phonological processes. *Proceedings of the 32nd West Coast Conference on Formal Linguistics*, ed. by Ulrike Steindl et al., 72–81. Cascadilla Proceedings Project.

Index

*3μ 30, 86, 102, 147

Abma 26, 28, 65
accentual lengthening 31, 78, 100, 119,
    193, 231
accentual meter 137, 139
āciriyam meter 126–9
adjective–noun order 165, 167, 190
Afrikaans 169
AIC$_c$ 181
ALIGNMENT 34, 106, 109, 114, 118, 131, 142
allomorphy (and weight) 9, 75, 95, 124,
    133, 144
ambisyllabicity 112, 176
Amele 154–5
Amharic 9–10, 71, 74
analogy, *see* leveling
anceps 126, 139
ANCHOR 106
Anguthimri 100
anuṣṭubh meter 145
anusvāra 120, 141, 156
aorist, reduplicated 2
apocope 99
apparent gradience 242–3
*APPEND 41
Arabela 26, 214
Arabic 66, 77, 80, 140, 176
    Baghdadi 75
    Classical 27, 68, 154
    Levantine 237
    San'ani 10, 26, 28, 66, 69–72
artificial grammar learning experiment
    95, 235
āryā meter 5, 120, 139–40
as far as clause 165
Asheninca 26, 28
Aṣṭādhyāyī 1, 160, 163, 170, 172, 178, 217
auditory adaptation, *see* auditory recovery
auditory recovery 214–15, 239
Avestan 138, 141
āytam 125

Badaga 134
beginning-weight 197, 204, 222–8, 230
Behaghel's law 160, 178
Belarusian 7, 231

Bella Coola 98, 101
Bengali 222
Berber
    Tamazight 140
    Tashlhiyt 11–12, 81, 143
Bernoulli process 144
Bhagavad Gītā 2
biases (constraint grammar) 237
biceps 63, 112, 149, 157
binary weight 1, 23–6, 64–86,
    98–145, 239
binary weight with bimodal phonology
    143, 156
BINMIN(φ, ω) 5
Bislama 12
Boumaa Fijian, *see* Fijian
branching mora 30, 59, 86–8, 103
brevis brevians, *see* iambic shortening
Buckeye corpus 6, 142, 176, 220
Buriat 99

cadence 110, 115, 145–7, 213
Caesar 114, 188
caesura 108–9, 111, 138, 151, 157
Cahuilla 10, 13, 26, 66–8, 99
Cantonese 224–5
Capanahua 26
Carib 18, 99
catalexis 157
categoricity 239–46
Catullus 153
CELEX 6, 93
Central Alaskan Yupik, *see* Yupik
Chickasaw 20, 26–8, 31, 49–52, 100,
    236
Chugach 28
Chuvash 71
clash 17, 34, 45, 58, 168, 185
clefting 165
clitic 98, 104, 116–18, 120, 175–6, 245
    adjunction 105–8
clitic group, *see* recursive prosodic word
coda 1
coda complexity (and weight) 10, 27, 35–6,
    39, 53, 69, 80, 86, 92–4, 98, 101, 141,
    145–7, 151, 176–7
Coda Prominence 15, 38, 59, 81–3, 87–8

coda sonority (and weight) 10, 12, 22,
    25–6, 92, 134–6, 148–51,
    174–6, 208
CODACOND 78
Coerced Weight 15, 27–30, 38–47, 70, 232
    geminates, *see* geminates
    minimality 99, 103
    positional 28
    secondary stress, *see* secondary stress
colometry 138
compensatory processes 6–8, 42, 56, 58, 74,
    120, 177, 196, 209, 239
complementizer, optional 165
complex weight 15–29, 35–63, 88–96,
    145–53, 239–46
compounds 68, 124, 155
    dvandva, *see* dvandva
    end-weight, *see* end-weight
    reduplicative, *see* echo reduplication
compression, see *muta cum liquida*
concurrence 119, 122
continua, *see* gradient weight
contour tone licensing, *see* tone licensing
coordination 162
copula, contraction 113, 165, 178
correption, *see* hiatus
counterbleeding 100
counterfeeding 85
counting 138
CRISPEDGE 109
cumulativity 193, 208
Czech 101

dative alternation 164, 200, 203, 225,
    229, 245
declination 221
degenerate foot 16, 103, 111–16, 131
DEP 109
dependency distance 200–1, 225
DEP-μ 30, 104, 106, 131
depth of field 229, 246
dimeter 139, 145
diphthongs (and weight) 13, 36, 43, 53, 81,
    96, 155
direct-interface, *see* phonetics–phonology
    interface
dīrgha (long) 1
distinctive moraicity 30, 40, 44, 70–1, 77
Diyari 100
dróttkvætt meter 153
durational invariance 8
Dutch 12, 80, 83, 124, 169, 196–7
dvandva 162–3, 169, 172, 217

Eastern Ojibwa, *see* Ojibwa
Eastern Popoloca 75
echo reduplication 162, 198–9,
    217–20, 223
edge-based decay 89, 93, 96
EDGEMOST 243
Eipomek 13, 27
elision 116, 131, 156
end-weight 5–6, 16, 25–6, 63,
    160–231, 245
    beginning-weight, *see* beginning-weight
    coda 174–7
    complexity 199–201
    compounds 162–3, 217–20, 223
    constructions 161–5
    frequency 165–6, 178–92, 212
    multinomial, *see* multinomial
    nucleus 169–71
    onset 171–4
    phonotactics 167–8, 175–6,
        198–9, 202
    rhythm 168, 198, 202
    semantic factors 166
    stress level 177–8
    stress modulation 210
    syllable count 178–93, 229
    syntactic complexity 166–7, 178,
        225, 228
    syntactic end-weight 228
energy, *see* total perceptual energy
English
    cluster duration 142
    compensatory processes 6–7
    end-weight 5, 161–231, 245
    loanwords in Tamil 124
    meter 137–43
    minimality 63, 98, 101, 245–6
    Old 6, 125
    South African 169
    stress 10–12, 15, 26, 84, 92–5
    syllabification 2
epenthesis 81, 99, 131
    stress 237–8
Estonian 7, 9, 80, 87, 101, 140, 231
Euler diagram 19
eurythmy 167
eutaxy 167
EXIST 38, 82
extrametricality 3, 8–10, 26, 33, 53, 68, 70,
    139, 151, 168
    Interval Theory 154–5
extraposition 163
extraprosodic 153, 156

f_0 220
factorial typology 234
Farsi, *see* Persian
features 19
fermata 139
Fijian 33, 64, 140
filler 141
final indifference 139, 149, 151–3
final lengthening 84, 100, 119, 139, 168,
   194–7, 202–3, 231
final strictness 139, 147
final voicing 86
Finnish
   allomorphy 9, 95
   compensatory processes 74
   end-weight 192
   gradient weight 95
   hiatus 154
   Kalevala 16, 147–9, 240
   meter 23, 140
   stress 15, 23, 26–8, 37, 57–8, 71, 73
fixed segmentism 219–20, 223–4
focus 166, 190, 201–3, 220
foot binarity, *see* FtBin
foot structure 9, 17, 28, 33–4, 53–5, 60–2,
   68, 98
*Foot⊂Light 115–16
forward-difference coding 148
French 81, 219
   end-weight 169, 173, 176, 185,
      190–2, 198
   meter 138
   stress 95
frequency (and word order) 165–6, 178–92,
   212
FtBin 22, 33, 103–4, 120, 157
Fula 47, 71

gaṇa 139
Gathic, *see* Avestan
gāyatrī meter 5, 145
geminates
   affix location 9
   coda 80, 87
   Coerced Weight 43–63, 72–4
   compensatory lengthening 8
   parametric moraicity 74, 97
   phonetics 25, 77
   relative to VC 64–81
   simplification 65, 81
   weight 10–11, 25–6, 28–9, 43, 48,
      64–77
   weight as onsets 74–7
   word-initial 8, 46

generative metrics 18, 112
genitive alternation 164, 167–8,
   178, 229
Georgian 26, 138
German
   end-weight 163, 169–70, 172–3, 192
   Thurgovian Swiss 4, 11, 76, 101
Goroa 28
Gothic 125
gradient constraint 33
gradient weight 3, 14
   meter 63, 137, 141, 145–53, 158–9
   relation to categorical weight 239–46
   stress 57, 88–96
   variable weight, *see* variable weight
   vs. variable weight 158
grammatical word 98, 104, 131
GramWd=PWd 34, 104, 131
Greek
   Aeolic 6
   Attic 124, 140, 142
   Homeric 16, 21, 63, 137, 145, 149–51,
      173, 192, 240
   Ionic 6
   Modern 163, 170, 192
   Samothraki 6
*GridStruc 49
guru (heavy) 1

haiku 138, 151, 156–7
harmonic bounding 44, 51, 206–7
Harmonic Grammar 14, 54, 90, 118, 147,
   206–10, 229, 234, 240–5
Hausa 140
*Hd, *see* *Pk
head-finality 139, 217, 224–30
heavy NP shift 163–4, 177, 225
Hebrew 192
   Mishnaic 164
   Modern 101, 164, 196
   Tiberian 12, 24, 65, 75, 83–4, 125, 237
hendecasyllable 153
hexameter 21, 63, 108–10, 112–18, 137, 142,
   151–4, 240
hiatus
   avoidance 167, 198
   correption 143–4, 149, 154, 156
   resolution 131
Hindi 10, 77, 124, 171, 224
   geminates 80, 125
   Gupta's 66, 68, 69
   Kelkar's 13, 27, 35, 27–36, 39, 53, 86–7
   meter 13, 140
Hixkaryana 99

hrasva (short) 1
Huehuetla Tepehua 11, 12, 24–6, 84–6, 134, 173, 238
Hungarian 140, 170–2, 187, 192, 225
Hupa 13, 26, 28, 88–92, 99

iamb 33, 58, 73, 139
iambic lengthening 33–4
iambic pentameter 115, 137
iambic shortening 28, 33, 102, 120
Icelandic 4, 8
ictus 17, 18
IDENT(long) 44
ideophone 102, 245
idiom 206, 245
Iliad 149–51
Inari Sami, *see* Sami
infixation 71
Inga Quechua, *see* Quechua
initial strengthening 78, 197
intensive 66
intermediate weight with unimodal phonology 144
Interval Theory 1, 96, 143, 153–9
    Vowel Prominence 156
Irish, *see* Munster Irish
islands of reliability 23, 174
isochrony 214
Italian 77, 96, 101, 108, 177

Japanese 87, 120
    beginning-weight 170, 192, 222, 224–6, 228
    meter 138, 140
    minimality 119
Jingpho 170

Kalevala, *see* Finnish
Kamban 123, 126–8, 150, 240
Kara 26–8, 62–3
karintaa chant 138, 141
Karo 20, 26, 214, 216
Kashaya Pomo 83
Kashmiri 3, 26, 28, 30, 32, 38–42, 149,
    see also Srinagar Koshur
Kashuyana 101
Kātyāyana 169
Kayardild 25, 140–1
Khalkha criterion 3–4, 10, 13, 24, 35, 64–74
    meter 140, 141, 158
Khalkha Mongolian, *see* Mongolian
Kilivila, *see* Kiriwina

Kiriwina 18, 33
Klamath 26, 28, 52–5, 69, 71
Koasati 8, 71–3, 83
Korean 193, 224–5
Koshur, *see* Kashmiri
Koya 65–71
Krongo 65–71
Kunama 65
Kuuku-Yaʔu 65
Kwak'wala 20, 22–3, 25–6, 134, 141, 149, 154

laghu (light) 1
Lamang 25, 134
lapse 17, 45, 168, 178–92
laryngeals (and weight) 13, 26, 66, 77–81, 88–90, 173
Latin 3, 28
    clitics 106–8, 116–18, 120
    Early 28, 33, 102, 106, 120
    end-weight 188–9
    intervals 153–4
    meter 137, 139, 140, 152–3
    minimality 16, 98–100, 102–20, 122
    prose 114
    resyllabification 108–18
    stress 33, 52, 69, 77, 103–4, 106, 114
    syllabification 2, 142–3
Latin criterion 3, 13, 16, 24, 35, 64, 77
    meter 137, 140, 158
layered moraic grids 37
Leti 11, 15, 71, 76–7, 101
leveling 95, 100, 120
lexical stress 23, 93
lexicality 106, 116–18, 131
lexicalization 107, 145, 206
Lexicon Optimization 99, 131
Lezgian 75
licensing place 77–80
Lithuanian 170
loanword 57, 85, 122–4
locative alternation 164
logistic regression 89, 93, 128, 148, 151, 180–4, 189–92, 227
longum 63, 112, 149
Luganda 75, 140
Luiseño 67

Macushi Carib, *see* Carib
MAIN→CODA 82
MAIN→VV 36, 28–38, 47–63, 81–3
Maithili 26, 28, 55–7, 71
Malay, *see* Pattani Malay

Malayalam 11, 15, 60, 71, 73, 132, 135, 140
Mam 26, 28
Manam 154
Mandarin 101
Marshallese 75
MATCH constraints 206
maximum entropy, *see* Harmonic Grammar
Max-μ 30, 130
Max-μ-V 30, 35
Max(place) 78
ME FIRST 166
Mechanical Turk 171, 175, 188, 195, 199
Menominee 101
metacondition, ranking 236
meter 5, 16, 25–6, 63, 137–59, 233
    constituency 138–40, 147, 149,
        156–7
    mora-counting 138–41, 156–7
    mora-counting meter 151
    resyllabification 108–10
    syllable-counting 137–41
    ternary weight 141, 145–7
metri causa 145, 148
metrical structure, *see* foot structure
metrical systems 13
metron 5, 63, 108, 112, 120, 137, 139, 147,
    149, 157
Milton 115
minimal pairs 93
minimality 4–5, 16, 98–136, 245–6
    cliticized items 105–8
    coda-specific 101, 122–36
    disyllabic 77, 98, 100–1
    exceptions 101–2
    geminates 101
    gradient 101–2, 121, 245–6
    onsets 98, 101
    opacity 99
    phonetics 100, 119
    phrasal binarity 5, 164, 194, 245
    prosodic explanation 98–100
    resyllabification 108–31
    root minimality 99–100, 105
    sonority 102
Mokilese 8
Mongolian 4
mora 3
mora-counting meter, *see* meter
moraic phonology 29–30, 36–8, 40, 70–1
Moraic Theory of Geminates 11, 15, 28–9,
    44, 64, 72, 101, 125, 232
moraic trochee 28, 60–2, 76, 99,
    see also trochee

μ (maxent HG) 237
*μ 30
multinomial 162, 178, 187, 211–13
Munster Irish 26, 64
*μ/R 130–4
Murik 31, 35, 39, 136
muta cum liquida 142–3, 149

N-gram corpus 160, 182, 190
Nankina 12
Nanti 11–13, 26, 28, 58–60, 81, 96,
    138, 141
Ndjébbana 75
Nepali 65–71
Ngalakgan 11–12, 15, 23, 26, 77–81
Nganasan 67
Ngarinyin 67
no-weakness principle 18
nonfinality 34, 36, 45, 104, 168, 178–92, 213
Nootka, *see* Nuu-chah-nuulth
normalization 144, 240
NOTMIN 38
nuclear stress 160–1, 201–28, 230
Nuu-chah-nuulth 25, 134
Nyawaygi 67

OCP (Obligatory Contour Principle) 167,
    175
Odyssey 149–51
Ojibwa 71, 100
Okinawan, *see* Tedumuni Okinawan
Old Norse 139–40, 150–4
Oneida 83
Onondaga 6
ONSET 109, 121, 131
onset complexity (and weight) 10, 12, 94–6,
    98, 101, 151, 156, 171–2, 208
onset sonority (and weight) 9–11, 20, 26,
    148, 172–4, 213–16, 238–9
onset weight 6, 9–10, 23, 26, 94–6, 101, 149,
    151, 171–4, 193, 197, 208–16, 232,
    238–9
    geminate 74–7
    Interval Theory 155, 156
    phonetic rationale 214–15
opacity 75, 84–5, 93, 147, 237–8
Optimality Theory 14, 33, 99–100,
    206, 234
ordinal scale 88
Orya 25
Ossetic 71
output-output correspondence 111
overlengthening, *see* supergeminates

overlong, *see* superheavies
Ovid 115

p-center 156, 214–15, 239
p-movement 202
pāda 145
Paipai 25, 134
Pāṇini 1, 160, 163, 170, 172, 178, 184, 217
paradigmatic model 192, 227
paraphonology 81
parity 5–9, 139–40
PARSE 54, 76
particle verb 164–5
Pattani Malay 6, 75
Peak Prominence, *see* PK-PROM
PEH-mapping 234–6
period 151
Persian 10, 13, 87, 140–1, 222, 225
persistent euphony 201
Phalaecian, *see* hendecasyllable
phonetic basis of weight 14, 25, 65, 76, 134
phonetic effectiveness 14, 233–37
phonetics–phonology interface 144, 216,
    233–44
phonological simplicity 14, 234
phonologization 100, 219–20
phonotactics, *see* end-weight
phrasal stress, *see* nuclear stress
Pintupi 100
Pirahã 26, 149, 209–14
pitch accent 6, 12, 72, 75, 83, 134, 145, 226
Pitta-Pitta 98
*Pk 38, 81, 82, 86
PK-PROM 32–3, 42
*Pk/X 32
planning 229
polysyllabic shortening 7, 100, 119,
    196, 231
Ponapean 8
Popoloca, *see* Eastern Popoloca
Portuguese 89, 96, 155
Praat 25, 133
Prakrit 5, 8, 124, 139
    geminates 125
    Māhārāṣṭrī 16, 101, 120–1, 140,
        141, 156
pretonic gemination 75
princeps 149
Principle of Equal Weight for Codas 10,
    64, 71
privilege 78
prominence-driven weight, *see*
    sonority-driven weight

prosodic end-weight, *see* end-weight
prosodic hierarchy 17
prosodic minimality, *see* minimality
prothesis 100, 109, 131
*P/σ$_\mu$ 31
Pulaar 3, 8, 13, 15, 26, 28, 36, 42–9, 73,
    125, 149

quantitative complementarity 2, 8, 71
quantitative meter, *see* meter
quantitative nonfinality 36
quantity-sensitive 4, 23, 83
quaternary weight, *see* complex weight
Quechua
    Huallaga 67
    Inga 25, 134
    Junín-Huanca 67
Quintilian 160

random forests 181
ratio scale 88
real-valued violations 240
REALIZEMORPHEME 68
recall 186–7
recursive prosodic word 17, 110, 206
reduced vowels (and weight) 9, 25, 56, 60,
    64, 81, 90
reduplicated aorist 2
reduplication 2, 8, 71, 224
reduplicative compounds, *see* echo
    reduplication
refrain 138
regression, *see* logistic regression
relative weight pathology 243
resyllabification 2, 16, 108–31, 136, 141,
    173, 198, 233
    meter 128–31, 156
Ṛg-Veda 5, 128, 145–6, 163
ṚH-CONTOUR 34
rhotics (and weight) 25–6, 122–36, 156
rhyme (poetic) 133, 155
rhythm, *see* end-weight
Rhythm Rule 212, 220–2
rhythmicians 149
Richness of the Base 68, 70, 99, 105, 130
Russian 95

saliency 157, 213
Sami 7, 87, 119, 231
San'ani Arabic, *see* Arabic
sandhi 122, 126–30, 133, 172, 173
Sanskrit 1–3, 68, 137, 140, 150, 214
    Brāhmaṇas 146

Classical 5, 6, 124, 139, 169
    end-weight 163, 170, 192, 217
    geminates 125
    syllabification 145
    Vedic 5, 10, 13, 16, 139, 143–7,
       163, 165
Sapir, Edward 88, 92
Sattasaī 121, 140
scrambling 225
second-position clitic 165
secondary stress 4, 22–3, 26, 31–2, 37, 39,
      65, 66, 75, 76, 83, 95, 154, 177
    Coerced Weight 45–63
Selkup 11, 22–3, 71
Seneca 83
Serbo-Croatian 177
sesquisyllable 101
Seto 71
Shakespeare 115
Shipibo 26, 28
shm-reduplication 219
Shoshone, *see* Tümpisa Shoshone
σ^2 (maxent HG) 237
$\sigma_{\mu\mu\mu}$→STRESS 32
$\sigma_{\mu\mu}$→STRESS 31–3
simplicity, *see* phonological simplicity
Skeletal Prominence 38, 59, 63, 81–3,
    87–8
Slavic 7, 231
śloka meter 2
sonority scale 19, 135
sonority-driven weight 9–13, 23, 25–6,
    37–8, 59, 64, 95, 102, 204, *see* Coda
    Prominence, Vowel Prominence
    209, 235
    end-weight 174–6, 208
    meter 149, 151
    stress 81, 84–6
SOV, *see* head-finality
Spanish 85, 96
Srinagar Koshur 26–8, 39
Stoney 68
stress 4, 22–97
    binary weight 23–6, 64–86
    complex weight 15, 26–9, 35–63
    exceptions 23, 35, 77, 92
    geminates, *see* geminates
    gradient weight 57, 88–96
    lexical, *see* lexical stress
    phrasal, *see* nuclear stress
stress-to-weight principle 31–3
STRESS→$\sigma_{\mu\mu}$ 31–3
STRESS-TO-STRESS 179, 203–4

StressTyp2 15, 23
stringency 18–20, 31–2, 204, 210,
    215–16, 232
strong element 17, 232
strong mora 34, 37
subminimal, *see* minimality
supergeminates 66, 80, 101, 125
superheavies 9
    avoidance in cadences 16, 145–7
    Coerced Weight 42
    mapping 32–3, 35
    scansion 141, 145
    weight 149
superheavy-to-stress principle 32, 80
Swedish 71
Swiss German, *see* German
Switchboard 177
syllabification
    coda maximization 158
    geminate 75–81
    judgments 155, 158
    meter 141–5
    variable 137
Syllable Contact Law 168, 175,
    198–9
syllable structure (and weight) 8, 25, 71,
    141–5
syllable-counting meter, *see* meter
syntagmatic model 192

Tagalog 172
Tamil
    coda place 78
    geminates 60, 124–6
    gradient weight 150
    loanword phonology 124
    meter 126–8, 150, 240
    Middle, *see* Kamban
    minimality 16, 101, 122–36, 233
    resyllabification 128–31
    rhotic phonetics 134
    rhotic phonotactics 133–4
    rhotics 26, 132–6
    stereotyped vocalism 219, 223–4
    stress 26, 28, 60–2, 71–2, 135
    supergeminates 66
Tashlhiyt Berber, *see* Berber
Taz Selkup, *see* Selkup
Tedumuni Okinawan 75
Telugu 60, 65, 101, 140, 235
Tepehua, *see* Huehuetla Tepehua
Terence 120
ternary weight, *see* complex weight

tertiary stress 55
Thai 6, 14, 140
Thurgovian Swiss German, *see* German
Tiberian Hebrew, *see* Hebrew
Tiriyó 31
t-mapping, *see* true gradience
Tocharian 138, 141
Tolkāppiyam 123
tone licensing 6, 14, 25, 75
topicalization 177
total perceptual energy 19, 25, 233,
    238–40
trimeter 145
trimoraic maximum 30, 86–8,
    103, 147
trimoraic syllables 32, 36, 86–8
Trique 6
trisyllabic window, *see* window
trochaic shortening 18, 33
trochee 33, 60–2, 69, *see also* moraic
    trochee, 90
true gradience 240–3
Trukese 6, 101
Try-and-Filter approach 205
Tsakhur 26
Tsou 101
Tübatulabal 71
Tümpisa Shoshone 20, 26, 214, 216
Tungus 171, 223
Turkish 171, 193, 222–3, 226–8
two-layered moraic grids 37

ultraheavies 146
unary weight 236, 239
unbounded stress 22–3, 39, 47,
    154–5, 244
underspecification 144–5
universals (of weight) 9–13, 24–7, 32, 68, 74,
    83–6, 100–1, 134, 205

variable weight 141–5, *see also* gradient
    weight
  vs. gradient weight 158
Vedic Sanskrit, *see* Sanskrit
Virgil 108–10, 112–18, 142, 152–5
Vowel Prominence 15, 28–29, 36–8, 47–63,
    81–3, 87–8, 232
  Interval Theory 156
VV < VC (rarity vis-à-vis VC < VV) 15, 24,
    83–6, 100, 167, 175, 200

Wargamay 67
weight percept, *see* total perceptual energy
weight-by-position 24, 30, 37, 47, 61, 78,
    102, 130
  by position 28, 65, 89
weight-to-stress principle 31–3
window
  disyllabic 60, 72, 88–90
  trisyllabic 33, 39, 52, 55, 69–70, 75, 89,
    96, 154
Winnebago 67
Wintu 67
Wolof 65, 71, 125
word shape controls 128, 148
wug test 94–6, 155, 167, 169–93,
    195–6, 199

X→φ$_s$ 204–5, 230

Yahi, *see* Yana
Yana 12, 23, 25–6, 28, 31, 34–5, 39,
    92, 154
Yapese 26, 28, 57
Yaygir 65
Yiddish 171, 219
Yidiɲ 98, 100
Yupik 65
  Central Alaskan 26, 27